Understanding Development Economics

Important parts of development practice, especially in key institutions such as the World Bank, are dominated by economists. In contrast, development studies is largely based upon multidisciplinary work in which anthropologists, human geographers, sociologists, and others play important roles. Hence, a tension has arisen between the claims made by development economics to be a scientific, measurable discipline prone to wide usage of mathematical modeling, and the more discursive, practice-based approach favored by development studies.

The aim of this book is to show how the two disciplines have interacted, as well as how they differ. This is crucial in forming an understanding of development work, and to thinking about why policy recommendations can often lead to severe and continuing problems in developing countries.

This book introduces development economics to those coming from two different but linked perspectives: economists and students of development who are not economists. In both explaining and critiquing development economics, the book is able to suggest the implications of these findings for development studies, and more broadly, for development policy and its outcomes.

Adam Fforde is a part-time Professorial Fellow at the Centre for Strategic Economic Studies, Victoria University, Australia, and he holds an honorary position at the Asia Institute of the University of Melbourne, Australia.

Economics as Social Theory
Series edited by Tony Lawson
University of Cambridge

Social Theory is experiencing something of a revival within economics. Critical analyses of the particular nature of the subject matter of social studies and of the types of method, categories and modes of explanation that can legitimately be endorsed for the scientific study of social objects, are re-emerging. Economists are again addressing such issues as the relationship between agency and structure, between economy and the rest of society, and between the enquirer and the object of enquiry. There is a renewed interest in elaborating basic categories such as causation, competition, culture, discrimination, evolution, money, need, order, organization, power probability, process, rationality, technology, time, truth, uncertainty, value, etc.

The objective for this series is to facilitate this revival further. In contemporary economics the label "theory" has been appropriated by a group that confines itself to largely asocial, ahistorical, mathematical "modeling." Economics as social theory thus reclaims the "theory" label, offering a platform for alternative rigorous, but broader and more critical conceptions of theorizing.

Other titles in this series include:

Understanding Development Economics

Its challenge to development studies

Adam Fforde

LONDON AND NEW YORK

First published 2013
by Routledge
2 Park Square, Milton Park, Abingdon, Oxon OX14 4RN

and by Routledge
711 Third Avenue, New York, NY 10017

Routledge is an imprint of the Taylor & Francis Group, an informa business

© 2013 Adam Fforde

British Library Cataloguing in Publication Data
A catalogue record for this book is available from the British Library

Library of Congress Cataloging in Publication Data
Fforde, Adam.
  Understanding development economics : its challenge to
  development studies / Adam Fforde.
  pages cm
  1. Development economics. 2. Economic development. I. Title.
  HD75.F494 2013
  338.9–dc23
  2013017459

ISBN: 978-0-415-86983-6 (hbk)
ISBN: 978-0-415-86982-9 (pbk)
ISBN: 978-1-315-88177-5 (ebk)

Typeset in Palatino
by Florence Production Ltd, Stoodleigh, Devon, UK

Printed and bound in the United States of America by Publishers Graphics,
LLC on sustainably sourced paper.

To my mother, who is a great deal smarter
than some of her children think she is

Contents

Abbreviations

ADB	Asian Development Bank
AFC	Asian Financial Crisis
AusAID	Australian AID
BRIC	Brazil, Russia, India, and China
CDA	critical discourse analysis
COR	capital output ratio
CoV	coefficient of variation
DE	developmental economics
DS	developmental studies
EBRD	European Bank for Reconstruction and Development
EOG	export-oriented growth
EPZ	export processing zone
FDI	Foreign Direct Investment
GATT	General Agreement on Tariffs and Trade
GDP	gross domestic product
GFC	Global Financial Crisis
GNP	gross national product
HDI	human development indicator
HPAE	high performing Asian economy
ICOR	Incremental Capital–Output Ratio
ILO	International Labor Organization
IMF	International Monetary Fund
INGO	international nongovernmental organization
ISI	import substitution industrialization
L&P	Lindauer and Pritchett
L&Z	Levine and Zervos
LHS	left-hand side
MAD	mean absolute deviation
MNC	multinational corporation
MITI	Ministry of Trade and Industry
NGO	non-governmental organization
NIA	National Income Accounting
NIC	newly industrializing country

NIE	neo-institutional economics
PRA	participatory rural appraisal
PWC	post-Washington Consensus
R&D	research and development
RHS	right-hand side
RRA	rapid rural appraisal
Sida	Swedish International Development Cooperation Agency
SAP	structural adjustment loan
SEA	Southeast Asia
SME	small and medium-size enterprise
SOE	state-owned enterprise
T&S	Todaro & Smith
TFP	total factor productivity
TP	technical progress
UNCTAD	United Nations Conference on Trade and Development
WC	Washington Consensus
WTO	World Trade Organization

Preface

This book is mainly intended as a study aid and teaching manual but is also useful as a monograph. It introduces development economics (DE) to those coming from two different but linked perspectives: that of economists and that of students of development who are not economists. Both are looking at what they would presumably agree is the same thing—development—but are doing so in different ways. Although these two perspectives can learn from each other, links between them are troubled and disjointed.

Important parts of development practice, especially in key institutions such as the World Bank, are dominated by economists. In contrast, development studies (DS) is largely based upon multidisciplinary work in which anthropologists, human geographers, sociologists and others play important roles. In the city where I live, Melbourne (Australia), economics departments are to be found in faculties of commerce or business, while DS sits in faculties of arts.

To start with, this means that students of DS learn too little about DE. Many economists assert that technical training in economics is needed to participate in their classes, so DE is not easily accessed by those in DS courses. But there are deeper issues related to the different approach to knowledge in mainstream economics compared to what is typical in arts areas. Economists usually assert their use of a scientific methodology, modeled on their understanding of natural sciences, and assume an objective reality that economic theory can access. From this follows their use of algebra and quantitative data.

Economists' views contrast with the tendency within arts to assume that truth is relative and judgments depend on the perspective taken. Arts methods tend to avoid algebra and prefer qualitative data. These two different approaches tend to have profoundly different implications for social or political action. These are generalizations, but it is fair to say there is a wide gap between what happens in DE courses and their counterparts in DS. This is problematic in educational terms but is also a pity for a number of other reasons.

First, it turns out that the attention DE pays to quantitative work has produced interesting and largely negative results. In terms of its own facts (see Box A, "Empirics and facts"), there appear few stable robust relationships globally between policy and outcomes (see also Chapter 2). So *anybody* (whether an economist or not) who uses such terms globally as "this leads to that" is skating on thin ice. This skepticism applies as equally to economists disputing the pros and cons of export-oriented growth (EOG) compared to import substitution industrialization (ISI) as it does to those arguing for participatory methods.[1] DS, therefore, has something to learn from DE. The approach of DE—its assumption of an objective reality that can be accessed through its theories—leads to consequences that challenge, not only its own position, but others deep within DS. So both sides, I think, can learn from reflection on DE. DE is not simply "wrong," and indeed the habit of seeking to assert that a position is wrong should undergo far more scrutiny than it usually receives. It does not necessarily follow from an apparent error in a position that its critic is correct, though this is a common argumentative technique (Dunn 2000).

Box A: Empirics and facts

I use the term *facts* to refer to an alleged reality specific to a particular set of practices or methodology, thus related to what could be called ways of observing or what have been called "observation theories" (Lakatos 1970). This makes it easier to discuss the idea that what one may be observing is not *necessarily* progress toward a better knowledge. Ways of coping with these issues are discussed in on p. 66 in Chapter 5. To my surprise, the word *empirics* is not in my dictionary. Please see "A note on language," p. xxvi. By it I mean that combination of ideas that define what facts are and those facts as they are used or deployed in a practice or set of arguments. Here I think I am following Lakatos in thinking in terms of the inseparability of a set of facts from "observation theory" that gives them their specific meanings "then and there" (Lakatos 1970).

Second, and more pragmatically, DE is important because its practitioners are powerful actors in international development who influence how significant resources are deployed. This is relevant not only for aid agencies and recipient country institutions such as ministries of finance, but also more generally, for the beliefs of politicians and their advisers, business leaders, and so on. Development economists' ideas and conceptual frameworks are part of influential belief sets. Appreciating how DE works is therefore useful to both understanding and influencing development.

Contrasting the different perspectives of DE and DS is also itself a useful exercise for students. For example, it is important to debate what exactly is meant, especially in terms of how arguments are developed, when we say that the DE methodology attempts to model itself upon an understanding of natural sciences. Since it is fair to argue that natural science now tends to assume the existence of some objective reality, rather than asserting it, this is an important issue. Earlier, natural science tended, in association with other common positions, to assert the existence of a knowable reality that could be thought of—like God (though not ineffable)—as fixed and unchanging even as perspectives and observers changed. Thus one finds frequent references in standard texts to "the development process," as though this were something as familiar and uncontested as a rainstorm. Further, DE's use of mathematics poses useful questions about the importance of formal rigor in argument and the value of systems that try to build formal propositions upon a set of axioms that believe in *apodictic* argument (see "A note on language," p. xxvi). There are accounts of the major problems created by views about the value of such methods (for example, Kline 1980). This situation means that DE offers students particularly valuable opportunities for considering the implications of choice of methods and approaches.

For students of DS the book presents a clear and accessible exposition of the core content of mainstream DE as taught in universities. It contains no algebra, though it refers to it, and examples may easily be found (and references are given). In my opinion it is possible to understand the basic logic of economists' models without working through their technical aspects. Indeed, in development practice, economists' arguments usually *are* presented in nonalgebraic terms. Getting into DE thus turns out to be more interesting and useful (and far easier) than may at first appear.

But things may not always be quite so balanced and reasonable. My experience discussing the arguments contained in this book with economists, and reflecting on their comments on earlier drafts, has shown me that the position the book takes may be experienced by them as confrontational. Its arguments challenge beliefs and the bases for those beliefs, especially within DE, but also those who value algebra and rely upon it. In explaining DE and seeking to develop an understanding of it, the book poses questions about empirics and methods that are not easily answered within DE, a problem that is hardly unique to economics. Indeed, these are hard issues for everyone. Few people are entirely consistent, and fewer still appreciate having their inconsistencies probed.

However, economists' commitment to data is praiseworthy. The central result of the seminal work by Ross Levine and Sara Zervos (hereafter referred to as L&Z) in 1993, published in the leading mainstream journal—that of the American Economic Association—was that almost no robust relationships existed between policy and outcomes globally. Yet many economists find L&Z's findings hard to deal with, and indeed citations of L&Z reveal that most economists rarely question the credibility of statements that economists know which policies work and which do not (Fforde 2005).

Examination of the canonical DE literature, specifically the textbooks used here, shows, I argue, that DS can learn much by understanding mainstream development economics. It is important to appreciate that one response to the tensions I am describing is to avoid confronting them, such as by not engaging with the arguments. Perhaps this explains in part why, as I mentioned, economics departments are now generally not sited close to their expected colleagues, such as political science, anthropology and other social sciences.

The book therefore has three interrelated elements to it: DE, views of mainstream DE, and development studies. These are separate but linked, and the book explains how. I will discuss key economics textbooks in order to explain DE to economic students, DS students and others, but at the same time I will also be pointing out drawbacks of the mainstream approach. Thus I exposit DE; I discuss views of mainstream DE (taking a step back from the exposition to discuss and evaluate mainstream development economics); and I consider what DS can learn about itself—about development and development intervention—from DE. This three-pronged approach means that I am explaining and critiquing DE and also considering what this may tell us about development work, such as aid. This approach means, for example, that when we come in Chapter 22 to consider experimental economics and randomized controlled trials, we are able to go deeply into the theoretical assumptions and empirical beliefs behind them.[2] There is a perhaps subtle point here. I hope that the value of the main theme of this book is that, while DE should not be taken at face value, the failure of its overall approach to generate robust predictive knowledge is extremely suggestive for wider problems in DS. The exemplar of such problems is belief in the known value of participation (the technique that involves aid project stakeholders in areas such as project design, monitoring, and evaluation) and its ability to ensure better development outcomes (Mosse 2005). DE failure to generate predictive knowledge suggests, in turn, that DE is best appreciated as explanatory, and an indicator of good explanations is their willingness to appreciate others' contributions—that is, to happily negotiate across disciplinary boundaries.

Some practical matters

The book draws upon a lecture series taught at honors (fourth-year undergraduate) level in Melbourne to a mixed group of students coming from both DE and DS. It consists of a series of concise chapters, with regular asides to encourage reflection and discussion as well as lists of useful questions. The chapters reflect the fact that the course was taught in two two-hour sessions a week. The usual format was an hour's lecture followed by discussions and student presentations. This explains in part why the chapters in the second half of the book are relatively short: as is not uncommon, students tended to delay their presentations toward the end of the semester.

I have not changed this pattern much here, and many of the later chapters are shorter, presented as problem-focused and therefore easily augmented by class discussion and presentation. The book thus takes the classic two-part form where the student learns various foundational aspects of the subject and then sees how they may be applied. I have tried to keep the book short and succinct.

The original course enjoyed a twelve-week semester, but, in transforming my lecture notes into this book, some lectures became two chapters. As a result, the book as it stands has, in effect, twenty-three chapters (plus this Preface) that cover twelve weeks if two are dealt with each week and one session left for revision, administration, or whatever suits the moment. If the class enjoys the fourteen-week semester common in the US, I encourage spending a week to discuss analyses of economic crises, such as the Global Financial Crisis (GFC), which started in 2008. Such crises are interesting, not least because most commentators fail to predict them, and this confusion can be observed by tracking reports and articles produced as the crisis evolved.

A good entry point to this is the speech by International Monetary Fund (IMF) Managing Director Michel Camdessus in 1999, just after the Asian Financial Crisis (AFC) of the late 1990s (Camdessus 1999), quoted in Chapter 1. Students, especially if they engage with this topic toward the end of the semester, may benefit from using what they have learned to research and discuss the different ways in which issues were addressed at the time in relevant forums (the press, journals, reports from organizations such as the World Bank, United Nations Conference on Trade and Development, and so forth). These may then be compared with the GFC a decade later.

The market for textbooks in mainstream DE is dominated by just two books. Based upon data relating to US universities, and assuming that these reflect the global pattern in English-language tertiary education, the two most used books in DE courses are Ray 1998 and Todaro and Smith 2006 (T&S).[3] That DE, as a tertiary subject, is studied through a limited number of texts suggests relatively little diversity. It also supports the idea that development economists tend to view development as concerned with finding and then implementing knowable (and known) problems to given solutions, taught in the same way as, say, engineers.

I would like to express my respect for *Development Economics* by Debraj Ray (1998), especially for its clarity and expositional punch. It is sinuously intriguing in the ways in which it addresses some of the more thorny issues, such as the origins of the abandonment of tariff protection by many developing countries in the early 1980s,[4] the welfare analysis of protection, and other concerns. These are mentioned in the following chapters. So far, it has only gone into one edition. By contrast, Todaro's work (*Economic Development*) is now in its ninth edition, and the original author has been joined by Stephen Smith.

Structure of the book

The book's structure reflects its use as a study aid and teaching manual. The first of two parts introduces ideas, arguments, and concepts, which are then applied and developed, mainly in Part II (Topics and Issues) but also in the closing chapters of Part I. A list of special terms can be found at the end of the book (see p. 323).

Part I, Development economics: theory and its application, platforms on some of the ideas already introduced in the Preface and starts by considering basic issues of the methodology and scope of DE and then moving on to examine ways in which development, construed as economic growth, is discussed. After a digression that introduces students to ways of assessing DE as a body of knowledge and presents some evidence of how economists construct their models (Chapters 6 and 7), a platform is provided for looking at various DE visions of the developing economy, which focus upon structural change; how DE texts approach issues of policy; and finally matters of poverty, globalization, and distribution.

Chapters 1, 2, and 3 pose basic questions about DE and developing economies, expand on introductory points, and discuss the possible impact of economic theories upon economic behavior and economic policy.

Chapters 4, 5, and 6 introduce DE and develop perspectives on DE arguments that economic theory should be applied to developing countries and look at some empirics. Chapter 5, which is crucial, steps back to offer students tools—for example, concepts such as epistemology—for treating economics as a body of knowledge among many others and so requiring choice as to how it should be assessed. The chapter also offers evidence of what economists do when they build their models.

Chapters 7 through 11 view in more detail established growth theory and some approaches, at times deemed radical, that have influenced policy. In another step to one side, Chapter 9 looks at the microeconomics that provides the so-called microfoundations of DE. This offers an explanation of the importance of concepts of market failure and links shifting beliefs in the extent of market failure to shifts in DE standard positions, above all, regarding state intervention.

Chapters 12 and 13 look more deeply at views of the particular conditions of developing countries, examining, in turn, theories that refer to the rural–urban divide and rural economic conditions.

Chapters 14 and 15 examine in more detail economic policy, stressing the powerful impact of earlier thinking upon current behavior, such as in aid programming, and ways in which difficulties are defined and then followed by policy prescriptions.

Chapter 16, the first chapter in Part II, Topics and issues, examines issues related to poverty, inequality, and the ways in which DE theories link these to issues of globalization.

Chapter 17 looks at the economics of factor markets in economic development. In the original course, case studies were brought in after this chapter over two weeks. This was because by now students have some understanding of DE and want to look at some concrete examples. The case studies were examples of national economic development policy and its assessment, but others could be used. The advantage of using national development policy is that the role of the state as a construed site of development intentionality is then made particularly clear, highlighting the conceptual self-positioning of DE.

Chapters 18 and 19 examine the effects of policy upon behavior in greater detail and, as a case study, the shift from ISI.

Chapters 20 and 21 look at globalization and the question of why East Asia succeeded economically. This engages with the issue of specificity—whether and how standard frameworks apply in different contexts.

Chapter 22 looks at experimental economics, which has come to be an important though varying element of DE courses and also offers very useful opportunities for students to discuss empirics, knowability and how this relates to development practices.

Chapter 23 concludes by looking further at economic theory, its empirical justification, and what can be learned from this. This permits further discussion of practices within DE and how empirical justification for some published positions was constructed. The chapter then provides examples of how powerful economic metaphors can be used to develop explanations that stress the economic aspects of important issues, suggesting the value of seeing economic issues often as the *effect* of wider processes and forces.

Personal perspectives

In this section, I attempt to state my own position as I see it. In presenting this book to readers, I feel it necessary to contextualize myself, as I did through my role as lecturer and classroom expert in the original course. This is in part because I wish to pose the question of whether, and if so to what extent, students think that subjectivity matters. Also, in the absence of stable predictive power, I think that DE is about explanation rather than prediction, and so the nature of the protagonist matters: perspectives matter.

To repeat opening remarks, a useful way of thinking about many of the differences between DE and DS is to reflect on their different ways of conceptualizing and managing subjectivity. When I taught the original course to a mixed class of economists and noneconomists, I chose to start with a presentation of my own prejudices and perspectives, partly because I was interested in the reaction. When I included my views in drafts of this book, comments showed interesting variation. Not infrequently, economists felt that my perspective was unnecessary, while those working in DS—such as anthropologists—tended to think it natural and correct. A class may wish to start by discussing this issue: do students want to know what I think my prejudices are? Why, or why not? If they do matter, are my prejudices usefully seen as biases? If so, what would an unbiased account be and how would students know it when they met it? In general, do students want to know about the context of a protagonist, or do they think this irrelevant? Why might reference to oneself in a presentation lead to negative reactions? What might such hostile or negative reactions assume about the nature of the knowledge presented?

Because my first degree was in engineering, I possessed mathematical skills that covered ranges well beyond those typically used in economics. This is important because economists often argue that economics' use of algebra per se adds to its authority, so they require facility with technical skills for participation and advancement in the discipline. Like others with mathematical skills, I did not quite know what to make of economists' expectations that their use of algebra made their views somehow more authoritative. Coming from a predictive science background, complexity and analytical rigor, however defined, was not itself valuable; what was valuable was what could be done with it. Mathematics in economics, I found, was viewed as a way of generating rigorous arguments based upon models of behavior where agents (mainly consumers and producers) maximize welfare or profits subject to certain constraints (see Chapter 9).

These models are used to generate conclusions based upon what are said to be reasonable assumptions about what constitutes rational behavior and the logic of the model. In that these conclusions are derived from such basic assumptions and mathematical logic, they are said to be *demonstrably* valid (apodictic). Much of the classroom experience of economics students is the exposition of these arguments in an algebraic format.[5] As can be seen from the footnotes of standard theoretical textbooks (Jehle and Reny 1998 is a good example), the textbooks give almost no operational *empirical* justification for the applicability of these models.

Yet things are not so simple. High school mathematics in the late 1960s, when I was taught, had been informed by changes in that subject before World War II, which stressed the *subjective* nature of logics. The idea that an argument was illogical was little more than saying it was inconsistent with a *particular* set of rules (Kline 1980). Questions as to which particular set of rules should be cited were, however, not easily answered without reference to such factors as the historical context. This raises the question of just how the particular logic adopted by any approach, including standard microeconomics, should be justified. Thus the value of approaches that stress the demonstrably valid nature of their positions has tended to erode. To put this in another way, it is not hard to be rigorous; what is hard is to offer a rigorous explanation that is empirically satisfying. As has been said, a good engineer is somebody who can make for $1 what any fool can make for $10.

I combined my education—an engineering BA with an economics minor, then a master's in economics in the mid-1970s, followed by a Cambridge PhD in economics and a post-doc (again in economics)—with forays into economic consultancy. In my mid-thirties, I worked for five years in Vietnam for Sida (the Swedish bilateral aid agency), after which I mixed consultancy and academic research in the 1990s. Feeling a strong desire to teach, at the end of the 1990s, I found a position at the National University of Singapore (in South East Asian Studies, teaching subjects such as comparative development policy[6]), after which I settled in Melbourne, where I now combine scholarly research, teaching, and consultancy.

I thus combine a natural science background with academic work in the social sciences as well as practice–development consultancy. Much of this work, in my case, is in a foreign culture and usually involves working in a foreign language—Vietnamese.

These experiences have shaped my perspectives. My background in mathematics and natural sciences meant that I was not intimidated by algebra and saw little reason to value its use, per se. My career has meant that I have been a scholar and a practitioner rather than a professional academic, but I have experience teaching at tertiary level. This means that I have less invested in supporting the authority of academic positions in general and DE in particular. My practical experience has also given me a strong antipathy to the imposition of solutions that do not engage with local political and social realities. And I have found that often such solutions platform either on weak empirics or upon apodictic arguments whose relationship to reality is vague at best.

If I attempt to list my predispositions, they are as follows.

First is a tendency to study *process*—how things change—and assume that *cognition* is part of this: ideas matter, ideas change, and nothing tends to be final. This draws upon the way I was taught mathematics: to be logical was simply to be consistent with a given set of rules.

Second, while I am happy to believe economic logics may be strong, they exist in what other people usually think of as a real world, meaning that the logics are *contextualized* and *contingent*: just how they work varies. Since other logics exist, negotiation of interdisciplinary boundaries is fun and valuable —in particular, listening to and engaging with anthropologists, historians, and sociologists.

Third—and deeply associated with these prejudices—is a belief that the assumption of *instrumental rationality* is neither scientifically nor rhetorically wise. I will discuss just what I think this assumption means in Chapter 2, but here it can be taken to mean that the beliefs and values of the people being studied do not matter to understanding them.

Fourth is a lack of faith in "one size fits all" approaches and a preference for the view that there are many ways to skin a cat. If I am going to support a particular approach, I want to be convinced: I want to know when and where a model is said to work and where it does not. I am skeptical by choice.

This attempt at self-explanation may—or may not—help readers to gauge the readings I select to illuminate the arguments to be found mainly in Ray (1998) but also elsewhere, and so help put them into contexts. It may also provoke reflection on whether my own position is worth knowing. If I were discussing engineers' solutions to problems, the question would be far easier to answer.

A note on language

Language is important, and, like many, I use a range of registers. Let me change register and say in my own way some things that may be useful.

The language we use is saturated with what could be called realist assumptions—that is, it refers to some objective reality, which is overlaid with other ideas and temptations. Technically, this view of how language is used and what it means is not realist in the classical sense of the word. The medieval scholastics, whose ideas still seem to echo in our confusions, were called realists because they believed in the existence of essences out there and beyond our thoughts—what are called *extra-mental* universals. The so-called nominalist revolution of William of Ockham largely destroyed the authority of these views, arguing that words were, well, just words. But this opened the door to a whole host of confusions, at root concerned with how we so often refer to some notion of reality as a way to convince others to our position. We add stress to our positions, seeking to add power to our efforts to persuade, by suggesting that we know what the truth is and the other person would do better to agree with this. Thus, to this day, we use a word derived from the French for truth to add stress ("very"), we say things are really hard when we say that they are very hard, we say that "actually" we are really sorry when we mean we are very, very sorry, and so on. What is confusing about this use of language is the way we use references to some idea of truth and belief in an objective and true reality to add stress and power to our statements.

These uses of language can be seen as attempts to influence whoever we are talking with, but superficially, at least, they refer to the idea that there is some knowable reality, whose nature the other person should accept. What is confusing is that while we seem mainly interested in persuading someone to do something—perhaps agree with us—such language also invites shared belief in some objective reality. I think these are two very different things. This is worth thinking about, but here is not the right place.[7] For me the central point is that discussions about social change—about development— get tangled up with issues of how things really are, when there is much to suggest that these discussions about development have limited predictive power, if any, and are far better seen as political— about human attempts to interact in ways that are of interest to various individuals and groups.

One of the things I am trying to do in this book is deal with a body of knowledge, DE, that largely ignores these questions of language and its use, which encourages students and others to believe that a set of equations, or a single equation such as a production function, represents something that is in some way real, and that its parameters can be estimated by adding an error term to an algebraic model and using a statistical technique called econometrics. I could call this a "neo-realist" approach, but nowadays realism, technically speaking, does not refer to the sort of untroubled idea that the medieval scholastics taught.

DE tends to encourage belief in things—its models—whose status (in reality) is not questioned by DE. In Chapter 6 I cite sociological research into economists' modeling decisions, which argues that usually models have only a vague relationship to reality, although within DE the ad hoc discussions that justify models take the form of statements about their correspondence with reality. To cope with how DE affects belief, therefore, is tricky, as it invites belief in the realism of its approach through exposition of its models and uses various devices to convince of their realism. In my experience, this leads to use of language that is somewhat convoluted and hard to understand. But I think that a main reason for these difficulties is that much of what is written about economics and development is, in the sense used above, neo-realist: neither is deeply interested in whether the terms it uses have any stable relationship to anything; rather, their languages seek a certain rhetorical power. This helps explain much about DE empirics and policy advice. And to cope with rhetoric requires proper attention to language and to words.

Dealing with DE, this book has to employ a number of terms often used within DE. It also uses a number of other terms that I think are useful for understanding DE. These words are included in the list of special terms at the end of the book (see p. 323).

To conclude, I hope this book will be of interest and value, both to those students of DE who are themselves either trained economists or students of the discipline, and to those in other disciplines who feel uninformed. Professionally trained in economics, I often find statements about economics as exasperating as statements from within it.

I hope this short introduction helps. You can always send me an email: adam@aduki.com.au [8]

Thanks

I express my thanks to anonymous referees, to Catherine Earl, Sheila Scopis, Suk Nyan Ng, Bob Smith, and Michael Webber for valuable and collegial comments on earlier drafts, and to students I have taught over the years. I thank Kathy Kaiser for excellent editing work. I thank Susan McEachern for her support. I also thank the Centre for Strategic Economic Studies, Victoria University, especially Professor Peter Sheehan; the Asia Institute of the University of Melbourne, and the School of Social Studies, La Trobe University. Mistakes remain mine.

Finally, my own experience teaching this course is that it sometimes produces (not always but often enough) that sensation in the classroom of the "penny dropping" that teachers usually find deeply satisfying. I thank my students for this. It confirms evidence from a range of sources that human understanding is often experienced as an awakening—a discontinuity (Rose 2003).[9]

Questions for discussion

1. Why do you think DE and DS are kept separate in university organizations?

2. What is the value, if any, of being told about the prejudices and perspectives of the author? Are these biases?

3. What deep assumptions do you think are being made when people say that their approach should or should not use algebra?

Notes

1   DS students will be familiar with participatory methods—the idea that elements of development practice such as project design and evaluation should not be done by experts acting alone but with the participation of stakeholders, such as local farmers if it is a rural development project.

2   Banerjee and Duflo (2011) argue that experiments and randomized controled trials offer reliable guides to predictively robust interventions.

3   Also widely used also are two collections: the multi-volume *Handbook of DE* (Chenery and Srivanasan 1995) and the collection edited by Deepak Lal (Lal 1992). Neither of these, however, is a textbook. Among textbooks, Ray and T&S dominate, with Ray significantly more popular; both are by orders of magnitude more widely used than competitors such as Gillis (1987) and Thirlwall (2003). Thus, results from Syllabus Finder (http://chnm.gmu.edu/tools/syllabi, accessed January 2008) show that Ray was used in 477 courses and T&S in 353 courses. This compares with the most successful of the next rank of textbooks, those of Gillis and of Thirlwall, neither of which were reported as used in more than 50 courses. The two other books (the *Handbook* and Lal's edited collection) were used in 316 and 152, respectively. Many courses did not use a textbook, it appears, since there were between 800 and 1,800 such courses (depending upon definition and search terms). This data and its interpretation are not definitive, but I conclude that Ray and T&S are dominant, with Ray well ahead in terms of coverage.

4   That is, the removal of high import tariffs (taxes on imports) so as to raise their prices on domestic markets, make them less competitive, and so support local producers. This was part of the common shift from policies that supported domestic producers, such as through tariffs, to enable the producers to take back their home markets from foreign suppliers ("import substitution") and so shift the economy toward exports (EOG).

5   DS students may consult any microeconomics textbook to see this process in motion. Jehle and Reny (1998) is a good example. Or they may simply ask a DE colleague or acquaintance. For a description of economists' practices and

comments on relationships between reality and their choice of models, see the discussion of work by Yonay in Chapter 6.

6   This course eventually saw the light of published day as Fforde (2009).

7   At a number of places in the main text I refer to the idea of ascriptivism—the notion that it makes more sense to consider discussions of cause and effect as concerned with the relatively mundane, but often very important, human issues of the ascription of responsibility (Stoecker 2007); see in particular Chapter 5, also Chapters 11 and 22. See the definition in the list of special terms on p. 323.

8   If you are interested in two books that, I think, tell us much about the beliefs and the drives to believe that underlie much of what is discussed here, try Woodside (2006) and Gillespie (2008). Woodside writes about East Asia and Gillespie about the West. I think these two scholars help put a lot of what follows into a broader perspective. However, neither mentions DE.

9   Rose is a fascinating study of poor people's experiences reading, going back to the seventeenth century. Apart from presenting a mass of evidence to argue that if you want to know what a text means to somebody, you should find ways to ask them rather than reading the text yourself, Rose reports many instances where readers were forced, by certain types of books, to decide for themselves what they meant. Often they referred to these as "classics" or some similar term and differentiated them clearly from others that were valuable also but simply for entertainment. Many accounts suggested that this experience was challenging but experienced as liberating if not exhilarating.

Part I

Development economics

Theory and its application

1 Ways to cope with development economics

In this chapter, I initiate a discussion about core questions that arise in dealing with development economics (DE) and offer possible answers. Central to this is the exercise of critical judgment, which requires a discussion of basics. Chapter 5 gives concrete references with which students may systematically develop ways of coping with DE as a body of knowledge. I am addressing issues of intentionality and agency—how people and institutions get involved in development. A central underlying issue is how far it is reasonable to believe that something that can be modeled with algebra can be driven by conscious intent.

This chapter starts a number of conceptual themes that I will develop throughout the book and are central to coping with the subject of DE. I view development conceptually as both something that *happens* and something that is *done*, with tensions between these aspects fundamental to understanding. I will contrast standard views of the problem of development (Box 1.1) with an alternative that grapples directly with these tensions (Fforde 2009). Adopting such conceptualizations is aimed at developing a discussion that allows treatment of ideas as well as historical processes, something at which DE is singularly bad. Including discussion of ideas and history facilitates discussion of ideas that consider development as something that is done, by various possible actors, as well as something that happens, which can be modeled with algebra.

I start by looking at development as an issue, taking as an example globalization and underdevelopment. This approach points to how discussions of underdevelopment usually refer both to what to do about it (possible actions) as well as how things are (reality). This raises the question of intentionality and specifically whether to follow the mainstream and think of development as a problem to which there are knowable solutions. I then discuss the issue of actors—those who "do" development—in the sense that development does not just happen. The two opposing tensions within ideas of development pose the puzzle of how a historical process that is said to be modelable with algebra (as in the growth economics that is central to DE and discussed in Chapters 7 and 8) can also be said to be doable. This leads to a discussion of how DE conceptualizes policy and how development is done, which turns out to be not quite as simple as it may appear.

Box 1.1 The problem of development

Many DS students will be aware of discussions of issues that arise from the problem of intentionality in thinking about change. One can argue that development is different from progress because it contains the notion of intentionality—development is something that can be "done." If so, some agency is required to host this intentionality.

A good example is an aid project, which, one can read in its documentation, is expected to do something—to effect certain changes in certain ways. But if these changes follow some logic, which can be and should be known beforehand, then what is the exact meaning of this intentionality? A tree grows according to some natural science logic; there is no "intention" in the same way as the farmer's intention to plant that tree, hoping, say, to build a house for his son when he marries. Once intention is included, then so do issues of values, ethics, and other factors that suggest that development should be done in certain ways. These very human themes do not sit easily beside the idea that development follows certain knowable logics or laws.

I discuss these issues further in Chapter 2, but here readers should be alerted to the deep issues underlying choices about how they choose to understand and define the "problem of development. Arndt (1981) was, as an economist, one of the first to point out the way in which the term *to develop* was used both transitively and intransitively. (See also Cowen and Shenton 1996 and Fforde 2009.)

Development as an issue: globalization and underdevelopment

Globalization: situation and problem

Most readers will be well aware of strong debates about the nature and impact of globalization.[1] Mainstream DE tends to support it, while much development studies (DS) does not. The concept is contested and arouses strong feelings.

These debates were further intensified by two major crises—the Asian Financial Crisis (AFC) of the late 1990s and the Global Financial Crisis (GFC) that started in 2008. Readers familiar with these debates will be well aware of the many definitions of globalization, many evaluations of its consequences, and, at the very least, that its fruits cannot easily be said to be have been shared equally, either within or among countries. Some readers may sense that such debates are in many ways old and may be related to the lack of agreement over important change processes. An aspect of global change processes, globalization is not only associated with development and underdevelopment, but many view it as a frequent *cause* of poverty.

Some commentators link these issues directly to apparent tensions in the global economy, such as the macroeconomic imbalances gauged by pervasive patterns of current account deficits and surpluses, and fiscal surpluses and deficits. In Chapter 23, students who work through the Question for Discussion will see how **National Income Accounting** (NIA) principles reveal that these imbalances are *definitionally* interrelated.[2] Globally, all current account positions must sum to zero, and the obverse of a current account surplus—a capital account deficit—must in accounting terms be the same thing (but measured from a different perspective) as net domestic savings. Those unfamiliar with the accounting systems behind these numbers may find this surprising. Further, the analytical value of such definitional equalities that help us think about relationships between things that at first sight appear to be unrelated (such as the US fiscal deficit and Chinese household savings patterns) is something that students may meet again when they reconsider NIA in Chapter 23.

A further aspect of the discussion is the possibility of relationships between globalization and *crises*, of which the AFC and GFC are examples. Since crises are inherently unpredictable, the question may be asked: do these events suggest that a process such as globalization has made the world riskier and more mysterious? And, if there are uninsurable (as unpredictable) risks, what are the consequences? If it is authority—statements that "this is the way the world is"—that underpins ways of responding to ignorance, what happens if dominant authority is challenged and loses prestige?

Consider the comments from the *Financial Times* journalist Martin Wolf, writing in 2009:

> First, we are seeing at least the beginning of the end not just of an illusory "unipolar moment" for the US, but of western supremacy, in general, and of Anglo–American power, in particular. The UK was the only power with global reach in the 19th century. The US held the same role in the second half of the 20th. The transition between these two eras was a catastrophe. Now we have a possibly even more difficult transition of power to manage.
>
> Second, the west, in general, and the US, in particular, have suffered a disastrous loss of authority. Assertion of an unchecked right to intervene destroyed trust in the US. The chaos that followed the wars in Iraq and Afghanistan and, far more, the financial crisis have destroyed the west's reputation for competence. The rest of the world was inclined to believe that the west, whatever its faults, knew what it was doing, particularly where running a market economy was concerned. But then the teacher failed the examination.
>
> Third, globalization has also fallen into difficulty. Thirty years of surging growth in private sector leverage, in the balance sheets of the financial sector and in notional profitability of the financial sector in the

US and other high-income countries has ended in calamity. The emergence of massive global current account "imbalances" has proved highly destabilising. Friction over exchange rates threatens even the maintenance of liberal trade.

Fourth, the provision of basic global public goods now demands co-operation between the established powers and emerging countries. This was shown in the inability to complete the Doha round of multilateral trade negotiations; in the rising influence of the Group of 20 leading countries and the parallel decline of the Group of Seven high-income countries during the financial crisis; and in the centrality of China, the world's leading emitter of greenhouse gases, in the climate change negotiations in Copenhagen.

Yet, quite rightly, the world also demands the provision of far more public goods than a century ago. Then a modicum of peace, monetary stability and open markets was all that was expected. Now the world demands that leaders not only sustain peace and prosperity, but also promote development and environmental sustainability. All this is to be achieved via co-operation among some 200 states of vastly different capacities. Meanwhile, a host of non-state actors, some benign and many malign, impose conflicting pressures. Sometimes, they subvert states entirely.

The *Financial Times* is not a left-wing newspaper. Such analyses offer powerful arguments that contextualize economic problems, especially historically and politically. They suggest that economic matters might well be the *effects* of wider issues. Economic order and progress, in such views, rely upon various preconditions. Central to these are authoritative views of why and how things are as they are, without which the world must be seen as risky and unpredictable. And Wolf's point is that authority can be both won and lost.

Consider also a speech by the outgoing managing director of the International Monetary Fund (IMF), Michel Camdessus, after the AFC. He argues that globalization has seen the arrival of a new breed of economic crises, with "the prominence of the private sector—financial institutions and corporations—on both sides of the equation as creditors and debtors." His analysis links this situation to the weaknesses of the global financial system itself, in that global politics cannot stop crises from occurring and cannot cope with them when they do happen, as is occurring with increasing frequency. Recall that he is referring to the AFC, which happened about a decade before the GFC. He says:

The task is certainly monumental. We are the first generation in history to be called upon to organize and manage the world, not from a position of power such as Alexander's or Caesar's or the Allies' at the end of World War II, but through a recognition of the universal responsibilities

of all peoples, of the equal right to sustainable development, and of a
universal duty of solidarity.

(Camdessus 1999)

If such men are fearful, then it seems reasonable to seriously consider arguments that globalization is not only problematic but capable of threatening
global order.[3]

Poverty and underdevelopment: the context of DE

There is, as we can readily see if we want to, much poverty, unhappiness,
and inequity in the world—more in some countries than in others. The
developed world enjoys much, materially and spiritually, while the rest of
the world does not. It is evident that some people think that something
should be done about this, and it is said—especially by economists—that
much of the problem is economic. If this view is accepted, the natural
expectation is for DE to offer solutions for what to do, how to solve the
problem, and how to build the bridge—that is, to argue that there is a
problem of development, mainly economic, to which there is a known and
reliable solution even if people may argue over the precise details of exactly
what this is. Yet, in many instances, the solution is not readily apparent.

Ha-Joon Chang's *Kicking Away the Ladder: Development Strategy in
Historical Perspective* (2002) is a short and accessible comparison of the
development paths of today's developed regions with those recommended
to today's poor. Chang argues that the policies and institutions of today's
developed countries did not exist when they themselves were developing,
and so are better seen not as suited to historical tasks of development
but as the *results* of successful development. This does not fit easily with
ideas that development is about known problems with known solutions.
Reference may be made to such historical issues as the high levels of import
tariffs in the US during the nineteenth century, the lack of democracy
throughout Europe at the same time, and frequent high levels of corruption
(such as in the US in the decades prior to World War I). In these situations
historical accounts of the causes of change often differ vastly from what is
now prescribed.

A search of the available literature shows that DE (unlike accepted
predictive knowledge, such as, say, civil engineering) exhibits a persistent
instability of positions both over time and between contexts. Thus Lindauer
and Pritchett (2002) ("What's the Big Idea? The Third Generation of Policies
for Economic Growth") offers a believable account of shifts in economists'
views over the past three generations and relates this instability to changing
social and historical contexts.[4] My point here is that a student of DE has to
cope with this instability—with a literature full of arguments rather than
one offering known and stable solutions. The argument is sometimes made
that this disagreement amounts to a pattern of progress, as mistakes are

replaced; we will consider this view. But Lindauer and Pritchett (henceforth L&P) argue that it is context—not progress—that explains mainstream views. I discuss this further later.

Meanwhile, out there in the world, inequality and unfairness remain. Some people (far from all) seem to do better, while others do worse; some who had been doing better now do not, while some seem mired in difficulties. This suggests that we do not yet know how to build the bridge. But a reader will find many aid programs, development strategies, and so forth that look like attempts to do so, and this prompts a striking question: if mainstream thinkers about development did not know what would work, why did they think they did? What does this suggest about their conceptualizations and practices?

This situation is interesting, of itself, some three generations after World War II. After spending considerable amounts of time and money on research to find development solutions that are reliably predictive, despite what may be said to the contrary by some particular school of thought or practice, there is no agreed set of solutions, and the dispute continues. This is *characteristic* of the literature on development but not of an accepted predictive knowledge, such as civil engineering.

Action and actors: the developers and what they do

Let us, however, choose to assume, as many do, that development is a problem with known solutions. This poses the question as to how we might defend this choice, but leave that aside for now. The assumption fits with the current situation, which is that the world possesses various development agencies, charged in various ways with doing development based on the assumption that development is a problem with known solutions. This assumption influences how they conceive of what they are meant to do and the contexts within which this happens.

Development agencies include the multilateral development agencies (the UN system and its agencies, the World Bank and other development banks, and the IMF), which work with, or sometimes against, developing country governments and their organs (planning committees, central banks, line ministries). There are also the social and political organizations of developing countries, as well as non-governmental organizations (NGOs).

Thinking of development as a known problem with known solutions, however, leads to considerable difficulties. The basic issue here is the instability of views, for, if knowledge is robust, then views may be expected to be stable over time and among different agencies. There will be an observable problem of development that these organizations are meant to solve. But if readers look at the literature and the positions taken, there is no clearly defined agreement or stability about what that problem is.

There are two important aspects to this variation over time and place: valuations and cause–effect logics.

Valuation is essential to any way of gauging success, yet there is a striking lack of agreed definitions of development, even though there are good arguments for a lack of agreement on how to value developmental outcomes (see Box 1.2). The conceptualization that *assumes* that development is a problem with solutions implies agreement on how developmental outcomes are to be valued.

Box 1.2 Welfare economics

Mainstream economics uses the idea of *welfare*—the well-being of individuals—to explore ways in which different situations influence the pattern of welfare. Do the poor benefit? Do the rich benefit? How can one think about this?

Generally, economics textbooks about welfare economics argue that such discussions are based on making intertemporal and interpersonal welfare comparisons—that is, comparing the well-being of different people and of the same person at different times. Such comparisons require some form of value judgment, even though values usually differ. So, within economics, good reasons exist for the lack of agreed definitions of something like development.

For an accessible, short and common sense overview, see Williams 1996, downloadable from www.york.ac.uk/media/che/documents/papers/discussionpapers/CHE%20Discussion%20Paper%20151.pdf.

If development is a known problem with known solutions, there should also be agreement about cause and effect. But securing agreement here also poses problems, because it requires getting people to agree about the identification and comparison of causes and effects, and of the nature of cause–effect relations across very different contexts. For mainstream developers, such as the World Bank, these assumptions include the idea that development is knowable. My point here is that something can be learned by characterizing the situation as a contest between people with quite different assumptions about the nature of the world.

If we reflect that these fundamental assumptions imply knowability, perhaps it is clearer how and why economists (rather than lawyers or bankers) should have been centrally placed in development practice since it is (or was) believed that they may actually know important things, assumed to be knowledge and comparable to that of natural scientists, that will predict what will happen if certain steps are taken. In other words, it was assumed that the best way to secure progress was through development, understood as a process like building a bridge, which could be planned, known beforehand, and expected to lead to unambiguous results—a river with a bridge across it. Further, it is believed that the best site for such knowledge is an agency that can supply a crucial input asserted to be in short supply: capital (thus a bank). And so a World Bank, heavily staffed by economists, should be a repository of the solutions to the problems previously discussed. The basic conceptual beliefs are reflected in organizational practice. But, we should ask, how persuasive are all these assumptions? Coping with DE and its positioning within DS requires being aware of these assumptions and where they may lead the discussions.

The problem of development

In the previous section, I argued that much development practice, and DE, assumes that development is a knowable process, characterized by problems and solutions and not so different from civil engineering. It turns out that these assumptions are slippery, if not treacherous, and should not be taken at face value. Part of the issue has to do with how conceptual choices embedded in economics deal with arguments, such as those of Wolf and Camdessus, which stress the dependence of economic processes on other factors. The idea that economic issues can be *separated* from others, however, is based on belief that economic logics powerful enough to warrant independent study—ideas clearly dependent upon notions of the knowability of such logics. Yet while economic issues are usually examined on theoretical grounds, I think it more interesting to look at the particular **empirics** associated with them.[5] These, rather than discussion of theoretical logics, offer more useful grounds for reflection.

But before looking at empirics, let me offer a contrasting and very different view of the issues discussed in the previous section. Rather than conceptualizing the problem of development in terms of known solutions to problems, it is possible to think of it quite differently. If the future is unknowable and unpredictable, yet development is something that can be done, then tensions between these two ideas can be thought of as central. That is, the key issue is the habit of thinking of development as both product and process, transitive and intransitive (Cowen and Shenton 1996; Fforde 2009). The resulting tensions lead to contending authoritative voices, who argue that they know what will happen, and so solutions are known in advance, when, at the least, they probably cannot all be right (whatever we mean by that). Thus, if we appreciate the problem of development as how mainstream concepts treat it as both a historical process and something that is known beforehand, this helps us understand what we find—the characteristic presence of different authorities with their contending positions. This suggests understanding the problem of development as primarily coping with tensions that arise in the evident unpredictability of social change, combined with the habit of asserting that difficulties can be addressed by action-based policy or some other vehicle for intentionality that is based upon assumptions of predictability. Given this, it has been argued (and I will discuss this in various ways later in the book, especially the next chapter) that we historically have seen two ways of solving the problem, though neither of these amount to more than coping strategies, as neither abandons the notion of knowability (Cowen and Shenton 1996).

The first, the Marxian conceptualization, argues that the only intentionality is the need for actions—such as development policy—to suit the laws of social change; for Marx, these were the laws of capitalist development as he understood them. It does not matter that mainstream economic theory does not predict, because policy will end up supporting capitalism. Readers may feel this is a tautology, and I tend to agree.[6]

The second argues that, in the face of evident unpredictability, correct development is what a given authority says it is.[7] If we want to know what works, we find an authority and believe what he or she says.

When presented in this way, for many people neither of these views is entirely acceptable. We are drawn to consider that what are presented as statements about known cause–effect relationships may be better seen—with less difficulty and inconsistency—as simply coming from within different belief fields, judged and valorized as such, rather than following some more general set of criteria (it is, to use a contemporary phrase "simply true for them"). An introduction to an anthropological treatment of policy is Shore and Wright (1997), which suggests thinking of DE as an explanation presented as predictive. If this position is taken, then what should be used are criteria suitable for judging what constitutes an acceptable explanation, accepting that these criteria are different from those of successful prediction. In this sense, DE's failure to secure reliable prediction does not mean that it is "wrong," because such a judgment means taking things at face value and adopting the conceptualization of DE that what matters is to "get it right" in cause–effect terms.

This situation, as I will discuss in Chapter 2, is consistent with evidence that the predictions of DE are not robust, which would suggest that we should best view and judge such theory as explanatory rather than predictive. To put it another way: if, as much economic research can be interpreted to indicate, the future is indeed unknown, then how do development practitioners live with this? The situation is made tense, though, by the **internal** practice of economics, which asserts, through the use of algebra, that the discipline remains inherently predictive (see Box 1.3) and so encourages ways of coping that treat it as such.[8] By contrast, when DS avoids explicit pretensions to prediction, it encourages different ways of assessing its positions (though the reader may wish to reflect on implicitly predictive claims, such as views that "participation works").

The reader may note that such puzzles and tensions do not seem to arise in the same ways in interactions between humans and nature—such as bridge building. Such knowledges, like those in social sciences, are of course socially constructed, yet it seems to be the case that knowledges associated with natural sciences is far more often experienced as predictive—that is,

Box 1.3 Time and causation

To quote Friedman 1966 [1953] on time and causation: "The ultimate goal of a positive science is the development of a 'theory' or 'hypothesis' that yields valid and meaningful (i.e. not truistic) predictions about phenomena not yet observed" (op. cit. p. 7).

For a softer and earlier statement that is very similar, see Stigler (1947): "Since economics is a science, it is appropriate to begin with an examination of the nature of science . . . The important purpose of a scientific law is to permit prediction" (Stigler, p. 3).

Economists' **models** deal with time by introducing a variable—"t." If a variable changes, and this leads to changes in other variables at higher values of "t" (that is, later in time), then the first is a cause and the second an effect.

Here also noneconomists confront an important, for economists, distinction between economic change viewed as "growth" and economic change viewed as "macroeconomics." Internally, the distinction rests on what is assumed to change and what is not. In the latter, a concept of "productive capacity," strongly related to that of a capital stock accumulated from past investments, is assumed to be fixed, so that the models aim to explain *levels* of utilization of that capacity. This is thought to operate in a "medium-term," historically with business cycles, and perhaps of five to seven years. The former, however, then treats that capacity as what can be explained by models (see Chapters 5 and 6). But note that in such models "time" is an algebraic variable (typically "t").

how we set about building airplanes, fixing cars, and so on.[9] We find that when we study such knowledges we do not need to know much about their historical origins or how particular approaches conflict with others. These knowledges have their histories, of course, and these usually involve at times strident contestations, but what we end up with, in terms of what we need to study, are usually a series of accounts that are relied upon to tell us that "X" will happen under circumstances of "Y." Of course, as we can see from the gathering crises of the environment, climate change and so on, these areas also show us examples of familiar human confusion, mendacity, and self-interested short-sightedness. But the knowledge associated with this seems to be able to converge to some predictive stability.

Other problems seem to arise in situations where judgments are being made about the actions and welfare of others. Was the aid project trying to do the right thing? That is, if, for example, it was meant to provide aid to refugees, was this the right thing to do? In the discussions of the "right thing" people typically include, often in familiar and muddled ways, discussions about what happened in terms of cause and effect, as well as discussions about what happened in terms of how to value it. In aid language, was the project trying to help the right people (and how do we know that it did?), *and* in trying to help whoever it was trying to help, was its cause–effect logic correct?

One take on this is that what humans appear to want mainly to do, when they discuss activities that may influence the welfare of themselves and others, is, at root, related to attribution of responsibility in the widest possible sense (Stoecker 2007) rather than any rationality of knowable cause and effect, which (no matter what the rhetoric and social pressures may suggest) is placed secondarily. Put simply, humans do not, when they think and behave as humans, act like natural scientists when they work on their models and run their experiments. Further, as we shall see when we discuss behavioral and experimental economics in Chapter 22, it seems reasonable to believe that humans are well aware of the difference between actually *being* in a particular situation, and pretending to be.

It would be limiting to conclude from this that DE is simply wrong. Interestingly, as already mentioned (and see Chapter 2), it is the pretensions to prediction inherent in the algebra that economics uses—and the use of statistical analysis to explore validity—that provide useful empirical arguments for the unknown nature of development. The issue here is not so much the assumptions but where they take their adherents.

Development economics and doing development

It follows that DE needs to be understood and not simply accepted or rejected. One approach is to look at variation in theoretical positions over time and place, and their roles within wider issues, such as the importance of policy in governance, social meanings, and organization. This is the approach I take here. This assumes that DE is justified, in terms of practice, not through a consistent predictive power but in other ways and places.

In this sense, DE is best studied first in terms of its *history* and *context*, and second in terms of its possible *impact* upon the of economic agents such as developmentalist governments, businesses, international and domestic capital markets, and families. Looking in both directions in this way can be of use both to economists and others.

For economists, this may resonate with deep tensions in modern economics—nagging issues such as, at the micro level, instrumental rationality (see Box 1.4) and, at the macro level, the meaning of intentionality in social change.

These problems have not been entirely ignored, for the discipline contains a wider range of opinion than outsiders sometimes realize. For example, the famous Robert Lucas critique of macroeconomic modeling arose in response to the view that the models' structures could not be assumed to be policy independent (Lucas 1976). This was powerful, especially coming from a

---

Box 1.4 Instrumental rationality

Instrumental rationality is the idea that it is unnecessary to distinguish between the real world and the decision-maker's perceptions of it. Simon (1986) provides a useful introduction, explaining that the assumption is required to support a way of understanding decisions and behavior which uses a formal algebraic model and treats humans as no different from a nonsentient machine (see Chapter 11).

Nobel Laureate. The issue here was, as in the case of developmental ideas, the instability of apparent knowledge—specifically, of estimated macro-economic relationships (such as between employment and inflation). Lucas attributed this instability to researchers not knowing the microeconomic relationships upon which the macro **data** presumably rested. His argument assumes, of course, that such relationships may be known and reliably aggregated to provide a basis for predicting what the whole economy would do.

But the central puzzle here is the apparent instability of economists' knowledge, which may be understood in different ways. L&P offer one option, which is to look at the changing contexts to explain shifting assertions of what is known (see Chapter 2). Another is to throw the question wide open: can humans be understood as though they were machines or plants, which are assumed not to change as observers' perspectives alter?

This question is central to the assumption of instrumental rationality: do the beliefs and perceptions of those who are being modeled matter, and, if not, are they being treated as objects rather than subjects? But why do these points need to be made at all? If economics were successfully predictive and associated with policy, in the same ways that materials science is associated with engineering, then little of this would be relevant. It becomes important precisely because this does not happen. And the reader may (I hope) start to feel deeply puzzled by the issue of instrumental rationality: how can this view be held by members of societies saturated with Judeo-Christian ideas that stress humanity's essential nature as defined by individual *choice*? One intellectual time line here stems from ideas of behavior, in some accounts derived from Darwinian zoology.

One possible answer leads from the alternative understanding of the problem of development I previously mentioned—that is, the central importance of the tensions created by the belief that development is both product and process. This answer has to do with the idea of "trusteeship"— the belief that the responsibility of the developed is to develop the underdeveloped, so they are rightly entrusted with the conditions thought suitable: power, assets, resources, knowledge, and so on (Cowen and Shenton 1996). The idea of trusteeship, and the practices supported by it, thus reinforce belief in asymmetry, related to an idea of social progress: the more advanced know more and better than those who are not. While common, such views sit uncomfortably, for instance, with evidence that the daily livelihood strategies of hunter-gatherers often required considerably more brainpower than those of modern technology-dependent office workers (Diamond 2005).

Driving many of these concerns is the persuasive but slippery idea that development is *knowable*. If knowing implies use of algebra and the instrumental rationality assumption, this constructs underdeveloped people as objects, behaving according to objectively known laws. Their own beliefs and perceptions, perhaps different from those of the observer and so excluded from the observer's model, will be in any case inevitably ignored in the analysis. This is one reason why economists' tendency to assume instrumental rationality is so important to understanding DE.

Something else that often accompanies these tensions is the lack of importance attached in DE to the values and interests of policymakers themselves. To appreciate how ideas about economic policy influence behavior, it is useful to appreciate that the focus of DE is somewhat one-directional—on the economy—and not on the effects of the economy on the economist. Yet such considerations are often vital for those who want economists' views on bond prices, on where a government will spend its infrastructure budget, on where middle-class families will send their children for education, on where small businesses will look to sniff out opportunities, and so on.

Assumptions of knowability and predictive power would appear to stress the importance of policy. Indeed, common in much DE is the tendency to think of policy, not simply as important, but as the key to change. The dominant source of agency in doing development is that of the state, for it is the state (guided by economists) that does policy. This not only fits with the idea that development is done but also validates views that stress the importance of DE as the source of ideas that enable this to happen and be delivered, as policy advice, to a state. As DE engages the task of doing development, it is driven toward a certain range of political positions.

These views, thus, may have major political implications. They fit, for example, with approaches to understanding politics that stress the importance of relations between state and society. There are others, such as a focus upon the "creation and maintenance of order" (for a discussion, see Almond 1988)—and with a not uncommon tendency among development economists to label misguided (in their view) but democratically supported policies as "populist." DS often stresses very different issues, such as the ways in which use of participatory techniques and reflective practice may avoid the denial of voice that often seems to plague aid project design. Characteristic arguments between economists and others may be seen as related to different ideas about how change happens.

Be that as it may, in terms of how the internal practices of DE may be assessed, if these assumptions of knowability and predictability are, as it appears, awry, and DE is better seen as explanatory than predictive, two important conclusions follow.

First, it is worth investing less in understanding formal policy logics than in understanding their prerequisites—government and the politics that makes governments. Studying DE can be a part of this as it shows the direction in which powerful noneconomic factors may be pushing.

Second, it may be better to form a view about what is happening *without* policy change. Institutions, for instance, may be thought to change by themselves.

Conclusions

This chapter has covered a wide field quickly so as to raise core issues. At the very least, I hope to have started the reader thinking that things may not be quite as simple or obvious as they seem. For example, I have argued that the mainstream conceptualization of the problem of development entangles ideas of development as something that can be done with the view that it is a knowable historical process. Granted the strong possibility that the future is better thought of as unknown, I argue that this tangle is usually resolved by maintaining that correct development is to be defined by authority. In turn, this suggests an alternative conceptualization: that the crucial issue is not to know what works, in predictive terms, but to appreciate, and so hopefully to cope with in some way (for example, by mitigating possible negative effects caused by denial of voice), current dominant ways of organizing development interventions, such as aid projects, that are built around spurious assertions of predictability. As we shall see, this goes to the heart of how DE may be positioned within DS.

Reflection on issues of valuation and cause–effect relations, combined with evident lack of agreement and the doubt, at times for good reason, whether agreement may easily be obtained, suggest that development is more than simply a known problem and solution. Above all is the need to develop critical judgment—that is, frameworks for assessing positions in the literature. It is striking that many people are not equipped to do so, especially economists. One issue that stands out is the *instability* of positions as to what is said to work, in DE as in DS, both over time and among proponents. Another is that to accept a proposition is to choose and, perhaps, to be persuaded. So the question is: how to choose?

For economists, there is the fact of competition with other disciplines and approaches, such as DS: where truth is widely accepted and presented as multiple and subjective, the apodictic propositions of DE face problems. It is this sense of skepticism—its origins and consequences—that underlies the structure of this book. Central to it is the emphasis on delving into underlying assumptions and where they lead so as to help readers form views about what they are being encouraged to believe as they engage with analyses of a development policy or aid project.

In the next chapter I will address **facts** internal to DE. This is one important aspect to coping with DE.

Questions for discussion

1.　What is your response to the idea that DE does not seem to present known correct solutions to problems?

2.　What have you learned in the past about how to make critical judgments of positions taken about what should be done about development?

3.　Should judgments that assert they can predict be assessed differently from judgments that say that they simply explain?

4.　What does it mean to have an explanation that does not predict?

Notes

1　It is easy to find reviews of this literature, both articles and books. I leave it to the lecturer, if this book is being used as part of a taught course, to guide students. Rodrik 1998 gives a simple introduction from a DE perspective.

2　NIA is discussed in Box 4.2 on p. 58 and in Chapter 7.

3　Readers coming from a DS perspective will probably be well aware of the so-called post-development literature, as well as the variety of arguments, old and new, that underdevelopment is caused by the dominant change processes present in the world. As we shall see, part of the issue in understanding the position of DE in DS is to appreciate how economics problematize such issues.

4　I will refer to this text frequently. David Lindauer is the editor of *Macroeconomics Readings* (1968), and Lant Pritchett has worked for the World Bank. I think it fair to say that both are mainstream economists, and I like the article a lot.

5　Lest post-modernists and others imagine that I assert that reference to empirics implies a belief in "objective facts," please recall Box A in the Preface. Inconsistency of an approach's "internal" facts is still of interest even if such facts are thought to be relative to that approach's observation theory, discursive status-giving, and so forth.

6　The possible interpretations of intentionality among Marxists and Marxians are important, but this is obviously not the place to discuss them. Here I follow Cowen and Shenton (1996). Some would argue, for example, that Marxian and other laws of social change are tendencies, subject to which people make history.

7　It has well been said that one can have power without authority, but one cannot have authority without power. This means that authority—the reasonable expectation of being obeyed or of one's opinions treated well— confers power. See Hindess (1996).

8   Those readers who are economists may notice that I am avoiding the phrase "formal model," which is common in many economists' discussions of their methods, in favor of "algebra." This is deliberate. For me the use of the term "formal model" to refer mainly to algebraic models, often with the accompanying adjective "rigorous," is misleading, as it seeks to assert that algebraic models are necessarily somehow more rigorous and formal than other structures of thought. I find this view impossible to accept. I would point to the lack of algebra in Einstein's major published works. More importantly, it does not follow from the use of algebra that the analysis is necessarily rigorous, in the sense that it avoids inconsistency. See Kline (1990) and especially his discussion of Gödel.

9   It may be asked how fixing cars is related to an interaction between humans and nature; my answer is that a car is an artifice—something made— and fixing it seems to rely far more on knowing, say, what happens if one changes the ignition timing and far less upon knowing, say, how to persuade one's son to hold the spanner (wrench).

2 Evidence and positions

Development economics and its facts

In this chapter, I start with a discussion of some of the facts of DE. I examine what these may imply and use this as a basis for questioning how we may judge propositions within DE. I then kick off a theme that will continue through this book and is central to it: how DE relates to other fields of inquiry. I commence by examining the robustness of the standard proposition that relations between policy and outcomes are known and then look at the stability of economists' views over time.

The empirics of development

Assessment of propositions in DE starts best with empirics, to see what DE's own internal facts amount to (see Box A on p. xvi). Let us examine the issue of the possible relationship between policy and growth across countries. This is central to the idea that different policies expressed in universalistic terms (such as **import substitution industrialization** or **export-oriented growth**)—see Box 2.1) can be known to work in mainstream terms—that is, across different contexts, so that "what works there works here."

Contrary to what one might expect, there is an evident lack of known robust relations between policies and outcomes across countries. This is shown by Levine and Zervos (L&Z) 1993, in an article entitled "What have we learnt about policy and growth from cross-country regressions?"[1] Using statistical techniques, their research found that if the specification was changed, most observed relationships (correlation) statistically went away. Changing the specification means altering the particular form of the formula used to express algebraically the idea that something is related to something else—that is, the **functional form** (see the list of special terms on p. 323).

L&Z's research looked at the *robustness* of relationships between policy "proxies" (see the list of special terms on p. 323) and economic performance and concluded that only two areas exist where policy has a robust relationship with outcomes: both the black market premium (the gap between official exchange rates and those on the free market, if different) and financial sector policy were related to economic performance. Otherwise, *no* robust relationships exist between policy and outcomes (such as growth).

Box 2.1 Export-oriented growth (EOG) and import substituting industrialization (ISI)

Study of DE usually rapidly leads the student to these two concepts, typically presented as alternative competing models for economic development. They are often placed central because of their importance in the history of DE policy prescriptions, which have debated the value of these as alternatives. This means that "what they really are" is best treated separately.

This said, ISI is the idea that economic development would occur if local producers were able to take back domestic markets from foreign imports, which implies that policies are necessary to protect and support local producers, such as through import taxes (tariffs) and targeted support—for example, credit schemes from which foreign firms were excluded. For EOG, by contrast, it is argued that economic development would happen if policy encouraged exports. Historically, ISI was mainstream doctrine up until around the late 1970s, and so EOG advocates needed to criticize it. (See Fforde 2009, Chapter 4; Waterbury 1999; and the World Bank 1993.)

Any statement that "it is known from the data that policy X creates outcome Y" (such as better growth) should not be accepted at face value.

There are at least two key questions here: first, the response of DE to the research; and second, why DE would assert that relations between policies and outcomes are known and robust, when its own facts imply that this is incorrect?

Taking the first issue, Fforde (2005) looked at citations of L&Z (1993) in the literature and found that, in general, economists had ignored the vital implications: only a minority interpreted the paper as concluding that linking policy and outcomes across time and space is a profound problem.

Turning now to the second issue—why DE could make assertions like "X causes more growth"—consider that a large number of empirical studies report that "X" causes "Y," with statistics to support their conclusions, as is found in the literature (Kenny and Williams 2001). Here an intriguing issue is the assumption of homogeneity—that there is a basic commonality across space and time: things are essentially the same and are related to each other through the same underlying mechanisms. This comes down, in part, to assuming that sampling is from a single population. Basic statistics will tell us that, if this is wrong, the statistical result would be spurious (see Box 2.2). The assumption of homogeneity is that what we are studying does not vary enough to change either our names for things as we move between contexts or our theories of how they are related to each other. This can also be called

---

Box 2.2 Spurious relationships

It is worth stressing that by "spurious" I do not mean "wrong" but rather "empty of meaning." If one uses a ruler to collect measurement data and is then told that the ruler cannot be assumed to be accurate, then the data collected has no meaning. Similarly, if one assumes a model to be correct, and this includes (as it must if its parameters are to be estimated) assumptions about errors in measurement, then any **statistical inference** based upon these assumptions become empty of meaning—spurious—if those assumptions are no longer thought to be true.

We will therefore find spurious effects in situations where researchers report spurious correlations—encouraging belief in cause-and-effect relations but where the apparent effects are actually not known in the sense of stable and predictable consequences. (See Granger 1974 and 1990; Cohen 1994.)

---

the assumption of **ontological** and **epistemological** universality, which I examine in Chapter 3 and also in Chapter 5, where I discuss tools for dealing with ways of understanding DE such as the notion of epistemology.

We will discuss this further later; the point here is that the particular internal empirical problems thrown up by DE tell us much about its use of empirics—that is, the belief that economics in general and DE in particular are concerned with known and predictable relations between economic variables, combined with a lack of attention to empirical evidence that denies this. The reader should note that to make these points I have not had to carry out any deep examination of the particular details of DE theory.

Development economists' unstable views

While it is easy to claim that such assertions by mainstream development economists have typically shown their instability over time, it is now useful, as we seek to gain a deeper understanding of DE, to start considering accounts of how these beliefs have changed. Owing partly to the belief that DE is about predictability and the use of algebraic models, explanations within DE tend to argue that this instability reflects a progressive improvement in the extent to which the economy is understood. In this description, theory converges to the truth. This can, of course, be questioned, and particular ways of doing so are discussed in Chapter 5.

L&P (2002) ("What's the big idea? The third generation of policies for economic growth") offers a historical account of economists' assertions. Looking back over forty years, they compare three points in time: 1962, 1982, and 2002. They situate their discussion within the overarching debate, which has a long history, about whether and how markets in general should be left alone, rather than, for example, suggesting that state policy should be used to secure development. The distinction between EOG and ISI (see Box 2.1) can be thought of in these terms: ISI requires state intervention; EOG, it is said, requires that the state intervene far less. These arguments, one should bear in mind, do not have clear and simple relationships to any reality; as we have seen, one implication of L&Z is that, if the argument is made in these very general terms, it runs up against the empirical result that almost no robust statistical relationships can be found between them. In terms of a debate between ISI and EOG, this implies that the world is too heterogeneous for these terms to be used safely; to put it another way, whatever is referred to by discussions about ISI and EOG would appear to refer to different things in different contexts, *even if the same words are being used*. Chang's point is relevant here, that the nineteenth-century US economy enjoyed high levels of protection against imports by imposing a rather high import tariff (see Chapter 1).

L&P argue that, for the immediate post-World War II generation of economists, mainstream opinion was generally against unregulated markets and in favor of state intervention, as was the case in 1962, but this had turned to support a generation later, in 1982. While, in both 1962 and 1982, economists had been certain about what should be done—what policies should be adopted and how social change should be managed— a generation further on, in the early 2000s, this was no longer the case. The article contrasts the earlier certainties with what the authors see as a current state of confusion that stresses contingency—"it depends"—and far less conviction.

The article offers a range of reasons to explain why economists thought what they did and so what policies they advocated at these three points in time. These shifts are not argued to reflect progress but rather changing contexts. Combined with the discussion on the lack of robust relationships between policy and outcomes, this takes us directly to the issue of how to judge different economic standpoints. The knowability assumption implies that economists' views change because of better understanding of some unchanged reality rather than changes in economists' circumstances. But the lack of robust relations between policy and outcomes combined with the contextual explanation of their instability suggests differently.

It is easy to find histories of economic thought that do not use the concept of linear progress associated with knowability. For example, Yonay 1998 discusses internal tensions within economics during the 1930s and 1940s as the possible empirical validation of formal models through **econometrics** (due to the creation of economic data as well as calculation techniques). The reader should recall the argument common in arts disciplines about the importance of the "subjectivity of truth" that stresses the effects of changing contexts and perspectives upon views taken. Such a perspective implies that any stability of the views within a discipline will be due, not to any inherent characteristics of what is being studied, but rather to unchanging characteristics of the discipline and its approaches.

The argument in L&P is that changing contexts led to changing views, which is quite different from any idea that mistakes were being corrected as economics came closer to a truth. For example, the confidence of 1982 derived in part from a certainty that the old views about the market were wrong.

The L&P article is useful because it is accessible and highlights the fundamental question of how to judge propositions in DE. The central issue here is how one, as an observer, interprets disagreement. If, to return to my earlier metaphor, one chooses to believe that social change can be known, this implies that problems of development are concerned with finding solutions to problems expressed in terms of "do this and that will happen." This is the "underdevelopment is like a river without a bridge over it" way of understanding development. If these truths are there to be found, then the basic yardstick to judge theories offered to one as possible truths is whether they predict or not. Positions that command authority, one may expect, will reflect this, while others that fail to predict will generally not command respect. But what happens if the ideas do not appear to offer predictive power but instead seem to vary—and to keep on varying— between different schools, agencies, and so on? Anybody seeking better understanding will then surely draw different conclusions. For example, given the lack of predictive power, if two positions in DE are contending, should that imply that one at least is (and will remain) wrong? I would argue that it should not.

A conclusion that may be drawn from L&Z (1993) is that DE is not, however it may appear, predictive. This in turn suggests that whether a position is right or wrong is different from what the algebra of economics implies. It seems obvious that, given the particular assumptions of the arguments, two different explanations may both be right, depending on perspectives, but two different predictions cannot both be right. However, things are not quite that simple.[2] To help cope with these issues, I will first discuss them in greater depth and then return to an alternative view, that from anthropology (Shore and Wright 1997), which situates economics as an element of policy and views it as part of organized belief and so contextually determined.

We turn now to discuss how, if not through prediction or some linear progress to better knowledge, propositions come to be treated as valid—that is, how they gain authority.

The authority of an economic position

Fundamental to this discussion is the source of the authority of a position. Authority strongly influences what is accepted at a seminar table, by the editors of a journal, or by the audience at a conference.

Developing critical judgment may simply be a process of positioning—that is, learning what is right and wrong in terms of what is authoritative. At this stage the reader may feel that these are open questions, and it is not quite clear how they are to be answered. This is quite reasonable. But part of the argument here is that DE does not appear to offer answers that go much beyond the pretensions to prediction inherent in its method. This means that the position of DE within the wider area of development practice needs to be understood by using intellectual resources from outside economics.

Let us now return to the simple account of changing mainstream views, which can be found in L&P (2002). The central conclusion to be drawn from the analysis is that while economic theory does not present its positions as variable and dependent upon economists' contexts, it nevertheless has its history. The best way to explain the ebb and flow of shifts in consensus, they argue, is by the contextual factors whose effects can be seen in economists' changing beliefs.

They argue that the dominant skepticism about markets around 1962 is explained by the experience of the 1930s; that the dominant optimism of the period around 1982 can be explained by the experiences of the 1960s and 1970s; and that the hedged and far less confident positions around 2002 are to be understood as confusion created by the widespread failure of the policies advocated with such confidence in the 1980s to generate clearly and emphatically the expected results. I discuss this further in Chapter 10.

There is nothing definitive about L&P's arguments. The reader may find other accounts of the history of economic views, and their empirics are weak. My point is that their accounts of history suggest alternatives that need to be addressed. To do so requires selection of criteria to underpin development of critical judgment.

The L&P arguments may be put into wider contexts. The central issue for L&P in describing differences between mainstream positions is the differing views taken of the value and direction of state actions—that is, which policies were deemed to be correct at the three points in time. Note that these views probably were not isolated from larger big picture issues, and in seeking a better understanding we would need to identify these issues as discussed in different historical accounts. Related to these positions, we indeed find a range of debates about the meanings, contexts, and consequences of these policies. Thus the policies of the 1980s, which were generally hostile to state intervention and confident that markets should be left alone, are often labelled "neo-liberal" or "Washington consensus." By contrast, the earlier 1960s' positions that assert the importance of state action in the face of the unreliability of free markets are given other labels, such as "interventionist." Put simplistically, this is reflected in the ISI vs. EOG debates (see Chapters 15 and 19 and Box 2.1).

The idea that development is a known problem with known (or at least knowable) solutions does not sit well beside L&P's argument that change in views is contextual, depending on the circumstances in which economists find themselves. Consider the issue of predictive failure: lack of robust relations between cause and effect (typically, policy and outcomes) means that interventions asserted to be correct in these terms will usually fail to lead to the hoped-for subsequent events. Unless "spun" into something more suitable, failure and success will not be related in a stable manner to policy settings. One conclusion is more research, another is to try harder, and another is lie and pay the right consultant to prove your point. But the alternative interpretation of the problem of development suggests that such failure is less a matter of prediction and more a situation that challenges the authority of (and behind) a particular position. This way of seeing things can make debates far less confusing, because *DE becomes an expression of important beliefs rather than a set of known solutions* (see Box 2.4, "Model vs. muddle").

As such, these beliefs are worthy of study. For example, although not yet discussed in detail, an important aspect of DE is the use of words and variables—**gross domestic product** (GDP) is a good example—that amount to universalized categories that helps it to embrace "one size fits all" policies and shows a tendency to think that "what works there works here" (see p. 27). This brings us to the point made by L&P (2002)—that the current situation is mainly characterized by far less certainty than in the past—whereas in the 1960s and 1980s economists were certain that they knew the problem and solution, L&P argue that there is a *qualitative* difference between these two earlier sets of views and the contemporary position, which tends to skepticism: there is no new "big idea" that offers people a formula, a set of "true and known solutions" to how to manage the economy. If forced conceptually into a **contingent** world where universalisms lack authority, this poses fundamental issues for DE and helps explain current tensions, such as the collapse of authority suggested by Wolf and Camdessus in Chapter 1.

Here we must ask to what L&P attribute the contemporary skepticism they identify and whether this points to a shift of economic method toward an arts subjectivity. Crucially, they return to the familiar argument that knowledge should be able to progress—that research has, *so far*, failed to discover stable relationships. They accept that things are unknown without confronting the idea that they may be unknowable in the terms they use. They may then explain failure to secure change through knowable cause–effect relations in the conventional ways with which they are familiar and which they presumably also teach; there is no issue of knowability, DE is thus believed to be consistent, and the problem is simply that progress along a path to knowledge remains limited. To understand such tensions we need both a far deeper understanding of DE, which is to come in later chapters, and also to equip ourselves with tools to deal with DE as a body of knowledge (in particular, see Chapter 6).

These ideas—and this will be confirmed by our examination of DE in later chapters—conform to a particular and uncritical interpretation of the role of *intentionality* in social change. Societies, through their governments, thus do development. This is manifested through an idea of policy based upon known cause–effect relations. DE contributes to this through its purported knowledge of economic change. L&P and other texts show clearly the limits faced by even these, by many contemporary economists' standards, skeptical members of the profession. While willing to argue that changes in economists' views are to be explained by context, the unchallenged belief we find in L&P is that cause–effect relations can be known, specifically and concretely through the methods of the discipline. Fundamentally, they take the position that the causes of social change are knowable and essentially *economic*, and should be used for prediction and as a basis for policy.

This is clear from L&P's conclusions, which are that cause–effect logics simply need to be better specified. By this, they mean that we should "ground our advice on a complete, coherent, and causal chain from a recommended decision or action to a desired outcome" (Lindauer and Pritchett 2002: 26). In other words, such chains can indeed be known.

But this highlights a central issue that consumers of such analyses confront, consciously or not. What criteria should be used to decide when this knowledge has been attained? The obvious internal answer of DE is when there is an ability to predict how economic variables will move in the future, and how this will change if we do something now, such as impose a tariff, a tax, or take some other step that the model says will lead to certain necessary changes. This is what is meant by the use of explanatory frameworks expressed in algebra, which contain reference to time (see Box 1.3 on p. 12).

Fundamental here is the assumption of knowability. L&P reveal their choice of a universalistic logic. They valorize (state what is good and what is bad) and list the elements of a correct approach to analyzing the economy, yet there is little to indicate, in ways that can be checked using their own facts, just why these factors are important. They include:

- The current level of income—GDP per capita: policies, they say, work differently at different levels of income. This assumes that theory may refer to the same policies in different contexts.
- The potential linkages with other economies (who are your neighbors?).
- Government strength and capacity (meaning that governments may be capable of implementing certain policies but not others).

L&P admit that what is meant by strong and weak states is not clearly identified but then treat the concept of policy implementation capacity as observable. This illustrates a characteristic use of categories: while not clearly linked to some **observation theory**, categories are still thought to refer to something in a rather uncritical manner, and so are readily thought of as something that influences economic growth. Significantly, this elucidates a situation where the algebra, despite its apparent basis in predictability, is essentially explanatory—no more and no less. This poses in turn the fundamental question of the origins and nature of the authority of such explanations, an important issue, but a matter of social psychology, history, politics, and many other things, none of which are the internal subject matter of DE.

We have learned from this discussion that assessments of DE should not be taken too much at face value. A useful point from which to judge positions is as part of the far wider issue of how to cope with the mainstream solution to the problem of development (see Chapter 1). If the problem is the tensions created by the belief that a historical process can be done, this accompanies the tendency to have recourse to authority when deciding what to believe and to rely upon assumptions of knowable cause–effect relations. Assertion of the value and existence of prediction can be seen as partly the solution to the problem. Yet confronting the issue of knowability, for economists, is a big task, precisely because, as we have already noted, while the formal structure of theory implies predictability, DE's facts suggest otherwise (L&Z).

Is knowability a necessary assumption?

We can now discuss in greater detail if one should assume there are known policy logics—that is, to accept statements that "this policy works." This means thinking more about the apparent lack of known robust global relations between policies and outcomes, reported by L&Z 1993 and previously discussed. I stress again that this is empirics: the result does not come from some postmodernist sociology but from the application of accepted statistical methodology *within* economic practice. It shows that DE beliefs in universalistic policies (such as ISI and EOG) are unfounded; more accurately, they are inconsistent with DE's internal conceptualization of relations between theory and facts.

This shows in many ways an important element of the internal practices of DE—respect for consistency. The L&Z research exists within a wider research program looking for regularities in relations between variables seen as possible causes of economic growth—policies and other variables— and outcomes in terms of per capita GDP growth. This is the "cross-country growth regressions" literature, which sought to discover what factors influenced growth in per capita GDP and explained differences in it, usually by carrying out a statistical exercise that made GDP per capita, or changes in it, the variable on the left-hand side of the equation and put what was argued to explain it on the right-hand side. Thus if the researcher argued that high import tariffs were bad for growth, the left-hand side variable would be GDP per capita and the right-hand side variable would be some measure (or **proxy**, see the list of special terms on p. 323) for the level of import tariffs. This model would then be applied to a set of data, typically a large number of countries over a given time period, and a result estimated that would imply something about the relationship, in that dataset, between the outcome—GDP per capita—and the policy (levels of import tariffs). This approach obviously has a wide possible range of applications. We can see it in a naive form in some remarks from Michael Todaro, arguing that tropical countries do badly at development:

> Almost all developing countries are situated in tropical or subtropical climatic zones. It has been observed that the economically most successful countries are located in the temperate zone. The dichotomy cannot simply be attributed to coincidence; it must bear some relation to the special difficulties caused directly or indirectly by differing climatic conditions. . . .
>
> There is growing evidence that tropical geography does pose serious problems for economic development and that special attention in development assistance must be given to these problems.
>
> (Todaro and Smith 2006: 73)

Here the proxy on the right-hand side, argued to explain economic growth, would be perhaps mean distance from the equator, or some variable that takes the value of 1 if the country is tropical and zero if it is not, and so on. It is obvious that the approach assumes that one model is valid across a range of contexts and periods.[3]

This approach generated (and to a certain extent still does) published but contradictory results: scholars publish papers that pass peer review and support their conclusions with apparently reliable statistics, but there is no consensus. Readers will find articles showing that open economies— economies that trade a high proportion of their output—grow faster than economies that do not published beside others that argue the opposite. Kenny and Williams (2001) is a readable and easy introduction to such research.

What is very useful to understanding DE is that this literature consists of a number of published individual research activities that are, viewed as a whole as a research program, inconsistent. We now need to discuss why this happens. One explanation is simple skulduggery (see Chapter 23), but there are other and more interesting explanations.

One is that something is wrong with untested and (internally) untestable assumptions, so that the statistical basis of conclusions is spurious. In this sense something fundamental about the approach of the cross-country growth literature is awry. Statistics 101 contains the pointed lesson that standard statistical analysis rests upon untestable assumptions, one of which is that the model (including the assumed pattern of errors) is correct.[4] If these assumptions are not met, the exercise will simply fail, generating empty estimates—that is, spurious results that are not wrong but meaning-

less. Under these circumstances, if two published articles argue differently—
one that openness is good for growth and the other that it is not—and if
both rely upon untestable but incorrect assumptions, then on these grounds
neither is reasonably said to be wrong or right in its conclusions. Spurious
results simply mean that no conclusions may be drawn.

So, what might be these deep assumptions, shared by all these articles in
the cross-country growth literature? A clear candidate, familiar to the reader
who has some understanding of statistical methodology, is whether or not
sampling is from a single population.[5] What may this mean? Kenny and
Williams 2001 conclude that this is related to assumptions of ontological and
epistemological universality (see Box 2.3).

Box 2.3 Ontology and epistemology

Ontology has to do with what things are said to be. Ontological universalism
then assumes that the nature of things—here, the apparent empirical
reference of economic variables—is essentially unchanged across different
contexts. This is equivalent in the natural sciences to assuming that rocks
are the same on Earth and on Mars.

In the arts, this is related to use of the term "essentialist," a common
pejorative term in contemporary humanities and social sciences.

Epistemology relates to how things are to be understood. Epistemological universalism thus assumes that the ways in which we understand—
for instance, the models we use to predict or explain—are the same across
different contexts. To use the natural science analogy again, this is to
assume that gravity (e.g. Newtonian models of motion) is the same on Earth
and on Mars. To say that gravity is the same is to argue that the same model
should be used in both contexts: gravity is part of that explanatory
framework.

Neither of these assumptions seems to me unreasonable as a starting point.
Why start by assuming that farmers essentially differ? Why start by
assuming that they respond to price signals with different behaviors—habit,
atomistic rationality, collective moral economy? Further, not holding to these
assumptions violates strong ethical positions, such as humanism and
assertion of the essential commonality of humans.[6] A fundamental element
of humanistic viewpoints is that humanity shares an essential nature, which
helps justify hostility to institutions such as racism.

But the combination of L&Z (1993) with a plethora of published results
accepted as statistically legitimate and that often contradict each other
suggests that the facts (of the discussion) question these universalistic
assumptions. This would assume that what works here does not work there,

---

Box 2.4 Model vs. muddle

The reader should think about the status of models in their own conceptualization. It was once put to me by a Vietnamese mathematician that one classic mistake in such thinking was to confuse the model with reality: to "absolutize" it (*tuyet doi hoa* in Vietnamese). This helps us think in terms of the contingency of a model: its reliance upon context. This is to say that persuasive accounts of a conceptual framework should include references to the practices within which the accounts are found: the discipline, its particular empirics (its observation theory), and so on, which are contingent. The model has no absolute existence.

A pithy restatement of this is to refer to confusion of "model" with "muddle."

A related issue is that of categorical thought. This refers to habits that use terms or categories with little reference either to empirics or to logical consistency. For an accessible introduction to discussions of deep historical antecedents of this confusion between what is said and what is thought, see the discussion of nominalism and the origins of modernity in Gillespie (1999) and at length in Gillespie (2008).

---

because, even if the words are the same, they are referring to different things, which are related to each other in different ways. Fundamental to the approach of DE, as we will see in later chapters, is precisely the belief in commonalities across different contexts: economic laws that apply universally to the same categories, such as, among others, GDP, inflation, exports, and foreign investment.[7]

The reader may start to feel that this is moving into very deep waters, and if so I agree. These deep waters do not question the practices of only DE, but pertinent questions may be asked of much within DS. For example, is participation in development (highly valued by many in DS) to be viewed as essentially the same thing globally and have the same effects across contexts? I have seen intense arguments between foreign experts and Vietnamese aid workers who wanted to adapt participatory methods to what they saw as local realities, suggestions that were dismissed as simply "wrong." As I argued earlier, DS may learn from DE. Here it is worth reflecting on possible parallels with various feminist debates and interpretations of "Third Wave" feminism that sees it as a rejection of certain constructions of gender meanings.

Now, one response is to reduce the height of the hurdle. Accepted statistical methodology allows changes so as to find more (or less) robustness in cause–effect relationships. One element of Statistics 101 is the idea that we decide what we mean by a reliable result—a 5 percent chance of error,

10 percent chance, and so on. These are subjective acts (see the discussion of McCloskey's work in Chapter 6).

An example is Hoover and Perez (2005), which reports that the world is indeed a nicer world for economists than L&Z implied, with more robustness in terms of what is "said to be known to work." Economic change, they say, can be about 40 percent explained. But this does not have to end the story. The new criteria could as well suggest that the height of the hurdle be raised, in which case even fewer relationships would be viewed as robust. Or they could lower it still further, and then report 70 percent, and so on.

If we now step back and bear in mind that we are examining DE and its place within DS, we have already learned a lot. Subjectivity is important, views are unstable, and things should not be taken at face value. The question is what happens next. What are the implications of these arguments for making judgments? Evidence suggests that citations of L&Z (1993) reveal that few economists saw any fundamental issue concerning the basic beliefs in DE of known and robust relations between policy and outcomes (Fforde 2005). This might be considered rather shocking in terms of the extent to which DE can be expected to be internally consistent. After all, the unreliability of common positions taken by DE is illuminating about what works where. Light is thrown upon the practices that led to the confidence of the 1960s' and 1980s' positions reported by L&P.

Now it is important to be fair: L&Z (1993) are simply doing good econometrics. The results are empirical in the sense that they work within the realm of economists' facts. However, it is not clear how DE might evolve if DE's universalistic assumptions were abandoned. For instance, recall the nature of most economic data. GDP is viewed as measuring the same thing in different contexts, so a rock on Mars and a rock on Earth are assumed to be the same thing. Assumptions underpin the definition of data and its creation, an issue long known to many natural scientists, such as the notion of "observation theory" (Lakatos 1970; see Chapter 6).

Conclusions

The discussion so far stresses the importance, in coping with DE, of critical judgment and not taking positions advanced by DE at face value. Pretensions to prediction are precisely that, and I have shown the tendency to reject evidence that goes against standard beliefs (Fforde 2005). This is a common human reaction; after all, many people in DS would probably find it hard to abandon belief in the efficacy of participatory methods (I would).[8]

I have used cross-country growth literature as an example, because it is accessible and helps make useful points. But the issue of empirics may be taken further. Algebra variables that seem to have real world referents imply that this is how the world is. If the algebra also includes a "t" (time) variable, the presence of causality is strongly suggested (see Box 1.3 on p. 12). Readers may examine standard economics textbooks, such as microeconomics, and look at the empirical underpinnings of positions taken. These underpinnings tend to be rather thin, if comparison is made with branches of natural sciences, such as fluid dynamics, that offer, based upon observation theory, operationable empirical reference as to what model is used where.

Returning to the particular empirics of economics, it is easy to investigate other sets of facts. A range of inquiries and practices within economics can, like L&Z, throw light upon the robustness of relationships between theory and empirics. For example, I have found evidence from experimental economics that mainstream economics lacks persuasive, factually based assertions about economic behavior which remain robust across cultures, times, and places (Fforde 2005; see also Chapter 22).

I next examine in greater detail the issue of interdisciplinary boundaries, which tells us more about the position of DE within DS. Within economics, some views stress the importance and inappropriateness of the instrumental rationality assumption (see Box 1.4).

Questions for discussion

1.   What is the value of treating facts as objective?

2.   Does it matter that English allows us to ask confusing questions like "How can you know that you know something?"

3.   If DE is founded on the assumption that its methods generate an internal empirics experienced as robustly predictive, and increasingly this assumption seems awry, what should happen next? More importantly, what should we expect to find within DE for this assumption to be more easily abandoned?

Notes

1   The article was published in the top economics journal, the *American Economic Review*, and its findings were not formally challenged. More sophisticated studies such as Fernandez et al. (2001), using Bayesian techniques, come to similar results.

2   What may be said to be right is not so simple as it may appear. Consider an exercise where the target of some activity is measured as "1001 blips, or zaps, or blurs." How is it decided that 1001, say, is so different from 1002 that a prediction of 1001 and an observation of 1002 should be taken to imply a failed prediction? And how is it decided that we shall agree to believe that whatever we are measuring was 1001? This is partly the point of thinking about "observation theory." See also the points made by McCloskey in Chapter 6.

3   Other issues may be raised. I live in Australia, a prosperous country that contains large tropical areas, such as most of the northern half of the State of Queensland. The country that I have spent most of my professional life studying, Vietnam, is

entirely tropical, and its rapid development since the late 1980s is usually attributed to a combination of historical and cultural contexts with two enabling factors: fast abandonment of hard-line Communism in the early 1980s and hard-won achievement of national freedom in the face of French and US military intervention.

4   See the entry under *econometrics* in the list of special terms on p. 324. There are, of course, other, heterodox ways of carrying out statistical analysis, such as those that use Bayesian methods, and these work differently. One could perhaps argue that the standard "model plus error term" methods used in DE match a tendency to an apodictic belief in proof by demonstration, after which the task of econometrics is simply to estimate parameters. See the discussion in Chapter 6 of McCloskey's views and the tensions created by estimations that suggest parameter values are not (statistically) different from zero. We may see here the expression of deep-rooted cultural beliefs in the value of apodictic arguments and their contrast with "open-ended" processes that expect ongoing adjustments to views as practice evolves (Gillespie 2008); Woodside 2006). These are very old arguments.

5   Readers may recall from their basic statistics classes that sampling is only meaningful if it is assumed that the sample is from a group whose relevant characteristics are stable, by which is meant that the group forms a single population. If not, the assumed relationships between the sample and group it is from are awry.

6   A vast set of writings is available in any good library on what people have meant by "humanism." Here I simply point to the tensions that seem to arise if, as this line of argument could take us, we started to argue that "we are all different," so that, for example, citizens of poor regions *should* be unequal before international sources of justice.

7   It is worth spending an hour or so with Samuelson (1947) (the book that played a major role in the mathematization of economics) to see just how his "metaphysical commitments" (above all, to constrained maximization behavior on the part of firms and consumers) drove his methodological interests.

8   If, like me, the reader finds that he or she is attracted to an understanding of participatory techniques, then they may wish to ponder on *why*. Is it the techniques' apparent efficacy or perhaps their seeming promises of democracy, or something else that drives one's views and emotions? To what extent is one usually aware of all this?

3 Interdisciplinary boundaries

The limits of economics

Readers may have asked themselves just why study arrives through discrete disciplines, such as economics, anthropology, and sociology, and why, accompanying these, they find study areas: for example, Development Studies, Gender Studies, area studies such as Asian Studies, and so on. They may have noted that academics tend to hold PhDs in disciplines rather than study areas and that study areas have an inherent tendency to be multidisciplinary.[1] This inevitably raises the general issue of interdisciplinary boundaries, another important aspect of coping with DE.

We come at this issue through the specific position of DE vis-à-vis DS. This position is clarified by the differences in methods that I have already discussed. Specifically, I argue that DE, mainly due to its use of algebra and its particular understanding of natural science, has a strong tendency to assume ontological and epistemological universalism. This means that many outside DE criticize it for ignoring differences and contexts and for too often taking positions that are ahistorical and ungendered. This criticism, however, risks doing little more than simply identify elements of DE's method. I have argued that there is a clear distinction between arts and economics, but, of course, this is a simplification; use of algebra and quantitative methods can be found in arts disciplines, such as practices associated with ideas of "rational choice." On the other hand are economic historians and their ilk.

"Universalism" and knowledge compartmentalization

I have so far mainly discussed the issue of universalism from an empirical starting point. I have not yet said much about the particular models DE uses (this comes later) but have instead stressed facts—DE's particular empirics. To develop the arguments, I did not have to say much about models other than their key characteristics: above all, their use of algebra, the assumption of instrumental rationality, and the treatment of time and so the pretensions to prediction. For me, this relates to my own experiences. With an engineering background and two-thirds of my career as a development practitioner, I want to know what the relevant people think works for them.

Practices such as medicine and engineering may be quite happy with situations where doctors and engineers assert they can predict but not explain outcomes. In engineering, a good example is crack propagation, important in the design of structures such as airplanes. When subjected to repeated stress, parts of these structures, it was found, developed internal cracks that grew slowly and could eventually lead to structural failure. For a while the only way designers could address these issues—for no theory worked for them—was by referring to a series of experiments that reported how cracks would spread under given empirical conditions. These were accepted as reliable enough to design safe airplanes. In the context of DE and DS, this suggests that a core issue may be the lack of observed regularity in terms of standard categories.

Within DE, we can find positions that deal with fundamental questions of method. The instrumental rationality assumption is central, not least because it suggests that subjectivity does not matter: humans can be modeled as though they were machines. Here, though, I need to stress that rejecting this assumption opens the door to a discussion of subjectivities. This may ease negotiation of interdisciplinary boundaries, for acceptance of the subjectivity of whoever is studied encourages discussion of *context*. This is where other disciplines may come in: contexts include culture, history, geography, politics, and so on. L&P (2000) may be read as groping in a similar direction, but in looking for "known logics" does not move far.

Consider now two anthropologists, Shore and Wright (1997), who allow us to gain a perspective on the issues at stake. They argue for seeing policy not mainly as a known cause–effect relationship but as having a central role in the social construction of meaning:

> policy increasingly shapes the way individuals construct themselves as subjects. . . . From cradle to the grave, people are classified, shaped and ordered according to policies, but they may have little consciousness of . . . the processes at work.
>
> (p. 4)

Shore and Wright pose a series of acute questions:

- How do policies work as instruments of governance? Why do they sometimes fail?
- What is meant, practically, by the idea that policy is essentially incoherent on close examination?
- What language helps to legitimate policy as it participates in the processes of governance?
- How do policies construct their subjects as the objects of power?
- How are changes in discourse made authoritative?
- How are claims made that define a particular problem and its solution, thus closing avenues for other alternative definitions?

This approach, obviously, is radically different from that of DE. It places issues, such as the ways in which beliefs are created and reproduced, centrally to its arguments. It shows that accessible and consistent accounts of matters related to policy avoid assuming that policy, and beliefs, such as the economic analysis that may accompany the policy, are mainly concerned with securing a robust knowledge of cause-and-effect relations. This approach provides a different meaning to questions such as what works and why. There is little sense that a given policy should be thought of as "correct," and so the criteria that Shore and Wright use to gauge their discussion of policy characteristics are quite different from those of DE.[2]

Thinking in this very different way can be useful. For example, it illuminates what may be happening when an assumption such as instrumental rationality is adopted. It suggests that, because DE can be seen as organized belief, the central issue in Shore and Wright's account of how an assumption could be adopted or abandoned is *social*—how economists' practices and beliefs may change—rather than (in a standard natural science comparison) how apparent inconsistencies—such as failure to predict—lead to change.[3] Of course, one could say exactly the same thing about anthropologists.

Understanding DE within such an approach would thus mean seeing it in ways that it does not itself share. This is my point: once we start to believe that DE is concerned with explanation rather than prediction, and so not fairly judged by predictive success or failure, the subject itself gives us little with which to assess its judgments. This can be confusing. Another way of putting this is to ask to what extent inconsistency matters. How significant is it to assert that DE is, in this sense, wrong? This is not the end of the matter at all.

For economists, why development economics?

I turn now to an interesting twist, which is how economists themselves have treated the basic issue of whether there should be a subdiscipline called DE. If the same laws apply everywhere (epistemological universalism) and these are applied to the same things (ontological universalism), then what justification can there be for a subdiscipline? Agricultural economics, relatively important within economics up to, say, the early 1990s, has since contracted significantly in the face of such arguments.

An example of this is the history of the attempt to use mainstream economic techniques in Australian rural development support practices, as discussed in McCown and Parton (2006a and 2006b). "Determinate" modeling (what they call "theoretical models") was pushed into these practices. These models took the form of algebra that would produce, it was hoped, ways of predicting, reasonably accurately, how farmers would respond (in terms, for example, of changes in what they were producing) to particular changes in their environment, such as prices. The models were introduced with confidence that it would work (an example of the confident application of mainstream economics) in terms of both predicting farmers' and providing useful advice to farmers. It appears to have failed to meet both goals, and McCown and Parton document this well.

Both in their different ways, the two following examples attempt to argue for the relevance of DE. Obviously, the very argument that such a subdiscipline is needed is associated with the idea that more is required than a standard economics theory when it is thought that development has particular requirements that standard theory cannot satisfy. This produces interesting tensions, and it is useful to see how these are managed. I start with Agenor and Montiel (1999), *Development Macroeconomics*. Both they and Bardhan (1993), who I discuss in the following section, argue that markets do not work properly in developing economies far more often than in rich countries.

Development macroeconomics

Agenor and Montiel self-identify as macroeconomists rather than growth theorists (see Box 1.3 on p. 12 and also the discussion in Chapters 7 and 8). Their arguments about how developing countries' economies really work reveal details of their *essentialism*—that is, assertions of fundamental characteristics shared across a wide range of contexts. Their arguments relate to the social and political struggles of the 1970s and later. The reader may note that they present their arguments as being essentially analytical, without much reference to political context.

Their self-identification as macroeconomists produces judgments centrally associated with tensions created by the focus of mainstream theory upon aggregate supply (see Chapters 7 and 8). By aggregate supply, they mean a conceptualization of the resources available to an economy for production: mainly its **factors of production** (land, labor, and capital). Examples of these tensions include issues of how to use large labor supplies or how to overcome particular supply constraints, such as domestic savings or foreign exchange.

Agenor and Montiel argue that standard macroeconomics textbooks use assumptions that suit developed, not developing, countries. One gains the impression that they believe that a characteristic of developed countries is strongly developed markets. They argue that working on developing countries requires, by contrast, a concern with the weak development of markets. These weak markets, they say, are evident from a range of phenomena:

- Financial repression. (Many capital markets are subject to fixed prices and so capital is rationed—who gets it and why?)
- Informal markets (the rule of one price does not hold;[4] the value of a good or service is contingent upon place, person, origin, ethnicity, and so on).

- Public sector production and activities (such as state-owned enterprises (SOEs), state marketing boards, and so on).
- Imported intermediate goods (one consequence of globalization processes). (Intermediate goods are used to produce other goods, such as the various parts assembled to make a car.)
- Ways of securing working capital. (Many small and medium-sized enterprises (SMEs) that often are family firms are likely to largely invest in fixed assets by using retained profits or informal capital mobilization rather than banks or the stock market.)
- Labor market segmentation. (Again, rule of one price does not hold; value of labor varies according to context/attributes.)

It is interesting to note the way in which Agenor and Montiel treat "behavioral functions" (how markets should be modeled). They argue that what they call "structural" features mean that economic patterns in developing countries are not expected to adjust smoothly—specifically, far less so than in developed economies. They attribute this to liquidity constraints in consumption, credit and foreign exchange rationing, and uncertainty and irreversibility in investment decisions. In the conceptual world of microeconomics (see Chapter 9), markets exist, ideally, for everything, and this should be borne in mind when considering their ideas. The reference point of conceptual comparisons is the characteristics of an ideal. Thus "liquidity constraints" has the conceptual significance that standard models do not apply, the ideal (allegedly visible in developed countries, with their "strongly developed markets") is "far away," and consumers cannot borrow to address problems in managing their spending and incomes.

There are two interesting points. The first is the form of the argument, which stresses a deviation from some ideal, here conceptualized as a perfectly functioning market. This analytical approach is common and underpins the notion of market failure. I warn the reader who is not an economist that what is meant by "perfectly functioning" needs discussion, and details of this don't come until later (Chapter 9). But the reader should also note the assumed links made between the applicability of models and the apparent nature of what Agenor and Montiel are talking about as they present and discuss their models. The reader should also ask if the models are usefully thought of as having stable relationships with some observable and measurable reality. This question needs to be asked.

We may ask just how empirically recognizable this picture is. For me, Agenor and Montiel are discussing, if anything that is persuasively real, relatively developed middle-income countries, typically in Latin America, whose institutions retain elements of the ISI common after World War II and (at the time they are writing) largely seen by the mainstream as bad policy. They stress the value and necessity of having well-operating markets, the actual absence of these, and so the need to have suitable analytical tools to study developing country economies, which, they argue, only have weakly operating markets.

Development economics as a valuable adjunct to mainstream economics

By contrast to Agenor and Montiel, Bardhan (1993), "Economics of development and the development of economics", offers a *historical* overview of DE. He discusses the question of which positions in economic theory, particularly DE, have had authority. The reader may note the ways in which this echoes the arguments of Shore and Wright (1997), which understand these issues in terms of their meanings within communities and organizations.

Bardhan argues that the early development economists focused upon important issues that have come back into mainstream focus. In his view (though this is a common theme in such histories), these were concerned with how to analyze economies where—compared with developed countries—rather high levels of economic transactions either took place outside markets or where markets did not operate "normally" because they were weakly developed. Therefore, like Agenor and Montiel, he is arguing for DE. According to Bardhan, DE took off after World War II,[5] and he stresses the inapplicability of much of the standard mainstream "Walrasian" toolkit to situations where markets neither dominated nor were well developed (see Box 3.1).

Before and just after World War II, economists tended to use graphical methods and far less mathematics than contemporary practitioners (see Chapter 9), but this changed from the late 1940s onward. In many historical accounts, the shift is linked to the economist Paul A. Samuelson, whose book *Foundations of Economic Analysis* was first published in 1947 and in many editions since. This book offered techniques by which economists could abandon their graphical methods for analyzing economic behavior of consumers and producers, and shift toward the use of algebra. Yonay (1998) judges that this shift had profound effects upon economics. I would argue that this tended to further distance economists from consideration of the limits of their discipline. Interestingly, the new algebra generally was little more than a restatement of what the old graphical methods were doing, though it made it far easier to think in Walrasian terms and opened the door to the development of new analytical techniques. It facilitated a shift in metaphysical commitment from "partial" to "general" equilibrium economic conceptualizations.

Bardhan then discusses a range of issues stressed by early development economists and argues that these issues later came back into mainstream focus due to two parallel developments.

According to Bardhan, the first development was from the 1990s, as orthodox economics became more interested in market failure partly

---

Box 3.1 Walras and general equilibrium

General equilibrium analysis, which arguably started with Leon Walras, refers to systems of modeling that view the entire economy as composed of consumers and producers whose interactions occur through markets where prices are sufficient to guide the system to a solution—an equilibrium. "Market failure" means that such models will not easily lead to a solution.

Related to this is the idea of a "perfectly competitive" market, where producers are so small that they have no effect on price (whether they increase or reduce output and sales), so they are "price-takers." Price signals are then sufficient for the model to work, in the sense of a solution in algebraic terms. This solution says what is produced and consumed, by whom, and at what prices.

---

because advanced modeling techniques made it easier to deal with: economists' algebra got better. In that way, mainstream economics could bring developing economics back into the fold, so DE ceased (like agricultural economics) to be treated as different. Bardhan argues that the second parallel shift was—and here he agrees with L&P 2002— that mainstream confidence in markets eroded.

These discussions in both Bardhan and Agenor and Montiel are associated with views that development is something that is done, and these views are linked to ideas of the importance of the state and so of policy. Recall that for L&P the key difference between the mainstream positions of the 1960s and 1980s was the attitude toward the state's actions in development. The shift they identified was from strong support for intervention to strong and equally confident opposition. This was followed in the period leading up to the early 2000s with a change to far less confidence and associated tendencies to skepticism. Bardhan's analysis supports this broad historical perspective.

The influence of context: an example

It is useful to look at examples of how the tendencies previously discussed project into practitioners' discussions of real situations. Many reports are available online, and the reader may find others for themselves. The Web is full of reports from such important agencies as the World Bank, the IMF, United National Conference on Trade and Development (UNCTAD), and various bilateral donors such as AusAID and the Swedish Agency for International Development (Sida), not to mention international nongovernmental organizations (INGOs) such as Oxfam. Good libraries contain copies of such fascinating documents as World Bank annual reports from the 1950s, which show just how different, if equally confident, analyses and prescriptions then were. It is useful to watch how viewpoints vary over time and between agencies. If we step back, we can start to see the tensions present in DE, especially when close to development practice. Note that a *minority* of the citations of L&Z (1993) reported in Fforde (2005) appeared to appreciate the major questions posed by that study: the almost complete absence of robust relations between policy and economic performance globally.

World Bank Report on Laos and intergenerational resource transfers

The World Bank Country Report on Laos referred to here (there are many) (World Bank 1994) is revealing, not for its mistakes, but for the approach taken, especially the willingness to conduct an analysis in terms of divergence from a theoretical ideal.

Laos was and so far remains a poor country, measured in terms of indicators such as per capita gross domestic product (GDP), and its people are mostly farmers. The report's sections on capital mobilization for development stressed the *absence* of formal financial institutions such as life insurance companies as a reason for slow growth. This is close to the argument of Agenor and Montiel that it is the *absence* of "normal" markets that is crucial, and it follows the standard argument of DE (see Chapter 4) that development is mainly economic. The report's focus is thus on institutions for securing growth through improved aggregate supply (recall the point made by Agenor and Montiel), and these institutions are understood in these terms. To look ahead, in Chapters 7 and 8 we will see how DE conceptualizes economic growth in terms of transformation of inputs into output (a "production function"). Is this an example of a comparison of model with muddle (see Box 2.4 on p. 30)? And does it reflect a human tendency to think that what is normal is what is familiar? These can be useful questions, and I myself suffer from similar tensions.

When I visited Laos, I found it interesting to observe the response of farmers living near Vientiane to the large demand for food from the capital. This demand stems from activities such as foreign aid, a Lao middle class, and the presence of rather high wages for simple manual labor. Rural areas around Vientiane showed surprisingly limited development of market gardening, even though common sense might suggest that this potential was important for possible future development. The markets contained strikingly high proportions of Thai farm produce imported to Vientiane from over the river on the west bank of the Mekong River (which forms the Thai–Lao border at that point).

Conversations with Lao farmers and others suggested that intergenerational resource transfers currently and traditionally were usually carried out through kin relations rather than financial institutions. Thus, a lowland Lao man with a new family would often obtain land and house through his wife and from his wife's family—in this sense, the society is bilateral.[6] It took me rather a long time to become aware of this because it is not the usual way of doing things in my own culture. Doing business between generations within the family seemed to work, helping to reduce risk, cope with information costs, and so on. But as I asked more questions other issues arose. Despite the opportunities offered by a market economy, low levels of formal female education and high levels of care-giving responsibilities seemed to reduce the extent to which women, powerful within their families, could engage with and exploit new opportunities. Some interviews I carried out suggested that the most adventurous villages were often those where Communist development activity (education, mobilization, etc.) had been useful in changing people's horizons. For me, this shows how the World Bank Country Report, I would argue typically and for understandable reasons, presents arguments that are fragile in the face of such accessible detail about farmers' lives.

This points to the ways in which such constructed knowledge works, especially its belief that what is seen as but a contingent alternative should be universally true. Concretely, the analyst looks for what is normal—for the World Bank, the use of institutions such as pensions and mortgages— and when he or she fails to find them, treats the economic situation as underdevelopment rather than asking how the people he or she is studying deal with these issues—in Laos, through kinship relations. I did not see the situation in quite the same way but was certainly relatively blind to the local practices of gendered economic activities. More practically, it shows the value of realizing that these habits of thoughts work and can be seen in operation, and how they may be grappled with by looking at the local situation and avoiding premature judgments. Voice does not have to be denied.

Under these circumstances, pointing to a lack of life insurance companies seems rather silly (see note 5 in Chapter 7 on how informal private mortgages underpinned late nineteenth-century London suburbanization). Further, the contrary argument is that economics explains not the lack of development but the lack of human development. And both of these arguments are expressed in the standard universalistic language of development.

The point can thus be made as follows: the World Bank study *assumes* that underdevelopment is the absence of the kind of institutions observed on a daily basis in donor countries, and it translates these assumptions through the lens of DE. We can see in practice what I have been arguing is an important aspect of DE: reference of some observed reality to a conceptualized ideal. In this case, DS offers different insights. For example, Robertson (1991) offers an interesting and useful discussion of variation in intergenerational resource transfer institutions between different societies. Chang (2003) argues that the institutions of today's rich countries are the *results* rather than the *causes* of their success, which is a quite different logical connection.

Conclusions

In Chapters 2 and 3, I have argued that the empirics (in the sense I use the term) of mainstream DE suggest a need for skepticism. This in turn pushes for the development of criteria with which to form judgments so as to avoid taking positions at face value. In Chapter 6 I will relate such concerns to ideas that seek to illuminate ways of assessing such positions—matters of method and epistemology. Granted this, which implies that DE is best seen as explanatory rather than predictive, what is interesting are the characteristics of its explanations: what it seeks to explain and how.

Questions for discussion

1. Are you more or less likely to accept a position if it is presented in logically consistent terms? If so, are you more or less likely to accept it if presented in algebra?

2. What are, for you, the most important implications of the World Bank report on Laos? Why?

3. What does it mean to suggest that a position in DE is wrong? What about DS?

Notes

1   One may hypothesize that one reason for this is the need for universities to be able to move resources into areas that they think may be profitable for a while but are then likely to be closed down at some point. Staffing study areas with staff with PhDs in the "core" areas—the disciplines—means they can be reassigned, and, perhaps more importantly, the study area built up and closed down far more easily. It is one thing easing into retirement professors of economics or history, and curbing their departments, journals, and committees, but what if Development Studies, Queer Studies, or Southeast Asian Studies all had the same sort of clout within academe?
2   Their book contains a number of interesting case studies.
3   We can find this approach applied to the history of economics and the understanding of economists' practices in the work of Yonay discussed in Chapter 6.
4   By this is meant that a good or service has the same price, adjusted for variations in things like transport costs.

5   This fits the common history of development as something that became an issue after World War II and the start of decolonization and the Cold War. DS students should be familiar with this and other, different, arguments.
6   There is a substantial and accessible literature here; for a contribution, see Ireson (1992). See also Ledgerwood (1995) for a discussion of related issues in Cambodia.

4 How DE categorizes development

Internal definitions

This chapter takes a step further into the internal workings of DE and attempts to show how the focus upon algebra limits categorization of development while constructing a core set of issues to be modeled. To put this another way, the specific adopted methodology frames what can be conceptualized; inherent in these choices are the accompanying use of only those categories that—it is thought—may be linked to algebraic variables and formulations. DS, with different methodologies, tends to regard DE as *excluding* important factors from the scope of analysis and discussion. Examination of the textbooks shows concretely how this is done.

Against the background of the first three chapters, here I examine internal definitions of the subject matter of DE. While the earlier chapters tried to put the subject into context, we now turn to look directly at how DE (through the **canonical** textbooks) defines key questions and states the central issues. In the next two chapters I will examine how these positions may be treated before returning in Chapters 7 and 8 to the textbook accounts that look at growth theories.

We will find that DE encounters problems in presenting economic explanations (economic models) of processes of social change—development—that are not easy to interpret as being essentially economic. By this I mean that, for many, development is *not* essentially an economic process but one that includes a range of factors. This means that if, as DE methods imply, economic growth is placed central and other factors peripheral, the question is how and why other factors are given less weight. We can observe how this argument is constructed in the mainstream textbooks, which is deeply bound up with issues of the negotiation of disciplinary boundaries. I start by taking the bull by the horns and attempt a quick summary of the central issue: the relationship between economics and development, as conceptualized by DE.

The central issue

For understanding DE, the central issue can neatly be expressed in the following question: what is said to be the relationship between economic change and the overall change process? Call the overall change process "development" so as to allow elements of intentionality to intrude (but choose to understand these elements of intentionality as "correct policy"). The question then is whether this development is a "known effect" or a "spurious effect" (see Box 2.2 on p. 21) of economic growth (that is, trend changes in the level of per capita GDP[1]). If development is a known effect, to understand development we need do nothing more than understand economic growth. This implies that DE should then stand in a distant rather than intimate relationship with DS, because, fundamentally, DE asserts that if we know economic growth processes we understand development, and we know economic growth through understanding economic models. Consequently, DE would not entertain a need to know much beyond its own positions and arguments.

This argument could be extended to any other core category. The point is to limit analysis to something that is said to be a known cause of development, and the most obvious candidate is trends in per capita GDP. If development is the known effect of those change processes said to be central, DE should be placed centrally—and rather alone—in a proper account of development.

If, on the other hand, economic logics for some reason are not said to dominate, then necessarily others logically do. Economic matters may be conceptualized as "effects"—for example, of changes in social and cultural values. It would then follow that changes in per capita GDP may simply be a spurious effect of economic changes, for no stable correlation would be found between them and GDP. To put the last point another way, what would be found in the economic growth literature is a series of inconsistent results—unstable correlations (each reported as known effects).

When there are suspicions that economic logics do not dominate, we look for evidence and argument that positive change—development—coexists with a wide range of observable economic growth rates and levels expressed in terms of GDP per capita. We may indeed interpret L&Z 1993 in this way. Readers may recognize the point made in many DS textbooks that development is not economic growth.

This chapter will confirm and then explore just how DE (understood through the canonical textbooks) asserts that development is a known effect of economic growth, linked causally to it. Second, it will explore how such claims assert the autonomy and importance of DE. I remind the reader that economics now typically situates itself outside arts and is academically separate from other disciplines keenly interested in aspects of change processes. Negotiation of interdisciplinary boundaries and its limits, this suggests, are intriguing issues worth studying. Chapters 7 and 8 show how economic growth theory works.

The relationship between economic growth and development

Development economics and the centrality of economic growth

What we find in both DE textbooks (Ray 1998 and Todaro and Smith (T&S) 2006) is the assertion, in various ways, of the importance of economic growth as a known *cause* of development and best understood via algebraic models. Thus study of economic growth will reveal the causal origins of development.

The first question for discussion in T&S shows a revealing perspective: "Why is economics central to an understanding of the problems of development?" (T&S 2006: 33). This phrasing encourages students to buy into the traditional theory and to ignore alternatives—that economics might not be central and that what is observed (such as changes in the NIA data) are no more than a spurious effect of other processes, determined by other logics, and beyond economics. Such familiar rhetorical devices counsel caution. We must ask, if we are to be persuaded by this positioning rather than simply accepting it, what justification is actually given. Is this based upon empirics or something else? How is the argument made?

The construction of such an argument may be clearly seen in Ray, who starts his book by dealing with the problem of the relationship between development and economics (Ray, Chapter 2). He *isolates* economics while situating it within development—that is, he works as though economics operated according to its own logics (the "laws of economics"). He does this in two steps.

First, he argues for the ability to track the *results* of development efforts. This asserts the existence of a cause-effect relationship—that between policy and outcome—so that we can, through correct policies, do development. The assumptions and thrust here should already be clear to the reader.

Second, moving toward a justification of algebra, he argues for the ability to measure and so to compare across contexts the *degree* of development. Again, the assumptions here should be clear to the reader. For example, measurement, given the presence of indicators such as GDP that are ahistorical and separated from cultural or social contexts, pushes for adoption of universalistic assumptions. One of the pitfalls of such mechanical (if not formalistic) comparison is the way data may assume ontological universalism, and, as we have seen, assuming that you are sampling from a single population can get you into a load of trouble. This is because if the assumption does not hold, statistical results will almost certainly be spurious, in which case it is hard to avoid reaching unreliable conclusions (see the discussion of "spurious" in Box 2.2 on p. 21).

But Ray's core argument is that, while development has many dimensions, these are *all* strongly linked to the level of per capita GDP: "The universal features of economic development—health, life expectancy, literacy and so on – follow in some natural way from the growth of per capita GNP" (Ray 1998: 9).[2] This is a clear and universalistic statement of the existence of known effect.

Ray argues that the issue here is not about development—about which, he says, people agree—but about whether development is linked to **gross national product** (GNP). This sidesteps a wide range of accounts that contest definitions of development. Indeed, large parts of DS would view the idea that people agree on what development is and expressions such as "universal features" as contentious: any DS course will tell students that there are many different definitions of "development."

To understand development, Ray asserts that it is worth reducing a larger set of issues to a smaller set through the use of economic theory. As he puts it, what must first be understood is the level and distribution of economic attainment:

> In this sense, the view that economic development is ultimately fuelled by per capita income may be taking things too far, but at least it has the virtue of attempting to reduce a larger set of issues to a smaller set, through the use of economic theory.
>
> (Ray 1998: 9)

In this way, theory is valorized in that it narrows the gaze: it is said to be good because it excludes factors from its analysis. This is not simply an exclusion of the noneconomic, for other possible aspects of an economic concept, such as economic change, are also excluded when the focus is upon per capita GDP.

We have then a clear positioning: economic growth is to be the central issue of DE. Chapters 7 and 8 will discuss this further, looking at algebraic models that focus upon determining economic growth—that is, changes in per capita GDP.

The problem of values: defending the centrality of GDP and economic growth

I have already reported the inherent conceptual problems that arise in comparing welfare between people and, for the same person, between different contexts (see Box 1.2 on p. 9). Attempts to use GDP measures confirm this. As we shall see, GDP is a measure of something called total **factor incomes**, and this is why it is part of NIA. This means that use of GDP (or GDP per capita) assumes that a comparison has been made about interpersonal welfare, for use of GDP inherently assumes that $1 of additional income should be valued the same no matter who is receiving the income and how much or how little they earn. This is not unreasonable, but my point is that it requires a choice about how to value a dollar of income. It would also be reasonable to argue that the economy did not grow if the incomes of 100 idle people rose by $5 but at the same time the incomes of 100 hard-working people fell by $3 (so that, in some people's eyes, there was no development). Such points are inescapable, and statements that GDP is an objective measure seek to hide them. Intriguingly, this is basic welfare economics, as any economist who was taught this properly should know.

What indeed do people value? The discussion in Ray assumes that this is not an important question, but we can ask the following questions: Who are we referring to? How are people different? What do they value? How do they do it? Even the range of opinion in one's immediate vicinity (for example, in a classroom) can show a wide range of possible answers to these questions. People are, it is easy to think, diverse and value things in different ways. A range of opinion surveys and other sources may inform us about these differences while making their own assumptions. For example, the United Nations Development Programme Human Development Report and Millennium Development Goals can be understood precisely as a reaction to the view that GDP should be accepted as the measure of development, as Ray seems to argue. Instead, the UN report argues that GDP should be thought of as part of a composite, along with other factors, such as life expectancy. But this way of looking at things is the outcome of choices and is as subjective as any other measure. Some people may and probably do value other issues more highly.

GDP as an acceptable indicator of development

Linking concepts of development closely to changes in economic magnitudes leads to discussion of the valuation to be predominantly carried out in economic terms. To be underdeveloped, if this premise is accepted, is to be associated with particular economic data showing this. It may appear trite, but this is fundamental to the separation of DE from DS. Again, it is useful to reflect on how this is closely linked to the assertion of DE's importance and autonomy as a discipline.

For example, in his Chapter 2, Ray moves from a discussion of the relations between economics and development to the data on national average levels of per capita GNP converted at market exchange rates. He notes that it shows a highly skewed distribution; in 1993, 85 percent of the world's population produced 20 percent of global GNP. This particular focus obviously both encourages and confirms viewing the extent of under-development through an economic lens rather than any other one. The focus is then shifted to the lens itself, and the exposition is developed by remark-ing on the likelihood of technical problems with GNP data. Ray notes that measurement error likely varies with per capita GNP, although he asserts that data is more correct in richer countries, and that the extent of self-consumed production (farmers may eat food they produce themselves) also likely varies with per capita GNP. Ray introduces another technical issue related to the ways in which the use of market foreign exchange rates reflects international trade. This is argued to mean that GNP will be underestimated in poor countries because the prices of nontradables (commodities, such as local services, that are usually not part of international trade) tend to be lower in poorer than in richer countries. This then leads to efforts to cope with this issue and construct better estimates of GNP measured at so-called purchasing power parities. I leave it to the reader to investigate their technical aspects, but the conceptual issues are clear enough.[3]

The reader will note that, it having been accepted that GDP is central to development, this core position is not threatened by a discussion of technical problems in measurement. It is the conceptualization that counts. In other words, although these problems have been noted within DE, they are ignored in modeling and empirics. As in other areas, as we will see, there is a mismatch between what is taught and what is practiced.

The economic narrative: expressing historical experiences in terms of economic growth

I have argued that the basic problematic of DE defines development essentially in terms of differences in per capita GDP, both over time and between social groups. If GDP is placed centrally, then historical accounts have to manage this. Ray (1998), Chapter 2, again offers us an example of how this is done.

He notes that between 1960 and 1985 the distribution of incomes globally was stable, with the top 5 percent and bottom 5 percent of countries staying in the same rank for that time period. Note that this assumes that "a $ is a $," in that the ranking takes a particular view of the value of income and expenditure. It chooses to value incomes and spending in terms of the actual monetary value rather than subjectively, so a dollar is valued the same for somebody who is starving as for somebody who leaves his air-conditioning on all day. In the middle group of countries, some that had been growing fast slowed, while some that had not been growing started to grow fast. This historical account offers a dualistic concept of global development. On the one hand, some countries move into and out of the group of "successful developers," while a group of low-income countries appear to not develop at all. Put simply, the problem is one of explaining either relative success or a failure to develop—that is, relative rates of economic growth or the absence of economic growth. These two attributes then provide a powerful division: successful vs. unsuccessful, or developers vs. nondevelopers. But some countries became failures and some became successes during the period, so it can be said that some shifting occurs between the categories.

So-called middle-income countries, Ray notes, seem most subject to mobility, shifting from relatively high or low rankings: some middle-income failures have become successes, while some successes have become failures. Two very different conclusions can be drawn from this. First, it illustrates how DE arguments view development as economic growth, understood as growth in per capita GDP. Second, if one holds to this assumption, it can produce some potentially interesting results—for example, the stability of a classification of countries by levels of development. As so often, much depends upon the particular view adopted.

Income distribution: defining an issue and predicating development upon economic growth

DE, however, takes further the argument for focusing upon economics. Obviously, variations in incomes are observed not only as variations in average per capita GDP *among* countries but also as variations within them. Ray introduces this issue in a way that is illuminating. He remarks that within developing countries income distribution is often highly skewed; the presence of both the very wealthy and those at global middle-class levels of well-being in countries that are relatively poor means that differentials are wide. But the twist comes in linking this idea to the view that levels of development are largely defined by economic development. A graph of income shares of the poorest 20 percent and richest 40 percent countries shows that the distribution gets worse (less equal) then better as per capita GNP rises.

The explanation tells a simple story, and such devices are common: both Ray and T&S use many of them. While possibly attractive, simple stories tend to invite the reader to adopt the universalism of DE as well as the idea that, at root, economic growth is the cause and development of the known effect of economic growth. They also encourage categorical thought (see Box 2.4 on p. 30). In this view, development without correct economic policies should be near impossible. It also follows that development cannot be diverse and must be knowable.

The argument about income distribution in Ray, Chapter 2, is that in very poor countries, the poor are close to subsistence and so largely self-sufficient, and the rest of the economy, which relies upon specialization and trade, finds it hard to support the incomes of the top 20 percent. As income starts to rise, some benefit but not all. The poor stay close to subsistence. As per capita GNP increases, incomes may be redistributed through taxes and public services. Thus economic growth creates the essential core of development, while inequalities remain, in part because so many remain relatively self-sufficient subsistence farmers. Whether these inequalities persist over the longer term is a matter for further discussion.

The reader from outside DE may well question this simple account. A fundamental issue is how (and whether) to conceptualize experiences across different contexts in this all-embracing way. One aspect is the assumption of ontological and epistemological universalism. But this does not take us very far. To answer Ray's account in its own terms is not hard. In the poorest countries, basic services—water, health, education—are generally not produced and distributed by markets. Instead, communities may take advantage of social structures such as village community networks that enable them to find local nonmarket resources for valued activities such as primary education. When these structures change and become less interested in such community action, while markets become more extensive, primary education may suffer (de Vylder and Fforde 1996, Chapter 6). When measured GDP rises, public service access may thus fall as markets replace public structures, whether of the government or of local communities. Here we see the movement between the 1962 and 1982 positions outlined by L&P (2002): what is varying is the underlying position toward the value of free markets, since it appears rather certain that without intervention (whether by communities or state) there will be less provision of health and education. Perhaps we are also reminded of Chang's view that the observed institutions of today's rich countries are the *result*, not the historical cause, of their development (Chapter 1).

The basic position adopted by DE may appear puzzling. On the one hand, it may be taken to imply that economic growth creates a possibility for increased spending on human development (growth first, schools and hospitals later). But the possibility also exists that human development itself may be necessary for economic development and so, in turn, for economic growth. Another view, which perhaps sits on the fence, is that growth is circular: higher levels of economic output support more education, and these in turn support higher levels of economic output. Placing economics central to an account of change processes takes sustained effort, and the reader may start to appreciate the tensions created for DE by its methods.

DE and the many faces of development

Both Ray and T&S confront the stress caused by placing economic growth central. This is clearly conceptually indispensable, if normal algebraic modeling is to be done. The core categories that these models use must be economic for DE to work, with the focus on GDP. But use of these economic models creates problems, because distinct and noneconomic (in the DE sense) concepts of development do not so easily go away. The position of DE within DS thus poses nagging if often muted questions. A central issue, which comes up in many contexts, is the argument that interpersonal and intertemporal welfare comparisons lack objective basis for their measurement (see Box 1.2 on p. 9). It would seem to follow clearly that there will be no agreement about the value of change, even if it is called development. As I have already shown in the case of GDP, any particular measurement embodies choices about how welfare is to be compared.

What is also important here is how DE, in this exposition, encourages the conceptualization that economic growth is something that happens separately from other aspects of change. There is an economic logic that asserts and rationalizes, though with peripheral caveats, an economic perspective on development. This does two things: it gives DE autonomy, and it states that, as such, it is worth knowing and studying. This is evidence for how disciplinary boundaries are negotiated and the position of DE vis-à-vis DS constructed.

These frictions have long histories, and it is useful to consider some accounts of them. We have already examined L&P (2002). Some discussion of the origins of their second generation position (the 1982 skepticism toward the role of government) is useful in understanding aspects of how economists think, and have thought, though this book is not a history of DE. I have already mentioned the existence of accounts that link this skepticism about government to the historical context. One important element of accounts of DE during this period is the development strategy of "distribution with growth" expressed in the important study of that name (Chenery et al. 1974). The core of this strategy was to find ways of using state and other structures to redistribute the results of economic growth to those believed to be more deserving than those thought to be benefiting. According to many historical accounts, such ideas arose in the 1960s in the face of evidence that there was little "trickle down."[4] In many accounts, the strategy of distribution with growth was proposed after countries with rapid economic growth were not reporting widespread improvements in well-being; in fact, income distributions deteriorated. In many developing countries, political leaders resisted slowing growth to improve development for a variety of political or pecuniary reasons. What many in DS would now see as the neoliberalism that justified structural adjustment and the excesses of rampant globalization may thus be understood to partly originate in what is now deemed to be unequal development—the idea that, viewed globally, change processes are inherently unequal and reflect shifts in underlying power relations.[5] As this chapter has shown, the logical objection is that DE, by privileging economics, positions itself somewhat unwisely: placing economics as central and treating development as its known effect treats powerful rhetorics such as politics as unimportant to the analysis.[6] We may ask, in this vein, why Third World leaders apparently failed to listen to the advice they were given in the 1960s about the limits of "trickle down."

In this section, I argued that two pillars underpin DE: first, the separation and definition of an economic sphere that can be organized conceptually as something that economic theory can explain; second, the assertion that economics, as the essential core of development, validates the questionable idea that development may reasonably be treated as something that can be compared across different contexts. In caricature, the first is the assertion "we believe in growth"; the second, that growth is globally real—it can meaningfully and without much risk be treated as the same force across different contexts, such as countries or regions (the assumption of ontological universalism).

Both assertions are not wisely accepted at face value. What is important and relevant is what may happen to human change processes when important actors accept them or not. Wolf (2009) and Camdessus (1999) are concerned about a collapse of the authority of such positions (Chapter 1). If this happens, it could also have serious implications both for the authority of important global actors such as the World Bank and the IMF, and, domestically, for the political influence of policy positions taken by governments, such as the value attached to free markets, the power of attacks upon ideas of the value of state and community actions, and so on. Further, underpinning the stability of capital markets, and lurking behind the concerns of Wolf and Camdessus, are investors' beliefs in the value and riskiness of their international investments. Ideas can matter.

Per capita income and human development

The idea that GDP per capita can and should be understood as part of an economic sphere analytically separate from and prior to other aspects of social change is both inherently fascinating and also basic to DE. Grasping this conceptualization is fundamental to understanding the position of DE within DS. It may be appealing, not least, as the reader should recall, because of the argument that good analysis requires a selection of certain variables and issues as central, and the associated exclusion of others. My refrain here remains that of asking readers to realize that something (what?) is happening when they consider whether or not to accept this argument— that is, whether to accept that DE's argument makes sense in viewing the world and how it changes in certain particular ways. A fundamental question is whether per capita GDP or GNP satisfyingly proxies for development. Ray and T&S both dodge this question, but it remains central, for without it, as we have seen, DE loses its position and its method.

Now, one way of arguing this is to return to empirics, to see whether DE and/or DS offer, as a matter of fact, a correlation between the components of any composite index that includes measures other than per capita GDP. Although a correlation can be found, correlation is not causation, and in some measures of development increases in GDP per capita are combined with human development indicators (HDI), including noneconomic measures, in the construction of overall development indicators. Here I focus upon thinking of the economic and noneconomic measures as separate.

Without going too deep, the reader may ponder this idea of causation. Which way might it go? Does more growth lead to better recorded human development measured in terms of HDI? Or does more HDI cause more growth? DE argues that *other* factors, which may plausibly influence HDI, are less important than economics. "Growth pays for human development" assumes that per capita GDP is the core variable. Is this reasonable? Put this way, I would be sympathetic with readers who throw up their hands and say that answering this means taking a view about issues that are too complex and diverse. I would reply that this means they should reject the assumption of ontological and epistemological universalism and refuse to think categorically in this way.

If we review the position taken by anthropologists Shore and Wright (1997), a better way out may be found than simply balking. More useful would be a discussion about interdisciplinary boundaries. DE, as such, obviously has little to say about noneconomic factors that plausibly influence human welfare and development, such as education and health, but ad hoc arguments to the contrary are easy to conjure. For instance, it is not hard to argue that causation may go in the opposite direction: a country that creates a disciplined, educated, and cheap workforce would find that economic development follows.[7] The point here is that the argument has simply to do with correlation and tells one nothing about causal direction. Causal direction must therefore be assumed (see the discussion of McCloskey in Chapter 6). Yet the push from DE is that economic theory is valuable because it explains economic change and because economic change drives development.

Structural features of developing countries

Once the centrality of economic growth has been established, DE can make concessions. The textbooks do this and discuss issues such as demography —for example, the "demographic transition," where changes in fertility rates appear usually to lag changes in infant mortality rates, leading to periods of temporary high population growth, often associated with rapid growth in labor supply.

Both texts (Ray 1998 and T&S 2006) also move on from the importance of economic growth to present standard stories about development which emphasize changes in occupational and production structures. Here we see an idea of a development process common to many different contexts, and thus capable and deserving of analysis by an algebra that assumes commonalities between different contexts. Development can be presented as an economic problem to which correct economic policies are the known (or knowable) solution. Thus both texts argue that countries with similar levels of per capita GDP may exhibit different structural characteristics. For example, one may be a highly profitable exporter of primary products, with therefore rather low levels of employment and output in other sectors compared with the other, perhaps a highly successful exporter of high-tech manufactures.

These accounts suggest that poor countries tend to be agricultural. For low-income countries (according to a World Bank definition), the proportion of GDP deriving from agriculture is about 30 percent. For the poorest forty-five developing countries, a higher proportion of the labor force—

around 70–75 percent—is rural. In middle-income countries agriculture is about 20 percent of GDP, and up to 60 percent of the labor force is rural. In richer countries, far smaller percentages of the labor force are active in agriculture.

This particular empirics helps make the point that most poor people in developing countries have usually been farmers, but, with the growth of "mega-cities," populations are increasingly urban. This starts to add to the standard narratives, because the question of urban–rural migration, for example, enters (see Chapter 12). It is said that people are pressed to leave rural areas by various factors and are attracted to cities, though many do not go into formal sectors (that is, sectors with recognizably "modern" characteristics such as legalized employment contracts, possibilities of unionization, and so forth). Urbanization is, therefore, a powerful influence—said to be more powerful if GDP growth is relatively slow. High rates of urbanization, it is argued, are one reason why so much GDP as measured in poor countries is produced in the service sectors. What we have here, then, is an opportunity to see how the standard narratives may be developed without abandoning their essential elements: the overriding importance of per capita GDP, to be explained by economics, and the assumption of knowability.

International trade

I have already flagged the importance of international trade as an identifier of different positions within DE. I argued that the distinction between the 1960s and 1980s positions presented by L&P (2002) is associated with the contrast between ISI and EOG policies (see Box 2.1 on p. 20). The skepticism of the current mainstream position, as L&P present it, partly corresponds to disagreement within DE of the relative value of EOG and ISI, and a lack of willingness to take a position that asserts the viability of *any* solution phrased in terms of global universal categories. So-called "one size fits all" prescriptions have become increasingly unpopular. This skepticism can be found in both Ray (1998) and T&S (2006).

Thus, according to Ray, there is no obvious relationship between the degree of openness to foreign trade and the level of per capita GDP. He notes that the composition of trade varies: developing countries are often exporters of primary products, also textiles and light manufactures, but not always, referring to China and India.

Simple economic theory contains the argument, based upon a particular model, that people will benefit from trade if something called comparative advantage (see Box 4.1) operates. We examine issues relating to this in Chapters 16 through 18.

The tensions within DE are evident in the ways in which both textbooks, while arguing for the view that economic growth is the core of development, also suggest that economic attainment is neither usefully measured in terms

---

Box 4.1 Comparative advantage

This term is one of the more confusing ones in economics, comparable to **moral hazard** and **rents** (as in **rent-seeking**) (see the list of special terms on p. 323). *Comparative advantage* is the principle that countries do best by exchanging goods, focusing on exports that contain more factors of production (nonproduced inputs: land, labor, and capital) that are *relatively* cheap compared with other factors of production, and importing those that are relatively expensive. It therefore does not mean that countries should simply export goods that they can produce more cheaply than other countries.

　　The reader should note here an example of the common tendency to argue in a rather short-term way, because the relative cost of factors of production may well be expected to change over time. The major debate between the Bank of Japan and the Ministry and Trade and Industry over post-war Japanese development policy saw the latter win out against the "comparative advantage" arguments of the former, leading to large-scale, government-driven restructuring and large guided investments in heavy industry (Johnson 1982).

---

of per capita GDP nor usefully thought of as having any simple and general relationship with development attainment. That is, both textbooks suggest both that economic growth is central and that economic attainment is not simply measured by GDP, while also presenting arguments that GDP per capita is not simply linked to measures of development. For me, these tensions, if they are not inconsistencies, are striking. They derive from the particular understanding of the problem of development that relates to the habit of viewing development as both product and process, and mirror the tensions and inconsistencies generated by this habit. It remains the case that DE, in its use of different methods from those of other disciplines, must position itself with respect to DS in ways that perpetuate these tensions.

Macroeconomics: year-by-year changes in levels of GDP per capita

How to treat time

If DE asserts that the core of development is per capita GDP, then how should time be treated? Examining this question illuminates just how DE deals with change. These issues are brought out clearly by Agenor and Montiel (1999), to which I now return. First, we need to clarify for non-economists the concepts behind GDP and hopefully also remind economists

---

Box 4.2 National income accounting

NIA is fundamental to the particular empirics of both macroeconomics and growth economics. They measure the incomes accruing to factors of production (land, labor, and capital) in a given time period and provide measures of the level of real economic activity when the effects of price changes are removed. Because the sum of these incomes must equal what is spent *less* spending on intermediate inputs (things bought to make things) and *plus* exports *less* imports, this appears as a set of real things — expenditure-based national income. (Intermediate inputs are called "final demand" — consumption by consumers and government *plus* investment, including changes in stocks.) If the constant price factors incomes are divided by sector (industry, agriculture, services, etc.) this is thought of as "output" constant price national income, called GDP.

It is immediately obvious that this latter measure is not "output" in the sense of so many tons of coal and so forth (see Chapters 7 and 8.) It is also obvious that this measure readily excludes subsistence activities as well as household production, though these can be estimated and added back in. Similar arguments can be extended to any activity deemed socially valuable and excluded from monetary income generation, such as, for example, family-based care to children, invalids, and old people, as well as to what could and should be left out, such as armaments. There is a wide range of choice here.

---

what exactly the data is. Central to this, which will become important when we come to growth models in Chapters 7 and 8, is to appreciate that GDP does not measure output in any simple sense but rather total factor incomes (see Box 4.2).

As already discussed, Agenor and Montiel (1999) position themselves as *macroeconomists*—as such, concerned with analysing activities measured in through NIA. By doing so, they argue that they are not *growth economists* who focus upon the supply of core resources—the factors of production that receive the incomes that GDP measures. The models that macroeconomists use assume that the central issue is the level of utilization of these factors in a given time period. These contrast with models of growth economists, which look at changes in the availability and productivity of those basic inputs.

As we already saw, Agenor and Montiel's view of the best indicators of underdevelopment is mainly related to the weak development of markets. Underdevelopment is thus defined in terms that reflect the basic difference between the two earlier positions—those of the 1960s and the 1980s—that we found in L&P: markets and attitudes to them. If economics is the core and markets work, then characterization of what is to be developed—and so underdeveloped—follows. Markets are thus placed centrally and poised to be a key element of policy.

How to treat markets: monetarist vs. structuralist views

The reader may start to sense that any attempt to leave out the broader historical context from discussions of how positions differ within DE results in frustration. Yet, while the arguments I have presented about DE suggest that this tendency is inherent, we can still learn, especially if we are aware of that context, from how the arguments are framed and developed. This helps us think of DE as a practice of significant importance rather than simply an area of at times awkward inconsistency.

In terms of their practice, Agenor and Montiel (1999) argue that *monetarism*[8] made a case that markets work and provided a benchmark to apply macroeconomic theories from developed countries to developing countries. Thus, in their interpretation, which is pretty standard, inflation is caused by monetary phenomena. Monetarism, in terms of their exposition —and this again is quite mainstream—was opposed to *structuralism*,[9] which came from Raul Prebisch's work at the Economic Commission for Latin America just after World War II. Such distinctions, which are commonplace in histories of development thinking, are detailed and as linked with the political and social histories of rich countries as anything else. I cannot go into these in proper depth here, so I leave it to the interested reader to research accounts of these debates and their contexts. Central to the importance of such debates, however, is the view within DE that structuralism argued from a particular empirical point (like many other known facts, abundant studies argue that this was not always true): because the terms of trade (see Box 4.3) facing poor countries were deteriorating over time, specialization as the market suggested was wrong and so intervention was required. Otherwise, locked into strategies focusing upon exports whose prices were falling compared with the prices of inputs (manufactures from rich countries), the outlook was dire. Intervention would entail protection, manifest as ISI, adopted widely in the post-World War II period in Latin America and elsewhere. Here we can see how a particular empirics links,

---

Box 4.3 Terms of trade

A technical term, terms of trade refers to the relative price of what is sold compared to the price of what is bought. All farmers know that if these improve, life is likely to get better; inputs get cheaper relative to the prices of what they sell.

through a particular modeling practice, to political prescription in terms of policy.

It is important to realize that DE, as represented by Agenor and Montiel (1999), assumes that differences between monetarist and structuralist positions can be expressed through differences between economic models. Political conflicts are then articulated in terms of different analyses with different policy implications. This particular understanding sees politics largely in terms of policy—whether it is correct and whether it is adopted.

With the field of battle thus defined and bounded in terms of arguments about algebra and models, we can readily see how advocates of different models should seek reasons to characterize developing country economies —and so development itself—in different ways. Agenor and Montiel develop and articulate the argument well. They argue that so-called *neo-structuralists*,[10] to give one example, argue that their models (to be "right") need to have the following characteristics: many agents possess significant market power; macroeconomic causality runs from injections to leakages;[11] money is often **endogenous**; and the structure of the financial system is important, as are imported capital and intermediate goods.

At this stage, the noneconomist should not be too put off by the highly specific terminology. Rather, this illustrates the point I am making, which is that these are the characteristics of certain algebraic models. That is, they are statements about the particular formulae and algebraic relations within them, just as the difference between macroeconomics and growth economics assumes (in the former) that variables that measure the overall supply of factors of production are held broadly constant. Those who create the model decide this: these are assumptions of and within the model, and cannot be entirely separated from it.

Further, the reader should appreciate that these models and ideas are (among other things) weapons in debates, often highly political ones, as histories of Latin America in the 1970s and 1980s readily show. Thus Agenor and Montiel, and their allies, argue that with their model it is easier to argue against the "shock treatment" that expects an economy to adjust easily and quickly in the right direction, and to a new equilibrium. The meaning of the analysis thus quickly moves into the political, as policy prescriptions are advanced and Agenor and Montiel seek to deny the validity of conclusions derived from situations where markets are thought to be working well and competitively. The standard reference point here, of course, is what is asserted to be the case in developed countries, and we can start to see how the power to carry this argument may have considerable political implications.[12] One may even point out that "to fight fire with fire," opponents of the politics associated with monetarism would be justified in developing counter-arguments that would work in such terms, even if they were not convinced by such models themselves.

In our example, as we can see explicated by Agenor and Montiel (1999), neostructuralists explain inflation characteristically and in ways that have certain policy implications associated with them. They focus upon a *passive* response of monetary policy to structural issues: slow productivity growth in agriculture, downwardly rigid prices, and wage indexation. This means that the area of political choice is changed, with the focus of debate on particular issues and policy options. Thus Agenor and Montiel argue that the situations they refer to—devaluation combined with tight fiscal and monetary policies—will lead to stagflation as prices remain stuck at levels that cannot guide economic resources to the right places for sound economic growth. An example, typical in such analyses, would be the idea that wages in the formal sectors, especially in public education and health, and in state-owned enterprises, are "too high" but cannot, without major political effort, be cut, due, for example, to the political power of public sector trade unions. In their view, this is an example of how markets in developing countries do not work well. These are, however, primarily the attributes of models; their empirical reference is another matter, as we have seen already (see also Chapter 6).

The DS reader who is not an economist may find this discussion somewhat tedious and not worthy of attention. That would be a mistake. Consider the wider context of these debates, which DE does not refer to (Ray 1998, for example, does not mention them in any significant detail). As I have argued, DE seeks to establish and defend an economic sphere that is analytically separate from and prior to other aspects of social change. What I encourage is to step back and appreciate the context of such discussions, not least the social unrest and problems encountered in many countries of Latin America in the 1980s. Like many political and social issues, it matters if it matters; that is the point of boundaries.

But it would also be unwise to treat DE in terms that are too limited to political or other contextual issues. It has its own internal logic and con-ceptual practices. For example, it is useful to realize the relative intractability to existing modeling techniques of economic conceptualizations where markets are, in the terms of DE, relatively undeveloped. Fundamental to what Agenor and Montiel are arguing is the proposition that developing countries often lack the attributes that would make them suitable to application of mainstream economic theory. This was highlighted in the example of the World Bank analysis of Laos (Chapter 3).

There is, as we shall regularly find, a strong link in DE between ideas about what makes markets work well and the relative ease of modeling them: in other words, good markets accompany tractable algebra (see Box 2.4 on p. 30). This problem would seem inherent, derived essentially from the drive to carve out a domain for DE and its position within DS, which is done by asserting the relative unimportance of variables outside that domain. Therefore, the algebra has to work. Yet, as algebraic techniques evolve, so does what can, in this practice, be studied (see the section on Colander on pp. 92–94).[13]

Conclusions

DE asserts the view that development is *necessarily* associated with economic attainment understood as per capita GDP. Students within DE who try to deny this proposition will usually face difficulties. Without this assertion, it is hard, if not impossible, to defend both the boundaries of the discipline and, perhaps more inflexibly, continued use of algebra. This assertion comes with various entanglements which include:

- Examples of negative as well as positive correlations between economic growth and development.
- Lack of agreement on how to measure development.
- Issues related to whether per capita GDP accurately measures economic attainment.

Despite this, DE stresses the view that economic change is the core problematic of development, which illuminates the tensions accompanying its position vis-à-vis DS. Notwithstanding, Agenor and Montiel (1999) may be read as stressing the contextual (and often political) basis of important differences in economic frameworks. In this, it is similar to ideas already encountered (L&P), and, like them, this point is not explicit. Rather, political differences of great importance are, in a way characteristic of DE, expressed as the differences between models. In this context, a problem facing economists in analysing macroeconomies of developing countries is that, if they assert that markets do not work smoothly, the more tractable models should not be used.[14]

Questions for discussion

1. Is it always wrong for an analytical framework to exclude factors from its analysis?

2. Discuss the advantages and disadvantages of the type of modeling practiced by DE.

3. What might happen to the way an argument is framed if empirics focus upon success and failure? Can this avoid discussion in terms of the problem of development as construed by Cowen and Shenton (1996) (see Chapters 1 and 15) and so define success in terms lacking robust empirical foundations?

Notes

1 See Box 4.2 on p. 58 on the NIA that defines GDP. For noneconomists, by "trend" here I mean changes over a reasonably long period of time, implying that factors influencing the extent to which productive capacity is utilized are conceptualized as minor by comparison with changes in productive capacity (see the discussion of the differences between growth and macroeconomics in Box 1.3 on p. 12). Productive capacity is usually gauged by proxies for accumulated physical and human capital.

2 GNP is gross national product—factor incomes generated by entities that belong to the nation, while GDP is gross domestic product—factor incomes simply generated within the territory controlled by the nation, and so including, for example, profits earned by foreign-owned companies. "Factor incomes" are incomes paid to factors of production—labor, capital, and land.

3 An accessible example of these technical aspects is Eurostat–OECD (2012), which is a manual; for obvious reasons, such documents are widely available on the Web.

4 This is the idea that inequality is needed if poor people are to see their lives advance: The benefits of development come first to the rich and then "trickle down" to the rest.

5 See Chapter 18 for a discussion of structural adjustment. Briefly, it is the idea, associated with the pro-market policies pushed by many donors in the 1980s, that securing rapid economic growth required profound changes to developing countries' economic structures, usually associated with the privatization of state-owned assets, reductions in import taxes, and cuts in state spending.

6 One issue confronting practitioners of DE is that often they have no professional expertise in political science or wider issues. Thus, just after World War II the standard British training for officials and others heading for responsible positions was the Oxford Politics, Philosophy and Economics degree, which meant that people could not study economics alone as undergraduates.

7 An argument could be made that this is what happened in Vietnam, where efforts by the Communists to secure planned economic development prior to the emergence of a market economy in the early 1990s created exactly such conditions, driving rapid growth from then on. However, based upon my own experiences working there, I do not think this is what happened. Hill (2000) looks at related issues.

8 This is a **straw man**, referring to a complex of views and positions underpinned by certain economic models and usually placed in opposition to Keynesianism. In shorthand, it may be understood as "1982" in L&P terms and "1962" viewed as its antagonist. See the quote from Dunn on p. 145 in Chapter 10.

9 In abbreviation, this can be understood as the equivalent, within DE, of L&P's "1962" when discussed in the context of Latin America. Inflation, thus, was attributed to structural rather than monetary factors, with these conceptualizations linked to different algebraic models and apparent political positions.

10 Another straw man, referring to contemporary positions that base similar views to structuralists upon "better" algebra, typically stressing market failure in ways that can be modeled within the mainstream.

11 These terms ("injections" and "leakages") come from ways of thinking about the economy in terms of NIA (see Box 4.2 on p. 58). Recall that this focuses upon the ways in which income leads to spending, which creates economic activity that creates in turn profits, wages, and rents (factor incomes). Additions to such flows may come about, such as through additional state spending, and these can be termed injections; and reductions (leakages) may also come about, such as

through increases in taxes. Reflection may suggest to the reader that increases in exports are like an injection, and increases in imports, since they shift factor incomes generation from domestic producers, are a leakage.

12 De Vylder and Fforde (1996), a study of the transition from plan to market in Vietnam, shows echoes of this discussion. It drew heavily upon an earlier study (de Vylder and Fforde 1988). My co-author had considerable experience in Latin America and so argued that the central issue in the Vietnamese transition was not to "get prices right" but to "make prices matter." Part of the intention here was to reduce the chances of donors advocating policies we thought unsuitable, since they assumed that poor economic performance was due to incorrect prices and pushed for that, not appreciating that (for de Vylder and Fforde) the main issue was the transition to a situation where, having got rid of central planning, markets and so prices mattered.

13 The so-called new growth theory (endogenous growth theory) is a good example of this, but we ignore this here. See Chapter 8 for discussion.

14 In my own experience, large areas of DE practice platform on a rather weak understanding of the algebra involved. Thus, mention of the formal assumptions within the techniques is often interpreted as an attack on belief, threatening metaphysical commitment. An example of this is the use of "consumer surplus," an analytical technique that requires making the assumption that the value of an additional dollar is fixed as income changes. Another is the basic result of welfare economics that interpersonal and intertemporal welfare comparisons involve subjective choice by the researcher. This helps to explain experiences such as the adoption and then rejection of formal farm modeling by Australian agricultural economists already mentioned (see McCone and Parton 2006a and 2006b).

5 Toward better management of understandings
Internal and external critiques of mainstream development economics

This chapter builds on what has gone before to take the reader through two different sets of approaches to assessing mainstream definitions of DE and so ways of seeing how DE may be positioned within DS. The chapter is rather long and "dense," and so may usefully, in a taught course, be split into two or even three sessions. The contrast between the first two sections speaks to fundamental issues of belief and, it might be said, **metaphysical commitments**—a rather old-fashioned label for the "untestable" assumptions behind approaches, that is, what the analyst has to assume for his or her research to avoid being spurious by definition.[1] (Chapter 6 offers some accounts of what economists actually do when they decide on the central element of their practice—their models.)

The chapter is trying to help students understand two main issues. The first is that much in contemporary social sciences strongly questions mainstream DE belief that it can know reality well enough to offer reliable guides to action—that it knows that "this will lead to that." In understanding this, students encounter various tools that help understand DE as a socially constructed knowledge. As such, I will argue, DE is best understood, not by looking at what DE practitioners say they study, but rather by looking at them and their contexts. The second issue is that these tools themselves require great care in their application as they easily lead their users into similar tangles as DE. Together, these two issues also suggest that DE, as something to study, offers the chance to examine knowledge that can itself recognize, if it wants, that it does *not* know, in a predictive sense, what will work.

The first section discusses an internal critique—that is, arguments from within economics—as an established development economist argues *against* what he says are standard mainstream assumptions. Given the apparent absence, as L&Z (1993) suggests, of observable regularities in the economics of development corresponding to those in natural sciences, the question arises as to just how to assess such an internal critique. The remainder of the chapter shows how this assessment is helped by shifting the overt perspective of DE from *outside* economics and into approaches, or, to use another word, matters of *epistemology*—that is, the study of knowledges.

The second section of the chapter thus discusses **external** arguments as to what is going on in DE, and offers pointers as to how and why its positions may or may not be accepted. Some readers may react negatively to the idea that development should be understood in the ways proposed by DE, especially the consequences of placing economic change as central and, in some ways, prior to other aspects of change. The second section of the chapter thus offers an overview of some basic approaches to the issue of how to assess economics, as one knowledge among many. (Chapter 6 presents discussions of empirical studies of economists' practices.)

The second section presents a brief discussion of various commonly cited approaches to the study of fields of knowledges (often called sciences). What is intended is not to cover these and related issues (and many will find others equally if not more interesting) in great length, since this is not the topic of the book, but to provide a path toward other aspects of an arts development subject. I do not even suggest that the areas I cover are the best, though they may well help readers work out ways of assessing DE and its place in DS. Rather, this section presents the basic idea that explanations may be discussed in structured ways, for the ideas I discuss seek to guide precisely in that way.

An internal critique: coping with the contingent— a case study

Rodrik (2003) starts with a fundamental question, which gets him into similar difficulties as Ray (see Chapter 4). This is how to make sense of the differences between economic growth rates between countries. Although this question inherently assumes there are commonalities, how should one explain China's rapid growth, apparently without what the mainstream asserts is a necessary condition—full private property rights? Looked at over time, what changed in India so that Indian GDP growth increased in the late 1980s? And why do the Philippines and Bolivia continue to stagnate despite sharp improvements in their **fundamentals** since the 1980s?[2]

The way the argument is developed and the questions Rodrik asks show that his growth puzzles are mainly concerned with anomalies: subjective facts that are thought not to fit a common pattern. This inherently suggests that these examples deviate from some set of underlying principles.

There are other ways of thinking about these issues. One is to ask why certain examples have voice—that is, why are they thought to be important. One simple answer is that they are said to be "successful," but, as we have seen, this raises the question of what exactly is meant by success, what that evaluation assumes, and whether we want to agree with it or not. But a central point of Rodrik's argument is the attempt to develop an analysis that is contingent and localized. The reader will judge whether he ends with a series of universalistic maxims.

Rodrik poses good questions, but what does he think constitute good answers? He uses a dualistic approach: on the one hand he argues that "deep" determinants of growth exist, but these are influenced in their manifestations by local and contingent factors. This seems to argue that there are indeed universals, which may be discovered when there is successful growth and correct policy, but they are accompanied by the local determinants of growth. This is then clearly a classic realization solution, common to most essentialist views of the nature of the world. Readers may recall Plato's famous vision of the light from the fire throwing shadows on the wall as a metaphor for the relationship between true conceptualizations and our experience of what we observe. Here, we may read a similar view in Rodrik: there are true, deep determinants of growth, but, like the shadows on the wall, their expressions in what we see and experience are mediated in some way—in his language, by the particular local conditions of a given region or country at a particular time.

Where do these ideas of what is basic come from? They derive from an augmentation of standard theory with additional factors. According to Rodrik, a simple statement of the standard basic DE theory is that total output results from a combination of resource endowments (that is, the available supplies of labor, physical capital, human capital, land, etc.) and productivity (technical and allocative efficiency). By the latter is meant the technological process of physically transforming resources, combined with economic institutions that ensure that the particular technology reflects the relative costs of inputs and how these change as the input mix changes, including the impact of demand (see Chapters 7 and 8). The simple idea here—and this can be illustrated with an algebraic model—is that markets, when combined with producers' behavior that is price-sensitive and profit-seeking, will *of themselves* lead to allocative efficiency. This is the standard vision of how an economy produces. We will return to this later (especially in Chapter 9).

To this idea Rodrik adds other notions: in particular, that accumulation (of endowments) and productivity growth are partly endogenous (influenced by and with trade and institutions), and that geographical situation should also be included as an explanatory variable. These factors are, he says, all well correlated with per capita GDP growth. Geography is allegedly important because it shapes the value of natural resource endowments and influences world market integration, colonial legacies, and so forth. Trade is important because it is widely believed to have a strong positive impact on growth. Institutions, too, are crucial because things like property rights, regulatory structures, and bureaucratic capacity are seen as vital. Rodrik asserts that opinion has moved from the view that institutions understood in this way arise endogenously to the opinion that they are essential preconditions of growth. He says evidence that institutions play a strongly causal role in growth can be found in the literature. As we found from L&Z,

this statement needs to be understood in its context: although a range of published results found this evidence, those results depended upon choice of functional form (the particular form that the algebraic formula takes) and other devices and are not robust.

What we have here is a straightforward example of the application of economic method and specifically the addition of extra explanatory variables to a model whose basic logic is not challenged. Anomalies are dealt with by adding to the range of factors embodied in the explanation. But this, Rodrik argues, poses methodological issues in the area of empirics. Clearly, he believes that empirics of some kind should be used, for persuasive power, to answer the question about which factors matter most. But here Rodrik finds some deep puzzles. To start with, "Econometric results can be found to support any and all of these categories of arguments" (p. 9). So this is not convincing. Further, "There is little reason to believe that the primary causal channels are invariant to time period, initial conditions, or other aspects of a country's circumstances" (pp. 9–10).

The language here is noteworthy, for the *existence* of these primary causal channels is not questioned, merely the extent of their impacts in different contexts. And so, to create arguments that can appear to address the specific variations he is willing to consider, he proposes the use of "analytic country narratives" that should "play a useful role in developing such contingent hypotheses and testing them" (p. 10). By such narratives he means stories about examples of development in different countries which explain (for him, and, one can assume, his audiences) how and why the deep determinants of growth that he treats as universal laws work themselves out (so they can be thought to be observed, like Plato's shadows on the wall) in particular contexts.

So the basic model is retained and defended by the addition of local contingent explanations to the basic model, or explanation. We can see, therefore, what exactly is being tested. The research *assumes* that the basic causes operate and is therefore only interested in proximate, locally contingent factors that defend the basic explanatory framework while adding to it. In other words, "we believe that XX works, we simply want to know how under particular contexts."

The reader may wish here to review the discussion of L&Z (Chapter 2) and the research into its citations (Fforde 2005), which showed that the majority of economists citing the L&Z article were not interested in considering the implication that the basic model was awry. This suggests that we are indeed dealing with a case of belief, founded upon "what has to be," given the particular theory (though this is not an entirely satisfactory explanation of what is happening).[3] A core issue is the reason for the beliefs—why groups of people (such as many development economists) believe in a theory.

When we consider Rodrik's conclusions, we may expect to find them to a large extent repeating what is *assumed* in the basic argument, which is that the basic model is correct. To this will be added, supported by the research, arguments that the add-ons he advocates are indeed economically significant.

Rodrik: conclusions from the country narratives

Rodrik draws six main conclusions from his research into examples of development in different countries.

1. *The quality of institutions—mainly public—is the key to economic growth.* This comes down to finding arguments that show that the institutions in the case studies—the country narratives—embody in some way the general principles advocated by mainstream economics: align economic incentives with social costs and benefits.
2. *Trade—specifically, government policy toward trade—does not play nearly as important a role as the institutional setting.* Countries benefit from trade, but this is not much related to public policies toward trade; openness and exploiting trade comes from endogenous rather than policy-driven change.
3. *Geography is not destiny.* His view here can be contrasted with that of Todaro and Smith that tropical countries face common developmental problems (Chapter 2). His point is that, with good policy, unfavorable geographical location need not prevent successful development.
4. *Good institutions can be acquired, but doing so often requires experimentation, willingness to depart from orthodoxy, and attention to local conditions.* Here, like many in the mainstream, Rodrik must address China. The problem, as can easily be seen from a range of studies, is that the country lacks what the standard arguments of DE say are required for rapid growth, such as clear property rights.[4] Rodrik argues for the value of what he refers to as various transitional institutions in China: dual-track reform; township and village enterprises; what he calls "Chinese-style federalism," though formally China is not a federation; and anonymous banking (by this he seems to mean that banks operate without paying attention to the class or any other status of their clients).[5] He argues that these institutions offered high rewards in terms of economic growth at low political risk and economic cost: "Successful institutions often have heterodox elements" (p. 13). Whether they offer similar potential benefits to other countries is, of course, the million dollar question.
5. *The onset of economic growth does not require deep and extensive institutional reform.* This is not conventional wisdom but shifts the initiative from policy to other possibilities, though Rodrik does not make entirely clear what this might be.
6. *Sustaining high growth under difficult conditions requires ever stronger institutions.* As economic conditions change, the causes of changes in

trend growth are different: a low-income and mainly agricultural economy responds differently from a middle-income export-oriented one. By this he seems to mean that institutions that may work at low-income levels (a striking generalization) will no longer be adequate at higher income levels. Just what is meant by strong and weak here is not clear.

These conclusions are fairly typical of such studies. They add to the mainstream analysis factors that the analyst thinks are important. Does this, though, do much more than protect the mainstream belief set? Or is the significance, as argued in the context of Agenor and Montiel (Chapter 3), the politics of positioning? In the next section we discuss evidence for how the mainstream links its views to reality. In other words, the issue is related to the negotiation of interdisciplinary boundaries and the extent to which the focus upon case studies is hiding unchallenged certainty about allegedly basic determinants of growth. The argument is thus consistent with the ontological and epistemological universalism discussed previously. The way in which the contingent is managed entails protection of the basic mainstream arguments and their assumptions. By this I mean that in such frameworks, where deep determinants of economic growth are said to work their logic in various local contexts, the approach has to find ways, as did Plato with his metaphor of the shadows on the cave wall, to explain what we actually see. We can also note that to explain anomalies, the methodology used often simply adds in variables *qua* additional factors.

Two points are worth adding here. First, some of the standard measures of statistical fit (especially the "R-squared") have the mathematical property that they "rise," suggesting an improvement in the extent to which the equation explains the data, if additional explanatory variables are included.[6] Therefore, simply adding explanatory variables offers better statistical results.

Second, statistical inquiry based upon apodictic approaches, which find difficulties in accepting the idea that, although the results report that a parameter is statistically not different from zero but it may still be important (for example, because the sample is too small), will also tend to seek publishable results that show evidence that the additional explanatory variable works. Both of these issues tend to create the plethora of published but contradictory results that are characteristic of the comparative economic growth literature that was discredited by L&Z (see the discussion of McCloskey's work in Chapter 6).

Assessments of economists' explanations: epistemologies and empirics

This section attempts to address wider issues that may arise if, as it should, the question is posed: how students may assess development economics as one knowledge among many. It offers a broader background to the problems that I am attempting to solve in bringing economics and more self-reflective sciences together.

The section therefore first discusses briefly the more accessible discussions of how DE may be understood. This offers students possible paths toward other aspects of an arts development subject. It also provides a situated, contextualized, and clearer picture—helping, for example, students to find ready-made bibliographies for putting together course papers. This is intended to avoid limiting the topics that students may address related to DE that could arise if there were no discussion of matters related to the history and philosophy of sciences. In this way the discussion is aimed to help students who are studying development, as well as to help economists better understand ways in which their discipline is understood.

I discuss ways in which DE, as a science or discipline, may be assessed and the typical issues that arise. In Chapter 6 I take the reader through some empirical work on economists, which shows how these issues may be addressed in practice—that is, by researching them.

Epistemology and ontology problematization: getting a grip by taking a step back

This section rapidly examines various approaches to the study of knowledges, such as DE. I argue that central to these approaches is the assumption that arguments are about what exists, what causes it, and how we may agree on answers. These are very old arguments.[7]

The age of these arguments, according to scholars investigating modernity, may surprise some readers. Consider the following, from Gillespie (2008). This is a study of the historical origins of ideas fundamental to Western culture, stressing the destructive effects upon various certainties of philosophical debates of the fourteenth century and the importance of these debates when considering modern ideas of progress and the advance of knowledge. Here Gillespie is focusing upon Western populations that have largely abandoned organized religious practice, which is far more common in Europe than in North America:

> [T]he apparent rejection or disappearance of religion or theology in fact conceals the continuing relevance of theological issues and commitments for the modern age. . . .
>
> [T]he process of secularisation or disenchantment that has come to be seen as identical with modernity was in fact something different than it seemed . . . the gradual transference of divine attributes to human beings (an infinite human will), the natural world (universal mechanical causality), social forces (the general will, the *hidden hand*), and history (the *idea of progress*).
>
> (pp. 272–273, emphasis added)

What actually occurs in the course of modernity is thus not simply the erasure or disappearance of God but the transference of his attributes, essential powers, and capacities to other entities or realms of being. The so-called process of disenchantment is thus also a process of re-enchantment in and through which both man and nature are infused with a number of attributes or powers previously ascribed to God. To put the matter more starkly, in the face of the long drawn out death of God, science can provide a coherent account of the whole only by making man or nature or both in some sense divine.

(p. 274)

This quotation engages with the fundamental question: why does DE purport to be about the modeling of empirical relationships when it may as well be interpreted as an attempt to create a place for algebraic modeling that appears arguably not to work in predictive terms? The question that arises here is whether beliefs, initially put in terms of religion, and so said to be about God, have been transformed in various ways and become (without fundamental change) beliefs about "man and nature." For me, this starts to illuminate the puzzle of why DE attempts to create belief in the deep determinants of growth, in the idea that economic growth is central to development? What are these beliefs? Gillespie argues that we may learn much from profound and largely unquestioned assumptions in Western cultures about language and belief that have long histories. Perhaps central to these are the belief that the essential order of the world can be truthfully known, a belief that exists *prior* to any testing of whether a particular belief is worth believing or not. Perhaps we can call this a "belief in belief."

The points being made here can be taken in various ways. Gillespie uses the telling phrase the "metaphysical/theological commitment" of an approach—that is, what those holding to that position *believe* to be the underlying order of what they are observing or doing—*an order that is a matter of belief*. He suggests that beliefs that were expressed in religious terms have transformed into beliefs about man and nature. For the trained economist, or indeed anybody familiar with statistical methods, the idea of such a metaphysical/theological commitment may be thought of as akin to the untestable assumptions contained in a statistical analysis.

The standard approach to the empirical investigation of an economic model relies upon econometrics. Put simply, an equation expresses relationships between variables: for example, the idea previously mentioned —that economic development, measured in terms of GDP per cap, is determined in part by whether the region is tropical or not—is conceptualized as the underlying model, and an "error term" is added to explain why observed values do not fit that equation exactly. Given suitable assumptions, statistical estimates of the parameters of the equation may then be calculated. As these are statistics, the procedure will also generate, again subject to various assumptions, indicators of the extent to which the estimated values may diverge from the true ones. Conceptually, this is similar to that of hypothesis testing, to which any student who has done Stats 101 will have been exposed. Be that as it may, the crucial issue here, which we will return to, is that any estimates made with these procedures rely upon crucial assumptions—any questioning of which raises big issues.

Here it is worth stepping aside to discuss basic statistical method, as this is often confusing, not least because of the language used. In my understanding, the so-called Null Hypothesis in standard statistical methodology is not, actually, a hypothesis as the term is generally understood. It is equivalent to using a stick that one assumes is a foot long to measure the height of poles in a manner that one assumes is generally valid. Given these assumptions, one can conclude that a hypothesis about the height of the poles is worth accepting or rejecting. But a second question is what one should conclude if the result suggests that the poles are, for the sake of argument, 100 yards high. If this makes sense, then those assumptions gain some support. If it does not, then they do not. Any judgment about this comes from outside one's work with the stick, such as what one has learned beforehand about poles, sticks, and so on. But if one concludes that the assumptions are not supported, then one can also conclude that one really has no idea how tall the poles are. This feels a little like a "bootstrap" problem, where the problem is not capable of solution with the resources available, like trying to pull oneself up by one's own bootstraps.

In basic statistics, one has to assume some underlying model or process that creates one's sample, which includes assumptions about how the sample relates to the population (this is related to the "error term" previously discussed—the conceptualization of how and why the underlying model is not actually observed). Basic statistics requires a story, like Plato's metaphor of the shadows, which reveal assumptions about the way in which the model (that cannot be observed) relates to what can be observed (the shadows). If the model is a simple algebraic formula that says that X—what one sees, say GDP per capita—is related to Y, then one option is that what one observes is subject to an error of a certain kind. Just what kind is largely a matter of assumption, though something can be learned from looking at the pattern of errors once the statistical exercise has been carried out.

On the basis of all these assumptions one may then infer things about the population, assuming they are true. But this is tricky ground if one starts drawing conclusions about these assumptions. Poles could be 100 yards high or the ruler may actually be 1 inch long, but with these techniques (and metaphysical commitments) one can only learn about reality by making assumptions. This is obvious. But note that what Gillespie is saying in his quote is that Western culture has a strong tendency to think that truth is there to be known, *and that belief is therefore to be encouraged, and skepticism discouraged.* The Null Hypothesis, like much else, is related to the idea that your basic assumptions are true enough to use them as a platform for the statistical inference that follows. If those inferences make no sense, for other reasons, that may tell you something about those assumptions, but just what is not too clear, not least because what you know is what you have inferred *on the basis of exactly those assumptions.*[8]

To quote Cohen (1994):

> What is wrong with NHST [Null Hypothesis Significance Testing]? Well, among other things, it does not tell us what we want to know, and we so much want to know what we want to know that, out of desperation, we nevertheless believe that it does! What we want to know is, "Given these data, what is the probability that H0 [the Null Hypothesis] is true?" But as most of us know, *what it tells us is "Given H0 is true, what is the probability of these (or more extreme) data?"* These are not the same, as has been pointed out many times over the years.
>
> (p. 997, emphasis added)

If we think about it, these basic assumptions include the idea that the world is knowable and ordered in ways that are independent of interactions with it ("the model is true" in standard econometrics) and that it is knowable through some logically coherent framework. To use the same term as Gillespie, this may assume that knowledge should be apodictic— that is, *demonstrably* true, arguably, because what it is about—reality—is also assumed to be coherent.[9] The pithy term used in much discussion of issues arising from this is the observation that much economic argument compares "model with muddle" (see Box 2.4 on p. 30)—that is, the arguments are demonstrably logical and coherent in their own terms (model), yet appear to contrast what they are ostensibly about (muddle). Gillespie's point is that such views may be linked to deep and typically untestable (and untested) assumptions about how the world really is and should be understood. The discussion of Rodrik in the previous section may be seen as an examination of such a contrast.

We recall that the responses to L&Z (1993), as mapped by Fforde (2005) through reference to citations, show that most ignored the possible implications: specifically that the data showed no knowable pattern of robust relationships between policy proxies and economic outcomes, when the relevant data sets were interrogated and the range of standard functional forms considered. This suggests that we are mainly observing a matter of untestable belief and metaphysical commitment.

To return to more mainstream discussions, probably more accessible to most students, we find various options. Often, exploring these options does not move far from the most basic assumptions and viewpoints of DE itself. Central to these tangles is the treatment of causality, which, like reality, is surely one of the trickiest terms that we encounter.[10]

Before I discuss these, however, I will rapidly discuss (somewhat tongue-in-cheek, as these arguments, while deadly serious, can become somewhat "precious") an insightful view, called **ascriptivism**, which suggests a rather different view of all this.[11] This comes down to the idea that discussions about cause and effect are usefully seen as being nothing of the sort; rather, they are part of human processes of negotiation, manipulation, mutual enjoyment, and so on.

While I was writing another book (Fforde 2009), a German colleague of mine suggested I read Lumer et al. (2007), a "heavy" book called *Intentionality, Deliberation and Autonomy*, written by professional philosophers. One chapter argued that people have a tendency to treat actions as mainly related to social interaction around issues such as responsibility, while viewing discussions of cause and effect as subsequent to this basic sense. In other words, they talk about causes and effects, but what they are really doing is deciding who gets blamed, praised, or ignored.

Discussions of cause and effect are, in this view, better seen as part of social processes related to the *ascription* of motives and responsibility entailed by attribution or responsibility via concepts of actions. That is to say that whether causes and/or effects generate predictability is of far less importance for humans than whether they generate judgments of responsibility, leading to praise, condemnation, or laughter, or whatever (Stoecker 2007). A range of jokes and the themes and subjects of drama suggest the power of such ideas.[12] What professional philosophers and others tell us is that, since logic and consistency may be somewhat alien to such views, those who act as though they believe in them may care (with happy passion) very little about apodicity.

A second useful piece of writing that may add to this perspective is a heterodox element within American political science, started by Converse (1964) reporting evidence about popular political beliefs (specifically, the general ignorance of the general population, from an elite perspective) and continued by Friedman (2006) arguing that evidence suggested equally considerable ignorance on the part of elites too. Thus:

> As Lord and his colleagues tellingly put it, their subjects' "logical sin lay in their readiness to use evidence already processed in a biased manner to bolster the very theory or belief that initially 'justified' the processing bias . . . making their hypotheses unfalsifiable . . . and allowing themselves to be encouraged by patterns of data that they ought to have found troubling. Through such processes laypeople and professional scientists alike find it all too easy to cling to impressions, beliefs, and theories that have ceased to be compatible with the latest and best evidence available. (Lord et al. 1979, 2107.)"
> (Friedman 2006: xxxvii and xxxix)

I would expect that one conclusion drawn from such observations is that it is unwise to take any body of knowledge simply on its own terms—but that is a very old idea.

The neo-Kantians and the creation of the term "epistemology": Kuhn, Lakatos, and Popper

A group of German philosophers working in the nineteenth century, concerned to handle tensions between contending schools of thought, coined the term "epistemology," in part to manage various inputs to such discussions—that is, to suggest systematic, ordered ways of discussing the issue. These scholars are sometimes called neo-Kantians, and the term epistemology has passed into more general usage. Thus, a view that quite different models should be used when circumstances differ may be said to argue against assumptions of "epistemological universalism"—that the same knowledge should work everywhere. A view that economists are uninterested in fundamentally questioning what they consider as economics may be said to mean that economists have no interest in epistemological questions. To say that knowledge should be internally consistent (logical) and have certain empirical practices is to say, from an epistemological point of view, something fundamental about that knowledge. To say that modern mathematics talks not of "logic" but of "logics"—the idea that being logical is to be consistent with certain stated and particular rules of logic (Kline 1980)—is to take an epistemological point of view, allowing for systematic comparison of mathematics as it was and now is, and so on. Epistemology as a concept gives one a language to discuss different uses of words such as "logic" without getting too worked up about whether this or that author is or is not being logical.

Up until, say, the 1970s, such discussions in the mainstream would usually have referred to at least three scholars: Karl Popper, Thomas Kuhn, and Imre Lakatos. These three are by today's standards rather traditional-minded (a polite term for out-of-date), for they are particularly interested in sciences, understood as developing—that is, progressing—fields of knowledge. I will contrast them with other authors such as Edward Said, Arturo Escobar, and Michel Foucault, who are more interested in questions about how and why knowledges such as science determined (or influenced) their own subject matter. This viewpoint is often baffling to economists, who tend to believe that what they study exists objectively whether they examine it or not. In this, economists tend to find the concerns of Kuhn, Lakatos, and Popper more accessible than Said and so forth. I will try to show, however, how the perspectives of both groups connect through questions familiar to economists such as "model choice" and "data creation processes." This should make the discussion in the next chapter more accessible to both DE and DS students.

Popper, working in the mid-twentieth century, argued that sciences, which could include economics as understood in mainstream accounts, advance through use of certain techniques. Central to these, he says, is a practice of *falsification*—that is, a science contains various accounts, or models, that interact with data and are said to fit data; if new data or models become available, models that do *not* fit data are abandoned, and this abandonment is said to mean that they have been falsified—shown to be untrue. This account can be found in Popper (1959; originally published in German in 1934) and is famous.[13] It is worth noting that he called his book, using a language that would now be seen as telling, *The Logic of Scientific Discovery*.

Popper does not appear interested in asking other questions about data and theory, such as their origins, "who the data and the theory belong to," and so on. Within this approach, the core definition of a science focuses upon interactions between data and theory. Of course, this is central to the internal of economics—what economists believe they do. This approach inherently assumes that knowledge as science progresses, so long as records are kept of what scientists do. More fundamentally, the view here assumes that there is something to know.

Kuhn, working mainly in the second half of the twentieth century, arguably treated sciences in a similar way, in that he also focused upon models and data. In his most famous work (Kuhn 1962, *The Structure of Scientific Revolutions*), he argued that most of the time sciences are mainly concerned with working out fine details, with reference to data, of modeling based upon certain fundamental ideas. This limited pace of progress changes fundamentally when and if models cannot explain data to some crucial degree. He focuses upon the possible existence of anomalies—data treated by the science as valid but apparently inconsistent with its knowledge. He argues that the accumulation of such inconsistencies eventually creates characteristic tensions, leading to the creation of qualitatively different sets of theories to underpin new models that are consistent with both what had been anomalies and pre-existing data (a new *paradigm*). Like Popper, this is a way of explaining progress.

Compared with Popper, Kuhn encourages interest in how such shifts happen, in historical terms. He also argues that in normal times a science is mainly interested in working out implications of theory that is considered true as it explains data (some of which is new). An important implication of Kuhn's views is arguably that what most scientists are normally doing is working through what their accepted theories have to say about data they encounter. Adding new components to the theory to account for apparent inconsistencies—as we may now see, this is what Rodrik was doing—is apparently quite compatible with Kuhn's account. This may often be simply discovering how a parameter varies under different conditions. Again, though, by contemporary standards, there is little interest from Kuhn and Popper in questions about the origins of theory and data, who they belong to, and so on. Neither shows much interest in asserting that knowledge is socially constructed, though both have a lot to say about the practices of what we now call knowledge production: the social processes that generate ideas that are seen and accepted as knowledge, such as civil engineering, DE, and DS, just to give some examples.

For mainstream economists, Kuhn and Popper make (and still make) considerable sense. They suggest that the acceptability of economic theory provides the basis for empirical work that looks for application of that theory, and that progress is underpinned by Popper's view that if theory cannot explain data it will be seen as falsified and by Kuhn's view that an increasing incidence of anomalies will result in pressures for the creation of new theories. Neither man stresses contexts, such as the historical, political, or social (this is what makes L&P such a useful accessible study). And, what is more pertinent for DE, neither broach the issue of what happens if the relationship between data and model, between empirics and theory, is increasingly experienced as vague, for that is one interpretation of L&P's characterization of the current situation.

Lakatos, working after World War II, arguably takes the discussion a considerable step further and/or sideways (for we should be careful about implying progress) (Lakatos 1970). For my purposes here, he may be read as arguing that data, in any science, cannot be separated from that science's practice. For him, the link is the idea of *observation theory*—the idea that data of itself is meaningless unless it is explained and given meaning by some theory or explanation. This point can be made in different ways. It may be argued that data is meaningless without some way of explaining it, and that this explanation is inseparable from the science itself. A simple rhetorical point here is that while most people know that Newton's third law says that force equals mass times acceleration, nobody has ever seen either a force or a mass. There is a need for explanation and also a need for seeing—for observation. And for those with some familiarity with relativity theory, clearly what is meant there by mass, and how data relates to that concept, is again different. For economists, especially those close to their econometrics lectures, the point is relevant to the extent that lecturers stress "data creation processes," not least in the construction of the ideas linking theory and data. The point here, again, is that data such as GDP per capita has to be created, through surveys and so on, and has also to be given meaning through observation theory; without both the data is no more than a set of numbers.

Lakatos poses the question of how data exists within science, thus pushing attention toward subjects of great interest to the next group of scholars I discuss: how can an account be given that explains the particular activities and beliefs associated with a science? Readers may already be concerned that DE's beliefs in deep determinants of things like economic growth, when combined with weak empirics and an apparent lack of too much concern over problems that arise from this, mean that we need to look outside DE for ways of explaining DE itself. And central to this is the usage of terms such as epistemology.

From a rhetorical point of view, it is not hard to pour petrol (or perfume) on fires of debate that accompany these issues. The lack of self-reflection and interest in interdisciplinary boundaries in DE is telling. For example, I recall a professor of economics, fluent in a Southeast Asian language, offering a seminar paper on the economics of migration in Southeast Asia that did not mention gender. When this was pointed out, he had nothing to say. I doubt whether most people in the audience, and certainly those who were not economists, found this omission either unexpected or unfamiliar. The lack of self-reflection and unwillingness to consider other factors beyond economics in DE makes it easy to ignore, in this case matters of gender (the trite point is that consumer and employment theory is, in the first instance, ungendered).

More contemporary treatments: Said, Escobar, and Foucault

Let us now consider, briefly, three other scholars: Said, Escobar, and Foucault. All three stress, in different ways, how a particular group's beliefs, in terms of its understanding, do not have to be explained in terms of a scientific truth. A group's understanding includes what is referred to as fact—that is, how data is created and how meanings are given to it.

Said, working toward the end of the twentieth century, is particularly important because of what he says about the construction by Western thinkers of the "Orient" (Said 1978). He argues that this process should mainly be explained by reference to characteristics and historical processes in the West. Thus, his account of the Orient is, at root, not about the Orient but what was said about it, by whom, how, and why. To put this (rhetorically) in an extreme way, Western literature about the Orient that Said examines is not to be explained by looking at, say, what Arab and other Muslims have written down or said, crafted, or sung, but by understanding Western issues, points of view, and interests.

The point of framing the issue (here of the Orient, but the method is of obvious wider application) in this way is that it teaches understanding of a conceptual framework by looking, not at what it says it is about, but at whom and what has produced it. This is a point of view far more familiar to DS students, for whom the basic building block of study is usually comparative rationalities and approaches.

This way of framing Western knowledge thus is not only striking for discussions of development but also of particular importance as China and India continue to grow economically far faster than Western countries (however defined). It might be said that for any group subject to the ideas of another, perhaps more powerful, this is tediously obvious.

Escobar, an anthropologist, offers clear and accessible accounts that suggest, using Gillespie's language, that metaphysical commitments are very much worth confronting. The angle he takes is that of *discourse*, focusing on how languages and accounts take belief in certain directions and away from others (Escobar 1995). For example, he argues that the terms used in development discourses (GDP, farmer, etc.) define what is to be included in development, and so what is to be excluded, and that these processes of definition reflect power relations. Thus, one might think, powerful people may support the idea that the correct way to discuss development is in economic terms, associating this with those ideas of economic efficiency that are part of DE.

For those interested in development, Escobar offers a clear account of how approaches such as DE work discursively, making certain relationships and situations appear natural rather than the result of human action.[14] He looks at three examples: integrated rural development (an idea sometimes popular among aid donors) and the introduction of small farmers to development with the green revolution; women in development (another term once popular among aid donors); and environmental issues and the idea of sustainable development. He argues for each that the discourse itself may act as a framework for an understanding, especially how certain things are made invisible or made visible within the discourse itself. An example would be comparable to the World Bank report on Laos discussed in Chapter 3, which was blind to ways in which local society coped with familiar problems. Women in development, for example, often tended to define problems of gender in ways that reflected the concerns of particular aid workers (Sylvester 1999). In this set of metaphysical commitments, the invention of underdevelopment—the fact that a discourse has effects—is thought of as an actor itself.

This can rapidly become very intense. Though only reference can be given here, vivid stories that juxtapose economists' confident accounts of what should happen with others' perspectives that contradict such accounts can readily be found, such as in the so-called "postdevelopment" literature. Ferguson (1997) is a good place to start. It is not hard to find even more extreme views of how the road to hell is "paved with good intentions" (Porter et al. 1991).

One useful way to start a discussion of Foucault is with the possibility of a "policy science"—that is, cause–effect relationships that would be equivalent to the experienced stable predictability of some natural sciences. This metaphor in some ways helps explain much of the language and stance of DE, because hopes for such a policy science appear often to have been ill-founded (Fforde 2010). A problem here is that natural sciences are clearly as socially constructed as anything else but tend to experience their empirics as robustly predictable, once it has been accepted that (after Lakatos) their empirics are internalized through observation theory so there is nothing objective about their empirics. But the failure of the policy-science project may be related, I think without too much difficulty, to Foucault's oft-referenced idea of the "construction of subjects." Ideas of human free will have been (or not) squared with notions of a self-constraining yet omnipotent creator (well discussed in Gillespie 2008). Whether this means that a socially constructed subject is capable of subjectively constructing anything it likes can be thought of as part of a "truth game," to use another phrase of Foucault. So far, it is hard to make water flow uphill, suggesting that taking such games too far is unwise, but you never really know, and to quote from another context, tomorrow is always another day.

Interpretations of Foucault I now leave to readers and their teachers to investigate. There are many entry points and, like many influential scholars, he has probably been more influential indirectly than through his own works.

Conclusions

This very rapid overview of these issues points to the main issues in studying DE. The first is that powerful currents within modern social sciences not only strongly question the ready assumption of DE that it can know reality in ways that may reliably guide action but also provide various tools for creating ways of understanding DE as a socially constructed knowledge best understood by looking at its practitioners and their contexts rather than at what they say they study.

Second, great care is needed with uncritically adopting these tools, as they often, especially when involved with development practice, slip into the very pitfalls they criticize in DE (Fforde 2010). In this sense, DE can be said to offer opportunities to recognize, with some degree of reliability, that it does not know, in predictive terms, what works.

A decent library and a range of reading lists are needed by students investigating ways of assessing DE. Much can be learned from such questioning, but it is worth noting that much of such criticism is equally applicable to policy advice that does not come from economists.

I once found myself saying to a student that "what is perfect is what works." The interested student may wish to read the study by Mosse (2005) that I criticize in Fforde (2010). This is a history of the failure of the injection by anthropologists and others (led by Mosse) of participatory methods into an Indian rural development project. Such methods sought to attain better outcomes by ensuring that poor farmers and others were given voice in the project in various ways. Although Mosse blames misrepresentation and incorrect analysis for the situation, his predictive confidence in the participatory techniques (which he was paid to help deploy) is not so different from many, such as development economists, who believe strongly in their ideas about solutions to development problems. To paraphrase the anthropologists Shore and Wright in Chapter 1: just because something makes apodictic sense as an account of the social construction of knowledge (no matter how cleverly constructed) does not make it a wise guide to action. Rigor is easy. It is the rest of it—the relationship, if any, between these ideas and the real world—that drops the anvil on your foot.

Questions for discussion

1.   Is Rodrik right in thinking that there are deep determinants of economic growth?

2.   Discuss but not too seriously: social science is as confused when it thinks it knows the truth as religions are when they think that knowledge of the Divine is the same as knowledge of the color of one's daughter's eyes.

3.   Discuss: agreeing about ontology is not the same as agreeing on what is out there.

Notes

1   Thus Gillespie (2008), quoted later in this chapter, and Box 2.2 on p. 21. More detail of basic assumptions in statistical analysis, which are confusing, are presented later in the chapter.

2   The "fundamentals" is a common term adopted by economists, which is hard to explain as it is usually not clearly defined. It tends to mean, in combination, elements of the context of the economy that support good growth, on the one hand, and parameters of the economy that do the same, on the other. For Vietnam, an example of the first would be its geographical situation in Southeast Asia, viewed as a dynamic region, and of the second the idea that the population is culturally hard-working. The term is rhetorically of great importance.

3   To repeat arguments I have made elsewhere, use of algebra means that the results follow from the working through of the algebra; they are apodictic (see the list of special terms on p. 323), necessarily true given the rules of the argument, and so dependent upon those for their validity. Whether the model may be said to have any empirical value is quite a different matter.

4   The importance of clear property rights is that they are *conceptually* linked to the apparent potential of markets to generate good outcomes under certain conditions (see Chapter 9). Thus is it argued that without clear ownership, firms and consumers will be unable to behave in the ways appropriate to this conceptualization.

5   Histories argue that patterns of racial and occupational segregation in American cities and suburbs, before and after World War II, allowed mortgage and other lending to lower status groups to be minimized, with important long-term effects. Internet search on the term "redlining" offers access to such arguments.

6   By statistical fit is meant the extent to which the exercise, with its assumptions, tells us that model and data are consistent. Here, using common methods, it is the case that adding in more explanatory variables will generate better metrics of statistical fit—simply doing so will make it look as though the model is better at explaining the data.

7   See the reference to "ascriptivism" later in this section and also Stoecker (2007).

8   This is, in fact, something that one can view as rather good fun. For example, see Granger (1990) and Granger and Newbold (1974), which report experiences running regressions on random data that produced correlations that, clearly, are quite spurious as the data is random. Cohen (1994) is a highly readable

introduction to the confusions that follow if one thinks that the hypotheses one tests through hypothesis testing are the same as the hypothesis in the Null Hypothesis.

9 Thus: "In his early thought, Descartes was convinced that he could construct an apodictic science on the basis of mathematics. Such a science, he believed, could represent all motion in thought so that human beings could truly master nature, ameliorating human misery, as Bacon had hoped, or producing the commodious life Hobbes desired, but actually making man the immortal lord of all creation (Descartes 1985, 1: 143)" (Gillespie 1999: 26–27).

10 DS and other students may be intrigued to know of a concept in econometrics called Granger causality, which comes down to little more than *post hoc ergo propter hoc*—"after it and so because of it." As McCloskey keeps hammering home, causality is a conceptual category, not of the data but of the chosen interpretation made of it (Chapter 6). Thus my use of the word "empirics" (see the Preface and Box A on p. xvi).

11 My mother used to label this as "really, it is all about who does the washing up."

12 My personal favorite is the Monty Python sketch about the academic and logician who has certain marital problems. This can currently (July 2013) be found at www.youtube.com/watch?v=FZqs36C5sgM.

13 As with many such important works, the reader is advised to read the original, but to bear in mind that the influence of such works is often through interpretations with which the original author may well have disagreed. In economics, a classic example is Hicks' interpretation of Keynes' work, which was early on largely used to teach Keynes, rather than the original. There is much debate about what Keynes really meant.

14 Bearing in mind the previous quotations from Gillespie, the popular term "God-given" comes to mind. For a decent account of critical discourse analysis, see Fairclough (1992). In German, I am told (I thank my friend Joerg Wischermann) that apodictic usually means "from on high," with pejorative sense.

6 Coping with facts

How mainstream economists decide on what is worth modeling

It is striking how economic textbooks that introduce theory to students give little empirical guidance—if at all—to which situations models are said to work in and where they do not. An anecdotal comparison would be with another knowledge area, fluid dynamics, where different models are used under different circumstances. Specifically, air in motion may be modeled as laminar or turbulent flow, with the transition from one to the other dependent on certain conditions. When a wing stalls, due to, perhaps, increasing angle of attack, the air ceases to flow smoothly, and, as the laminar flow model (students are told) ceases to apply, the plane starts to fall from the sky. A host of similar instances can be found to guide model selection generally, based, as in this example, on an experienced predictive capacity. Standard microeconomics textbooks, however, lack this empirically founded guidance (e.g. Jehle and Reny 1998).

The superficial form of modeling taken by economic analysis is that of mathematics. If variables include time—"t"—and are part of determinate solutions, then, like the natural sciences for which the mathematics was originally developed, there is some expectation that the analysis has some robust relationship to observables: basically, predictive capacity. Though much can be made of different epistemological positions (Kuhnian, Popperian, Lakatosian, "naive,"[1] etc.—see Chapter 5), it is quite clear that economics, as practiced, lacks predictive power. Through its emphasis upon statistical significance, econometrics may for some researchers finesse this, but the basic issue remains. Nobody knows what GDP will be in, say, twelve months' time, and nobody can accurately forecast prices. It seems far more consistent to interpret the determinate *form* of economic positions as simply one set of explanations among many. This means, of course, that it is risky to use economic knowledge as a reliable input to organized activities that rely upon cause–effect logics to organize what they do (Fforde 2009, 2010).

From this line of argument it follows that the available studies of economists' modeling practices should tell us that model selection is largely *not* driven by what various naive views of natural science would suggest: above all, concerns with failed predictions or the need to secure better prediction. Instead, to develop robust explanations that fit the data, the studies should stress what could be called *sociology*: that is, the importance of human elements in our diverse and evolving explanations. These elements include changing modeling techniques, concerns about the state of the world, career rivalries between economists, institutional tensions between university departments, and political opportunities and constraints. And these sociological factors are what we may find if we search for studies that can inform us. But partly because of the determinate form of economic arguments and hopes for predictive capability, the relevant literature is rather thin.

Here I refer to three interesting and rare empirical sources: McCloskey (1985) on the forms of economic arguments (what she calls their rhetoric), Yonay (1998) on economists' practices, and Colander et al. (2004) on changes in economists' interests, focusing upon what they call the "cutting edge" in the early years of the first decade of the 2000s.

Economics as rhetoric

Deidre McCloskey's famous book *The Rhetoric of Economics* has gone through two editions and is widely cited. The book by the respected US economist appears to have two main goals. First, it shows how economists' arguments are rhetorical, in the technical rather than the pejorative sense; that they deploy various techniques to persuade their audiences and that these techniques are not very different from those used in other areas. This discussion is persuasive, in part because of its close attention to the textual forms of important economic arguments. In passing, McCloskey also argues that these persuasive techniques are drawn from the same tool kit as those used in the natural sciences and humanities. In this sense, the study informs economists that natural science is, like economics, rhetorical: it seeks to persuade and uses various techniques to do so. Her arguments seek to explain in some detail how economists' arguments are linked to empirics and how these link to other aspects of their rhetoric, such as the claims to rigor attributed to the use of formal arguments (mathematics) and appeals to fundamental axiomatizable propositions about behavior (rational choice). Much of the book is devoted to an extremely thorough and interesting discussion of these issues.[2]

Second, it digs deeply into the specific nature of economists' empirics. For my arguments here, this is particularly interesting. Chapter 8, "The Rhetoric of Significance Tests," reports empirical research into economists' empirics. However, it is preceded by Chapter 7, "The Unexamined Rhetoric of Economic Quantification," whose central argument is that quantification requires subjective judgment and that much economic argument fails to recognize this. To quote:

> The question of whether prices are closely connected internationally, then, is important. The official rhetoric does not leave much doubt as

to what is required to answer it: collect facts on prices . . . and *test* the hypothesis. A large number of economists have done this. Half of them conclude that purchasing power parity works; the other half conclude that it fails. The conclusions diverge not because economics is arbitrary but because the disputants have not considered their statistical rhetoric.

(McCloskey 1985: 109–111)

What McCloskey means is that there is far too little recognition that subjective discussion, to answer the question "How large is large?" is bound up in these judgments. People vary and so these judgments are likely to differ. We may conclude from any lack of convergence in the empirical literature that either the truth has not yet been found or that we are seeing a reflection of the different perspectives and approaches of researchers. This, in a sense, supports the basic approach of many, if not most DS courses, which is to teach comparative rationalities—how approaches to doing development vary over time and between different agencies and actors.

The characteristics of the research published—in particular, whether it converges or not—thus tells us a lot about the subjectivity of the researchers. In this it is not unreasonable to argue that it is economists' **priors** that drive the results—their known facts.

McCloskey's Chapter 8 reports on a study of the empirics of relevant papers published in the *American Economic Review* during the 1980s. What energizes this research is the view that economists, whose quantifications using econometrics rely heavily upon statistical significance tests (see Chapter 5), often confuse judgments about economic significance with judgments about statistical significance. As she puts it:

> The numbers are necessary material. *But they are not sufficient to bring the matter to a scientific conclusion.* Only the scientists can do that, because "conclusion" is a human idea, not Nature's. It is a property of human minds, not of the statistics.
>
> (p. 112)

And:

> It is not true, as most economists think, that . . . statistical significance is a preliminary screen, a necessary condition, through which empirical estimates should be put. Economists will say, "Well, I want to know if the coefficient *exists*, don't I?" Yes, but statistical significance can't tell you. Only the magnitude of the coefficient, on the scale of what counts in practical, engineering terms as non-zero, tells you. *It is not the case that statistically insignificant coefficients are in effect zero.*
>
> (p. 118)

The point that she is making is, in some ways, trivial, which is what partly gives it its power. She quotes Wallis and Roberts (1956): "In statistical usage, 'significant' means 'signifying a characteristic of the population from which the sample is drawn,'" regardless of whether the characteristic is important (p. 123). In other words, she is reminding us that a basic assumption in statistical inference, in economists' terms, is that the model is correct. The problem then is how to gauge its parameters: by analogy, for example, with those who believe that participatory methods lead to better project design and then assume that participation has an effect before they can estimate how much difference participatory methods make. A project that imposes experts' views and ignores participatory methods, in this way of looking at things, results in "X," while a project that is based upon participation, results in "Y," and the statistical methodology allows one to gauge the difference between "Y" and "X." But to do so means assuming that the model and one's assumptions about why observations differ from what it says are correct. Statistical methods then say that if one can explain how one's observation differs from the essential truth (the model proposed), one can then say something about the estimates made through the statistical exercise of the difference between "Y" and "X." What is important here is to appreciate that one has to make assumptions to create a platform upon which to rest one's statistical estimates. (See the discussion of the Null Hypothesis and the assumptions behind statistical inference in Chapter 5.) It is not generally appreciated just how powerful these assumptions are, which is what McCloskey is trying to show.

Given the data, econometrics permits estimation of the parameters of the model and gives measures of the statistical significance of those estimates. What this means in terms of our discussion is that it is the assumptions—that the model is correct, that the observations differ from what the model would precisely predict in certain ways, and that steps are taken to manage errors in measurement (usually that samples are randomly taken)—that allow statements to be made about how accurate the estimates are likely to be—that is, their statistical significance.

This poses the crucial question of what may be concluded from finding that a parameter estimate is not statistically different from zero. To go back to the previous example, the exercise may lead to the statistical conclusion that, given the errors involved, "X" is not different from "Y." But what if one increased the power of the sampling, such as by increasing the number of observations? It is obvious that this will probably make the conclusions more reliable, but this depends on what is meant by "more reliable," which depends upon how much reliability is wanted. In international development aid practice, how much does the reliability of estimates matter? To whom? As McCloskey points out, "it depends."

In the specialized language of statistical analysis, a parameter estimate that is statistically different from zero does not *necessarily* say that the relationship is important.[3] Indeed, under reasonable circumstances it would be reckless to assume on that basis that it was. It depends upon judgments, such as about the risks to being wrong. McCloskey's point is that what she calls the rhetorical unawareness of economists, as part of their practice, is striking. And this leads them to interesting and characteristic behaviors, such as a tendency to a somewhat naive (see note 1 and Chapter 5) view of natural science methods. One thing, though, that we learn from McCloskey's discussion is that their metaphysical commitments encourage economists to seek, somewhat intensely, arguments for accepting or rejecting the model (rather than simply gauging estimates of parameters). We can recall that the entire econometric exercise may be thought of as based upon a procedure that requires, for the moment, assuming that the model is correct. Therefore, she is wise to focus squarely upon an analysis of what is being done when a parameter (in our example, the difference between "Y" and X") is estimated as being not different from zero. What she is arguing is that this does not *necessarily* mean that in the real world it is different from zero. In epistemological terms, perhaps what we see here are the consequences of a willingness to believe that the model either is or is not about reality.

McCloskey and Ziliak (1996) published the results of their survey of empirical papers that had appeared in the *American Economic Review* during the 1980s. They posed a range of questions for each paper, exploring the relative importance attached to statistical inference. For example, question no. 16 in their questionnaire is: "Is statistical inference the conversation stopper, conveying the sense of an ending?" The findings of the research confirm that, while statistical method platforms on powerful assumptions to permit researchers to gauge estimates of parameters of models, the main thrust of economists' investigations is to support or attack models as they stand (see also Cohen 1994, quoted above in Chapter 5). For example, only 30 percent of the papers distinguished statistical significance from economic, policy, or scientific significance (p. 131). Only 31 percent reported descriptive statistics, such as the means of the regression variables that would allow the reader to judge the economic significance of the results (p. 131).

These results suggest that published results, and so beliefs, are not reliably based upon robust prediction; it is unwise to conclude that robust predictive power (or its absence) follows from published results, showing that parameters are (or are not) statistically significant. Given the lack of robust prediction, quantification is driven by the subjective tool of significance tests. This goes along with, or at least so it appears, a choice of descriptive metaphors that may be weakly linked to empirics, thus strengthening the influence of already existing beliefs and other priors. Such metaphors take many forms, but one obvious one is the use of proxy variables; in Chapter 23 we discuss how a concept of *economic openness* is used rhetorically, on the one hand, and then inserted into an empirical exercise by constructing a proxy variable said to measure the degree of economic openness. Statements about the laws of economics, in epistemological terms, do many things, but here the most important is that they assume epistemological universality—in natural science terms, that the same laws of gravity may be used to explain and predict here as on Mars. Here the reader may wish to review the discussion about a World Bank report on Laos (Chapter 3).

The sociology of economists

I turn now to examine work to better understand how economists' particular views form. Yonay (1998) (also Yonay 1994) is a historical study of conflicts between institutional and **neoclassical** economists just before and during World War II. In his account these conflicts were concerned with control over key markers of power and influence, such as journals and senior academic positions. He argues, further, that a central goal of the institutionalists was to use the rapid increase in data availability to seek empirical regularities;[4] by contrast, the neoclassicals held to their beliefs *a priori* in the value of their models. Trained as an economist (Yonay 2000) and sociologist, he then turned to map what economists actually do in their central core practice— the creation of models (Yonay and Breslau 2006). These models are represented by many economists as rigorous and examples of scientific explanation. My own interest here is to examine just what is said about their subject choice. As Yonay puts it:

> The truth of economic statements is thus the product of economists' success in enlisting the support of other economists, data, whole economies, mathematics, and other agents, rather than adherence to an established and rule-based method.
>
> [W]e want to ask how neoclassical economists themselves make the connection between their models and economic realities. . . . [O]ur goal is to elucidate the "epistemic culture" of economists that guides their own routine work of model-building and their evaluation of their colleagues' models. Such empirical studies of economics are strikingly missing, despite economics' allegedly huge influence on economic policymaking, and consequently on the lives of us all.
>
> (pp. 5–6)

Although in a different style and framework, Yonay is addressing similar issues to McCloskey. He discusses what he calls economists' "non-experimental practices" (p. 7). This comes down to model-building, for, "according to our observations and interviews it is the keystone of the economic discipline" (*idem*). Model-building, for Yonay, is a social but in many ways isolated practice largely done by individuals working alone. But what they do, what it means to them, and why they chose to model in certain ways and not in others is part of Yonay's account. His own empirics are interviews—here it is worth recalling his professional training as an economist—with economists working and publishing in the mainstream.

His central point about model-building is his question: "What does a model do? . . . [E]conomists want to explain economic phenomena; they discuss economic facts and use them as evidence; and they aspire to reveal the 'real' mechanisms behind the phenomena they study" (p. 16). He concludes that a central issue for economists is what is referred to as "motivation"—that is, the economic significance of the model, which is of "major concern to economists." This refers to "the importance of the model for theoretical and practical concerns" (*idem*).

> Choosing what model to construct, that is, what phenomenon to explain, is a challenge emphasized by most of our interviewees. The challenge is not to find a suitable topic but to choose among many potential ones. The economists must gamble on what would interest their colleagues, and once they choose a topic . . . they actually speculate on their ability to show the intuited mechanism. . . . Obviously, the importance of the topic is a feature of the community, and individual economists test the wind before choosing in which direction to sail.
>
> (pp. 17–18)

The nature of modeling activity, according to Yonay, typically comes down to "building a simplified model of the real-world economy that shows how the (rational) conduct of maximizing agents under specific conditions leads to that phenomenon" (p. 18). Thus, models are given assumptions that allow a rhetoric to show how a previously excluded issue can, through the model, be explained. But in this practice a model with the approved building blocks (statements about agents' preferences etc.) and an analytic solution may still be challenged on the grounds of plausibility. Here Yonay and Breslau's discussion is interesting, for this is not a predictive criterion:

> Referees and editors often cite implausibility as a reason for rejecting articles. They use their sense and knowledge of the economy to assess whether a model offers an important explanation of an economic phenomenon. Thus, an article can handle an important subject, be rigorously constructed, and still be rejected if the referees and the editor believe that it fails to address a main mechanism behind the phenomenon in question.
>
> (p. 28)

Yonay and Breslau suggest that, for the mainstream economists they studied, "this is basically an internal dispute over the relative importance of simplicity versus generality within the same epistemic[5] culture" (p. 31). One should not, then, be too surprised that econometrics was marginal to the work of the economists they studied, who considered its position as subservient (p. 32).

The most striking conclusion from their research is the limited, one might even say ad hoc, relationships between modeling activities and empirics. This fits with McCloskey's findings. Their conclusions would not support a naive view of systematic iterations between theory and facts, leading to progressively better predictive capacity. Yet, as Yonay and Breslau report:

> [E]conomists were very concerned with the way in which their models matched reality. . . . They knew they were being judged according to the compatibility of their models with reality (*as considered by their peers*), and they judged other economists' models according to how well those models agreed with reality, *as they perceived it. Yet, the way they conceived of reality and the methods they regarded as appropriate for understanding reality differed from the conceptions and methods employed by most other social scientists.*
>
> (p. 33, emphasis added)

This supports my point: the ideas about reality that guide model-building, and so economists' expressed and articulated views about the economy, are specific. If you want to know how economists view the world, look at their explanations of it. And these come more from whatever facts and approaches they have at hand than from the hard slog of empirical work, which is not highly valued. Thus:

> What is distinctive about model-building in economics is the process that mediates between the microworld (the economic models) and the ostensible object of the research. Rather than involving scientific instruments or data-gathering procedures, this mediation is accomplished by vaguely defined but generally accepted conventions regarding the movement from reality to models. . . . There is no pretence that the model actually resembles reality. Rather, the concern with realism is a concern with the plausibility of the mediation between the reality and the model.
>
> (pp. 33–34)

Thus:

> The model is not a proof but a demonstration of a possible mechanism. The audience is not expected to accept the suggested mechanism as the cause of the phenomenon, but rather as a proposal of a conceivable economic force.
>
> (p. 35)

It would seem, then, relatively clear that the specific models that receive approval from economists, as an epistemic community, should not—unless with great care—be treated as guides to action. This is only partly because of the risk that peers' judgments about what is important and true is "wrong." More deeply, the issue has to do with what is meant, in terms of peer review, by wrong, for such studies are peer reviewed and published. I feel comfortable using the distinction between understanding and predictive knowledge, concluding that the former, given the different values and preferences of economists' peers, is quite different from any conclusion that these models are predictive. Hopes for the untroubled sharing of empirical beliefs across contexts experienced as different are weakened by the presence of only vaguely defined conventions that govern relations between models and reality. These are not wisely to be treated as *predictive* models. While the superficial form models take may appear to offer a robust basis for prediction, or at least for tracking reality, that is not their intended purpose; in simple terms, they are meant to be consumed by people who find these exercises valuable and important—as a peer group and in terms of their particular understandings. For me, this is quite different from a *predictive* knowledge. *Reader beware.*

I turn now to look at a third study of how economists' concerns and motivations change, and the reasons for what they are at any point in time. This can be accessed through a study of those within the epistemic community, who are seen as being at the cutting edge. This combines with McCloskey and Yonay to support my argument.

Changes in economists' interests and the cutting edge

Colander et al. (2004) specifically focuses on "the process by which economic thinking changes" (p. 1). Indeed, they title their book *The Changing Face of Economics: Conversations with Cutting Edge Economists*. They implicitly assert that this change is progressive, based on their detailed interviews with economists considered to be at the cutting edge. One striking element of their assessment of current trends is the treatment of empirics, for their main focus is not so much upon the economy but upon other economists. Thus:

> What is making it possible for these ideas to take root now ... are advances in analytic technology that have made it possible to study much more complex models than before, development in computing capabilities that have allowed one to study problems that do not have analytic solutions, and advances in other disciplines relevant to economics.
>
> (p. 4)

They see the shifts as driven by elites within the discipline, who become "open to new ideas" (p. 4). Thus change, according to the authors, mainly comes "from within" (p. 5). As they show through their own methodology, the central issue here to understanding change is to review the subjectivity of those at the cutting edge within economics. Ideas, initially expressed in workshop papers and then published in well-known journals, diffuse downward. The lag time is relatively stable ("up to ten years" (p. 11) and largely determined by hierarchies and internal relationships within the discipline—what Colander et al. call its "sociology."

To start with, this casual empiric is naive. The presence of studies such as that by Yonay and others are not referenced, and such an important parameter as the lag time is simply mentioned in passing. Yet, if we take a long step sideways, and consider the periodicities associated with changes in development doctrines, which form the core of DS courses, we can find similar time periods. One can relate these to typical times-in-post for aid workers (3–4 years), aid project cycles (3–5 years of implementation preceded by perhaps 2–3 years' preparation), and so on.[6] Colander et al. appear uninterested in just why this lag should be stable, as they believe it to be. I would personally be very surprised if major advances in predictive sciences exhibited stable lag times.

The reported stability of such time lags tends to suggest that it is the *internal* characteristics of the community that determine the lag time—the yearly teaching cycle, the number of years required to acquire bachelor's and master's degrees, grant applications, promotions, time taken to set up new journals, and so on. In development practice and aid work, similar matters influence the rhythms of development cooperation—the time-in-post of program officers, the need to develop new ideas within career structures, and so on. Such characteristics of both communities, which are a vital piece of knowledge for anybody who works with them, indicate the relative robustness of the internal in its interplay with its environment.

These considerations have far wider implications. If we choose to stop thinking that development knowledges such as DE are primarily to be understood by reference to what they say they are about and instead focus upon how they are produced, evidence that the sociology of their producers appears to generate stable patterns over time is valuable. For those trying to cope with varying donor beliefs, for example, the existence of these time lags and cycles suggests that better strategies assume that they will change, to keep up with economic ideas, according to a system that has built-in lags of around a decade. Thus, a department in a government ministry responsible for managing relations with aid donors wisely spends resources monitoring changes in donor ideas, expecting them to change. Further, if we reconsider L&P (2002), we can conceptualize the change as moving cyclically between important dualities, as in the dualities of state and market, which, L&P shows rather clearly, are concerned with shifting views of the prescribed balance between "state" and "market." This view is productive. Consider the following:

> The paradox is that cyclical movement reappeared, whatever the purpose of progressive development, in the intention to develop. It was the

intention to development which embraced the internal [the idea] of development, namely the conscious authority of autonomous being to determine and realize its potential.

(Cowen and Shenton 1996: 54,
quoted in Fforde 2009: 100–101)

What this means is that once produced knowledge loses a decent empirical footing, and becomes dominated by "vaguely defined but generally accepted conventions regarding the movement from reality to models" (to quote Yonay again), then it is the subjectivity of the researchers that dominates.

It is not possible to summarize here the interviews in Colander et al., but what comes through most strikingly is the "artisanal" nature of personal histories, the focus upon modeling, and the vaguely defined relationships between models and reality, as understood by these economists. These support the pictures offered by McCloskey and Yonay.

Conclusions

As I have already mentioned, mainstream economists' practices vary: undergraduate teaching has different content from postgraduate, which in turn is different from what Colander et al. refer to as the cutting edge. Again, though, if we ask epistemological questions, possible responses include empirics—studies of what economists actually do. These studies focus upon the "heavy lifting" *core* of the discipline, in terms of what is published in the most highly ranked journals, such as the *American Economic Review*. They argue that these journals strongly affect prestige within the discipline, and we have already seen how development economists apparently need to argue that their particular concerns are valid and should be treated as important by their peers. Given this, it is not surprising that development may pose particular problems to economic analysis, not least as it involves powerful stakeholders whose views are quite powerful enough to ignore what economists say, no matter how prestigious.

Based upon the examples of such studies that I have referred to, we should conclude that economists' explanations mainly tend to reflect what they, in their particular contexts, think are important to other economists. These explanations should not be viewed as predictive, despite the use of models that are estimable and that contain time as a variable. Rather, they are better seen as an example of an explanatory knowledge, which is aimed at and valued by a peer group. Therefore, there is little reason to suppose that practitioners will be socialized, such as through training, to be sensitive to cultural differences or to cope with institutional and empirical differences. On the contrary, one should expect the explicit and implicit meanings of their models to be linked by strong but thin cords to what economists see, at any point in time, as the important elements of *their* realities as they and their peers understand them.[7] It would be quite wrong to deny the importance the discipline gives to links between models and reality, as such. Hopefully this chapter has offered some information as to what these links tend to be.

Questions for discussion

1. From an epistemological perspective, what are the main characteristics of DE, in terms of the way it construes economic development and how to analyze it?

2. What might the variation in economic orthodoxy over time suggest for variation in economic behavior?

3. What are some possible implications of the ways in which social development indicators show far better results globally than do economic indicators?

4. What assumptions are common about the nature of economic policy and the knowledge said to underpin it?

Notes

1   By "naive" I suggest approaches that are neither reflective nor responsibly self-informed by investigation of literature and others' research.

2   McCloskey tends to assume that economists' debates are founded upon deep beliefs in the importance of persuasion. For remarks about the role played by the famous US economist Anne Krueger in the politically driven purges of those with "wrong views" in the World Bank in the early 1980s, see Rodgers and Cooley (1999). Careers were made and destroyed.

3   For those who find this language baffling, it means that if you measure something and you are not sure how accurate the result is, even if the result says that the real measurement *could be* zero, it is unwise to assume that the measure really *is* zero, particularly if it is dangerous if it is not zero. You do not wisely assume that you know for sure that it is zero.

4   Institutionalists are of some importance to DS because they had, in part through the institutional prestige of a man called Wesley Clare Mitchell, considerable influence upon the economists who staffed and guided the institutions of the US New Deal and of the United Nations immediately after World War II, where a number of the same people worked. The line runs through a chairman of the Federal Reserve, Arthur Burns, and perhaps through to Paul Volcker, born in 1927 and famous for the "Volcker Rule" that called during the Global Financial Crisis for a restoration of the separation of banking functions in the US similar to that imposed after the financial problems of the Great Depression.

5   The reader can look up this term; for me it means a group with shared beliefs in what constitutes knowledge.

6   For a valuable study of such aspects of international development work, see Fechter and Hindman (2011).

7   As an Italian FAO official once put it to me, "what they see out of their window." While unkind, this remark points to how others see these practices. The "other," as followers of Said might argue, is thus mainly to be understood with reference to the self.

7 Established theories of economic growth

Standard theories and implications for policy and practice, Part 1

In this and the next chapter we examine central aspects of what DE has to teach us about economic growth. We are now back on a simpler path, where, drawing upon the work done so far, we may sit back and see how DE, having defined problems of development, offers answers. We can be relatively confident that we do not need to take these positions as a given and can therefore appreciate them on their own terms, as we are now equipped with various options for assessing what to do with them. Again, I remind the reader that I am treating our two texts (Ray and T&S) as canonical indicators of DE. Although some economists may say that their approaches are not widely accepted, these are by far the most dominant textbooks in the field (see the Preface). The discussion (of Easterly 1999) in Chapter 14 argues that old ideas may have a long shelf life and enduring influence. I focus upon Ray, whose Chapters 3 and 4 take the reader directly into this core area of DE.

Growth models: overview

It is obvious that a focus upon economic growth as central to understanding development encourages us to select and focus upon certain core questions. (This push was discussed in Chapter 3.) The method and perspective of DE leads to certain ways of understanding development, which isolate the economy and argue that the economy changes according to certain rules—in other words, that it should be modeled formally. This leads to various arguments expressed in terms of growth models, which are typical of mainstream development thinking and practice. Familiarity with these arguments explains enduring elements of mainstream economic thinking about development. We may therefore ask some questions:

- What are/were the policy implications of these theories?
- What is/was the basis for any influence these theories may have—for example, via policy—on economic behavior?
- Are the theories correct?

- Are they persuasive? If so, for whom, and how?
- Are they authoritative?

The internal of these approaches to growth modeling involves a number of building blocks. We will address these in turn.

First, we will review National Income Accounting (NIA)—the statistical practice that underlies the construction of data such as Gross Domestic Product data[1]—what it is, what it is not, and how some important things are measured. Certain aspects of this may be surprising for many, including economists. Second, we need to review "production functions"—ways of thinking that use algebra to advance an account of how certain inputs lead to certain outputs in a determinant manner. Third, since these production functions are a good example of DE's use of algebraic modeling, we will need to review what is meant by a model. After this, we will come to the core of the chapter, which is a discussion of the so-called Harrod–Domar model. The chapter will conclude with a discussion of possible implications of *belief* in the explanatory power of an approach that uses models such as the Harrod–Domar for economic behavior. This discussion will touch upon issues already mentioned: the idea that economic growth is knowable, ways in which the approach suggests that ontological and epistemological universalism is an acceptable (or wise) assumption, and the more important and enduring idea that economic growth—in this approach, development—is essentially supply or input driven.

By the end of the chapter I hope that readers will be aware that such views are tangled, as we will see from the discussion of NIA, especially with conceptual tensions over the meaning of capital: should it be seen as a physical input, best thought of as like so much electricity or steel? Or should it be seen as something that generates a return to its owners—a return to a factor of production, such as wages (paid to labor) or rents (paid to landowners or owners of other real estate)? Obviously, such returns may vary without any change in the physical quantities of inputs; their prices, for example, may change.

Review of NIA

Economists define economic growth in terms of changes in the value of GDP when the effects of price changes have been allowed for. Measures of GDP are calculated based upon various conventions, which are technical but worth knowing.[2] These conventions are used to create a system of NIA, which measures total factor income—that is, the income received in a given time period by certain entities that are assumed crucial: owners of capital, owners of labor, and owners of land and similar assets that are not produced yet receive a return. It is at once clear that total factor income, which equals GDP for reasons I am about to explain, is in no sense a measure of physical output—for example, so many tons of steel or so many meters of cloth—in any normal English usage. For example, if we look at measurement of economic activity in, say, agriculture, the total output (tons of rice, meat, etc.) may well increase, but if input prices rise faster than output prices, total factor incomes may well fall. It is intuitively obvious to some people, but not all, that total factor incomes in an economy must equal the measure of spending that excludes inputs bought by producers other than factors of production for use in the current period. This measure of spending, called "final demand," equals current spending by consumers and government plus investment. Again, it is intuitively obvious that, if there is foreign trade, exports have to be added to this measure of spending and imports subtracted from them. (Some people get their minds round this by realizing that exports generate factor incomes *here*, while imports generate them *there*). Investment may be divided into fixed assets and stocks (inputs and outputs kept in store).

Factor incomes are—obviously—measured in money terms. The expenditure measures can be adjusted to take account of price changes, usually measured through surveys. This leads to what is called "constant price expenditure measures," equal by definition to GDP and so available as a constant price measure of GDP. In a similar but more complicated way, the total (physical) output of sectors can be remeasured in constant price terms, as can nonfactor inputs, and the difference offered as a sectoral constant price measure of each sector's contribution to GDP. And then, bingo, one has sectoral constant price GDP, or, in the usual terminology, the output of the basic sectors referred to—agriculture, industry, and services. The reader will then see that reports that industrial output in China rose 10 percent refer to statistics that estimate changes in total factor incomes in industry, adjusted for changes in prices. It is important to realize that this is what the statisticians are meant to do: focus upon factor incomes (thus National Income Accounting). In this basic vision, the issue is to understand how society can generate certain levels of factor incomes and their distribution, perhaps conceptualizable as an effect of various processes.

But the picture is further complicated by a range of issues. These are rather easy to understand if it is borne in mind that GDP is a measure of total factor incomes—payments to owners of capital and land, and for certain types of work done (not all).

Obviously, this system is designed to measure payments of money for activities that rather directly generate things that can be sold. The list of activities therefore quite deliberately *excludes* important contributions—for example, the work done in families (cooking, housework, etc.) to support family members who get paid. In class, it is worth discussing what these activities might be, not least as this implies judgment as to what causes those factor incomes—those activities that are paid for (and vice versa). That is, it depends on people's conceptions of the economy. There are many potential candidates for activities upon which factor incomes are said to depend. Definitions can be found in the relevant manuals that statistical bodies are meant to follow when collecting and processing data.³ Such manuals may (or may not) tell statisticians to include: caretaking that is not paid for, such as child care and aged care; reduction in the value of things excluded by the NIA framework and therefore in effect treated by it as free, such as the environment and stocks of nonrenewable resources; and, finally, "social capital"—the profitable activities often associated with the destruction of local societies under colonial rule, slavery, and other forms of domination. More radical positions could include social destruction wrought by radical reforms—for example, the effects of reforms upon large parts of the Soviet economy in the 1990s, which saw life expectancy fall sharply.

A second issue is the treatment of capital. As I have argued, in NIA, capital per se does not appear directly; NIA measures incomes that flow to owners of capital via profits. Statisticians generate measures of the monetary value of the capital that is generating these returns in various ways, such as adding up past investments or by holding surveys of "real"—that is, physical— assets. But it is apparent that the relationship between these measures and factor incomes is not immediately obvious. Statisticians generate, based upon these measures, adjusted measures of GDP in order to take into account the depreciation of assets. Lurking behind these exercises is the issue of the pricing of capital, which is not simple. For example, at any point in time, markets do not directly value most existing assets. If *expected* profits fall, perhaps because of political worries, it is plausible that their owners will think that the value of the physical assets will also fall. They will consider selling them at a lower price, and, if thinking of buying them, will want to pay less. But should statisticians reduce their estimates of the value of the stock of fixed assets?

Now, if this is what GDP is all about, and if, as we have seen, economic growth is measured by changes in GDP, then what models do we find that explain development by explaining economic growth, so measured? This happens through the idea of a production function. But before we get to that, keep in mind NIA and especially the identities of the NIA framework: the way in which its internal logic means that certain things are equal by definition (incomes = spending = consumption plus investment plus exports less imports).

Production functions

A production function is a piece of algebra that says output equals what you get when you combine, through the algebra, various inputs—typically land, labor, and capital in the way defined by the function. This leans on the metaphor of an individual production process—for example, frying eggs —where so-called "real"—physical—inputs are related to real outputs. This could be made more complicated by thinking in terms of vectors (of inputs and outputs) and matrices, but crucially in this metaphor there is no need to aggregate—you use *this* frying pan and *that* egg to fry what you eat for breakfast at a particular time and place. What the production function approach suggests is that it makes sense to think of the economy in the same way. The term *aggregate* is worth thinking about here. If metaphor is used to think about the economy, then the issue is how to think (and measure) in and at aggregate levels, so that aggregated real inputs (labor, capital, land) are related conceptually to aggregated real outputs. This poses questions: How do you aggregate? How do you choose how to aggregate? Aggregation means finding ways of adding together things that are both similar and different, choosing to ignore differences and stress similarities. Thus, you have to choose whether the egg you fried and ate alone this morning is to be measured and considered the same as the egg you fried, memorably, for your uncle on the last day of his life, in that hut by the lake where he took you for holidays as a child. This is a deliberately extreme and emotive example, but is it different from considering whether $5 for a starving child walking with their parents to a refugee camp can be added, one-for-one, to $5 spent in Starbucks? Choice is involved in deciding how to cope with this.

I need to point out that output in this sense is not obviously the same as in the NIA sense: constructing an argument that supports the production function approach requires making links between concepts of total factor incomes (which is what NIA measures) and aggregate concepts of capital, labor, and land inputs. And this is tricky.

What is a model?

Before coming back to how growth economics in various ways links economic growth to ideas of capital and other inputs that may be related to the metaphor of "real inputs that combine to produce real outputs," we need to think more about the status of these ideas. Just what is the production function meant to do?

If it is about explanation, we can start to see core elements of the argument: more inputs should give more outputs, certain inputs are to be left out of the account, and so on. More subtly, however, recall that NIA is a system of accounts, and within such systems many things are true by definition. For example, GDP measured in terms of expenditure (as final demand) by definition equals total factor income; it is the same thing measured in different ways and given different labels. As we shall see, this strongly influences just how growth theory operates, including the idea that things that are true by definition may also influence prediction.

What I have said so far about growth economics already suggests confirmation of important characteristics of DE and so its position within DS. The idea that economic growth can be understood through a piece of algebra that links levels of GDP to various inputs confirms much of what has been already been discussed as deeply nested within DE—its metaphysical commitment. It suggests that change processes are knowable—economic growth is determined by something. And it deals in universals —the assumptions that relationships between such measures can be discussed in isolation from context; in other words, the relationships and what they are said to be about are epistemologically and ontologically stable enough. For an engineer, that translates into "rocks here are the same here as there, so the same theory should be applied," but is this the same for capital or labor or land? Certainly one can find measures of GDP constructed for different places and times, but this is not to say the data has the same meanings, even if it has the same label.

Perhaps more interesting is the powerful notion that economic growth is about the way in which increases in the availability of inputs determine increases in output. If expressed in algebraic form, one obvious conclusion is that underdevelopment is mainly the absence of suitable inputs, capital being the main candidate. But this again poses the question of the meaning of capital, which appears in NIA as an income paid to the owners of capital but in a production function as an input. The perceptive reader may here be pondering why development banks (suppliers of capital) should have become such important players. In Chapter 14 (work by Easterly), I discuss ways in which the importance of capital to changes in GDP is integrated into lending practices *and how limited is the empirical evidence that this view is well-founded.* All this suggests that the idea of economic growth modeling has important implications for economic behavior. And the models have names.

The Harrod–Domar model

We now examine ways in which growth models are used in DE. To quote Ray, "We sense . . . the big payoff, the possibility of change with extraordinarily beneficial consequences, if one only knew the exact combination of circumstances that drives economic growth" (p. 47). This is the desire to construct economic growth as a *dependent variable* that can be isolated from *independent variables*, which can then lead to intentional realization of the possibility of change, as and if the independent—explanatory—variables are conceptually linked to policy settings. But Ray considers it unwise to expect that one could derive this from theory, because the world is so complicated. But he argues that growth theory helps us to understand economic change and through that development. So what is to be explained?

Ray stresses that the rates of economic growth (GDP trend change) experienced since, say, 1800 are both far faster than before and seem to be accelerating. For modern developed countries, the period of, say, 1870–1978 shows per capita GDP rising by factors of between 3 (Australia) and 16 (Japan). The argument gathers pace: "A sevenfold increase in real per capita GDP in the space of a century cannot but transform societies completely" (p. 49).

What is interesting about such statements is their *causative* positioning: it is growth that transforms. This is consistent with the overall aim of privileging DE and offering an account within which its realm can be treated as autonomous and so determinative of others. One could also argue, in the reverse direction, that it was the massive transformations of many societies that in some cases *caused* the observed changes in recorded constant price GDP, as an *effect*—an observed change in GDP per capita which platforms on a wide range of noneconomic social changes. But then what would DE have to say about those transformations, in a competition for disciplinary status and autonomy?

Ray then broaches a key problematic: is development (understood as economic growth) one where poor countries catch up with rich countries? Is there, over time, convergence among countries in levels of per capita GDP? Underlying this question is the more profound one of whether development is possible, in terms of the emergence of common standards of living and other indicators across the world. On the one hand, this relates to the issue of whether the development of today's rich countries, which took place in a world where there were no developed countries, is therefore best seen as qualitatively different from current conditions. And this, in turn, as much of the literature in DS argues, poses the question of whether contemporary underdevelopment is in any way linked to, if not caused by, the presence of rich countries. At an extreme, this leads to economic theories of imperialism, ideas that offer explanations of the creation and perpetuation of underdevelopment. In such senses the apparently technical issue of whether the particular economic growth model chosen implies convergence has wider meanings. For example, if the chosen economic model indeed shows a pattern of convergence, then an obvious implication is that there is little need to invest time and effort in learning about international politics, to see if it implies the existence of considerable asymmetries of power, so that, in some way, rich countries may prevent poor countries from becoming richer.

In mainstream manner, Ray defines economic growth, "at its simplest," as the result of abstention from current consumption, to create savings that are equal to investment. This offers an explanation for growth and so for development. Savings, he argues, come from household decisions not to spend all income on consumption: "By abstaining from consumption, households make available a pool of funds that firms use to buy capital goods" (p. 52).

An abundance of historical accounts offer alternatives, such as the importance of cultural and social events to patterns of historical change—for example, in eighteenth-century England, as the Industrial Revolution got going.[4] An economic gaze would tend to ignore such events in favor of factors that can be included rather easily in the modeling approach. Such factors would include technical change, for example. Yet there are histories that argue strongly against reading an economic logic into change in the UK at that time.[5] And we can also recall that many business histories report that initial capital formation in businesses often comes from retained profits, in part because this is more attractive to their owners than external sources of finance (perhaps because banks are not trusted or have high transactions costs).[6]

This relationship between deductions from incomes (here attributed to thrift) that create final demand in the form of invested savings (rather than consumption spending) is the basis of most models of economic growth. The basic equation that sets GDP equal to a function of returns to factor incomes related to factor inputs thus leads (in the DE world) to an equation where the rate of savings (which equals the rate of investment because savings equals investment in this model) divided by the capital–output ratio equals (as an accounting identity) the proportionate rate of increase of output less depreciation (p. 55).[7]

This is simple algebra and may be intuitively obvious to many. If not, it is worth dwelling on. The equation is an *identity*, always true given the conceptual framework and its expression in NIA. But it also looks like a recipe—a behavioral model—implying that if you change one variable on the left-hand side (LHS), the others will stay the same so that the right-hand side (RHS) will change.[8] For example, if you increase the savings (i.e. investment) rate, you will get more growth, or if you use capital more efficiently (reduce the capital–output ratio), you will get more growth. It is easy to think in these terms, but it is important to be careful about the nature of the *causality* implied by these statements. Since the relationships are identities, *they are always true*.[9] Other arguments are needed to justify thinking in terms of causal relationships. Any situation where recorded GDP is increasing will thus generate data that shows, apparently (in other words, depending upon the assumptions made to generate empirical results), that there are links between these variables. The conceptual issue is just what, if anything, to make of these links. Use of identities is therefore fruitful in that it encourages relatively free thinking.

It does not take much knowledge of history to appreciate that ideas behind economic planning in many places, such as the USSR and India (the Mahalanobis model), seem to have been influenced by the idea that economic growth is *caused* by increases in inputs, especially capital. Indeed, the identities encourage various ways of thinking. Note further that you can amend the identity by expressing all the data in per capita terms: divide everything by population. Again, it remains an identity.

To return to Ray's exposition, he argues that the adjusted Harrod–Domar model "combines some of the fundamental features underlying growth: the ability to save and invest (captured by s), the ability to convert capital into output (captured by the inverse of the capital–output ratio)" (p. 56).

Here we can see how the conceptual development offers an explanatory framework that platforms upon the NIA identities. This is another example of metaphysical commitment—the idea that increases in output (recall that

GDP measures changes in factor *incomes*, not factor inputs per se) stem from *economic* factors that entail cause–effect relations that are knowable.

This can be further developed, conceptually. For example, Ray suggests thinking in terms of a disaggregation of investment—for example, separating rural from urban investments. Here one can start to think in terms of the different effects of such investments in a poor country where a high proportion of workers' incomes are spent on food, so that investments in rural areas will have different impacts upon production of consumer goods. Again, we can think in terms of the different effects of investment in production of wage goods compared with investments in sectors producing investment goods. If the data is available, this enriches the account of what is happening, based upon these basic identities.

But as this occurs, conceptually, we need to consider the various ratios implied by the elements of the model, for depending upon what is thought to be going on these may change. For example, the basic assumption that more investment leads to more output implies that the investments actually get used—in other words, that the ratio between increases in the capital stock (investment) and output is fixed. What countries with high levels of investment actually often find is that this ratio *increases*. At the level of planning commission thinking, they find that beyond a certain point their massive expenditures (for example, the infrastructure costs of a city like Bangkok) are associated, not with the same increases in output experienced earlier, but far less. Also, taxes required to pay for such spending may also be thought to have negative effects on growth. What is happening here is that the core relationships within the explanation of growth based upon the Harrod–Domar model are experienced as, not fixed, but variable. Thus, students find themselves engaging in somewhat ad hoc discussions about issues that are crucial within this framework:

- What influences the savings rate?
- What influences the capital–output ratio (COR)?
- How do the savings rate and the COR interact?

As the discussion digs deeper, students often find either that it becomes more and more influenced by ad hoc abstract thinking in terms of various categories or that it becomes increasingly influenced by the particular historical and institutional details of the case study. These influences, clearly enough, start to erode the basic idea that economic growth is the driver of change, for these factors take the account further from economic growth in the terms suggested by the models here.

Yet, as I have argued a number of times, this way of thinking may encourage certain changes to behavior—if people believe in it, then it matters. For example, officials in state planning agencies might accept the basic logic of the model and assume that a crucial issue is to stabilize the COR—to ensure that investment in new fixed assets can be used. And this may (and probably did in some cases) lead to doing everything to guarantee that these assets were utilized. Thus, if planners were thinking in terms of increases in industrial capacity, they would do what they could to make sure that training of workers, infrastructure, and other public goods, such as public health services, were all pushed to the goal of ensuring that the investments in industrial capacity could be used fully.

To take another example, consider issues associated with the determinants of savings. As Ray asks: is this a variable that can be influenced by policy? Because the approach suggests that it can, you can argue that the savings rate will be influenced by variables such as the level of per capita GDP, as well as how it is distributed. And, as noted, this requires the reader to accept the value of thinking in ways that abstract from a particular setting and so encourage the use of the basic universalist assumptions. From this one can conclude that savings are essentially the same in different places, so that low levels of income accompany low levels of savings (p. 58). This view is empirically challengeable.[10] But, reasoning consistently within this framework, Ray concludes that "there should be some tendency for the savings rate to significantly rise as we move from very poor to middle-income levels" (p. 59).

This leads to the idea that the savings rate should change as per capita GDP changes. Clearly, the conclusion does not come directly from the model but from some simple additional theorizing. Along similar lines, it can be argued that population growth will vary with levels of per capita GDP, though we are reasoning in a way that assumes a sufficient commonality for use of such terms across different contexts. The assumptions of ontological and epistemological universalism may lead us to believe that we are sampling from a single population and risk blinding ourselves by treating them as positions that we leave untested.

The Harrod–Domar model thus shows how a series of identities obtained from the NIA framework encourages thinking in particular ways and may influence economic behavior. We now turn to the Solow model, which shows how powerful currents in DE argue about the determinants of important variables within the overall NIA approach to understanding economic change and so development.

Solow model

Recall that mainstream DE views the return to capital as essentially a return to a physical input. At aggregate levels the metaphor used is that of a factory: so much goes into production and so much output results. Thus standard naive DE theory argues that there should be "diminishing returns" to all inputs, including capital.[11] This changes the algebra to make the COR dependent on the level of per cap GDP and opens the way to a discussion of the possibility of convergence, which is delivered through a production function. The standard idea is that "this represents the technical knowledge of the economy" (Ray, p. 65)— that is, it relates output (GDP) to capital and labor inputs. Some of the questions that arise here, especially the conceptualization of just how factor incomes (which are measured) can be related to physical inputs of those factors, are discussed in greater detail in the next chapter. This requires discussion of how these factor inputs are priced. Here we simply assume that these matters have been conceptually resolved.

The algebra shows what is intuitively obvious. If GDP is functionally dependent upon capital and labor inputs, and the population increases (for some reason), eventually the economy grows to a point at which diminishing returns to capital "creates a downward movement in the capital–output ratio as capital is accumulated faster than labor" (p. 67). The lower capital–output ratio then brings down the rate of growth of capital in line with the growth of labor, so that the long-term capital–labor ratio is constant, driven down to the rate at which increases in the capital stock lead to no increase in output; all output gains come from increases in population, so that per capita growth is zero. GDP growth equals the population growth rate. The rate of savings does not matter—an increase in savings simply increases the capital stock so the returns can fall even more. A higher per capita capital stock simply raises the ratio between capital and output. This is simply algebra, but also, if the conceptual framework treats capital as a physical input, leads to some puzzles.

The Solow model implies there will be convergence, as richer countries with more capital experience diminishing returns to capital, and so their growth slows. But there is no obvious convergence—capital is not more productive in poorer countries. And this leads to problems with the initial idea—that capital viewed as a physical input should experience diminishing returns. One problem is that if it does not, then here and now all firms should invest without limit, since the more investment, the higher the return. And this challenges the idea that the economy is stable, with tendencies to equilibrium, for without this tendency, algebraic formulas that generate solutions said to explain in which direction the economy has moved and so where it ends up will be implausible. After all, if the formulas cannot generate solutions (in an algebraic sense), then what are they doing?[12]

In this way of thinking, what stops diminishing returns? The simple answer is the introduction to the argument—that is, to the model—of a variable called "technical progress" (TP), which means that the additional output deriving from given increases in capital stock (i.e. investment) does not actually fall as it would if returns were diminishing. TP pushes the COR downward, and this can be fed into the Solow model, retaining its apparent value to understanding economic growth. Conceptually, this leads to ideas that richer economies remain richer *because* they overcome the diminishing returns to their large capital stocks through TP, which keeps making it cheaper to secure increases in output.

But this apparently simply idea, like others, leads to tangles. For example, is TP embodied in investment goods? Or is TP something that operates on labor, treated as an input, as it also operates upon investment goods (to stop diminishing returns)? If the latter, then the focus is upon education, training, organization, production of public goods such as health, and so on; if the former, upon programs to improve technology. Again, a big idea pushes the discussion either into increasingly abstract ways of integrating such arguments into the algebra or into local, historically influenced discussions where the modeling increasingly loses explanatory power, as the basic idea—that economic growth drives change—has to engage with discussion of other change processes. These tensions are shown by the discussion in Ray of convergence, which is viewed as a global general issue, for otherwise it is not meaningful in DE terms.

The Solow prediction of convergence without TP is fundamental to the Solow model, but comes in different flavors. At its most abstract is the idea of "unconditional" convergence. In this approach, we choose to assume that all countries have essentially similar basic characteristics (those of the model), and economic growth then means various interactions, such as between TP, savings, population growth, and capital depreciation. Then the model will conclude (its algebraic solution in the long run, when "t" is very large) that all countries will converge to the same steady state, where capital per efficiency unit of labor is the same for all, despite any differences in starting points. Empirically, Ray accepts that there are problems testing this. What the data shows him is that, over a long time period, few countries appear to develop rapidly, so you appear to get convergence, but this actually shows that currently successful countries are basically "the same." Get rid of this way of looking at countries, and there is no convergence. If more countries are examined over a shorter time period, it is hard to find any evidence for convergence (pp. 74–87).

When these parameters are allowed to differ, we can consider so-called "conditional" convergence. If you think that technology is the same for all countries, but savings rates and population growth can differ, then you will expect to see convergence to different sets of steady states, with each set defined by what is left, as diminishing returns push down the extra output created by savings, investment, and increases in the capital stock, offset by population growth and TP. So the various steady states are simply defined by the varying rates of TP and population growth. Again, though, these steady states are *independent of starting points*—that is, the initial settings of the model specific to each country have no influence, algebraically, upon the final steady state.

There are two ways of assessing empirical work here. The internal, which assumes that the Solow model can predict, advises using the algebra to solve for the steady state suited to each TP and population growth rate set, and see whether convergence is conditional on this. But the external view requires assuming that you can use the model to predict growth. The problem with this, in statistical terms, is that the model does not say that "this" is determined by "that" but relies heavily upon a series of definitional identities from within the accounting identities of NIA, which measure the same thing in different ways and give different names to each, and tries to say that this is a model. The RHS variables are not independent of the LHS variables. Even so, even for the internal of the approach, the data shows that the Solow model does not explain much in predictive terms. But what it does offer, as we have seen, is a big picture explanation of the economic growth process that offers various entry points while avoiding core issues concerned with the relationship between the issues raised and, apart from on an ad hoc basis, noneconomic factors.

Conclusions

Growth models show clearly the ways in which DE works to offer explanations of how economic growth happens. To appreciate this, it is worth recalling the NIA framework and how it is used. Key questions should be borne in mind.

First, investment in NIA is a recorded *change* to the capital stock, but this is different from changes in the recorded *value* of the capital stock: which of these two are we interested in?[13] The Harrod–Domar/Solow framework shifts the focus from this issue by assuming that the two are the same, and yet they are not. It is intuitively obvious that in any observed economy any estimate of the value of the capital stock will vary as factors such as prices and expected profits shift.

Second, NIA measures the factor incomes generated in a time period, using various social structures, institutions, physical things (such as steel and electricity), and so on. They tell you almost nothing about the capital stock, which is usually calculated quite separately.

Third, the observed lack of convergence suggests that something happens to maintain the investment share in a developed country's GDP, which leads to discussions of just how the level of profits are determined and other savings behavior mediated into investments in various ways. Calling this anything to do with diminishing returns seems to obscure what is happening.

Fourth, the Harrod–Domar framework is simply a look at NIA. In comparison, the Solow model uses an aggregate production function that assumes that you can relate the capital stock data simply to the NIA data, which is risky. A big issue is how capital is valued in whatever data you have, and that is a big question.

However, both these models stand as explanations of economic growth, which is why they are presented in DE textbooks. As such, it is easy to shift perspective and to ask from a DS perspective how they potentially influence behavior. At a fundamental level they support ideas that classic policy rationalities (Fforde 2009) make sense and can be used to influence economic change and so do development in the ways these models imply. They also suggest that thinking within what is essentially an accounting framework may, without too much difficulty, be rethought as thinking within a model, where intentionality operates through economic policy (for example, to encourage technical progress) and so "does development." We can see how the conceptual framework tends to add on assumptions about aspects of the so-called essential nature of economic change viewed as a globally valid category that is part of the development process and linked to practice. Finally, we can see how such discussions, for all their apparent power, tend to lead to tensions as the particular local conditions that arguably influence key parameters draw the discussion away from the strictly economic (in DE terms), which will be resisted as incompatible with the preservation of disciplinary autonomy. Recall the question: "Why is economics central to an understanding of the problems of development?" (T&S 2006: 33).

In a normal DE classroom situation, such a question cannot so easily be answered in the negative; it assumes that economics is central. Rather, DE looks for developed ways of adding to its own internal—that is, economic—explanations, as we will see in the next chapter with ideas of endogenous growth that address certain internal problems with the theories of economic growth discussed in this chapter.

Questions for discussion

1. Are there examples of other disciplines taking the same view as DE when it argues that economic growth is central to development?

2. Is there any defensible common-sense reason for calling GDP "output"?

3. Like NIA, balance-of-payments data is also based on accounting identities. So, because the balance of payments always balances in that system, how can there be a balance-of-payments deficit?

Notes

1 NIA is discussed in Box 4.2 on p. 58 and in Chapter 7.
2 It is useful to spend an afternoon with one or other of the standard manuals on NIA that are readily available. The trick question is "What is the factor cost adjustment?" Once you can answer that honestly you are pretty much home and dry.
3 These are easy to find on the web—an example can be found at http://unstats.un.org/unsd/nationalaccount/sna.asp
4 For a contemporary look at just how power structures within and beyond English villages shifted incomes from ordinary people to landlords and others, see *Rural Rides* by William Cobbett, a radical journalist who had fought for the British Crown during the US War of Independence.

5 For example Clark (2000), who, in a masterful study, instead stresses the importance of religion on the grounds that it was central to the world views of people of the time, arguing that imposition of later ideas of history is anachronistic, heavily dependent upon factors such as class that cannot be made to fit with the perceptions and behavior of contemporaries. This can be seen as close in its criticism to attacks upon the assumption of "instrumental rationality" (see Chapters 2 and 11).

6 An interesting point here, encouraging skepticism about explanations of economic processes that stress the importance of the formal institutions seen daily in rich countries (especially formal capital markets and their institutions, such as bank mortgage lending), is that the first substantial suburban housing growth, in nineteenth-century London, was largely financed by local private mortgages. Arranged by local worthies such as solicitors, these saw a handful of investors (such as the richer local tradesmen such as butchers, undertakers, etc.) lend individual mortgages, usually at call (Ball and Sunderland 2001). Absent problems of moral hazard linked to twenty-first century central banking ideology, it is not so easy to argue that these were less efficient, taking into account the costs of bailouts during crises such as the GFC, than contemporary intermediation methods. Compare the discussion above about Laws in Chapter 3, pp. 41–43.

7 The "proportionate rate of increase" means the change in the variable divided by the value of the variable; more simply, the percentage rate of increase.

8 Here I deliberately use some algebraic shorthand. LHS is the left-hand side, where you put the notionally *dependent* variable, which equals some formula on the RHS (right-hand side). But the mind tends to the idea that *if* the RHS changes, then so must the LHS, as this is an identity, and then looks for ways this could happen.

9 Since it can cause some confusion, may I remind the reader here that the term *identity* means a relationship that is true *by definition*. Within NIA there are many identities, essentially because the same thing is being measured in different ways. Thus a household's income—for the sake of simplicity, its incoming cash for a particular period—is identical, if it neither borrows nor saves, to its spending. The money can be measured when it is earned, or when it is spent, but it is the same money. This of itself says nothing about causality.

10 Vietnam is a useful counter factual here. While remaining poor in mainstream terms, domestic savings rose sharply in the early 1990s with marketization and capitalism. In some accounts, this was associated with opportunities offered by SMEs combined with business-oriented SOE behavior.

11 By diminishing returns is meant the idea that as more of a particular input is used, so more and more is needed to generate the same proportionate increase in output, so the return to its use diminishes.

12 Readers may wish to reflect on how the ability of the algebraic method to generate solutions (in terms of the formulas) may be taken to confirm the analytical independence of DE, since no reference to anything external of DE is needed to complete a given account. Further, it appears that, since these contingencies are hidden (for example, just how is capital measured and what does a given measure depend upon?), such propositions appear *necessary* and so offer possibilities for apodictic reasoning.

13 If this sentence is baffling, consider the following: in a given year the reported cost of all investment spending was X, but because of a sharp increase in hydrocarbon prices the value of some important fixed assets—such as coal-powered electricity generators—fell sharply, by more than X, so that the total value of fixed assets could have actually fallen.

8 Established theories of economic growth

Standard theories and implications for policy and practice, Part 2

What endogenous growth models are trying to do, according to Ray, is to improve on the basic Solow model, which, as we recall, is production-function based. This new modeling approach originated from various issues that arose within DE and specifically what was learned from the application of the Solow model. Recall that the empirics meant that the Solow model explained only a part of observed correlations. Importantly, given the basic physical metaphor of the economy as a production function, dominated by relationships between inputs (factors of production) and output (as GDP), the question is why the productivity of capital appears to vary much more than the conceptualization—the theory—predicts. This leads to a search for a better theory that can explain more: how important variables vary and, above all, how they may be conceptualized as being determined *within* the model—as being *endogenous*.[1] Thus, while Technical Progress (TP—see Chapter 7) may be thought important, it was left unexplained within the Harrod–Domar and Solow models. So the question can be posed: where does TP come from?

This poses classical questions. Is it reasonable to assume that technology flows freely from country to country? If TP is embodied in capital goods so that it can be treated as simply something that is brought with them as they are purchased, that does not solve the problem of its origins. This leads to the prospect, so potentially fruitful in a methodology that seeks to model, of the inclusion of additional variables—inputs—in the production function.

With technology, what other inputs could/should be included in the production function apart from labor and capital? Within this approach, the problem is that, in empirical terms, there is too little variation in the rate of return on capital. Poor countries simply do not show a high enough rate of return on capital to fit this explanation: if they are capital short, then, surely, returns to capital should be high. This problematic clearly views capital as something that, like other resources, should move in response to relative prices that reflect relative scarcities between different contexts (but see the discussion of Zebreg's work in Chapter 20). One internal possibility is that variation in types of labor explains the lack of variation in the rates of return to capital. One may indeed note that capital markets show no great need to move capital from rich to poor countries. Indeed, the international pattern of balance of payments capital account surpluses and deficits reveals that a dominant feature of the world economy from the 1990s until at least the early 2010s was the flows of savings from China and other poorer countries to rich ones, especially the United States.

This is unlike labor, which does seem to move (if allowed) in ways that fit this metaphysical commitment, as relative prices would suggest, from poor to rich areas. If thinking in aggregate conceptual terms, one might ponder that the price of labor is set by something like supply and demand but that the price of capital is not. The reader may recall Ray's earlier argument that abstention from consumption creates a supply-price for capital, in contrast to a demand price in terms of investment opportunities, so that one may construe capital as a commodity (like labor).[2] There are contrasting arguments (e.g. those of Polanyi, in Chapter 17) that assert this is incorrect: capital is not a commodity with a supply–demand determination of its quantity and price.

Human capital and growth

The endogenous growth approach starts by considering that rich countries have a capacity to make high levels of investment in human capital: skilled labor that can create new ideas. This is contrasted with the unskilled labor of many poor countries. Conceptually, this may imply that poor countries have low returns on capital because their labor is unskilled—returns to human capital are low—and this offsets the higher return to physical capital (because these countries find themselves not so far along the path of diminishing returns).

The revised model then splits savings/investment into two streams: one increases physical capital and the other human capital. The algebra shows that the steady-state equilibrium is set by the savings rate and the propensity to invest in human capital.

The most important implication of this is to preserve the basic conceptual positioning: the metaphysical commitment to the existence of economic forces that explain what is observed. Thus, while diminishing returns to capital exist, there is no convergence in per capita income (although rates of growth converge). ("Diminishing returns" means that the partial derivative is negative. This can be expressed in terms of proportionate rates of change as well.[3])

Once you are back in a modeling world of broad constancy of returns, the savings rate and the rate of investment in human capital influence growth rates—therefore called endogenous growth models—and the rate of growth is determined within the model. But if you add back in a sector that uses unskilled labor, this reduces the effects of the productivity-enhancing skilled labor, and we get back to a normal Solow picture. We then have an explanation of the failure of markets to work, in the sense of the absence of convergence, which uses the idea that people in richer countries are more socially valuable, allegedly because they are better educated and more skillful, due to higher investments in human capital, than those in poor countries. It also suggests that people in rich countries are better paid because they are more productive, rather than (for example) because they belong to social groups whose competitive position is based upon control over such institutions as labeling (which gives them rights to high-paid jobs), "gatekeeping" and so on.[4] There are important questions here: just why do some people earn more than others and enjoy those incomes in places that offer opportunities that raise (such as through good provision of public goods) the value of these earnings? The empirics of research that gauge relationships between human capital and productivity are not quite as clear as the modeling approach we are discussing could have us believe (see Gundlach, discussed in Chapter 23).

This comes up in the discussion of conditional convergence in Ray, Chapter 3. Looking at many countries in a short time period, he suggests there is little evidence for convergence in per capita GDP. What happens if you re-examine this, taking into account different levels of human capital? However, it is difficult to reliably measure human capital. Ray cites work by Barro (1991 and 1996) that used school enrolment, but this proxies output with input. However, if, despite these difficulties, we regress growth in per capita GDP for human capital proxies, it appears that, while high per capita GDP slows the rate of growth, high human capital speeds it up, and the two factors offset each other, so the regression shows no overall convergence.

What is meant by technical progress in endogenous growth models?

Recall that TP is crucial to offsetting diminishing returns in the Solow model. It is obvious that if some fixed factor of production (e.g. labor) exists, without something like TP growth rates must slow if we have constant returns to scale for the other factors of production—land and capital: this is how algebra works. ("Constant returns" means that the sum of aggregate factor incomes equals output.) Ray's basic point is that human capital theories and the Harrod–Domar model answer the question by arguing that diminishing returns happen at the level of the individual production process (frying eggs) but not at the level of aggregate economic growth because something offsets them: for example, investments that increase human capital and so labor productivity—the basic insight of endogenous growth modeling.

Here we can see DE developing the argument of the value of growth modeling so as to make it more plausible but without deviating from the basic and unchanging metaphysical commitment to explanations that involve markets. Where does TP come from? Ray (1998) remarks that:

Technical Progress does not happen in a vacuum. Many years ago, such advances were the result of spontaneous insight or the lonely work of individuals. It is a characteristic of recent history that research and development is carried out by firms, who deliberately divert resources from current profits in the hope of future profits.

(p. 108)

Ray stresses the "modern" way in which companies allocate resources to research and development (R&D) and how the results become patented. He then classifies TP into two gains:

1. In knowledge, caused by deliberate allocation of resources. The gains are produced in expectation of a return, which requires an ability to appropriate the return (we could also call this the commoditization of knowledge rather than treating it as something that should be freely available to all).
2. Acquired as a transfer from the producer of that knowledge. This requires externalization of the value of the innovation in some way.

Thus TP becomes an output, produced for profit, and can therefore, like human capital, be added to the model to offset diminishing returns. By including a model of TP, this offers obvious scope for developing the basic model of economic growth. A sector is added to the model that produces innovations as inputs to TP. To do so, it uses a fraction of the available human capital (the rest is used to produce all the other goods). This construal is then supported by the image of a line of machines, some invented already, some not (Ray 1998: 109–110). New machines offer both better productivity than old ones and also a wider range of opportunities to combine inputs to generate outputs or to generate product variety in consumer demand.

You then do the algebra and end up with a determination of the rate of economic growth per capita where the rate of TP is determined by the stock of human capital, and how much of the stock of human capital is used in R&D is what determines TP.

In the internal of DE this offers a developed form of the basic growth model that makes sense in DE terms. It is worth noting various points. First, nothing in this theory talks to us about functional forms and so nothing tells us exactly what these are (see Simon's points quoted in Chapter 11). This is actually important for, as we found from L&Z, most of the apparent empirical results are not robust—the statistical significance usually disappears as the functional form is varied. It is also odd, from a natural science perspective, to encounter theory that has nothing to say about functional form.

Second, an important issue is how, conceptually, one may construe an explanation of how human capital is allocated between R&D and other activities. (It is instructive to read Ray 1998: 111–112, to see how the argument develops.) For example, this allocation could depend upon the extent to which there exist institutional devices that influence the realizable value of R&D, such as patent protection laws; expectations that the laws will be enforced; societal values that reduce pirating, and so on. Other factors could include the availability of public investments in basic science and military spending, and the presence of opportunities to appropriate public knowledge and make it private (e.g. genetic codes). As before, we see how DE rapidly encounters other disciplines, such as political science, history, and so on.

Externalities, technical progress, and growth

Another way of modifying the basic Solow model to offset the internal issue of diminishing returns is to consider positive and negative externalities. **Externalities** are costs and benefits external to the calculations of a particular consumer or producer but caused by their behavior (see Chapter 9 and later in this chapter). To repeat, this is within the basic metaphysical commitment to a world where production at the national economy level is best viewed as the transformation of factor inputs into output (GDP), a transformation that is a metaphor for the apparent use of physical inputs at the micro level—the production line, the fried egg, and so forth.

This second option focuses upon externalities generated through acts of local capital accumulation or R&D. We will see in Chapter 9 that externalities are a classic example of market failure, usually seen as leading to situations deemed "bad" in terms of the expectations DE offers for their effects upon public welfare, and so warranting state or societal intervention in the free operation of markets. It is therefore interesting to note the stress here upon positive externalities, for these are usually seen as produced at suboptimal levels without intervention. *Externalities* takes us into the realm of microeconomics, which is discussed in the next chapter. The term means the effects of an individual or a company's decisions that influence others, but not them, so, if they are only trying to maximize their own profits or well-being, they will (in this view of humanity) ignore those effects. If the effects are "positive," they are thought to be good, whatever that is assumed to mean, and, if "negative," bad. I make the distinction between positive and good, and between negative and bad, to stress the need for subjective evaluation to decide to assess the outcome. A standard example of negative externalities would be pollution caused by a company, which arguably does not affect its own profits (so long as there is nothing to "internalize" these costs, such as consumer boycotts or special taxes to "make the polluter pay"). An example of a positive externality would be the effects of a company's decision to give remedial literacy classes to its migrant workers, which improve the profits of another company that hires them later.

Ray's example is the effects of a big capitalist putting a railway line into a town, which others can use and thus produces a wide range of so-called "multiplier" effects. In this way, the presence of the railway line stimulates economic activity so that the overall effect of the investment is a multiple of its cost. For example, reducing transport costs encourages other business activities. On the other hand, negative externalities could come in the form of pollution from the railway engines, which could affect nearby towns. Ray thus encourages the reader to note how both R&D and acts of capital accumulation (human and physical) may have big external effects—both positive and negative. His rhetoric encourages us to think that the externalities may be important in some significant way to the pattern of economic growth.

We can see that this is a quite different conceptual positioning from DE's simple notion of economic growth as processes where inputs came together to produce outputs, easily expressed in algebra. Here, the notion of economic growth has developed, and so the discussion can be seen now to platform on a broader notion of economic activity rather than focusing upon GDP. Economic growth, in this view, is now more than just increases in GDP. In terms of economic growth modeling, however, the algebra now adds to the production function of each company a factor that measures the overall productivity gained from simply being part of the same economy as the other businesses; this factor is dependent upon total capital accumulation within the economy. Firms will then invest even when their own investments alone cannot make enough profit.

This development of the model of economic growth pushes into areas that are conceptually hard to handle with algebra yet powerfully persuasive. An element of this is the question of complementarities (Ray 1998. 114–116). Here Ray engages with the topic of expectations and investors' beliefs, which are a type of externality that changes, not the level of profits or utility, but the ranking of other companies' alternatives. Firms' expectations of profits depend upon what they think other firms will do; if they think their sector will be expanding, offering potential falling unit costs because of scale economies, they will see that strategies within the sector are complementary. Thus companies' *beliefs* may be part of self-fulfilling investment behavior —with different equilibria (solutions to the model). At a low level, all companies are pessimistic, total investment is low, and so is growth; at a high level, all are optimistic, growth is endogenous, TP and human capital gains offset diminishing returns to physical capital, and growth is high.

By this stage Ray has said most of what he has to say about DE and economic growth modeling. We can note that tensions over negotiation of disciplinary boundaries do not really go away. We now come to a final element of the picture, the oddly named "total factor productivity" (TFP), which plays a prominent role in discussions about growth efficiency and international competitiveness.

Total factor productivity

For students, it is vital to appreciate that TFP is basically no more than a measured *residual* found when a production function approach is applied to historical data.[5] It is the proportion of observed economic growth that the particular model selected cannot explain by changes in inputs. Obviously, this depends heavily on the selection of functional form, which involves making choices about what is happening to returns to each input as things, mainly the level of output, change. How does the amount of labor used, and what it gets paid, change as more labor is used? An answer to this and similar questions about land and capital inputs is necessary to explain the particular functional form used. As already mentioned, DE theory has little to say about the precise functional form. Equally obvious, a conceptual link needs to be made between factor incomes, as measured within the NIA framework, and factor inputs, which are not part of GDP. To repeat, GDP is a measure of constant price factor incomes.

In terms of the selection of functional form, if you assume constant returns to scale and **perfect competition** (see the list of special terms on p. 323), then you are assuming that factors (inputs) are paid their *marginal products*. Here we encounter a term, like externalities, that is used in microeconomics, which we discuss in the next chapter. The marginal product of an input is, at a given level of output, the ratio between changes in that input and changes in output, with other inputs unchanged. Imagine a situation where labor is increasingly unproductive—for example, if a muffin maker works for two hours making muffins, then an additional five minutes' work is required to make an additional muffin, but if she works more—say for five hours, then an additional ten minutes' work is required to make the additional muffin (the *marginal product*). The additional output "at the margin" —the marginal product of ten minutes' work—has fallen from around two muffins to only one.

As we shall see in the next chapter—and this is intuitively obvious for markets to work properly—producers and consumers must adjust their situations until trade-offs are those offered by prices. Since trade-offs act at the margin, it follows that trade-offs, such as marginal costs and benefits, need to have the same ratios to each other as prices; thus, factors need to be paid their marginal products.

If we return to the muffin world, if the worker is paid $6 an hour ($1 for 10 minutes), and all other inputs stay fixed (perhaps because the shop has the same amount delivered daily), and a muffin made is sold for $1, then the manager would find it profitable to offer the worker more work when she was working two hours but probably not when she was working five hours. The reader may feel that thinking in these concrete terms is rather odd, when the thrust of the DE approach is in terms of algebra. This is perhaps because when we think of a concrete example all sorts of other questions come to mind, such as the weather, the mood of the worker, and so on. These points are trite, perhaps, but worth thinking about as they pose questions about the relationship we think exists between the model— the algebra—and any particular real situation. The epistemology here is important to understanding DE, and the reader may wish to refer to the discussion in Chapter 2 and Box 2.4, "Model vs. muddle" on p. 30.

But this is just a conceptualization of what is called perfect competition, which, as we examine in the next chapter, means that producers and consumers take prices as given. What this means in terms of how a market is conceptualized is then relatively open: what matters is the algebra, which links factor incomes to factor inputs.

What these assumptions permit is that treating the NIA categories of factor incomes as measures of factor inputs makes sense, because factors get paid their marginal products, and these have a simple relationship to average product. Because of constant returns, factor incomes are a good proxy for factor inputs. If you accept this argument, it is legitimate to treat a production function with these characteristics as a suitable model of an actual observable economic growth process. Given this, and the idea that deviations of observed values from those of the model are caused by random errors, an estimation can be made and, from this, measurements of TFP (see the discussion of assumptions in Chapter 11).

Now, it is quite obvious that this conceptualization is vulnerable to a wide range of criticisms. It is also clear that many DE discussions include references to TFP as an important indicator of matters of competitiveness. In dealing with these issues, Ray (1998) advises the reader to note the following (pp. 118–119).

First, the *level* of TFP is irrelevant; because it is a residual, what is measured is changes in it.

Second, there are problems with how the total labor input is measured. One "standard method" (p. 118) is to proxy this by population growth, but this "error is particularly pronounced in countries where the participation rate in the labor force has significantly altered over time" (p. 118).

Third, apart from problems in measuring the total labor input, are even greater issues in measuring aggregate stocks of capital. As Ray puts it, these "may be useful in a theoretical exposition, but [not] in practice" (p. 119). His expressed concern is simply that different parts of the capital stock may be growing at different rates.

Finally, though, Ray (1998) makes the highly destructive point that the entire edifice

> runs into problems if either factors of production are not paid their marginal product or if the production function is not constant returns to scale. In either of these cases, we cannot use the observed shares of a factor (such as labor) in national income to proxy [for measures of factor inputs]. . . . We lose the ability to measure these variables, and once this happens, we can no longer get a handle on TFP growth.
>
> (p. 119)

Ray offers no evidence of the extent to which factors are or are not paid their marginal product. Yet simple observation would suggest that there is plenty of evidence that consumers and producers influence the prices they face—they are not "price-takers"—and that production functions often do not exhibit constant returns to scale (cost per unit varies with the level of production). When buying a retail durable good, such as a television, I will usually seek to negotiate with the dealer, and do the same when buying materials such as stationery for my consultancy business, and choose my suppliers accordingly. Despite this, or perhaps because of this exposition, Ray can now turn to examine DE and discussions of the rapid rates of economic growth enjoyed by East Asia since the mid-1960s.

Total factor productivity and the East Asian miracle

As Ray (1998) points out:

> Based on the many theories that we have studied, we can trace high growth to one or more of several contributing factors: among these, the most important are capital accumulation, both physical and human, and technical progress.
>
> (pp. 119–120)

As we will see, Ray is pointing to the value of skepticism in assessing authoritative results, even as he is expositing them. He reports that rapid growth in East Asia led to discussion about the sources of growth. Given the stance of DE toward conceptualization of growth (as discussed in this and the previous chapter), many researchers thought in terms of inputs and approaches based upon the use of production functions. Reflecting on the quotation just given, we can ask whether this is a statement about economic theory *or* about certain economies and how they have (actually) changed. Are the factors referred to important because they are important in the theories or through empirical argument? Here we need to note the problems with empirical analyses that Ray has just cited.

Examination of NIA for successful East Asian economies indeed shows high rates of savings and investment but not that high relative to other economies. Private investment is higher; they are net capital exporters; and human capital indicators are high compared to other countries with similar per capita GDP levels. A crude question can be asked: to what extent is their growth due to increases in inputs or in the efficiency with which inputs have been used? This is the "perspiration or inspiration" question posed famously by Paul Krugman (Krugman 1994). And it can be related conceptually to institutional questions.

Thus, what happens to measurement of TFP growth? A famous World Bank study argued that high TFP growth in East Asia from the 1960s through the 1980s was caused by EOG policies that enabled effective and productive utilization of high rates of investment and human capital development (World Bank 1993; see also Chapter 18). Ray argues that this was misleading. He quotes another study (Young 1995) that carefully deconstructs inputs (changing participation rates, structural shifts from agriculture to industry, etc.) and concludes that much of the Bank's conclusions came from underestimation of inputs.

This is an interesting and revealing argument, which appears to rely upon assumptions that factors are paid their marginal product (that is, there is perfect competition) and returns are constant. What is the justification for this? We need to be careful here. On the one hand, we can bear in mind Ray's fourth point, cautioning us that if we are skeptical about assumptions that there are simple links between factor incomes and factor inputs, then the validity of the modeling is questioned. Indeed, we can argue that all of these positions generate spurious results, in that the assumptions required to make their statistical results meaningful are clearly somewhat reckless because there is so little evidence that factor incomes and factor inputs are closely linked. But if we treat these as competing explanations, linked to reality in ways that DE deems suitable, we can see this as an argument of considerable importance. Recall Yonay's point that economists adopt "vaguely defined but generally accepted conventions regarding the movement from reality to models" (Yonay and Breslau 2006: 33–34).

The usual argument (see Krugman 1994) is that to secure high TFP growth requires more than a combination of vast supplies of rather cheap labor and massive investment. This is in part a political view. From a political or developmental point of view, how useful is it to place great emphasis upon the validity of these approaches? We may choose to see this as a debate about the value of certain explanations and their relationships to policy positions. We are not simply saying that the approaches are right or wrong. Ray is arguing for a historical interpretation that gives less weight to the idea that certain market-friendly institutions (such as companies' freedoms to hire and fire due to a relative absence of trade unions) were important in generating growth, based upon the idea that inputs, if properly measured, have increased far more than the World Bank reported. Thus, he is attacking the Bank's argument that efficient institutions are the primary reason for East Asia's growth. In the DE world, this is, as Yonay reports, a powerful and important argument—and perhaps elsewhere, too.

Conclusions

This chapter and the preceding one have shown us how DE works to create an economists' account of change expressed in terms of algebraic models. On the one hand, we can see the importance of retaining the assumption of diminishing returns (especially to capital) that accompanies use of production functions underpinned by the idea that capital is subject to a supply–demand analysis where prices rise and fall to create an equilibrium.

This shows important underlying elements of DE, and in the next chapter we examine the microeconomic conceptualizations upon which this platforms.

Further, if we ask what empirical evidence is offered to support belief in the value of the Solow model in its various versions, and bear in mind Ray's concerns, one answer is that empirical evidence in any simple predictive sense is weak and unreliable. This fits with the L&Z result that the data on variations in economic growth between countries shows few robust relationships between these variations and policy settings. These models therefore need advisedly to be taken as explanatory, although it is clear that they do not appear as simply explanatory but clearly present as predictive for many. This implies, as I have argued, that DE sits squarely within the basic problem of development, asserting predictability (development as a known immanent process that can be done) but on troubled empirical grounds. This is now familiar and shows that DE occupies a rather easy relationship with much DS practice, even if there are also considerable tensions. Reconsider arguments in DS for the value of interventions such as use of participatory methods, where the poor actively participate in designing projects for themselves. Many DS texts argue that use of such methods will lead to good results, but what is the evidence and how robust is it? Like for those in DS keen on participation, DE encourages statements that accept robust knowledge of the future, but internal evidence suggests, in different ways, that this knowledge is not so reliable.

Various characteristics of DE are also evident. DE encourages thinking along certain lines: conceptualizations are highly aggregated (e.g. labor inputs in the national economy) and supported by data that measures these aggregates. We find added-on ad hoc explanations, at a highly aggregate level in universalist terms, that treats capital conceptually as a physical input like others—for example, labor—and comparisons between such terms across different time and place that are, from other perspectives, very different. This allows engagement with issues such as donor technical assistance and lending policies, which are expressed in these same terms. To say that they are simply wrong does not end the game.

Questions for discussion

1. Are we better educated because we are richer or vice versa?

2. Does DE suggest that higher education in rich countries should, in the first instance, be seen as consumption rather than investment?

3. During severe recessions, will TFP growth be measured as negative because of slow growth and continued payments to land and capital?

Notes

1   This obviously fits with how Popper and Kuhn (see Chapter 5) understand science—as progress related to interactions between theory and data founded on experience of problems with predictive capacity.

2   The demand-price is the price at which an amount of the good will be bought, and the supply-price is the price at which an amount of the good will be sold. Ideally, the former falls as the amount increases, while the latter increases, notionally offering opportunities for the two to be equal at the equilibrium price, all other things being equal; we come to the study of such interactions in the next chapter when we look at microeconomics.

3   For those who either forget their high school math or never got it, a "partial derivative" simply means how X varies with Y; for example, 1 kilogram of raw sugar cane gives you 100 grams of refined sugar. If returns are constant, you get the same for the next kilogram. If they are falling, you get less than 100 grams. The "marginal product" is the additional amount you get for the additional input and is a ratio. As we shall see in Chapter 9, trade-offs start to look nice when these ratios equal price ratios, for then, intuitively, you won't get more by changing output or consumption levels.

4   *Labelling* refers to situations where access to jobs relies upon the job-seeker meeting certain criteria, such as having the correct accent or at least some standard dialect, acquired socially; *gate-keeping* refers to ways in which pressures to change such labels may be resisted, such as by controling definitions of what correct accents or dialects are said to be. Similar arguments apply to matters of dress, deportment, apparent attitude, and so forth.

5   If the terminology is baffling, try thinking of a residual as the difference between what the model says "X" will be and its actual measured values, "Z." If the model says that, given certain inputs, output should be "Y," but it is higher, then the difference between Z and Y is the residual—what is left over once the model's algebra equation has done its explaining/prediction.

9   Microfoundations

This chapter supports students in thinking about the microfoundations of development. Histories of DE show major shifts in beliefs about the extent of "market failure," and I argue that these shifts are more to do with changing *empirical* judgments about the extent of market failure, and are only weakly linked to theory. Indeed, some theory arguably suggests that, on conceptual grounds, markets in large parts of poor countries, where families both produce and consume, always fail. Changing beliefs among economists about the extent of market failure, I will argue here, are an example of ways in which the economy—as a concept, measured and observed as such, is an *effect* of factors acting outside economics.

Microeconomics encourages discussion in terms of ideal types—consumers, producers—and the use of these concepts in models of whole economies. DE platforms upon microeconomics for core ideas, such as economic efficiency and the idea that markets have the ability to secure good outcomes. In doing so, it assumes that markets operate according to some logic that algebraic models may capture, but this creates tensions between assertions that "markets result in good outcomes" and arguments about the extent of market failure in practice. Any empirical basis for judgments about the extent of market failure is, of course, central to the extent to which these things should or should not be taken as reliable guides to action.

As we have seen, because the conceptual motor driving the positioning of DE vis-à-vis DS is the prioritizing of economic growth, DE deals mainly with large-scale economic issues: the economies of entire countries or regions. As the main focus of DE places *economic* change as central to development, it downplays other factors and preserves a relative autonomy for economics compared with other disciplines or fields of knowledge. Economics courses include a range of other elements of the discipline, and we need to address a major set of issues for what is usually taught as *microeconomics*, which develops models that offer explanations and predictive possibilities for its main chosen categories: consumers, workers, and companies. Such a focus is usually referred to as the *microfoundations* of the discipline: an explanation of what underpins the macroeconomics of growth theory. Microeconomics is particularly important because of the role, as we will see, that arguments about market failure play in what DE has to say about what the state should or should not do.

Furthermore, new analytical tools available to economists have enabled the development of new models that have become part of *development microeconomics*, a process marked by the publication of a specific textbook aimed at this (Bardhan and Udry 1999). Such models, arising from practices studied by Yonay (reported in Chapter 6), then become associated with the cutting edge and thus publishable. Often, the models are concerned with market failure situations and respond to the need to cope with the shifts from the 1982 second big idea discussed by L&P (2002) and the associated confusion. The reader should recall that while the first big idea (of 1962) was strongly and with certainty *against* markets and in favor of state intervention, the second one (of 1982) was strongly and with certainty *pro* market and against state intervention, while the third (of 2002) was rather uncertain whether to take such a position at all.

As we have seen, mainstream development thinking often tends to view development as something that is done, requiring intentionality and a site for that intentionality—that is, the focus of many arguments is that the agent that can do development is the state, so policy is all-important. Thus the ways in which DE justifies state intervention, or argues against it, help to explain DE's place within DS. Arguments about market failure are not mainly about macroeconomic or economic growth but about micro-economics: what happens when consumers and producers interact through markets.

In what follows in this chapter, we will need to understand how micro-economics works in its own terms. This can at times be confusing. A central point, which may help prevent us from being unable to see the forest for the trees, is that much, but not all, of the thrust of microeconomics is to develop the argument that, under ideal conditions, markets lead to optimal results in terms of the maximization of consumer welfare, taking account of alternative ways of producing what consumers purchase. As we shall see, the famous economist Joseph Stiglitz states very clearly that "*markets result in Pareto efficient outcomes*" (Stiglitz 2000: 77). Pareto optimality means that a characteristic of the equilibrium (solution) of the algebraic model is that a deviation from it would make at least one consumer worse off without making any other consumer better off. A Pareto efficient outcome is the main result, for Stiglitz, of his argument up to that point in his book. But, as we shall see, he then goes on to discuss arguments about the conditions required for that conclusion to hold, which can be read to imply that they are unlikely to be met. These conditions are about market failure. Appreciating this tension, between the position that "markets are good" and the position that "the conditions for markets to be good are perhaps only rarely met" is central to understanding the position of microeconomics in DE.

Here it is important to appreciate that, while they appear to be closely linked, arguments about *change* (understood by DE as essentially based on economic growth) are different from arguments about efficiency, and *that microeconomics is mainly concerned with efficiency*. The links DE makes between them are fascinating. Economists learn that how resources are allocated in a model, given various assumptions about what does not change, can be interpreted in terms of efficiency criteria (that is, in terms of the model). Crucially, these criteria are seen as conceptually separate from matters of growth and refer to *static efficiency*. Ideas of comparative static efficiency are concerned with comparing how a given set of factors and other inputs may be used with different degrees of efficiency, both in terms of production and also to satisfy the varying needs of consumers. [1] In terms of the algebra, as we shall see, that which is assumed to stay fixed—supplies of factor inputs—is exactly what is assumed to change when the focus shifts to economic growth. Typically, these are variables such as the capital stock and the labor supply. Thus DE's arguments about microeconomic issues are not immediately linked to those about economic growth, though the impression can easily be gained that they are. Economics lacks a clear concept of *dynamic* efficiency to match its clear notion of static efficiency.

This conceptual issue is important. At least two elements are worth considering. First, is the question of the possibility of *negative* relationships between static efficiency and growth. In the US economy of the late nineteenth and early twentieth centuries, it can be argued that the "robber barons'" use of bank and railroads monopolies created severe static efficiency losses, yet it can also be argued that the rapid growth of the US economy at the time was linked to the large economies of scale that their activities exploited and that were protected by their use of cartels and corrupt politicians.

Second, arguments that a situation is inefficient in static terms, compared with what the models suggest would be an efficient outcome, tell us little about what could happen while moving between the two. As mentioned, in many areas, DS has a tendency to compare model with muddle, to argue that an imaginable alternative would be better than what is experienced in the here and now, implying that we should move to that alternative. Common sense indicates that between the ideal and the present situation there may be different paths. In economics, so-called "theories of the second best" encourage reflection on this and arose precisely because of the conceptual problem generated by a methodology that focuses upon model rather than muddle.[2] This need for caution arises because microeconomics tends to argue that markets work well unless something prevents this from happening.

This encourages a metaphysical commitment that sees the world in these terms. For example, in DE, as in mainstream economics, a *rent* is understood as a return to an economic resource that competition cannot remove, either because of the nature of the resource (for example, land of good quality or an asset generating increasing returns to scale) or because of social institutions that stop competition from working—for example, trade unions or rent-seeking (see the list of special terms on p. 323) caused by state intervention. The models show, in terms of the internal of the discipline, that *if* competition (as defined) were allowed to work, "good things" would happen. DE defines these good things in terms of characteristics of the modeling results, and how these results suggest, under the given conditions, an optimal outcome in terms of consumers' welfare. The precise nature of this optimal outcome may be discussed, but this is the basic argument. This cuts across arguments that cartels, state intervention, and trade unions, at different times and in different places, have been associated with rapid economic growth.

It is important to appreciate, as many do not, that the concept of static efficiency has more to it than meets the eye. For many, inefficiency is related to idleness—the idea that resources are not fully used, that workers should be at their place for longer hours, that capitalists are "fat cats," and so on. Rather, economists differentiate between *production efficiency* and *economic efficiency*. The former refers conceptually to situations where, for a given set of inputs, output is as high as it can be; as the inputs are used in different proportions, so the efficient—in this sense—level of output changes. The latter refers to situations where, given the different ways consumers trade off having more of one good and less of another, production choices and consumer choices are linked so as to produce outcomes that both maximize profits and the value to consumers. This is a much more subtle point.

Examination of various course outlines available offers an interesting opportunity to see what is taught as "development microeconomics." A Google search in mid-2010 provided information on about a dozen microeconomics subjects taught at various tertiary institutions globally (including Harvard, Princeton, and other well-known establishments). Of these, most used the textbook by Bardhan and Udry published in 1999. These courses show how the trend has been to use improved algebraic techniques to focus upon models that offer analyses of market failure.

Examination of the two textbooks treated here as canonical (Ray and T&S) shows that neither offers a focused treatment of microfoundations. They both tend to assume that their audience is made up of economists for whom many of the conclusions of microeconomics will be familiar and valorized—that is, treated as a reasonable basis for belief. This chapter therefore offers a review of this knowledge. Central to this is the view that government action is appropriate only when markets fail, because mainstream theory argues that, under certain conditions, markets left to operate freely will lead to good outcomes. What is meant by all this in theoretical terms will be discussed later in the chapter. A central issue, it will become apparent, is the status of these ideas in terms of their metaphysical commitments—in more ordinary language the ways in and the extent to which ideas about microfoundations are accepted within DE as explanations. I will argue that a central issue to explaining change in what DE has tended to argue is the variation over time in mainstream beliefs about the extent to which markets actually fail in reality. While the experience of the Great Depression encouraged belief that market failure happens a lot, on the eve of the major political changes of the early 1980s views had shifted back to the belief that this happens rarely. Arguably, at the time of writing, the situation is one of uncertainty, with the AFC and the GFC tending to support views that market failure, especially in capital markets, is widespread. Yet, as we saw in Chapter 6, we should not expect—and do not easily find—empirical bases for such views comparable to those found in natural sciences.

Background of microeconomics

Microeconomics is best understood as behaviorism with algebra. It is not behavioral in the sense of being interested in underlying motives or perceptions but rather seeks to find ways of modeling what can be measured by an observer. It holds to the instrumental rationality hypothesis (Chapter 11) as it focuses upon generating models that explain what is consumed and produced, and how these are linked through markets. Microeconomics' central focus is on the role of price as the information required to link consumers and producers. Intuitively, we can see how an idea of competition will encourage producers seeking to maximize profits to find ways of producing what they can sell, at a price that is profitable to them and that consumers are willing to pay. In like vein, consumers seek to allocate their income between various products to balance what they gain (products) against what they lose (the price they pay—the cost to them of buying the product). Again, we can construct a way of understanding this to create *equilibrium*: higher prices reduce demand and increase output, so at some price for the product—what consumers pay, equal to what producers receive—demand will equal supply, and things will stay as they are. This concept underpins the meaning of the algebra—a system of equations: the economy has been "modeled." Whether this model is acceptable or not, as already argued, depends on a host of factors.

This basic structure of microeconomics can be seen from the textbooks. They tend not to follow what could be thought of as a natural science pattern, starting with observed regularities and then discussing which models should be used under which empirical circumstances. Rather, they start with a presentation of the particular techniques they wish to use and then discuss how these can be used to manage algebraic models for each of the basic micro categories previously mentioned (consumers, workers, and companies). These are treated separately—that is, models of what companies do and what consumers do are developed independently. These two categories are usually stressed far more than models of labor.

Thus Jehle and Reny (1998) starts with a Part I, "Language and Methods," that contains two chapters that rehearse technical methods: Chapter 1, "Sets and Mappings," discusses mathematical techniques, and Chapter 2 "Calculus and Optimization." This prepares for the use of mathematical techniques that offer models of how companies maximize profits and consumers maximize their welfare (i.e. get the most value and satisfaction for their money).[3] Part II, entitled "Economic Agents," contains two chapters that look at consumers ("Consumer Theory" and "Topics in Consumer Theory") and one chapter that looks at producers ("Theory of the Firm"). Part IV then builds upon this to discuss how these models offer a way to conceptualize an economy built upon interactions between consumers and producers, which occur through markets. This then enables discussion of matters of welfare, referred to as "Social Choice and Welfare" (Chapter 8):

> With only a few exceptions, we have so far tended to concentrate on questions of "positive economics". [4] We have primarily been content to make assumptions about agents' motivations and circumstances, and deduce from these the consequences of their individual and collective actions. In essence, we have characterized and predicted , rather than judged it or prescribed in any way. In this chapter, we change our perspective from positive to normative, and take a brief look at some important issues in welfare economics.
>
> When we judge some situation, such as a market equilibrium, as "good" or "bad," or "better" or "worse" than another, we necessarily make at least implicit appeal to some underlying ethical standard. People often differ in their systems of ethics and so differ in their judgments on the merits of a given situation. This obvious fact need not discourage us and make us despair that normative economics is "just a matter of opinion". On the contrary, there is such a thing as consistency in reasoning from premises to conclusions and so to prescriptions. Welfare economics helps to inform the debate on social issues by forcing us to confront the ethical premises underlying our arguments as well as helping us to see their logical implications.
>
> (p. 334)

It is noteworthy that this section comes *after* the preceding chapters, which define what is important to understanding—that is, what should be modeled, and so, logically, have already defined what is deemed unimportant. I leave it to class discussion to consider what has thus been rendered invisible.

It is also interesting to have some understanding of the histories of microeconomics. Prior to the arrival of a famous textbook on mathematical techniques applicable to economics (Samuelson 1947), the conceptual framework already outlined was taught, not through algebra, but through graphical methods, which continued through until the late 1960s in some places. These techniques dated back to the nineteenth century, including such elegant creations as the Edgeworth box, and were important to what is usually called the "marginal revolution" that saw such techniques focus on how firms could maximize profits and consumers the value of their spending.[5] Such lines of thought tended to lead to ideas that such processes required firms and consumers to arrive at positions where minor trade-offs between alternatives did not improve their position (in terms of their profits and welfare, respectively). At these points, graphs met, so that trade-offs were equalized at the margin, at rates equal to relative prices.

These methods can be found in such examples of past canonical texts as Stigler 1947, a textbook used at Oxford in the late 1940s. They require far less formal mathematical training than modern examples like Jehle and Reny but come to similar conceptual positions. Recall the already cited study in the history of economics (Yonay 1998). His main contrast is between what he calls "institutionalists" and "neoclassicals." The latter, whose metaphysical commitment was to the existence of a reality corresponding to the basic microeconomic conceptualization discussed here, used graphical methods and argued against a re-examination of theory in light of changed empirical opportunities. The institutionalists, who in his account become far more important than other popular modern histories argue, called for a re-examination of theory. Yonay argues that both schools, in the end, lost out to the mathematicization that embraced mainstream economics after Samuelson. An interesting idea, which I do not develop here, is that one consequence of the mathematization was to encourage a development of the basic microeconomic conceptualization previously outlined, which deals with firms and consumers, into a concept of the entire economy viewed in the same way—a general equilibrium (see Chapter 3 and discussion of Walras, Box 3.1, p. 40). Prior to that, when graphical methods were dominant, thinking tended to be more limited to what is called *partial equilibrium* and somewhat unwilling (and largely unable, for technical reasons) to attempt conceptualizations that would model the economy as a whole. It seems obvious that graphical methods tend to discourage thinking of the whole economy in such terms. They are not, on the face of it, candidate components of a vast system of equations.

As we have seen, the basic conceptualization of microeconomics is the division of the economy into producers and consumers, who in turn seek to maximize, respectively, profits and the value to them of their purchases. This poses analytical difficulties if producers and consumers appear as the same entity (such as a subsistence farming family). Similar technical problems arise with joint production, when the same resource is being used for more than one end, so that it becomes hard conceptually to see how the use of that resource can be managed within a maximization conceptualization of the economy (see the discussion of "economies of scope" in Chapter 23). It is quite clear that the most basic feature of the algebraic models used to model consumer and producer behavior is that of maximization. That is, producers and consumers both seek, subject to constraints, to maximize something; for producers, this is profits, and for consumers, it is welfare in the sense that they cannot do any better for themselves by buying less of one thing and more of another. Thus, "rational behavior" is simply behavior that can be modeled algebraically by a model that allows for the generation of a result—an equilibrium—where profit for producers and welfare for consumers is maximized. A little thought will suggest intuitively that the foundation of this sort of exercise is the ability to hold things constant as the maximization occurs (which is why, for example, price-taking is so useful for the algebra, as it means that prices can be assumed not to change as consumers or producers increase or reduce what they respectively buy or sell). And so if there is joint production or if the producer is a consumer of the same product (as is the case for subsistence farmers), the approach faces considerable problems. This shows the tensions created by the view that the most important element of rigorous economic modeling is the idea of constrained maximization embodied in an algebra. Be that as it may, we need to consider what is meant by market failure in the context of microeconomics.

Microeconomics and market failure

As previously stated, the reference point of microeconomics is the conceptual situation where prices are sufficient sources of information for the maximizing behavior of consumers and producers to lead, in the algebra, to modelable situations. As this happens, relative prices match the relevant trade-offs made as consumers and producers adjust what they buy and sell, so that when they are managing to maximize profits or the value of what they consume, the equilibrium of the model argues that the situation is *optimal* and any intervention would be unwise. The argument is made (and supported by the algebra) that any interference in the situation would make one party worse off if it made the other party better off (what is called "Pareto optimality").

Central to this conceptualization is the idea that, as producers and consumers examine possible trade-offs (for example, by having more of this good or using less of that input), *prices do not change for them*—that is, they are price-takers, so their actions do not influence price directly. Thus, if a producer is large enough to influence price (if it increases output, price falls, which will happen once the producer has a significant share of the market, so long as other producers do not reduce output to try to keep prices up), and this also allows it to reduce unit costs (perhaps because of economies of scale), it will increase profits and the model will be unstable. Worse, without intervention, and to maximize profits, the producer will *set output levels lower than would suit the interest of consumers*. In this sense, the model shows an example of market failure.

The point can be illustrated differently. Consider a situation where some of the benefits of consumption (such as the enjoyment of a classical art course or the smell of a frying egg) accrue to others—those who listen to the satisfied student regale them with accounts about the class or the scent of the frying egg. These are another example of the externalities we have already discussed in the previous chapter. The trade-offs that the student and lecturer examine when deciding on whether or not to transact take no account of these (here non-financial) effects, as they are external to their decisions. *Prices do not reflect adequately all the information that is relevant, in the sense of influencing the behavior of the entities we are trying to model algebraically and whose decisions determine exactly how much is produced, and so sold and bought.* This is because the decisions by the producer and consumer ignore these external costs and benefits. The boyfriend's enjoyment of the smell of the egg, in this logic where empathy does not exist, does not influence the girlfriend's decision to fry the egg that she eats. Conceptually, it would seem that the effect of such positive externalities is to have fewer rather than more such courses (or fewer fried eggs), because those who benefit are excluded from the decisions taken by the producer and consumer. The decision on how many courses to schedule or eggs to fry, in this approach to how decisions are taken, will tend to ignore these benefits, and so on.[6]

In general, market failure is thus a characteristic of the microeconomist's conception, expressed in algebra, of economic interactions between producers and consumers. In this characterization, the point of reference is situations in which producers and consumers are price-takers, and prices are adequate to reflect the relevant information. Under such situations, the models show (and this is intuitively acceptable) "good things happen" in terms of the maximization of the welfare of consumers and profits of producers, and deviations from this are therefore suboptimal. This offers a reason for comparing muddle with model. It is elegant and clever.

Standard textbooks offer examples of market failures. Consider the discussion in Chapter 4 of Stiglitz's *Economics of the Public Sector* (2000). In these situations, "without intervention" can usually be conceived of in terms of output levels being either too high or too low:

> [M]arkets often seem to produce too much of some things, like air and water pollution, and too little of others, such as support for the arts or research into the nature of matter or the causes of cancer. And markets can lead to situations where some people have too little income to live on.
>
> (pp. 76–77)

Two other issues, though, are important: first, the *extent* to which the problem arises empirically; second, what should be done about it. Again, though, we need to be aware of the tensions created by economic method —above all, the slippery relationships between model and anything else, such as reality. Thus Stiglitz starts his discussion by asserting that his previous chapter *"explained why markets result in Pareto efficient outcomes"* (p. 77, emphasis added). His own theoretical work, for which he won the Nobel Prize, argued for the importance of "informational asymmetries" in

modeling market failure. As we are about to see, the presence of informational asymmetries is sufficient, in these algebraic models, to prevent the
generation of solutions where "good things happen" in terms such as Pareto
optimality. Yet, based on understandings of what it is to be human, it may
be argued that *all* human transactions are marked by such information
asymmetries, and so *all* market transactions will exhibit market failure. In
this sense, while markets as modeled may result in Pareto efficient
outcomes, *none may ever actually be experienced.*

Stiglitz, quite conventionally, refers to six situations under which markets
will, in this specific sense, fail. The following list will inform the reader of
how economists engage with the relationships between their models
and reality. He offers (as again, quite conventionally) no empirics to guide
the reader as to where and how extensive these conditions may hold.
The situations are primarily *conceptual*, related to aspects of the model, and,
as we have seen, Yonay discusses how this relation between model and
reality works: "this mediation is accomplished by vaguely defined but
generally accepted conventions regarding the movement from reality to
models" (pp. 33–34).

The first in Stiglitz's list is *failure of competition*, which is the absence of
so-called "perfect competition," where consumers and producers are price-
takers. Perfect competition is best understood, above all, as conditions
applied to algebraic models of supply and demand, where, for reasons to
be given (see next paragraph), the equations used to link individual
consumers' and producers' desired levels of purchases or sales are such that
changes in these levels do not change prices. These individual equations are
then added up to provide, at that price, what producers and consumers in
the market would want to sell or buy at that price. This essentially algebraic
condition has then, as McCloskey would put it (see Chapter 6), to be given
an economic meaning, for algebra is simply algebra. In understanding DE,
it is useful to consider how this is done, for it invites, in interesting ways,
the reader to link conceptualization to some reality. This we can find in Jehle
and Reny (1998):

> In this section, we examine when the firm is . . . a perfect competitor
> . . . [when] it believes the amount it produces and sells will have no
> effect on prevailing market prices. The competitive firm sees the market
> price for its product, assumes it will remain the same regardless of
> how much or how little it sells, and makes its plans accordingly. Such
> a firm is thus a price taker. . . . One way to interpret the fact that the
> firm takes prices as given is to suppose that the firm has a choice
> regarding the price at which it sells its output. . . . If it attempts to sell
> its output at a price above the prevailing one, then it will make no
> sales, because in a competitive output market, consumers are perfectly
> informed about the lower price . . . elsewhere. On the other hand, the
> firm can sell all it desires at the prevailing price . . .

> While the assumption [here] . . . is extreme, they [*sic*] provide a tract-
> able model of the firm, that is capable of yielding important insights.
>
> (p. 236)

One may note that they do *not* argue that this modeling offers predictability. Rather, they seek to create belief that it is about certain conditions
that apply in reality, while "extreme" (which suggests "unusual," but that
is not the word they use). It is valuable, as an exercise in epistemological
research, to examine how different textbooks manage the task of offering an
explanation of how the concept of perfect competition may be related to a
reality. This varies, such as over time, though of course the basic algebra
does not. Stiglitz's argument implies that in *any* situation where a producer
or consumer influences price, the outcome will be suboptimal.

In the second situation *public goods* will "either not be supplied by the
market or, if supplied, will be supplied in insufficient quantity" (p. 79). Such
goods have two critical properties: first, if a consumer enjoys their benefits,
this costs nothing extra (an additional person using street lights at night does
not raise the cost of lighting the streets); second, a consumer cannot be
excluded from enjoying such benefits. The second point can be interpreted
to mean that a producer cannot get paid by such a consumer. An example
is the services of a lighthouse, where a ship that enjoys its services doesn't
have to pay for it, as it would pay for, say, fuel. Any ship that can see the
light benefits from it, and an additional ship does not change the costs of
running the lighthouse.

One interesting device useful in considering broad brush economic
history is to compare the social conditions that lead to abundant private
goods with those associated with abundant public goods. This was a central
point of the famous book by J.K. Galbraith, *The Affluent Society*, originally
published in 1958. His pithy phrase was "private affluence and public
squalor," referring to situations where goods that could easily be sold at
profit were abundant, while those, such as public goods, were too often
lacking, leading to squalor. Further, it may be argued, as Galbraith did, that
the one discourages the other—weak production of public goods forces
societies to focus upon lifestyles characterized by an emphasis upon what
can be bought and sold. This is thought-provoking. The microeconomics
discussed here, however, simply treats these options as largely, if not
entirely, determined by noneconomic forces; the balance is an *effect* of such
causes and beyond economics.

Third are *externalities*—situations

> where the actions of one individual or one firm affect other individuals
> or firms; where one firm imposes a cost on other firms but does not
> compensate them, or, alternatively, where one firm confers a benefit on
> other firms but does not reap a reward for providing it.
>
> (p. 80)

Here the origins of these conceptualizations required by the algebra are particularly clear. The modeling focuses upon individual producers and consumers, and this drives the argument. The illustrative examples that conceptually link these ideas to reality are typical: the effects of pollution, of urban congestion (as negative externalities), and of an orchard upon a beekeeper (a positive externality). Stiglitz is clear that "whenever there are such externalities, the resource allocation provided by the market will not be efficient" (p. 81). Yet this remains confusing, not least as the comparison here is with conditions that would or could correspond to perfect competition, and as we have seen just how these may be thought through is not entirely clear, perfect competition is an explanation for certain requirements imposed on the algebra.[7]

Again, we are given no indication of the extent of such situations. As we saw in the discussion of endogenous growth models (in Chapter 8), such externalities can, conceptually, be very broad. Recall the example of an externality given by Ray: the effects upon investors' confidence of particular economic acts (Chapter 8). This may be taken to imply that externalities can be conceived of, like information asymmetry, as an inescapable part of human interactions, and so, again, implying that markets always fail if we choose this aspect of the basic conceptualization.

Fourth are *incomplete markets*—situations where "private markets fail to provide a good or service even though the cost of providing it is less than what individuals are willing to pay" (p. 81). Public goods are conceptually similar to this concern with incomplete markets in that they offer arguments as to why the ideal situation suggested by perfect competition may not come about. But Stiglitz here is attempting to broaden the discussion to enable him to include other markets, such as insurance and capital markets. The argument again is that if these are incomplete, in the sense that consumers and producers cannot insure against all possible situations or obtain unlimited amounts of capital at a price, then the ideal situation suggested by perfect competition will again not hold.

Here recall my remarks in Chapters 7 and 8 about the ways in which DE treats return to capital (as a factor income in GDP) as a payment for an input. Here we find arguments that it is not quite so simple. Much of Stiglitz's discussion is concerned with matters of racial discrimination and selective support for politically important groups such as farmers, so that arguably insurance and capital markets are not perfect.

He also develops an argument about *transaction costs* and *enforcement costs*, which weaken the extent to which firms will actually market products:[8] "This basic principle—that when there are asymmetries of information and enforcement problems market may not exist—has been shown to provide part of the explanation[9] of many missing markets" (p. 83).

A second point he makes when discussing incomplete markets is the importance of *complementary markets*. Here enters the issue of joint production and consumption—the basic conceptualization that producers and consumers make decisions with reference to *single* products that can be compared with other single products. Once there are complementarities, the basis for the model used to argue why markets result in Pareto efficient outcomes breaks down. We will see how this challenges the basic conceptualization of development microeconomics when we discuss how Bardhan and Udry deal with family-based farming in the next section. The issue here, partly technical, is concerned with the *separability* implied by the algebra —that consumers and firms make their decisions in ways that are kept algebraically distinct, that this or that product has this or that price, and output decisions for each, like consumption decisions, are separate from those for other products. Joint production and joint consumption, and intersubjectivity issues such as empathy and vicarious feelings, deny such separability. Without separability, the algebra lacks the ability to carry the basic conceptualization. Again, if we ask the extent to which such complementarities matter in reality, we get no answer from the text.

The fifth situation is *information failures*; this section is revealing. Stiglitz starts with a textured discussion of the institutional reality he faces (US government regulation of information disclosures by firms in areas such as consumer loans). He considers information as being, in many respects, a public good and considers its role in the assumptions underpinning the models, which led him and others to deduce "the fundamental theorems of welfare economics" (p. 84).[10] These include the requirement that there be perfect information —"more precisely, that nothing firms or households did had any effects on beliefs or information" (p. 84). In effect, this means that the only information required (other than internal information about the values of goods in consumption, or how inputs may be transformed into outputs) is price, which is shared by both buyer and seller.

The final situation, *unemployment, inflation, and disequilibrium*, is treated in a way that is odd. Bearing in mind the AFC and the GFC, and the importance in understanding the role of such episodes (including the pre-World War II Great Depression) in much modern history, it would seem clear there is a problem here. But Stiglitz avoids the issue:

> Most economists take the high levels of unemployment as prima facie evidence that something is not working well in the market. To some economists, high unemployment is the most dramatic and most convincing evidence of market failure. . . . The issues raised by unemployment and inflation are sufficiently important, and sufficiently complicated, that they warrant a separate course in macroeconomics.
>
> (p. 85)

We can conclude that, for Stiglitz, microeconomics has little fundamental to say about these issues.

Conceptually, what Stiglitz has to say is clear. Market failure is above all a characteristic of certain algebraic models. From this, he argues that, if certain conditions are met, and there is an absence of market failure, "markets result in Pareto efficient outcomes" (p. 77). The discussion of market failure (Stiglitz's six basic market failures) may be interpreted to say that markets always fail, though this is simply choosing one among many meanings of the stories that accompany the narrative, for no operational empirical basis is given to encourage the reader directly to one or the other position: is market failure widespread or not, under given historical conditions?

Here it is interesting to see how Stiglitz concluded an early (1976) paper on information issues, work on which contributed to his stellar academic reputation. The paper was entitled "Equilibrium in competitive insurance markets: an essay on the economics of imperfect information." To quote:

> We began this research with the hope of showing that even a small amount of imperfect competition could have a significant effect. . . . Our results were more striking than we had hoped: the single price equilibrium of conventional competitive analysis was shown to be no longer viable; . . . and finally, and in some ways most disturbing, under quite plausible conditions equilibrium did not exist.
>
> (Rothschild and Stiglitz 1976: 648)

My reading of this—I am sure there are others—is that for Rothschild and Stiglitz introducing imperfect information issues creates major problems for the basic conceptualization that markets work and work well.

Let us return to L&P. Their first big idea, 1962, can be seen as the general view among the economists they are referring to that markets fail a lot. The experience they cite is not a series of market studies but conclusions drawn from the broad historical sweep of the times—the Great Depression and other economic disasters. Similar arguments apply to their second big idea, 1982, where there was belief, similarly founded, that markets fail rarely. And perhaps the experience of 2002 is that markets probably fail often but that, more importantly, economic theory offers no robust basis for taking a view. At the same time, as we explore in the next chapter and as L&P suggest, policy failure remains hard to understand—as we might predict that it would, given what we have seen of DE empirics.

Let us turn now to examine another canonical text that focuses specifically upon development microeconomics. Recall the results of my Google inquiry about the readings commonly used in development micro-economics teaching in mid-2010.

Markets and the failure of standard analytical methodology

Chapter 2 of Bardhan and Udry (1999), entitled "Household Economics," is the first substantive chapter of their book and shows how DE works, conceptually and methodologically. The chapter starts with the observation that many people in developing countries earn at least part of their livelihood by working in their own enterprises (often farms) and often consume a significant part of their own output. They therefore

> make simultaneous decisions about production (the level of output, the demand for factors[11], and the choice of technology) and consumption (labor supply and commodity demand). This mixture of the economics of the firm and of the household is characteristic of the situation of most families in developing countries and provides the starting point for our analysis.
>
> (p. 7)

This statement is worth reflection. It is common internal knowledge in economics that while the standard models tend to work for men, they usually do not for women (in terms of the internal empirics of mainstream economics) (Fforde 2005). This raises the question of just what is driving their statement. Is it the tensions created by the apparent inapplicability of standard theory to many people in developing countries, or is it that once one reflects on how families tend to make decisions, that theory is far more widely, if not generally, inapplicable? How plausible is it to argue that decisions about remunerated work— work done for wages outside the home— are separable, as the algebra requires, from all the other decisions? It is surely plausible to argue that families make their usual human and messy decisions (both monetary and nonmonetary) based upon a range of activities that include home-based production (housework) and consumption (eating) as well as wage and nonremunerated activities away from the home. This appears even clearer when the family is involved in farming and consumes its own food produce, and this vision underpins the rhetoric of Bardhan and Udry's quotation.

In developed countries, average working hours per week (by which is meant hours spent working for cash remuneration) are perhaps thirty to forty hours, out of a far larger total of waking time. In better-off households, as is common in developed countries, households equipped with a range of humans and their machines are involved in production of a wide range of services that are consumed locally (such as vacuumed rooms and cooked food). What people typically feel as burdensome and productive activities in households includes housework, shopping, caring for others (both those deemed to be dependent, such as the old and young, and those not, such as idle teenage children). What people typically feel as essential but not burdensome I leave to class discussion. Sociologists and anthropologists tend to argue that these activities require negotiation and discussion with others, conceptualized in a host of ways that may be mutually incomprehensible if not antagonistic. Thus any separation of the economics of production and of the household would seem to exist mainly in terms of the conceptualizations of DE and mainstream economics, and is not widely shared.

Bardhan and Udry (1999) initiate their discussion by viewing markets as complete, meaning that everything has a price and so everybody can calculate trade-offs in monetary terms. Inherent in this conceptualization is that decisions exist by themselves, and so, among other things, it is possible to develop an algebra that separates the production decisions of the household from its consumption decisions. Then the original microeconomic conceptualization appears valid, since there are in effect two households—one a producer and one a consumer. This provides a standard against which to develop the analysis further. However, they conclude from their empirical references that "In most developing-country contexts, the separation property seems more useful as a benchmark for comparison than as a basis for empirical work" (p. 11). By separation property, they are referring to the argument that the algebraic model of consumption decisions may be kept separate from those of production decisions: that the decisions are separate, mediated through markets. The value of a benchmark here, as mentioned before, is as a conceptual reference point against which to judge, usually in terms of static efficiency, other situations as modeled. This conceptual reference point works in terms of argument the same way as the tensions Stiglitz exploits between the notion of perfect competition and its absence—market failure. The same economic efficiency outcomes associated with perfect competition are read into the results of an application of algebraic models that separate the consumption and production decisions, attributing them to separate consumers and producers whose relationships may then be modeled as occurring through markets and the prices of what they consume and produce; this is a model of "efficient households," where the models generate optimal outcomes.

Bardhan and Udry then grapple with an imagined situation where markets are incomplete—that is, agents cannot optimize welfare and profits with respect to relative prices as gauges of the values of trade-offs. Their example is a situation where farmers have no land market (the amount of land held is determined in some other way so it is simply a given), and a local labor market experiences unemployment (understood to mean that people will not work for wages lower than some amount[12]). They then conclude as follows, effectively abandoning theory:

> The available empirical evidence casts serious doubt on the validity of the unitary model. While the available work is mostly supportive of the more general model of efficient households, there is some evidence, particularly in Africa, that calls even this weaker model into question. More research is required before the general validity of the efficient household model can be accepted. *If the efficient household model cannot adequately account for the intra-household allocation of resources, it appears that it will be necessary to move towards more detailed, culturally and institutionally informed noncooperative models of the interaction between household members.*
>
> (p. 18, emphasis added)

Two final points need quickly to be made. First, histories of DE will usually report that, just after World War II, important contributors to the discipline argued that market failure was common in underdeveloped countries and that this had important policy implications (see the discussion of Bardhan in Chapter 3). Before the dominance of pro-market radicalism (call this the Washington Consensus, but this is simplistic), the various institutional aspects of standard prescriptions reflected deep pessimism about the extent to which markets could be trusted to work properly by themselves. In this chapter I have linked these views to the *empirical* judgment that market failure is widespread, and I have argued that such judgments are only weakly linked to theory. Development microeconomics can indeed be argued, on conceptual grounds, to imply that markets in large parts of poor countries, those where families both produce and consume, always fail. This suggests that these changing views are an example of the ways in which the economy is—as a concept, measured and observed as such—an *effect* of factors acting outside economics.

Second, it is useful to stress how, as we saw in the discussion of Yonay's work, microeconomics encourages discussion in terms of ideal types— consumer, producer—and their projection into models about whole economies. This is facilitated by the ontological universalism, which inhibits tendencies to question whether such terms should have stable meanings across contexts. Bardhan and Udry point out that such assumptions make no internal sense when production and consumption take place in a single unit.

Conclusions

As we have seen, DE platforms on microeconomics, referring to various positions it supports and the arguments these generate. Ideas of efficiency and the ability of markets to secure good outcomes are central to these conceptualizations. Less obvious perhaps is the idea that the operation of markets has some underlying logic that microeconomic models may capture. The idea of market failure offers a way of discussing, with reference to ideas of efficiency, particular experiences that may be used to encourage or discourage state intervention in markets and to offer relevant explanations. The central tension within microeconomics, as we saw from the discussion of Stiglitz, is between assertions that "markets result in Pareto efficient outcomes" (Stiglitz 2000: 77) and arguments about the extent of market failure in practice.

As we have seen, understanding their views of the extent of market failure helps to illuminate positions held by economists regarding national development strategies and the value or otherwise of government intervention. These views, as elsewhere, are best seen as only vaguely linked to empirics, as outsiders to DE would perhaps usually expect. As explanations, clearly they have considerable importance and power. As guides to action, wise people should again be wary.

Questions for discussion

1. What do you think Bardhan and Udry seek to do when they show, as the chapter demonstrates, that standard microeconomics does not work in large parts of poor countries?

2. What is meant by "when the supply curve starts to slope downward," and what is its conceptual significance?

3. What is the political significance of "when the supply curve starts to slope downward"?

Notes

1 Economists' arguments about efficiency here have a specific meaning concerned with how one particular solution to the algebraic model is compared with another (for example, with a different tax rate); each solution is seen as "static," in the sense that nothing is changing—it is a solution to the model—and one is to be compared with another (with the different tax rate). The method is thus often called *comparative statics*.

2 I leave this reference unexplored further as the reader simply needs to know that this point has been discussed and economists therefore should be aware of it. The basic point is valid, which is that how you get there makes much difference to whether you actually want to go there, and that the DE theory here discusses only what it would be like when you had got there.

3 I choose my words carefully here. Early consumer theory argued that consumers chose what they bought to maximize the total utility of their consumption, but this was thought vulnerable to criticism (what really is "utility"?) and was reworked. Modern expressions of the theory now argue that consumers choose what to buy so as to get to their highest "indifference curve"—that is, to the highest in terms of their ordered preferences of a range of bundles of goods. The basic results, in terms of how consumer behavior is modeled, are pretty much the same. The algebra creates what some find interesting results, such as the distinction between variation in demand for a good when income is held constant (the so-called Marshallian demand curve) and when utility (or its equivalent) is held constant (the so-called Hicksian demand curve).

4 See the quotation from Milton Friedman in Box 1.3 on p. 12.

5 It is worth spending some time reflecting on the historical importance, in the development of this mainstream microeconomics, of graphical rather than algebraic techniques. As mentioned in the previous chapter, important characteristics of the results of these models occur at points where rates of change are equal—on a graph, where two lines touch. As Yonay (1998) shows in good detail, the mainstream neoclassical economists of the 1930s used graphical rather than algebraic formulations of their ideas, of which the Edgeworth box is an example. The famous "Marshallian Cross," where two curves on a graph, whose axes are price and quantity, can be shown to intersect at an equilibrium point, under certain conditions, is part of this tradition. Yonay argues that this approach was swept aside in the 1950s and 1960s by mathematical (algebraic) methods. Samuelson (1947) is worth revisiting in early editions as its rhetoric is revealing

of the hopes for a natural science of economics, similar to those expressed by Friedman and Stigler and quoted in Chapter 1 (see Box 1.3 on p. 12).

6 The issue is, of course, clearer if we think in terms of externalities that have clear financial implications. The logic, though, is similar. Financial implications appear clearer than others—costs or benefits appear in money terms—but behavior may as well be strongly influenced by costs or benefits that are not financial, such as the prestige a lecturer may feel from putting on a certain course, which his or her superior is unaware of, or the discomfort felt by a student who feels that he does not fit in during classes, about which the lecturer is unaware.

7 To stress the point already made, it is an interesting exercise for students to compare how this is done in different microeconomics textbooks, including those published at different periods. Each needs to present a narrative or explanation of what perfect competition is, and these stories vary, often in interesting ways. But the algebra stays the same.

8 Neo-institutional economics stresses the importance of transactions costs (see Chapter 11). A simple conceptualization would be that they refer to the costs of doing business, of transacting, so that market prices alone do not sufficiently explain the incentives influencing behavior. Enforcement costs are conceptually thought of as concerned with the costs of enforcing a contract, so that again, if a seller may welch on a deal, market prices alone do not fully explain incentives.

9 His use of the definite article here is telling. Are there no other explanations that he would countenance?

10 I have not thought it useful to go through the details of this exercise, which is highly apodictic in the particular way in which it uses algebra and what are called a series of assumptions (I prefer to call them conceptualizations) to draw the basic conclusion that "markets result in Pareto efficient outcomes." It can be found in any microeconomics textbook and in Chapter 3 of the book by Stiglitz discussed here. Since the assumptions are only vaguely linked to empirics, it is better and less confusing to call them simply the characteristics of the particular models used. As we see in this section, when discussing market failure, Stiglitz, like others, sees no need to give an *operational* basis for establishing when and how these conditions are satisfied. They are thus best seen as conceptual in nature.

11 That is, factors of production—land, labor, and capital.

12 Here readers may note how the methodology requires no reference to non-economic factors, or to other disciplines; the algebraic method permits this.

10 Contemporary internal radicalism

The Washington Consensus and after

The reader will have noticed that many of the DE arguments in the book so far, especially in the last chapter, are concerned with the value of markets in development. For some, it will not have been immediately obvious why this is so important within DE. Others may have noticed that these arguments often appear to be positioned so that support for markets is presented as opposition to state intervention, and vice versa. These positionings resonate strongly with the historic series of "Big Ideas" we find in Lindauer and Pritchett (2002) and discussed in Chapter 1. Recall their view that 1962 was a time when economists were often mistrustful of the market and advocated state intervention that was often associated with ISI and a range of measures to protect and support domestic producers. Recall also their idea that by 1982 many positions had turned around—to a mistrust of the state—and were associated with attacks on ISI and support for EOG.

Yet the fundamental question remains as to whether it was reasonable to believe that these policy stances would, in fact, lead to the expected outcomes. Further, given the empirical tensions within DE (the combination of predictive rhetoric with evidence that reliable predictive power is absent), we need to examine how positions within DE cope with situations where it appears that policy should have worked but did not. A useful entry point is the belief that the consequences of the pro-market measures of the 1980s were two "lost decades" (Easterly 2001). Readers familiar with the DS literature will be well aware of the many accounts of severe social costs —such as higher unemployment, decreases in life expectancy, increases in infant mortality, and family stress—experienced in many poor countries after these measures were taken. Beliefs, thus, may come up hard against empirics.

In the last chapter we saw how Stiglitz first argued that markets lead to optimal outcomes and then went on to present a range of reasons why markets, through market failure, would not lead to optimal outcomes. It is useful to view this logical shuffle not as a mistake but as a familiar characteristic of DE. Readers should be reasonably clear by now that the extent to which markets fail empirically is not something that DE provides any clear answers to and should perhaps suspect that the "2002" position reported by Lindauer and Pritchett, of relative uncertainty, is linked to the lack of expected results from policies driven by confident belief in the value of free markets of 1982.

In this chapter we examine discussions within DE of how to explain and hopefully predict economic growth. (We looked at this in some detail in Chapters 4, 7, and 8.) We start to grapple with a tender and painful issue in the application of DE: what if the policy that economists advocate does not work? Central to this is the interpretations of the widespread adoption of pro-market policies from the early 1980s and the arguments that they have tended to fail—unexpectedly and at great cost. These will help to clarify arguments used to justify these policies, which were a major departure from the previous orthodoxy and were widely expected to generate rapid economic growth in poor countries (Easterly 2001; World Bank 1993). Often, the shift to adopting them required major changes that were heavily criticized for the social costs they imposed on the developing countries. The question of predictability is therefore central. But, as we have seen, while the algebra used by DE *suggests* predictability, there are many reasons to interpret the central thrust of DE as instead concerned with *explanation*, which is very different. And this will also require us to engage with the related question of how DE had earlier (1962) supported anti-market policies.[1]

To manage a first stab at this, I will contrast statements by Williamson, author of the canonical text on the Washington Consensus (WC); by Stiglitz, who sought to offer a post-Washington Consensus (PWC); and by Fine, who criticizes the PWC. In the next chapter I will further develop arguments as to how all this may be critiqued.

The mainstream and the Washington Consensus: continuities

Most serious courses in development will cover something called the "Washington Consensus," usually treating it as a central element to histories of development doctrine. As with ideas such as EOG and ISI, and indeed development itself, students easily find a range of definitions, but it is useful to provide some discussion as debates about the WC continue to be important in understanding DE. In caricature, as we shall see, the WC is usefully understood as sets of ideas (sometimes inconsistent and variable) that support deregulation of economies and tend to assert that free markets should be central to, and will help obtain, successful economic growth and so development.

Clearly, explanations as to why this is the case or why such views may be incorrect should rightfully include a wide range of arguments, including the political and cultural. Here we are concerned with understanding DE in its own terms. From what we have already discussed, it is clear that a range of factors internal to DE encourages assertions that markets fail rarely, implying (given the importance played by ideas of market failure in how DE discusses markets) that markets left alone will tend to lead to good outcomes. We have seen the central point a number of times—perhaps most clearly in Stiglitz's assertion that his chapter "explained why markets result in Pareto efficient outcomes" (Stiglitz 2000: 77). Recall also the problems of framing discussions in standard conceptual terms under various particular conditions arguably common in poor countries, due to lack of separation of production and consumption decisions, when an economic entity, such as a farming household, both produces and consumes (Bardhan and Udry, Chapter 9). Crucially, microeconomics uses the idea of perfect competition as the basis for most of what it has to say about market failures, but that point of reference becomes increasingly impotent if perfect competition is considered increasingly unlikely in practice. The more markets fail, the further away the conditions of perfect competition appear. Yet, as we have seen, while Lindauer and Pritchett report a major shift between 1962 and 1982, the evidential basis that would answer questions about the actual extent of market failure was and remains weak. Views about the extent of market failure are therefore contentious, no matter the confidence with which they may be presented by those holding a particular position. It is common sense that we attempt to assess these positions within their wider historical and political contexts, as was already suggested in the discussion of Agenor and Montiel (1999) in Chapter 3.[2] But this is difficult to do, not least as DE itself gives us very little guidance.

Consider the view of Dunn (2000), a political scientist, commenting upon the shift from earlier ideas that supported state intervention (what he calls Keynesian ideas) to the pro-market views that, in DE, are referred to as the WC: "It is extraordinarily difficult to see clearly and steadily quite what is at stake in this drastic shift . . . Some of the judgments required are essentially causal. . . . [They] are enormously complicated and inherently highly uncertain" (p. 73).

Dunn argues that the broader history of such changes is likely to be contentious, not least on scholarly grounds.

> In the case of the massive impetus towards economic liberalisation of the last two decades of the twentieth century . . . it is natural to see this [as] the discovery of ever clearer and more reliable techniques for fostering economic efficiency . . .
>
> This is very much the way in which a whole generation of economists actively engaged in public service have come to view it, just as their Keynesian predecessors a generation or so earlier saw the previous move in a roughly opposite direction. Viewed epistemologically, however, the sequence looks strikingly different. . . . [I]t was the increasingly evident falsity of one set of false beliefs, not the steadily growing epistemic

authority of their replacements, which did most of the work. . . . The clear result is the negative result.

(pp. 184–185)

Dunn suggests that the situation described in L&P 2002 is simply the rejection of one set of false beliefs and the ensuing realization that the new set was equally false. What we learn from the examination of DE is that it offers basically two sets of false beliefs (in Dunn's terms), each predicated on the idea that it offered a solution. Given that the immediate pre-World War II history argued against free markets, and that political trends of the 1970s were hostile to the status quo, this opened the door to a situation, supported by internal dynamics in economics that go back at least to the publication of Samuelson's seminal work in the late 1940s, that saw the internal of DE match political opportunities of the time.

In terms of canonical texts, for WC we have Williamson (1990) as a clear statement of what the WC was. A decade later (2000), he reviews the WC, and this gives us an opportunity to see whether he has changed his views. Realizing that the WC was at the time radical (rejecting earlier views that market failure was extensive), Williamson's concern in 1990 was in part to ensure that the WC's basic ideas remained, as the Reaganite high tide of the 1980s receded.[3] We need to appreciate that the WC is about policy—what states should do—and is therefore inherently political and institutional. It is striking that Williamson is clear about practice; he argues that the term WC reflects, not the imposition of policies from Washington, but a process of intellectual convergence. We should also note that the term WC is now used differently from how he wants to use it; it now refers to market fundamentalism, neo-liberalism, and other terms. In other words, WC is and always was contested. Williamson (2000) expressed fears that the reforms favored by many—macroeconomic discipline, trade openness, and market-friendly microeconomic policies—would be rejected because of irrational and unfounded hostility to these ideas.

We may now consider Easterly (2001), which suggests how mainstream DE deals with its internal facts. Easterly argues that, even though many poor countries started implementing market-friendly policies around 1980, poor countries shifted from trend per capita GDP growth of around 2.5 percent in 1960–1979 to 0.0 percent in 1980–1999. In other words, the rapid economic growth that was predicted to follow policy changes apparently did not come to pass; rather, the situation deteriorated. Easterly argues that this happened despite two pieces of evidence:

1. That growth before the 1980s was determined by various policy settings.
2. That policy proxies then moved in a positive direction after 1980 (positive in the sense of expecting them to lead to better economic performance).

He asks the question why and gives only two possible explanations (Easterly 2001: 137), revealing how he manages the tensions created by apparent predictive failure. The first is that the research before the 1980s was spurious. He suggests that the regressions were misspecified because the studies tended to see how a stationary variable—growth—was determined by nonstationary policies and initial conditions (such as levels of education *before* the period analyzed). This means that, in his view, there was no reasonable empirical basis for belief in the policies, though he does not put it quite like this.

The second explanation is that other things were happening to *offset* the favorable policy shifts. What could these have been? Easterly looks for—and finds—correlations that point to other factors: the developed country growth slowdown in the 1980s and common shocks—especially the rise in interest rates—slowing both rich and poor countries' economic growth. This, of course, serves to preserve the basic beliefs underpinning the research, which does not make them wrong but arguably fails to make them a wise guide to action, *if wise action is predicated upon known cause–effect relations*. The central point here is the attempt to argue, similar to what we found in Rodrik (Chapter 5), that the basic core set of beliefs is correct. Fforde (2005) reported the citations of Levine and Zervos (1993) as showing how a majority of economists were unconcerned with the study's basic empirical result—that there were almost no robust relations between policy and outcomes globally (Chapter 2).

We can ask, thus, whether Easterly is persuasive. He does not back-check to see what these factors implied for the period *before* 1980. And, more profoundly, we can ask the central L&Z question of whether the data contained robust regularities or not; this provokes reflection that perhaps the research had *not* identified robust cause–effect relations, and basic theory should better be thought of as only working in explanatory, not predictive, terms. Easterly does not consider this (he does not cite L&Z). Nor does he consider the possibility that the main driver of belief in WC policies was not empirical—that is, sufficiently robust to cope with the test of application—but rather a combination of belief in theory with vague empirics, which is suggested by studies such as that of Yonay (1998; Chapter 6).

The Washington Consensus

Williamson (1990) argued that through the 1980s most people in Washington had come to think that policies good for developing countries could be summarized as follows:

- fiscal discipline;
- redirection of public spending toward fields with high economic rewards and redistribution: primary healthcare, primary education, and infrastructure;

- tax reform to lower marginal rates and broaden the tax base;
- interest rate liberalization;
- competitive exchange rate;
- trade liberalization;
- liberalization of inflows of Foreign Direct Investment (FDI);[4]
- privatization;
- deregulation (to abolish entry and exit barriers);
- secure property rights.

These characterize good policies in terms that clearly require the belief that markets rarely fail. Looking back, Williamson (2000) asks the question: do WC policies work?—that is, do they reduce poverty? His answer is that it depends on how WC is interpreted. According to him, populist interpretation identifies it with laissez-faire Reagonomics, and he does not think that such policies offer an effective agenda for development. He refers to one area where, according to him, there is almost always market failure—education: "We know that poverty reduction demands efforts to build the human capital of the poor" (Williamson 2000: 257).[5]

In Williamson's opinion, the inner logic of the original WC included the idea that inflation caused by lack of fiscal discipline was regressive in its effects on distribution (the first point in the list of WC policies). [6] The other points were all seen as pro-poor in various ways, and he argues that the results of privatization depended upon how it was done.

> Deregulation in general involves the dismantling of barriers that protect privileged elites (even if some of them, like trade unionists, have difficulties thinking of themselves as an elite) and hence there is a strong presumption that it will be pro-poor.
>
> (p. 258)

The question of financial market deregulation and interest rate liberalization is complicated by two big issues: first, the possible effects of financial market deregulation on causing the AFC; second, the role played by capital market controls in some East Asian success stories.

Now, the standard story of how East Asia did it refers to government control of interest rates. This is the financial repression referred to by Agenor and Montiel (Chapter 3). By keeping rates *below* market clearing levels, so supply was less than demand, governments could learn from the rationing systems that had to be put in place to allocate credit (see Chapter 14). Controlling interest rates by setting them at low levels created excess demand for credit, and so some rationing system was needed to decide how credits were allocated, giving whoever controlled that system considerable power to decide which companies and sectors would be able to borrow. Arguments that this allowed officials—for example, from Japan's Ministry of International Trade and Industry (Johnson 1982)—to spot winners and maintain high levels of competition went against standard DE thinking, as Williamson confronts here. (See also Chapter 18 on the World Bank's "Economic miracle study" of East Asian success.) Even the World Bank supported export credit subsidies, keen as it was on prescribing export-oriented growth.

Williamson argues that the original formulation of the WC should have stressed much more the need for financial supervision. But it does not follow from this that directed lending (as in some East Asian countries) is pro-growth and so ultimately pro-poor. He concludes that most of the WC reforms "are at least potentially pro-poor" (p. 258) and so should be retained. These ideas are familiar to anybody who has either read the standard DE positions of the time or comes across their adherents, originally (in the 1980s) radical and now often institutionalized (and due for retirement in the 2010s) as professors, heads of research departments, and directors of institutes. Williamson (2000) speaks to and for them, while Easterly (2001) tells us something about how tensions between weak predictive power and explanatory authority are managed; the core issue seems to be preservation of belief.

I now discuss two very different critiques of the WC: those of Stiglitz and of Fine.

The post-Washington Consensus

Stiglitz

The position taken by Joseph Stiglitz (Stiglitz 1998) illuminates again the importance within DE of the view taken of the extent of market failure. Stiglitz was important historically as part of pressures to push the World Bank and the IMF, under the Clinton administration in the 1990s, away from the WC. For understanding DE, the trajectory in terms of ideas and of contemporary pro-poor doctrine is important, though, recalling the previous quote from Dunn, complicated and likely hard to understand.[7]

Stiglitz does not endorse the original WC but believes it should be superseded, because the implicit policy objective is inadequate, focusing too much on economic growth and adding in democracy as well as other objectives, while he believes that policies should focus more on making markets that work to support development. Influenced by post-Soviet Russian experiences, the 1990s saw the growing acceptance of the importance of building the institutional infrastructure of a market economy, he argues.

Stiglitz starts from a critique of the WC:

- Development policy needs more instruments to get well-operating markets.[8]
- Development policy needs to change its objectives in order to attain goals of sustainability, equality, and democracy.

- The basic lesson of the Asian crisis was that the state often had done too little rather than too much—that is, poor regulation, especially financially.

Stiglitz also argues that East Asian success showed that the WC was wrong, in that it did not explain the success, which stemmed from state intervention. He argues that the main economic weakness of the WC was that it tended, in its stress upon trade liberalization and deregulation, to ignore other issues. What were these? Most important was *competition* and how to use it to get markets that would allocate resources efficiently; the WC also tended to ignore education and technology, because it believed these things would happen once the state got out of the way. The WC, therefore, believed that macroeconomic stability and liberalization would be sufficient to secure economic growth (and so development), and that the governments of poor countries should focus, in a limited way, upon securing these. This can be seen as the belief that markets rarely fail, that market failure is not widespread, and conditions close to perfect competition are common. Just what this means in terms of empirical measurement is not clear.

By contrast, Stiglitz argues for a post-Washington Consensus that adds:

- financial sector reform, understood as a combination of deregulation and reregulation;[9]
- government as a complement to the private sector;
- enhanced effectiveness of the state.

But all this platforms upon the idea that these are necessary *because of the extent of market failure*, so central to Stiglitz's argument is the scope and necessity for state action when markets are thought to fail often rather than occasionally (whatever that may mean empirically). He comes back again and again to the view that regulation and competition policies are needed to attain less distorted and more efficient markets—this is what the state has to ensure. An example he gives of what he sees as excessive confidence in the market are the effects of privatization on the creation of monopoly. Here the story is that privatization of large SOEs with strong monopoly positions *without* at the same time putting in place restrictions to prevent them from exploiting their monopoly once privately owned is a mistake. Another classic error of WC, he argues, was to liberalize financial systems without advocating enough reregulation to cope.[10]

In a rhetorical step that is telling, for it goes into areas deemed taboo by many, he is willing to argue that ISI need not stifle competition but depends upon the state of domestic competition and competition policy. With a similar logic, Stiglitz criticizes WC blanket hostility to SOEs, because, in managing a transition, step-by-step privatization may have better economic results (he compares China and Russia).

He relates PWC ideas to the widespread lack of competition in the real world, which should lead to clear new tasks for DE (as we shall see in the discussion of neo-institutional economics in Chapter 11), focusing upon issues arising from market failure—such as externalities, public goods, imperfect information, and incomplete markets. The political implication of this is that governments have to play a role to make markets work better, because markets fail and adjustments need to be made to address this.

But this poses the obvious question of how this is to be done and what an economist can tell us about it. For Stiglitz, this points to the issue of how to ensure good policies, for the quality of institutions influences economic outcomes. His practical suggestions are an example of a confident economist attempting to negotiate interdisciplinary boundaries. He lists the following:

- reform government in developing countries (he argues for change basically along Western normative lines—independent judiciary, separation of powers, and reduction in the scope for arbitrary actions by officials);
- make better use of markets (e.g. in procurement);
- govern better—use participation;
- broaden development goals.

So one interpretation of what happens when a clever economist tries to produce a political analysis is that his own local (what is around him and seems normal to him) is valorized. The idea that there should be a formal separation of powers is not universal in the West but is a typically North American position. One may sense that these are ad hoc arguments. From the apparent apodictic clarity of formal economic reasoning, under histor-ical conditions where the application of that reasoning is (once again) constrained by the idea that markets fail a lot, the focus is pushed *away* from DE and toward other disciplinary areas. For Stiglitz, the sequence is that a heavy focus upon economics leads to the conclusion that it is institutions and politics—not economics—that determine what will happen in countries where policies are changed—a fine conundrum, as it suggests that the economy may not be much more than the effect of processes outside it.

We turn now finally to examine a quite different view of the PWC, that advanced by Fine.

Fine

Fine (1999) presents an analysis of the PWC, focusing on its relation to ideas of social capital and the developmental implications of these ideas. He characterizes the PWC, in economic terms, as

> broadening the scope of what constitutes market imperfections. These are now organized around informational imperfections and asymmetries

of various sorts, including the presence of transactions costs, so that market outcomes depend upon who has what information before, during and after the economy's passages in and out of exchange.

(p. 2)

He argues that social capital is the most revealing aspect for how these PWC arguments project representative individuals (consumers or firms) into macroeconomic analyses based upon microeconomic models. Thus, a national economy is presented as being made up of firms, consumers, and so on, with common characteristics, so that how they are said individually to behave can be used to partly explain how the whole macroeconomy works. Thus, a particular image of the American consumer may be conceptually linked both to the microeconomic narratives based upon the models we saw in Chapter 9 and to what is happening to the US economy as a whole. This conceptual method, he argues, parallels attempts to apply maximization approaches to areas previously outside economics (such as analysis of marriage).

We have met this before in the discussion of relationships between macroeconomics and the so-called "micro-foundations" in Chapter 9. In microeconomics, as we saw in that chapter, producers and consumers (the microcosm) optimize profits and welfare respectively, and interact through markets. Ideas derived from this are then projected into macroeconomics.

Fine argues that central to this PWC thrust remains the explanation of social structures and institutions based on individual optimization that we found in microeconomics. This explanation offers the ability to explain the macrocosm—the wider social pattern—in terms familiar from microeconomics: "Mainstream neoclassical economics now has the power to offer an explanation of the social, without taking it as **exogenous** as previously" (p. 4). DS readers may be familiar with the application of so-called rational choice ideas to fields beyond economics. Here, as in microeconomics, individuals are to be analyzed through uses of algebra and rationality, understood as choices that maximize, as in microeconomics where producers seek to maximize profits and consumers aim to maximize welfare.[11]

So what is the notion of social capital? It is something over and above other forms of capital that can be attached to the conceptualization of the economy in a functionally positive way, explaining levels of economic performance. Here we recall how the idea of perfect competition offered an explanation for how societies with economies that had markets with, or close to, the characteristics of perfect competition were more developed (Chapter 3) and should grow faster (Chapter 9). We can also recall from Chapter 8 how endogenous growth models worked in a similar way. Fine argues against a simply *physical* notion of social capital by arguing that more social capital is not necessarily good for development, nor does thinking about it necessarily lead to better policy advice. This is because physical notions of capital try to avoid the fact (for him) that capital is essentially social in character and the literature tends to avoid this, by using physical analogies, most importantly that social capital, for example, electricity generation, can be thought of as measurable: more of it is better.[12]

A number of useful points come out of this. Fine notes from the start that the PWC is an attempt to dominate the debate by defining agendas and stating what good development policy is. We have seen already how negotiation of interdisciplinary boundaries came into Stiglitz's discussion. Fine also has some interesting remarks on the way in which ideas are contested: "The notion of market imperfections suffices as a proxy for social capital within the economist's vocabulary" (p. 11).

While recognizing the importance of noneconomic variables, Fine argues that Stiglitz does not include them in his analysis of the PWC. This can be seen as preserving the basic autonomy of economics—the idea, which we saw in Chapter 4, that economic growth is central to development, and so its analytical framework can be kept separate. The economy is *not* the effect of noneconomic forces but has its own independent logic, expressed in the algebra of economists' models.

Fine argues that the PWC "allows the World Bank to broaden its agenda whilst retaining continuity with most of its practices and prejudices which include the benign neglect of macro-relations of power, preference for favoured NGOs and grassroots movements, and decentralized initiatives" (p. 12). He adds that the PWC identifies only a limited number of areas where state intervention should take place, which are linked to how market failure is conceptually part of microeconomics. As we have already seen, technical advances at the cutting edge change the extent to which market failure can be modeled and the ways in which market imperfections can be used to justify state intervention, bringing in sources of market failure, such as informational asymmetries and transactions costs, to be dealt with in formal DE terms. This preserves DE as an area of model development (see Chapter 6), and the basic conclusion of DE is that *institutions exist to cope with market failure.* Economic logic remains central and, to quote again T&S, students may be asked: "Why is economics central to an understanding of the problems of development?" (T&S 2006: 33, quoted in Chapter 4).

Detailed discussion of this takes us well beyond DE and the basic scope of this book. Recall Dunn's view that arguments about the historical factors at play "are enormously complicated and inherently highly uncertain." Fine, who has his own strong priors—his own metaphysical commitments—argues that a central element of such accounts should be the renewed import-ance of the state, mainly related to the effects of crisis and of globalization, requiring enhanced state capacity for regulation and for support to capital. To retain hopes of being relevant, organizations such as the World Bank need to have a view of the state's role in development.[13]

Conclusions

Understanding DE, and so having a better chance of coping with it, is enhanced by consideration of these issues. Easterly and others show clearly that the hopes of WC reforms (asserted by their advocates as relatively certain) have proven unreliable. Although we may note the 2002 confusion reported by L&P, this has not (yet?) produced any major crisis in a Kuhnian sense (Fforde (2005), Chapter 5 here), and perhaps, given what we have studied of how DE works, this is not surprising.[14] Market failure is crucial, but the extent to which it is viewed as extensive or rare lacks much clear empirical foundation, even while at the heart of major changes in economic development policy prescriptions.

Questions for discussion

1. Why does Stiglitz state that the PWC requires government reform to be carried out along a particular subset of Western normative lines— independent judiciary, separation of powers, and so forth?

2. Contrast the political implications of the WC and the PWC.

3. Why Washington in the Washington Consensus?

Notes

1 I use the terms "pro-market" and "anti-market" as useful shorthand. The reader will easily find analyses of particular countries that combine assessments of the overall economic policy stance in these terms with evidence that reality was far more complex.

2 The reader should recall that Ronald Reagan, US president from 1981 to 1989, was responsible for many radical changes that reversed long-held policies of state intervention in the economy. Similar policy changes were introduced in the UK under Prime Minister Margaret Thatcher, who held power from 1979 to 1990. Arguably, neither of their radical agendas was fully completed, with Reagan followed by George H.W. Bush and then Clinton, and Thatcher by John Major and then Tony Blair.

3 See the previous footnote.

4 It is called "direct" investment because it refers to investments by foreigners directly into economic activities, by the construction of factories, perhaps in joint ventures, rather than by indirect investments into assets such as government bonds.

5 Recall the point made by Ha-Joon Chang (Chapter 1) about the periods when rapid industrialization was occurring in many now rich countries. If we take the late nineteenth-century US as an example, does it make much historical sense to argue that rapid reductions in poverty were based upon efforts to build up the human capital of the poor?

6 "Regressive" means that consumption tends to shift *from* relatively poor people and *to* relatively rich. If it was the other way round, it would be called *progressive*. In general, studies usually argue that income taxes are progressive and direct taxes (that is, taxes on consumption such as a VAT or a sales tax) are regressive.

7 During Stiglitz's distinguished career (he has a Nobel Prize), he moved from a position in the Clinton administration to the World Bank in the mid-1990s, from where he was a vocal critic of IMF policy prescriptions during the AFC. He argued that they were far too radical and pro-market, labeling them as WC, and his discussion here of the PWC arguably reflects this political positioning.

8 The term *instruments* borrows from the language associated with algebra and belongs to the set of variables not determined by and within the algebraic model but set by policy. They are a type of exogenous variable that can, to use another language, carry the intentionality within the historical process of development (see Chapter 1). An example would be fiscal policy, or interest rates, or import tariff levels.

9 If deregulation means reduction in the level of government control, then reregulation is a telling phrase once one appreciates the historical context. Deregulation refers to the *removal* of controls put in place as part of earlier anti-market views ("1962" in Lindauer and Pritchett terms; see Chapter 2). Stiglitz, had he wanted to ignore this history, could as well have used the word regulation.

10 Histories of policy advice before the 1997 AFC may inform the reader of the extent to which advisers advocated caution as they also advocated deregulation.

11 The reader may wish to review the discussion of instrumental rationality in Chapter 2 and skip forward to the relevant section of Chapter 11 (pp. 34–36).

12 In passing, similar points can be made about concepts of power viewed as a measurable quantity; see Hindess (1996) and, for a summary, Fforde (2009), Chapter 5. In a simpler register, it does not make much sense to treat power as a knowable attribute that *determines* beforehand what will happen in encounters, yet this is how people often employ the term.

13 The reader may wish to revisit the quotations referring to crises from Camdessus and Wolf (pp. 5–17). Such views suggest that the World Bank is a minnow in the face of such powerful forces, a view confirmed, perhaps, by the evidence from Easterly about the apparent failure of the "big idea" of the times—1982, in terms of L&P's periodization.

14 The reader may recall the discussion of Kuhn in Chapter 5. He argues that big shifts in patterns of thought occur when the knowledge community comes to think that its facts no longer fit its theory. But the experience of natural science, Kuhn argues, is that this is only a necessary condition; for a major change to occur some new theory is needed that can explain, with a stable empirics that is likely to be experienced as predictive, the anomalous facts that earlier theory could not explain.

11 Alternative economic theories

In this chapter, I will discuss a few alternative perspectives to mainstream DE. These include neo-institutional economics (NIE) and Marxian views. I will also cover some deeper issues posed by overtly reflexive approaches, such as discourse analysis. My main point here is that while much is made of the value of knowledge as socially constructed and of deconstructing positions, this often obscures how such positions themselves reconstruct alternatives preferred by their protagonists, which usually lack reliable predictive power yet often assert the contrary in that they are proposed as guides to action—that is, policy. This does not necessarily make them less preferable than other explanations, but, as so often is the case, they do not escape the risks associated with any metaphysical commitments to confident certainties.

DS students, familiar with DS topics such as women and gender in development, should be able to bring some interesting contributions to this discussion. Thus, "Third Wave" feminism arguably rejects particular deconstructions as reconstructions that are unacceptable. For example, Springer (2002) talks about how black feminism was "drowned out" by the first and second waves of the women's movement in the United States, leading to an effective "disregard [of] the race-based movements before them" (p. 1061).[1] Springer may thus be read as rejecting histories of the women's movement in the United States as unacceptable because, while radical, they construct a history that ignores subgroups, here understood as black American women. Sylvester (1999) talks of "disparate tales of the 'Third World'" (p. 703) and reports that she has "conducted research in Zimbabwe comparing perspectives on women workers and their needs, as expressed by development agencies ... (most of whom see themselves as engaged in alternative development work), with views expressed by women identifying as women workers. The gaps between women's self-conceptions and views held about them by the resourced development agents have often been wide enough to drive a lorry through" (*idem*).

This chapter is heading toward the idea that apodictic arguments face important risks if they don't have robust predictability. From the perspectives of this book, both mainstream DE and DS views that are confident about what will work take the same risk, which is that faced in general by assumptions that debate may progress through apodictic argument— that is, demonstration of the validity of a position mainly through logical argument. Clearly, this starts to develop the possibility that it may be wiser, so long as stable and predictive knowledge is unavailable, to treat knowledges as better if accompanied by dialectic argument, in the sense of being consciously process-oriented, with acceptability criteria understood as contextual and multiple.

As an engineer turned economist turned development practitioner, I may be taken well out of my depth, but I think this is useful. Coping with ignorance is a much undervalued ability (Fforde 2011a), and at times it is useful to share one's confusion. In part, this is because it is not wise to accept views simply because they are clearly and logically presented, and founded upon persuasive assumptions (a basic endeavor of apodictic arguments). For example, humans are often persuaded to do or buy things that are not entirely in their interests—the technique of being "spun." But this may sometimes be felt "like a splinter in the brain" (to quote the Matrix) or generate discomfort, like the "Uncanny Valley" that causes audiences to reject computer-generated images when they are "too real."[2]

I start by discussing critique and remark in passing that I believe *all* concepts can be deconstructed and *all* arguments can be critiqued. Like the notion of misrepresentation, sometimes the notion that deconstruction or critique is valuable carries with it the idea that one can avoid an infinite regress, which seems flawed (unless it stops because of boredom, lack of resources, or some other element that is not part of the argument per se). It assumes that deconstruction, or critique, can stop *because it has reached a point of truth*. This for me is simply that fear of ignorance often drives people to seek beliefs, at the end of the day, without too much regard for their accuracy.[3]

Knowledge is sometimes presented in ways that do not involve questioning but as accepted. If the same knowledge is then used to guide action, it may be called belief. Belief is important because it influences not only how people behave but also how they judge others. But sometimes knowledge is not accepted without question. Why? Such knowledge can be perceived as not meeting its own internal criteria—for example, within economics, the illegitimate use of econometrics or some other formal element of the practice.

In these terms, the knowledge can be experienced by the recipient as challenging. Much of the thinking of people like Popper and Kuhn (Chapter 5) is related to identification and elucidation of internal inconsistencies. These are generally identifiable through policing mechanisms internal to disciplines, such as canonical textbooks.

The knowledge can also be perceived as fitting external criteria that challenge it. These criteria are not easy to identify within the practice or discipline itself (though they may be, as the discipline defines itself through difference).

An example would be the frequent criticism of nonalgebraic methods from within DE and mainstream economics generally. These issues of perceived inconsistency may perhaps be as much felt intuitively as conceptually formed in any clear manner. Recall the definitions of literary classics cited in Rose (2003; Preface) where many poor people reported sensations of awakening as they encountered literature that, they said, forced them to think for themselves. And also reflect upon notions of the "splinter in the brain" or the idea that once you are aware of propaganda, it ceases to have power over you.

This takes us to an implication of the notion of epistemology, which is that through study of such concepts people can learn critical methods. But there are many other possible reasons why an approach is criticized: it may simply have opponents, there may be academic incentives to publish challenges, and so on. But it is striking that presentation of knowledge may or may not be accompanied by ways of assessing it. As Dunn (2000) suggests (Chapter 10), it is often acceptance of the falsity of an antagonist's position, rather than the value of the protagonist's, that seems to work rhetorically in getting the reader or listener to agree. This may in part reflect people's preference for avoiding confusion rather than ignorance: they prefer certainty and ignorance to the alternative—uncertainty and knowledge of it.

Development economics and critique

A large part of the problem posed in studying DE is in the tensions that exist between two tangles. First are the evident reasons for questioning much of what is presented as credible knowledge. These are many: L&Z (1993) and how their results were treated (Fforde 2005), the apparent failure of the Washington Consensus, the pattern of historical change in the discipline (L&P 2002), practices such as cross-country growth regressions that simultaneously express and challenge core beliefs, and so on.

Second is the apparent lack of internal practices that explain how to confront these and other reasons for questioning what is presented. One aspect of this is the lack of operational empirical reference in textbooks to tell students when models work and when they do not. For example, the question of the empirical extent of market failure is striking.

But these tensions coexist, on the one hand, with pretensions to a "naive" scientific method that lacks predictability, and, on the other, with the strong tendency of DE to seek to explain.[4] Indeed, while explanations and predictive theories seem to require very different criteria to evaluate them, mainstream DE's commitment to formal modeling and naive natural scientific method prevents it from investing more in developing its own standards of explanation.

Much of what is called critique, with its reference to post-modern ideas about the relativity of knowledge, tries to abandon any idea of predictive knowledge. This is not exactly what I have in mind here. For me, prediction is as much a social construct as anything else. What intrigues me is why some human practices experience predictability and others do not. The core issue is what to do when questioning something presented as knowledge. As far as I can see, many of the problems are due to inexperience in dealing with situations where presented knowledge needs, for various reasons, to be questioned.[5]

I now turn to Marx, who offers what seems to be an economic explanation that combines pretensions to prediction with arguments about what determines consciousness. As we saw in the discussion of the problem of development in Chapter 1, as conceptualized by Cowen and Shenton (1996), the Marxian response was the only alternative to the mainstream one: that correct development is what authority says it is.

Commoditization and ignorance: linking economics to critique

In this section I want to link an economic argument to justification for critique. This argument is highly apodictic in its own way; furthermore, it offers an explanation said to be both true and predictive that draws upon an idea of a "veil of illusion" created by the nature of commodities. This critique asserts that only one step is needed in a proper deconstruction of how we initially conceive of the world. This is, of course, an interpretation of Marx, but there are two interpretations (at the very least) of what Marx means.

The first, which can be found in the writings of many mainstream economists, is of Marx as an economist. Arndt (1987), thus, stresses the influence of Marx on various statements about the problems facing the world and different views about what should be done about them (Marx himself argued for revolution)—Baran, structuralism, Prebisch, Frank, neo-Marxism, and so on. These statements, found in a wide range of articles and books, tend to think in terms of capitalism rather than market economy, but the focus is economic (though different from mainstream DE). Whether Marx is indeed best thought of as an economist is doubtful, because he certainly did not treat economics as a domain separate from his main interests, which were change processes.

A central concern of much of this literature is the same as that of the economic growth theory as discussed by Ray (1998; Chapter 7). Why is there no convergence? Why do some countries stay richer and some stay poorer? This often leads to a focus on whether capitalist development can exist in developing countries and to a theory of development in economic terms, where the economy is seen as closely linked to, and analyzed with, the political, social, and so on. Such arguments were usually highly apodictic, attempting to prove their point. This could lead to funny (both strange and ironic) results, as shown by the so-called Warren thesis—that capitalist development in the so-called "periphery" (typically of ex-colonial countries) was actually happening, contrary to most theories of underdevelopment. Since this contradicted what they had often shown to be the case, the response from many important scholars was highly negative.[6]

The second interpretation is to see Marx as a student of capitalism. The early Marx was concerned with freedom and the ways in which capitalism denied self-determination in various ways. Marx's analysis of capitalism[7] focused upon exploitation as something occurring in production, as workers' labor power interacted with capital to generate products whose values in sale exceeded the value embodied in those products—the theory of "surplus value." But value here is *abstract*—it is labor power treated as a commodity: another $3 espresso rather than what it is—a cup of coffee brewed by particular person (say "Sarah Ward" in a good mood) at a particular time (say, 8 on a Thursday morning, overcast with hopes of sun later) and place (say, in Collingwood, Melbourne, Australia). So fundamental to Marx's analysis is the idea that things—products—are not as they seem that a veil of illusion is created by the nature of capitalism in which products are commodities, and then this veil is thrust aside by the analysis. Thus, based upon Marx's analysis of commodities comes a theory of knowledge, which could also be said to be a theory of ignorance (Fforde 2011a).

The labor theory of value explains why competition among capitalists seeks to drive down the value of commodities by reducing the abstract labor in them but always enabling capitalism to expand since separation of labor from the means of production means that surplus value can be created.[8] It also explains why products that are bought and sold under capitalist conditions are not seen as they really are: because commodities embody abstract labor, buying and selling them—actually a relationship between the specific people (above "Sarah Ward") who made what is exchanged and those who buy it to consume it—are the purchase and sale of a commodity. This illusion—commodity fetishism—is generated by capitalism itself and hides real social relations under market relations.

Thus, fundamental to this interpretation of Marx is a need for a critique that may reveal what is really happening compared with what capitalism presents to an observer. Marx's view is that capitalism itself is generating the false knowledge (bourgeois ideology), so that false knowledge is specific to capitalism and in some sense serves it. And all this, which is highly apodictic, is no more than an attempt, through rhetoric and assertion presented as analysis, to generate belief in his views.

Beliefs about the nature of reality

The idea that knowledge comes in chunks and may reflect historical trends and interests is not solely Marxian, but Marxian ideas have had a pervasive impact upon ways of carrying out a critique—that analysis may reveal a hidden reality and that the nature of the hiding of that reality needs to be explained.[9] And this leads to the possibility of believing that DE is simply

part of the power structure, reproducing it and supporting it. By participating in constructing belief and "naturalizing" what is experienced, DE may
help to make people believe that what they are experiencing is normal and
natural, and therefore not something they can change. It reinforces the veil
of illusion in the interests of a group.

It is the common experience of students that the theory of knowledge that
comes with approaches such as Marxism poses valuable questions, not least
because DE offers little that is overt or simple to guide the construction and
evaluation of *explanations*. This is not to say that the possible answers given
by Marx, Marxists, or Marxians are to be preferred, but they may help to
open the mind.

A central issue in all this, of course, is the peculiar sense of disorientation
that may accompany discussion of nonpredictive explanation. I have no
answer to this. It seems as risky to argue that there is a known development process as to assert that "There are no general patterns of development
just as there is no general definition of development. Each people must write
its own history" (Arndt 1987: 147, quoting Jameson and Wilbur 1979: 31).

This sort of statement can be somewhat trite: if we tend to believe that
everything is unique, this can be taken to suggest that explanations may be
expanded without limit. If it suggests, on the other hand, that we gain from
knowing about the contingency of particular explanations, that is a far
weaker statement. In this sense it can readily be argued that there are general
patterns or general definitions of development, but the point is how we
accept such ideas. A Lakatosian sense, that data as empirics is always related
to some set of meanings, may help us avoid rushing into an infinite regress.
By this I mean that any statement may be questioned and deconstructed ad
infinitum, so long as the resources and interest are there to do so. As I
previously remarked, rigor is easy; it is the rest of it that drops the anvil on
one's foot.

Recall the common view that all statements are relative. It can be argued
that such statements are contradictory and assume something similar to
ideas of misrepresentation—that it is fair to criticize particular statements
for their relativity while asserting that one's own statements are somehow
better. This suggests that the scientific method of economics, if viewed as
an "agnostic realism," is not methodologically as weak as some might
say. The problem is the lack of observed regularities. The issue, then, is concerned with context. In areas related to practice, such as development, it
follows that for DE and DS the central issue, if development interventions
are to be organized in ways that expect certain things to happen, is what
to do about the evident lack of predictability and the contrasting tendency
to assume determinacy that accompanies the use of algebraic (and other)
metaphors embodying ideas of cause and effect. This discussion is not
really helped much by asserting that knowledge is socially constructed, with
the exception, as we shall see in Chapter 15, of possible harm reduction.

Ignorance, thus, is a better guide to action, while knowledge of ignorance is a better guide to prevention.

DS students, especially if they are being taught by human geographers and anthropologists, will probably be well aware of how ideas of the social construction of knowledge have been driven in part by something called *critical discourse analysis*. Although vast amounts of text state they are using this approach, or variants, it is usually hard to pin down precisely the acceptability criteria. After pestering colleagues without much success for an agreed canonical statement defining critical discourse analysis (CDA), the nearest thing I could come to was Fairclough (1992). CDA is often challenging (e.g. Escobar 1995 as an example of particular value to DE) and often relies heavily upon the rhetorical or argumentative step that goes from assertions about the relativity of others' empirical references to assertion of the value of their own. Here we can see possible similarities with the shift from 1962 to 1982; recall the quote from Dunn arguing that it was the *rejection* of what came before that drove the shift in beliefs.

Neo-institutional economics

We have already seen how mainstream microeconomics treats human behavior—modeling it in ways that apparently require little attention to the particular subjectivities of consumers or producers. We now turn to examine neo-institutional economics (NIE) as an alternative approach that attempts to grapple with this issue, for leading figures within it argue that the mainstream approach adopts the instrumental rationality hypothesis (see Box 1.4 on p. 14), implying that this should be relaxed, so that local meanings and institutions matter.

NIE is rather hard to define, in part because it can be construed narrowly or widely. It can be seen either as a better economics or as one part of wider theories of history and institutions. In Chapter 9, I reported how the pre-war institutionalists in some accounts had important effects upon post-war DE. Some histories limit the role of pre-World War II institutionalists to J.C.R. Commons, Wesley Clare Mitchell, and Thorstein Veblen, while others do not, arguing that it was a far wider movement (Yonay 1998). As I discussed, there was a major debate between the institutionalists and neoclassicals in the 1930s over methodology: what to do with the wide range of data and computational power that was being introduced (Yonay 1998). The basic argument was whether to search for theories that fitted the data or to keep to the neoclassical paradigm. The institutionalists lost.

What comes through from contemporary work by NIE is the desire to view markets within their social and historical contexts. North (1995b) is a rather subtle reading, because it combines the basic position of mainstream economics regarding the potential of markets to generate good welfare outcomes with a rejection of the instrumental rationality assumption. He argues that "When it is costly to transact, institutions matter" (p. 18).

Is this a tautology, and, if so, why state it? Does he claim much more for NIE than an ability to assess the relative efficiency of different organizational forms—a universalist position? Why is it that his position seems to make it easier to engage with development? For North, NIE maintains the fundamental assumption of scarcity and hence competition but abandons the idea of instrumental rationality—the assumption that has made neoclassical economics institution free. He refers to Simon (1986):

> If values are accepted as given and constant, if an objective description of the world as it really is can be postulated, and if it is assumed that the decision-maker's computational powers are unlimited, then two important consequences follow. First, it is not necessary to distinguish between the real world and the decision-maker's perception of it: he or she perceives the real world as it really is. Second, it is possible to predict the choices that will be made by a rational decision-maker entirely from a knowledge of the real world and without a knowledge of the decision-maker's perceptions or modes of calculation (of course, his or her utility function must be known).
>
> (p. 17)

How does North argue this through? Conceptually, in such a world, institutions, ideas, and ideologies do not matter. But it is hard to argue that this is the world we live in. Because information is incomplete and mental capacity is limited, human beings impose constraints on human interaction in order to structure exchange. In such a world ideas matter and play a major role in people's choices, and the existence of transactions costs lead to inefficient markets. Cognition can be thought of as the mental models people use, which are contextual—culturally derived as well as learned by the individual—and so vary a lot. Each individual can have a range of models, which need not be consistent within one individual or between individuals.

The presence of transaction costs means that people transact to reach *toward* the optima suggested by the zero transaction cost model;[10] these are then manifest as costs of measurement, enforcing agreements, and so on. In this conceptualization of why economic institutions exist, they form to cope—that is, to reduce uncertainty in human exchange—and, with technology, they determine the costs of transacting. In this way we can try to understand economic performance over time. North thus defines NIE as fitting in with neoclassical theory, because it:

- starts with scarcity and hence competition;
- treats economics as a theory of choice subject to constraints;
- employs price theory as an essential part of institutional analysis;
- sees changes in relative prices as a major force leading to institutional change;
- argues that NIE modifies or extends neoclassical theory;

- modifies the instrumental rationality postulate;
- adds institutions as a critical constraint;
- analyzes the role of transactions costs as the link between institutions and production costs.

From this point of view, NIE extends economic theory by including the analysis and modeling of the political process as critical to economic performance, as the cause of the diverse performance of economies, and as the explanation for inefficient markets. But we can note the fundamental world view—the world as we experience it—is defined by reference to an ideal that cannot be attained and is therefore unobservable.

Interpretations of perfect competition

The thrust of North's argument is that institutions exist because we do not live in a world of perfect competition. This therefore takes us back to the conceptual reference point we discussed in Chapter 9: the ideal to which competitive markets will, it is said, take us toward (if not actually to), in the absence of market failure.

North's argument is similar to Stiglitz's view of "why markets result in Pareto efficient outcomes." The statement relies upon the reader accepting an explanation of what is observed, which includes comparison with what cannot be observed. But it leads to rather different perspectives that add to the DE mainstream. The reader may here recall the quotation from Gillespie (Chapter 6): It is odd but familiar to us (to whom would it be unfamiliar?) for the power of an argument to rely upon reference to something unobservable that is construed as perfect—a conceptualized state of markets in their ideal but arguably impossible to realize state.

A basic question asked by NIE is: what is needed for the social environment to support economic change? The answer appears to be that institutions evolve to support productivity-raising activities, but there is no guarantee this will happen. Those who read around in NIE will find, however, a common view that this idea leads to a competition among institutions, so that those that survive are better in terms of their contribution to economic efficiency and so, in terms of mainstream DE, to economic growth and so development.[11]

> The fundamental issue ... [is] that successful development policy entails an understanding of the dynamics of economic change if the policies pursued are to have the desired consequences. And [this] entails as an integral part of that model analysis of the polity, since it is the polity that specifies and enforces the formal rules.
>
> (North 1995b: 22)

Thinking about this may lead in a different direction from the standard DE view that market failure justifies intervention. It becomes far easier to cope with the idea that the state is neither exogenous nor benign; in a nutshell, states matter, while getting prices right by itself will not work. Yet still there is the belief in forces drawing humans (all of us?) toward the ideal purportedly offered by perfect competition. The solution to the problem of development is therefore "adaptive efficiency" attained through continuous interaction of institutions and organizations, competition, and an institutional framework that selects skills and knowledge with the highest payoff. This far more historical approach includes awareness that perceptions derive from people's mental constructs and that institutional change is overwhelmingly incremental and path-dependent. This offers a chance to present accounts where observed change is not simply in the direction of efficient outcomes but *aiming* in that direction. And so the issue of disciplinary boundaries comes back; how certain is North that economics can explain change? For him, how central to development is economic growth? Yet he states that "It is simply not known how to transform ailing economies into successful ones" (p. 24).

This suggests that for him the extent to which economics can explain change is limited. Thus his advice tends to be pragmatic rather than dogmatic and that institutional rules and norms change at different rates— formal rules shift fast, while informal norms change slowly. Further, adopting formal rules is not the end of the story as the informal norms must also change:

> Polities shape economic performance because they define and enforce the economic rules of the game. Therefore the heart of development policy must be the creation of polities that will create and enforce different property rights.
>
> . . .
>
> Political institutions will be stable if organizations have a stake in them; therefore reform must create such organizations.
>
> (p. 25)

For successful reform, institutions and belief systems must both change. Adaptive rather than allocative efficiency should be the guide to policy. Norms of behavior are needed for new rules to work and this takes time; in their absence, policies usually will be unstable. Short-run growth under autocratic regimes can happen, but, in the long term, institutions need the rule of law and the protection of civil and political freedoms. Informal constraints are necessary (but not sufficient) for good economic performance and can sometimes offset bad political rules: "The key is the degree to which the adverse political rules are enforced" (North 1995b: 26).

North, thus, offers the seduction of a persuasive explanation rather than the stridency of an apodictic demonstration. This is informative, not least because of the role that North's attack on the instrumental rationality hypothesis plays in helping him to negotiate more effectively across disciplinary boundaries. An element of this is his professed lack of certainty, which contrasts with much of what we have encountered in DE so far.

There are interesting tensions between NIE, in North's account of it, and the PWC position. We need to be aware that some accounts of NIE turn history into a determinate account, where a history of social Darwinist processes is known (and demonstrated in the arguments deployed) to winnow out institutions that do not reduce transactions costs. [12] But North is careful to state that what actually happens depends on many things—not just economics. This suggests that North is inherently non-universalist and openly skeptical about certainty a priori—he maintains a high degree of "it depends." It is hard to imagine him arguing that highly specific institutions such as an independent judiciary were necessary for development. Stiglitz, though, in his exposition of the PWC, is relatively certain about what can and should be said; his view appears in this sense very different from North's, and he was very sure that such specific institutions as an independent judiciary were necessary. The PWC's role as a guide to action, to policy prescription, and to valorizing positions is different from North's. North seems far more interested in negotiating across disciplinary boundaries and far more likely to say "I don't know," while Stiglitz treats development as a problem with knowable solutions.

Debates about the importance of realism in theoretical assumptions

In this final section I will discuss the issue of the realism of assumptions. Students and others frequently confront economic positions, such as microeconomics, by arguing that the basic assumptions are unrealistic. Arguably because of their metaphysical commitment, which is fundamental to thinking of economic realities in terms of their deviation from ideal states (perfect competition), mainstream economists usually reject such arguments. In this they are sometimes supported by the views expressed by scholars (such as Friedman 1966 [1953]) that it is not the assumptions that validate a theory but its predictive and/or explanatory power. Such arguments usually are, in my experience, sterile: neither side changes their position. The reader may have noticed that my own position here regarding DE has been to point to the *lack* of predictive power, on the one hand, and problems with explanatory power on the other.

This issue of certainty, of the tensions created by confusion, and the risk of rejecting the view that if you are not confused you are misinformed can be found in a range of critical writings. As I have already mentioned, and DS students will be well aware of this (see Chapter 15 for examples of post-development critique of mainstream DE), much modern radicalism takes various positions critical of mainstream thought, drawing upon Marx and in many ways the view that dominant ideas reflect the requirements of capitalist development. Fine is a good example of this (Fine 1999).

His exposition and critique of the WC and PWC was discussed in the previous chapter. As a Marxist, he aims to elucidate the roles these ideas play in supporting capitalism and what their particular nature reveals about the issues that the state and development policy must try to address. He also aims to show how the particular positions taken by those who support WC and PWC are inconsistent or reveal their origins in the requirements of capitalism rather than of progress. Thus, Fine notes that the concept of social capital (see Chapter 10) permits analyses to ignore macro-power relations (class, international relations, etc.) and enables them to make statements isolated from such issues as what the state should do. For him, this helps to explain why organizations like the World Bank express a continued preference for working through certain NGOs and decentralized initiatives (bypassing possibly contentious macro-power structures). In the same vein, he argues that the PWC is highly selective in how it addresses the role of the noneconomic in economic performance; it can therefore ignore critical approaches, whether from international perspectives, class-based, or whatever. This is a clearly expressed and powerfully argued critical analysis. But how certain is Fine?

We can contrast two different types of position in such debates:

1. Those that contrast errors in others with correctness in the author.
2. Those that encourage investigation of the particular and contingent (what works where) and so do not take a strong and total position a priori about what works where and when.

From this point of view, critical positions like the WC and PWC share the first characteristic.

Conclusions

The core issues, clearly, come down as usual to the persuasive power of DE positions in different contexts. Many people who have been exposed to such approaches as microeconomics react by arguing *against* its assumptions. They find them unrealistic and unpersuasive, and are wary of them. For me, this suggests that they follow the method that rejects an approach (here, microeconomics) on the grounds of the weakness of its explanations. Yet, is it fair to do so on the grounds that the assumptions are *unrealistic*? This would seem familiar and linked to deep-rooted ways of confronting positions. In part, the ways in which positions are opposed or supported often reflects common tendencies to consider and evaluate positions based on the congruency of their metaphysical commitments with one's own. Here the reader may recall the ideas of Philip Converse and Jeffrey Friedman discussed in Chapter 5.

While I previously mentioned that little seemed to come from philosophical ponderings on the nature of action, for me a much more valuable discussion followed from the view that much human debate about cause and effect is *ascriptive*—that is, political and concerned with praising, blaming, and other human activities that influence who has to do what or not, and so on. And, while there are no easy answers to such matters, it does make discussions about the assumptions of microeconomics easier to think about. As already quoted, Milton Friedman (1953) argued that "The ultimate goal of a positive science is the development of a 'theory' or 'hypothesis' that yields valid and meaningful (i.e. not truistic) predictions about phenomena not yet observed" (p. 7).

If this were widely accepted, then economics would have long been abandoned, since it has long been evidently incapable of prediction. Theoretical assumptions would have to be queried on the grounds that the models built upon them were failing. The example of the L&Z study and the responses to it shows that DE is concerned with very different things than prediction. When assumptions are criticized for being unrealistic, therefore, we had better consider this in terms, not of the internal of DE, but of its explanatory power in a range of forums. And this is not a matter of proof and refutation but shows the contextual factors that influence the rhetorical power of a particular apodictic argument.

Such arguments can obviously be deployed against overconfident views in any walk of life. Clearly, views that "participation leads to better development, and we know this to be the case for the following reasons" (here I create a straw man) can be better understood and appreciated if we have learned to cope with DE. What DE adds (and here it is singularly important) is its use of algebra for formal arguments combined with its capacity to digest considerable amounts of data subject to the insights of statistical analysis. This, as we have seen, produces robustly negative results both at the micro level and for international relationships between policy and outcome using the standard categories (L&Z). It also shows how DE tends to be isolated from other approaches (the rest of DS, to start with) and, associated with this, its view that its subject matter (economic growth and economics) must be *assumed* to be the platform upon which change (development) rests.

Questions for discussion

1. What is the difference between a theory of knowledge and a theory of ignorance?

2. Do you think that knowledge construction is organized to find what may be said to be known rather than what may be said to be unknown, and if so what difference might this make?

3. Discuss areas of human life that are conventionally understood to be areas of ignorance and how people are expected to cope.

Notes

1 What is happening here is that allegedly ungendered analyses of society are allegedly deconstructed by first- and second-wave approaches that then recon-struct in ways that ignore certain groups, here black American women.

2 A useful maxim for applied researchers is "If you are not confused you are misinformed." I first heard this from Professor Robert Cassen, who was inter-viewing me for a job (support and contribution to Cassen 1985). Before me he had a meeting with an impressive American holder of a Rockefeller Foundation grant, and we overlapped. The American was describing with great confidence, and in great detail and with impressive logic, the political situation in a left-wing African state. When they left, Professor Cassen turned to me and asked whether I "bought all that." I replied no, as the situation surely could not be so clear. The point is that the combination of great confidence and analytical power did not convince. "Uncanny Valley" refers to a discovery among producers of computer-generated animations, which was that viewers' acceptance of their films would start to decline *once the level of realistic accuracy reached too high a level.* Information about this is readily available on the web and elsewhere. I discuss issues of spin in DE on pp. 303–308.

3 An interesting question here is just what is experienced as ignorance rather than mystery. If God were thought of as female, for many people this would probably be different, though I have no idea exactly how. To quote the poet Wilfred Owen, "Courage was mine, and I had mystery; Wisdom was mine, and I had mastery."

4 I use the word "naive" because of the general lack of interest from economists in many important questions related to data—as to how it is created, validated, and given meaning. In this sense Lakatos appears to be rather far off main-stream DE radar screens (though any good econometrician is well aware of the implications for what sits, as metaphysical commitment, in the Null— the assumption that the model is correct). See Chapter 5.

5 Interested readers may wish to investigate arguments that formal empirical practices, such as statistics, are far more focused on discovering or confirming knowledge than denying it. A starting point is Cohen (1994). See also Granger, an important figure in econometrics, on spurious regression results (Granger and Newbold 1974 and Granger 1990). See also the quotation from Cohen (1994) on p. 74.

6 Warren (1971) and the ensuing debate.

7 This is what I think; others differ.

8 The reader may wish to review what was discussed in Chapter 1 about the so-called Marxian solution to the problem of development, as Cowen and Shenton (1996) understood it. This conceptualization argues that there is in reality no intentionality since actions, such as development policy, must suit the laws of social change; for Marx these were the laws of capitalist development as he understood them. It is the logic of capitalism, thus, that enables capitalism to expand.

9 At this point it is not uncommon in arts and DS courses to mention an Italian scholar, Gramsci, and his notion of ideological hegemony. Here is not the place to explore this, and readings are easily accessible.

10 The idea that transactions costs may be assumed to be zero can be found as one of the explanatory assumptions of microeconomic algebra that does not include such costs in the models it uses. As with perfect competition, but harder to find, the narratives that explain why this assumption makes sense can be found and compared in different microeconomic textbooks as a useful student exercise.

11 The reader will recall the various ways in which DE has a tendency to view development as being marked by the existence of developed markets (Chapter 3).

12 By social Darwinist, I mean the idea that competition among types of institutions sees the better ones prosper and others die out. This appears to fit well with the idea that markets in richer countries are less imperfect than those in developing countries.

12 Other visions of the developing economy
Uneven growth and exclusion

This chapter starts to focus upon particular topics and offers the reader comparison of one addressed by Ray (1998; Chapter 10) with a similar issue as managed by a noneconomist. The topic Ray addresses is that of duality: the idea that developing economies are concerned with the division of the economy into two sectors that change in different ways as development happens. These, as we shall see, can also be thought of in different ways: as urban and rural, as advanced and backward, and so forth. This leads to the question of how people may experience development differently, with those in the less advanced sector being excluded from the improvements enjoyed by those in the other sector. This poses the wider issue of exclusion: the possibility that only some people may be fully included in the gains from change. And this in turn suggests that economists' methods may *limit* how they contribute to conceptualizations of matters arising from the use of dualities such as rural/urban or excluded/included.

This, we shall see, poses questions about what economists can learn about data and data creation from studies carried out by noneconomists. The example I use here is Jonathan Rigg's (1997) *Southeast Asia: The Human Landscape of Modernization and Development*, Chapter 4, "The Experience of Exclusion." In my opinion, with a suitable interpretation (or reinterpretation) of the internal standards of DE, much indeed can be learned by DE from what Rigg, a human geographer, has to say. For economists, the basic lesson, as should have been taught in any decent econometrics course, is to understand the data creation process. Like many of the later chapters in this book, the discussion lends itself to augmentation by student presentations and extended class discussion. The key here is to illuminate issues arising from the particular epistemology of DE through examination of alternative perspectives.

Rigg's central point offers such an alternative. He argues that social change leads to uneven growth, and a key concept he uses to discuss this is *exclusion*, which he platforms on the conceptual distinction between "the village and the town." The basic meaning of this concept, which is richly developed in his book, is that one can identify social processes and structures that systematically include some and exclude others from participating in the gains from economic change. His approach is thus explanatory and depends upon the use of powerful concepts, which he treats rigorously. I will contrast this with what Ray has to say about the rural–urban divide, given his stress upon algebraic modeling techniques.

Why should economists read geographers? For economists, such texts are valuable in that they may

- Reveal what is behind the data, both in terms of incidence and behavior.
- Suggest caution and the value of challenging commonly held assumptions so as to get closer to the data.
- Open the door to engagement with other disciplines and approaches.

Exclusion as more than poverty

An important part of the analysis, which offers possible access points that link to the DE approach to related issues, is how Rigg shows us a view of exclusion "from above"—that is, from the standpoint of central government, national policymakers, and so on. An interesting addition to this can be found in Scott (1998), which provides a fascinating analysis of how such "views from above" emerged historically and how they work.

Rigg argues that issues associated with poverty are often quantified, based upon the idea that the incidence of the perceived problem can be accurately gauged, usually through surveys. For him, this is not entirely plausible, for a number of reasons. One is that it risks treating what cannot be measured as not entirely real and so something to be ignored. He quotes Robert Chambers (1995)[1]: "It then becomes the reductionism of normal economics, not the experience of the poor, that defines poverty" (p. 108). Thus development (and DE) "obscures the real effect of the process on individuals, their lives and livelihoods. It is clear that people are not excluded from development merely because they lack income" (p. 110).

Examining the issue of exclusion thus adds to poverty studies and poses questions of who gets left out of the reckoning. Awareness of data creation processes and Lakatosian observation theory make this point still more strongly than Rigg, as this reinforces the point that information by itself —raw data—is meaningless. Thus, thinking about exclusion highlights the ways in which knowledge and its production define categories, exclude others, and lead analyses: poverty surveys create data and therefore problems to be solved. Rigg argues that survey work often defines the solutions as it defines the data that defines the problem: it identifies development *materially*, when other definitions may be as or more important. It is quite obvious to me that people may well value intangibles highly and perhaps more highly than tangibles. If this is not obvious to the reader, then consider a story told by Robert Chambers (I cannot recall the source). Apparently, a researcher had examined welfare levels in a South Asian rural community, and returned some twenty years later to repeat his investigations. When he presented his results to the village, he reported they were worse off than before. Villagers replied that they disagreed: when he had carried out his earlier work they had been subject to violent repression from local land-lords, which made them feel ashamed, and since their removal, villagers felt far better off, no matter what his data showed. It seems silly to ask who was right.

So one thing that we can learn about DE from Rigg is just how much understanding is put at risk when an approach decides what its empirics are to be. He presents a wide range of issues that may take economic analysis in certain directions. These include the value of participatory methods: if those surveyed like the changes they have experienced, then these positive reactions, even if not easily measured, if at all, arguably should be included in the account of what has been happening, even if the survey says that the participants are worse off—that is, according to external measures (done by somebody else). Here we have a clear example of the importance of the awareness, from basic welfare economics, that interpersonal and inter-temporal comparisons of welfare are not objective but "done" —that is, choices are made, and others may disagree with them (see Chapter 1 and Box 1.1, p. 4). To say that a choice is being made is to ask questions: Who is doing this? Do other people agree with how they are doing it? What are the choices about? What Rigg (and Scott 1998) and others are arguing is that answers to these questions are important.

To repeat, and to recall McCloskey in Chapter 6, numbers by themselves mean nothing until some social practice (and the question is: which?) says what they mean. Rigg then goes beyond this to the risks of participatory methods themselves: who do the poor themselves exclude? We can add to this another element of subjectivity: the possible effects upon the practi-tioners of the data that is created; for example, empathy toward people who are unhappy and troubled often draws analysts in, who seek to link the meanings they give their data to these intuitions and moral sentiments. Alternatively, and here we can recall the quote from Sylvester in Chapter 11, analysts or practitioners may create beliefs about such people that are far from what the poor themselves have to say.

Another issue is the effects of instability on the situation of the poor, so that categorizing them is risky. Much data on poor people suggests that poverty is multidimensional, with shifts along each dimension not well correlated, so that improvement in one dimension may accompany deteri-oration in another.[2] Finally, there are semantic issues: what is meant (in a data creation context) by terms such as wealth, income, and deprivation? Researchers usually find much variation in use both among the poor and between them and the poor. As is common, discussions of poverty may exert powerful forces upon debate about change and development that, unless muted, challenge many assumptions and positions. For example, survey data in Vietnam through the first decade of the 2000s increasingly showed that it was not lack of recorded assets that was associated with, on average, high ethnic minority poverty, but the relatively low return on them compared with other groups (Fforde 2011b). This pushes the analysis toward looking at factors that exclude certain groups, but, as a local study reported:

> Although poverty is multifaceted, the lack of data prevents us from covering all of its dimensions including ... participation in decision making and social inclusion
>
> (Vietnam Poverty Update Report 2006: 18)

Such quotes show clearly how the assumptions driving data collection are important, and how certain issues can be inaccessible, if not invisible.

A core point that Rigg is far more easily able to make than mainstream DE is the possible relationship between exclusion and heterogeneity of people—the sheer variety of humanity and its experiences. Clearly, use of algebraic models ostensibly requires stable relationships between variables and what conceptually underlies the data. This tends to mean that if heterogeneity exists, such models encounter difficulties, and so there are pressures to assume homogeneity, not least for comparative purposes. Yet, as Rigg points out, many groups can be excluded from development where economic growth is uneven, and the mainstream appears to fare far better than minority groups and marginal peoples such as hill tribes and forest dwellers. Governments are often opposed to shifting cultivation (often called swidden or "slash and burn"), leading to the attempted exclusion of those who practice such techniques. Maps that show the incidence of populations excluded from development ("maps of exclusion") often show how poverty is apparently higher in forest areas.[3] In survey data, such categories therefore often overlap with—and offer correlations with—indicators of income and other measures of poverty. Measures of ethnicity often **correlate** well with measures of welfare and well-being. Concepts of modernization also often refer to homogenization as part of nation building, and, in the context of development, there can be exclusion of some groups referred to as "backward." As Rigg points out, exclusion or marginality is often driven by particular ways in which people are excluded from development while yet being part of it—prostitutes active in sex industries, forest dwellers active in illegal logging, and so forth. Due to these interactions, the situation could as well be described, he says, as a combination of constraint and coercion, because the process of development itself creates forces of inclusion and exclusion.

Appreciation of texts such as this one by Rigg, in my opinion, makes for better economic analysis. They show much about important issues:

- What is behind survey data—data creation and the dataset—both empirically and also in terms of what the data means (behavior).

- Why it is easy for DE to lose arguments and why so much quantitative work is defensive. The reader may reflect on the difficulties a quantitative DE analysis would have in coping with an attack on it that uses the arguments Rigg deploys.
- The value of qualitative work.
- The problems in coping with and managing decent economic research.

This suggests that while mainstream DE, for relatively clear reasons, exerts pressures to avoid such issues, they can be mitigated. I turn now to see how Ray, in his Chapter 10, addresses similar questions.

Mainstream development economics: the rural and the urban

Ray (1998) starts Chapter 10 by arguing against his earlier position:

> The literature on economic growth, a good part of which we studied in Chapters 3 and 4, might tempt you to view economic development as a process that transforms all incomes and all sectors in some harmonious and even fashion.
>
> (p. 345)

What this means is that economic growth theory encourages analysis in terms of the "big numbers." Recall how I argued that treating GDP as a measure of changes in levels of economic activity requires making a choice about the value of the incomes of different people (Chapter 4). This point confronts the same issue that Ray makes: it can be risky to think in terms of such aggregates. Rigg and Chambers make the same point, which suggests the value of deconstruction of any aggregate measure and an awareness of what arguments expressed in those terms are doing— in part how they work rhetorically, to use McCloskey's term. But the problem is partly due to an assumption driving the approach, which is well-expressed by T&S (2006): the idea that economic growth is at the centre of development. Ray poses the question, but continues using these aggregate concepts and so obeys the internal consistency rules of DE.

Thus, Ray argues that the most important structural feature of developing countries is the distinction between the rural and urban sectors. To support this view, he reports that in such countries a large share of both people and output comes from agriculture and that important relations exist between agriculture and the rest of the economy. Clearly, *if* development is understood as economic development, and *if* we are to conceptualize underdevelopment in these terms, then it follows that decreases in these shares—of the so-called backward agricultural sectors—are definitionally part of development. Conceptually, therefore, this is a dual economy view, where development is seen in terms of both a backward and an advanced sector. The rural is seen as backward, not least because its markets are weakly developed, and the urban is seen as advanced. This can have pernicious effects across a wide range of social practices, which Rigg has already alerted us to. The rural sector is a source of labor supply; of food supply, if food imports are not available; and demand for urban products. He does not develop these ideas in an open dialectical manner but presents them as a useful framework. If we question this choice of framework, it is possible to imagine alternatives.

One can also look for any simple structural feature that may be conceptualized as universal, common to all (or most) developing countries. We have already met this with the remark by T&S (see Chapter 2) that "Almost all developing countries are situated in tropical or subtropical climatic zones." As most DS students would know, a standard critique of such views—that development consists of changes that replace the backward sector by the advanced sector—would be that this is simply modernization theory, where development is defined as becoming like others ("us")—that is, industrialized and urbanized.[4] Therefore, the rural areas are "the past" and the urban areas "the future." One problem with this view is the deindustrialization that took place in rich countries in the closing decades of the twentieth century.

In developing his conceptualization, Ray divides the urban sectors of the economy into formal and informal. The formal sector is made up of "firms that operate under the umbrella of accepted rules and regulations imposed by government" (p. 346). Such firms, he states, are often unionized; adhere to regulations and receive, in turn, the benefits of state economic support; and pay taxes.

The informal sector employs a high share of the total labor force and is "a loose amalgam of organizations that escape the cover of many of these regulations and do not receive access to privileged facilities" (p. 346). An example of such organizations would be the informal arrangements in which market traders organize transport for their goods.

This distinction between the two sectors is common and clearly not solely economic. One may reflect on the possible effects of the shift to WC policies upon the growth of informal sectors and of earlier ISI policies upon the growth of formal sectors in the first place, as state-related activities contracted. In Vietnam, as the state sector shrank sharply in 1989–1991, normal Southeast Asian patterns of street life returned as traditional socialist controls were abandoned. With extensive small-scale trade and services returning to provide many products, people who had left the state sector rather easily found new jobs (de Vylder and Fforde 1996). Many in other countries were not so lucky. One can also reflect upon the possible importance of success in state-led human development (public health, sewers, etc.) upon the ability of cities to carry large informal populations.

But we can also ponder how this dualistic conceptualization works in its own terms. For example, in rural areas, even on farms, surveys from some

countries show how family income may have a large non-agricultural component. This may be more evident when growth is rapid and without much
land loss, so that subsistence needs can be met rather easily and there is both
scope and opportunity to explore alternative sources of income, especially
if urban living costs are high. In Vietnam this is referred to as "leaving
agriculture but not leaving the farm." But Ray focuses upon a view of the
rural areas as mainly agricultural, using a sample of Indian villages as
representative: "The volume of data now available . . . provide rich insight
into the functioning of typical rural economies" (p. 349).

Here again we see the powerful tendencies of DE to portray a particular
situation as typical. Ray argues that the villages (of the survey) are diverse
in terms of soil fertility, rainfall, and cropping patterns; and production
involves subsystems (avoidance of monoculture), thus requiring management of a wide range of variables and response to changing conditions. We
can recall how the microeconomic framework of DE met insurmount-
able problems in dealing with complex situations where the same entity is
both consumer and producer (Chapter 9). We may surmise that here Ray
may be signaling his own personal dissatisfaction with the analytical
framework he is explaining, as its explanations may appear rather simplistic
when set beside accounts of the rich diversity of life in the villages surveyed.

Ray then develops the argument to consider rural–urban interactions.
He focuses upon two fundamental resource flows: agricultural exports and
a food surplus. There are, of course, others: markets for industrial and consumer goods, and agricultural exports as a source of foreign exchange. He
does not mention the possibility of rural financial savings mediated through
informal capital markets and other more formal institutions into firms,
perhaps situated in urban areas (an East Asian phenomenon?).[5]

This leads him to discuss one of the important models of DE: the Lewis
model, a classic, like Harrod–Domar and Solow. It goes beyond the simple
structural duality of industry and agriculture to think in terms of the
transformation over time of a traditional into a modern sector. It is a dual
economy model, by now well mined for papers and insights. The power of
the idea shows in the ways in which it can be plugged into a range of
definitions of the two poles of the duality. The Lewis model goes back to
the 1950s and argues that the fundamental determinant of economic growth
is the accumulation of physical capital in the modern sector (where labor
productivity is higher). We can recall how endogenous growth theory sought
to explain higher incomes in richer countries through notions of human
capital (Chapter 8), relying upon the idea that education and other markers
link simply, through the idea of a production function, to higher output.

The core idea in the Lewis model is that a large surplus of labor in the
traditional sector conceptually can leave the sector without a significant
reduction in output there. This means that the marginal productivity of labor
has been forced down to zero levels and that only when a significant amount
of labor has left the sector will incomes there start to rise. This is likely to

happen often when there is a lot of underemployment and job sharing (such as in an informal services sector), and may not be simply because of a high population density. Ray discusses various issues with the surplus-labor model. Centrally, if the marginal productivity of labor is zero, then something has to be noncapitalist in the standard DE way of thinking. This is because of the assumption (see Chapter 9) that factors will be paid their marginal product so long as producers are behaving as optimizers—that is, seeking to maximize their profits. The conceptual position is then that if people are paid despite their marginal product being zero, those who use their labor are not trying to maximize profits and so this is not really a market economy. There are lots of reasons to argue why the traditional sector may act like this (not paying workers at rates equal to their marginal product), such as conceptualizing its production methods as using little capital that is not priced or using forms of economic organization that are social (involving, for example, income entitlement). This may be linked to assumptions about services and informal sectors, the importance of domestic servants, and so forth.

The concept can also be developed in other ways. For example, some economists have broadened the explanation of surplus labor to ideas of *disguised unemployment*, where levels of employment are recorded higher than the true value. This helps preserve the peace of mind of those who think in terms of production functions, for under such conditions it can be thought that people are paid their average product. It is also possible to think in terms of surplus laborers, so the ones left behind in the backward sectors, as others leave for the advanced areas, work harder to keep up total traditional sector output. On many farms, the work is there to be done, and if one leaves another has to do their chores.

The concept also leads to thinking about factors that can be modeled to explain the evolution of the agricultural surplus, and this opens the door to ways of modeling structural economic change. Ranis and Fei (Ray 1998, p. 362 et seq.) modified Lewis' model to exposit how the dualism may stop. Much depends upon parameters and functional forms, but in this conceptualization the algebra expresses the idea that development is both the transfer of labor from agriculture to industry and the simultaneous transfer of surplus food production to industrial workers. Much depends on when agricultural wages start to rise, because this is a major turning point in the process as modeled. If the traditional wage starts close to subsistence (the marginal product of the departing worker), then industrial wages will have to rise steeply in order to drive the process.

The next turning point is when traditional wages are exceeded by the marginal product of labor in the traditional sector, for then capitalist forms are feasible in the traditional sectors (firms can pay wages equal to marginal product there) and so the concept leads to a search for indicators of the commercialization of agriculture. As the economy modernizes, therefore, labor in the traditional sectors stops being paid what social norms say it should be paid and is instead paid what it is worth on the market. Thus, in this model, capital accumulation in the industrial sector is the engine of growth, for this drives the demand for labor there, sucks labor out of agriculture, and eventually pushes wages up enough for the entire economy to be one where all labor is paid its marginal product. Obviously, this conceptualization is underpinned by the idea that, as Stiglitz put it, there are good reasons for supposing that "markets result in Pareto efficient outcomes" in the absence of market failure. And this exposition, of course, assumes that markets fail rarely, so their extension into areas where they had not been dominant is economically productive and, in addition, good for the well-being of the population. Note here how arguments about static efficiency slide across to support arguments about growth.

Ray rehearses various policy issues that accompany this conceptualization. What about agricultural taxation? If it is assumed that capital accumulation in the urban areas, in industry, is crucial, this would appear to justify taxing agriculture. If wages in the traditional sector start to rise, as total income there rises and average product increases, it is intuitively obvious that, with suitable parameters and functional forms, the model will show that this reduces the agricultural surplus (that is, because agricultural incomes are higher, people will eat more), and this pushes up modern sector wages, reducing profits and therefore economic growth. But this is saying that industry *should* tax agriculture to stop this from happening, and this may lead to unexpected consequences. Many of the negative stories of "late ISI" refer to parastatals, which were given monopolies over the purchase of agricultural export crops, leaching off earnings and squeezing farmers' incomes. It may be thought that the issue here is political, but from the point of view of DE, the core political economy issue derives from the basic model, which focuses upon the issue of who or what subsidizes growth and encourages the idea that resources to subsidize growth must come from the backward sector.[6]

A second issue dealt with by Ray is agricultural pricing policy. This is similar, but comes from the other direction: how to ensure food supplies at acceptable prices for the urban areas. The argument goes that favorable procurement prices (that is, prices that farmers and procurement agencies like) face urban complaints about high food prices (workers hate them, as do urban security forces that will have to cope with riots if food prices are unacceptable). One natural result is a heavy fiscal burden from government subsidies to reduce food prices. Ray argues that an overvalued exchange rate can have the same effect.

Such ideas heavily influenced views of the effects of and rationales behind ISI. As we shall see (Chapter 19), this particular model suggests that there are risks. The state uses its power to intervene but ends up in a mess, having created vested interests and a tricky political economy. The majority of the population is still in the rural areas, isolated from the main areas of dynamic change and growth, which are urban and protected by the government. Arguably, this will make it hard for politics to change the situation. And it is likely that economists will calculate static efficiency losses caused by the interventions by linking (in these analyses) to the price distortions caused by tax and subsidy policies. Dynamic efficiency losses will be far harder to calculate. It was within such analytical frameworks that DE contributed to the debates associated with the end of ISI (see Chapter 19).

Rural–urban migration and the Harris and Todaro model

The dual economy models of Lewis and of Fei and Ranis were later augmented by a classic model of rural–urban migration: the Harris and Todaro model. This sits within a problematic that considers whether private migration choices may be out of line with social goals or policies, implying that there can be over- or under-migration to cities. Again, we see the conceptualization orient toward a metaphysical commitment that assumes it is sensible to compare observed realities to some ideal construct. The Harris and Todaro model is, like that of Lewis, driven by a conceptual dualism: a formal urban sector pays high wages, and this helps to create urban unemployment partly through a simple supply–demand mechanism but partly through the basic logic of the model. These high wages can be attributed to a range of factors: unionization or government policy that seeks a modern sector for display purposes (see Chapter 14). Again, we see DE look for interventions in markets to explain distortions. By contrast, it is possible to find analyses that explain segmented labor markets in endogenous ways, referring, for example, to the effects of risk and economic fluctuations upon workers' strategies.[7]

But the underlying thrust of Harris and Todaro is that any problem is caused by market distortions imposed by unions or government (a microeconomic perspective). Again, we can see how this conceptualization leads to certain ways of thinking about the world, and so influences how people may respond.

They start with a two-sector model—rural and formal urban—where wages are flexible in both. They view absorption of labor in each sector, so as labor moves, wages rise in the sector it is leaving and fall in the sector it is going to; thus movements in labor between sectors can lead to an equilibrium in the model. Note that this requires little in the way of assumptions about human behavior. And, if formal wages cannot move below a certain level (in this line of thinking, the obvious culprit is unions) then, of course, this equilibrium does not happen, and labor absorption in that sector is reduced below the equilibrium level. At that wage level (above the level associated with the proper equilibrium that would arise if markets were allowed to work), agriculture cannot employ all the workers who want to work. If that wage level is imposed, there would be unemployment, but the argument then goes that workers cannot stay in the rural areas because wages there are flexible, so they migrate to the cities.

The algebra is then explained further by the suggestion that those workers who are leaving agriculture believe they have a chance of getting one of the high-wage jobs in the cities and prefer this possibility to staying in rural slumber. This probability can be proxied with reference to something (such as the share of formal in-total employment in the urban areas), and the *expected*[8] urban wage for a migrant is then listed as an equilibrium because it must equal the rural wage (perhaps also adjusted in the same way). The algebra then works in terms of producing a solution to the model.

This conceptualization can then be used to discuss policy issues, which are developed in clear examples of apodictic argument. We note that the basic assumptions of the argument push these policy issues in certain directions. Ray discusses "the paradox of urban job creation," for in this view the informal sector is caused by wages that are too high in the formal sector, which slows the pace of migration. Reduce formal wages in some way, and migration will be able to accelerate (more low-paid jobs are better than fewer high-paid jobs). But, given the political assumptions underpinning the algebra, this will be opposed by planners and city authorities who are driven by the incentives that the model assumes operate upon them (such as the desire to preserve the "modern" urban sector), rather than being far-sighted and able to see the logic of the model and the need to keep formal sector urban wages down so as to stimulate economic growth.

What are the implied policy responses? One consideration is the idea of accelerating labor absorption in the formal sector *without* reducing wages, an unpopular option with workers and their supporters. But to slow the informal sector's growth in this way, the expected urban wage must rise as the system adjusts, because the share of informal employment falls, although offset by increased migration. In terms of the algebra, all this does is speed up the Lewis aspect of the process by accelerating accumulation, so a policy designed to reduce the size of the informal sector ends up increasing it (by simply pushing the underlying process). Indeed, in the model, the only way to cope is either to restrict migration (coercion) or reduce the formal–informal wage differential in some manner, along the way reducing the efficiency losses caused by it.

One interesting option for the latter is to subsidize labor in agriculture, which keeps people in the rural areas where the budgetary costs are likely lower. Conceptually, such subsidies could be set at a level that would put an end to the informal urban sector—that is, rather than migrate and risk failing to get a formal sector job, it makes economic sense to stay in the rural areas and enjoy the subsidies. This provokes questions about the rationality of human development as a development policy and the result of high levels of social policy spending in rural areas. If we consider issues of reproduction relations and the effects of gendered migration—women combine farming with work to reproduce the labor force by caring for children and old people, while men look for urban jobs—this would suggest that strategies that value light manufactures exports with a predominantly female factory labor force are missing something.

A minor point, of course, is who or what pays for the subsidy and/or social spending in the rural areas. Ray suggests a profits tax on firms repaid to them as a wage subsidy, an intriguing idea.

The Harris and Todaro model can also be used to think about other issues, including risk and risk aversion.[9] If the conceptualization is developed to include the idea of risk aversion that varies with income, this can be used to augment the model. We have a good example of the process of model selection and development described by Yonay (Chapter 6). Ray gives no clear empirical justification for including this in the model, but clearly it generated sufficient interest among economists for it to be developed. In this line of thinking, more risk-averse people are less likely to migrate. Here we can see DE treating "risk-averse" as a personal characteristic that is as given as natural hair color. By contrast, we may consider that social institutions influence risk aversion (such as providing access to free public health facilities) and that such institutions are constructed, not God-given. Note that Ray takes preferences as given, as exogenously determined, and compare this with North, who would more easily consider institutions as endogenous—that is, to be explained conceptually.

Ray then brings in institutions such as insurance, which relate to his view of rural society as possessing social capital based upon information and low mobility, but he does not consider such institutions politically. Similar issues arise from consideration of family structure and with similar problems. In Chapter 13 we will discuss a study that considers in detail an account of how views of risk change (Rutten 2000).

Conclusions

In this chapter we have seen two very different conceptualizations of structural divisions in poor countries. Juxtaposition of Ray and Rigg is useful to view how the particular conceptualizations frame discussions of cause and effect, and therefore policy options.

In combination, they offer ways of thinking about the economic logic of institutions, which ease problems related to the assumption of instrumental rationality: that institutions are given rather than constructed, and so their local contingency and their endogeneity may be ignored. This points to ways of avoiding the WC trap of policy advice to governments, which risks harming, mainly through the narrowness of its conceptualization, the non-economic prerequisites for better operating markets, which are arguably necessary for that very policy.

Questions for discussion

1. Research the history of agricultural export marketing organizations in developing countries, such as Tanzania, before and after independence. Do you think the problems are caused by the form they take (state-owned) or by the political context?

2. Discuss the differences in political styles and rhetorics associated with apodictic and other arguments. Which do you find more persuasive and why?

3. Discuss the policy and political implications of Lewis' conceptualizations compared with the approach of Agenor and Montiel (Chapter 3).

Notes

1   Rigg's quotation is from Chambers (1995: 180). Chambers is famous in DS for his influence upon the development of participatory techniques for creating knowledge and understanding, later formalized as *rapid rural appraisal* and *participatory rural appraisal*. While rarely discussed from a DE perspective, these can be understood as creating data situated within an empirics founded upon models of local behavior that are meaningful to those modeled. These empirics are thus likely to support both better explanations (in that they are persuasive locally) and avoid many errors that applied researchers are familiar with; above all, crass mistakes arising from reading-in to data priors drawn from familiar but exotic realities.

2   From this point of view, of course, poverty as measured does not necessarily rise or fall, as it is multidimensional; it may show an increase in one dimension and a fall in another.

3   A vast literature (Rigg himself is a good start) offers explanations for these situations, discussing how changes in the types of crops grown relate to changes in where and how they are grown and where the cultivators live. In these narratives the views of governments, often criticized as hostile to such populations for various reasons, are often given considerable attention. Scott (1998) is a good text for class discussion.

4   I am assuming that DS students are well aware of what is meant by modernization theory; DE students unaware of it can find it discussed in any standard development studies textbook.

5   I follow a common categorization here in suggesting that this is perhaps an East Asian phenomenon. There are many accessible accounts of how buoyant rural incomes combined with investment opportunities in other parts of the world.

6   Here we see the political importance of these ideas, for they may be used to justify extraction of resources from agriculture to support industry. The reader may want to review the discussion of the political importance of modeling by Agenor and Montiel in Chapter 3 (pp. 37–39).

7   Urban economists often make such arguments—for example, Ball and Sunderland (2001) referring to the labor markets of nineteenth- and early twentieth-century London.

184 Development economics

8   By this is meant the product of the chance of getting a job and the actual return
    if you get it. If the chance is one in four, and the income $100 a month, then the
    expected return is $25. This, in terms of the algebra, is the price that drives
    behavior.

9   Risk-averse people are those who think that, given the possibility of gaining, say
    $100, their chance of actually getting it is rather low. Thus the expected return
    is less. If this risk aversion is imagined to be a parameter, this can be included
    in the algebra of a model. It can also be used, as we saw, to generate an empirics
    and collect data (the example was the share of formal employment in total urban
    employment that could be used as a proxy for the chance of getting a formal job).

13 More visions of the developing economy

Rural economy

In this chapter we examine rural economy and in particular how land is treated in DE. In rural areas, land is a key factor of production and how access to it is secured is often highly important. By referring to land as a factor of production, we already risk, whether we are aware of it or not, taking sides in an area where political and social tensions often have considerable potential for conflict, often violent. This comes down to arguments about the reasons why owners of land are paid: it is not always clear what the owners are paid for doing nor who or what is doing the paying. In a poor area, the powerful people in a village may be many things apart from landlords: They may be local political leaders, they may have religious positions or influence, they may be involved in local development activities such as supporting mass education, and they may have important social and other links to the wider world, and these may involve activities (such as securing support in times of trouble) that are valued. Or they may be unpleasant and self-serving, and in consequence unpopular. The people who pay them rent may be their loyal followers, or they may be deeply hostile and supportive of radical political movements pushing for land reform and the break-up of landlords' estates.

These issues can pose considerable problems for economic analysis, precisely because they are often not economic in character. But we can learn much about DE from seeing how these tensions are managed. Central to this is the wider question of why factors of production (land, labor, and capital) receive the rewards they do. Land is particularly interesting.

Because land is not produced (though its productivity is, of course, influenced by investments in improvement, such as ditching, leveling, and soil upgrading), part of what is paid to its owners is not a payment for costs incurred in any simple sense. Land ownership in many societies (but not all) is associated with high (sometimes very high) social status and conspicuous consumption, as well as considerable political power, not only in local communities but also in national politics. To say that land is a factor of production (rather than, say, a basis for social position) is thus to risk arguing that it is best seen as an *input* to production, and so, like other inputs, deserves to be paid.

As we shall see, while Ray (1998) gives a thorough presentation of what mainstream DE has to say about the economics of land, he ends up with the position that, precisely because land ownership tends to confer political power, this is an area of analysis where the inability of DE to deal with noneconomic factors is for him particularly troubling. The core issue for him is land reform, for while the *economic* arguments for breaking up large landholdings may be strong, these may not offer acceptable explanations, as political and social (noneconomic) logics may better explain what is so often seen: stable patterns of landholdings that generate high rewards, both in terms of social and political position and well-being, for landowners.

In some parts of the world the economically powerful in villages or at higher levels are involved in a range of markets: they own land, lend money, sell inputs, and buy farmers' produce. As we shall see, Ray starts his discussion with an analysis of how ideas of market failure may be used to explain institutions—how land is held, how money is lent, and so forth—and then goes on to frame his analysis in terms that examine how markets may interact in a rural economy.

For mainstream DE the economics of land is, however, treated in terms of economic logics—algebraic models of markets and market failure—and arguments based on these techniques have been deployed at times to identify the pervasive economic costs of landlordism, as well as the benefits here as elsewhere of private property. The reader should recall examples of how economic arguments may usefully be seen as part of political debate (for example, Agenor and Montiel in Chapter 4). In the histories of rich countries, social position based upon rural land ownership was for a long time viewed by the mainstream as vital to social order. In these histories, the rise of other groups has often involved contestation, with historians taking sides. Conservatives have stressed the value of landed property as a basis for social hierarchy and order, while radicals have often opposed landed groups, especially if they have used political power in ways that are thought to hurt the interests of others (an example is the debate in the United Kingdom in the early nineteenth century over the Corn Laws, which put tariffs on imports of food, aiming to support farm incomes but pushing up urban labor costs).

Although historians and economists have differing views in such debates, that does not mean that nothing can be learned from their analyses. I also discuss accounts that point to the social determination of productivity-enhancing institutions, which avoid what some models predict would happen.[1] Central to this, as we shall see, are ideas that under certain conditions landowners will invest in their land, improving its yield and productivity. The question then is what institutional setups will encourage this. As we shall see, this discussion can have implications for concluding from model failure that behavior is irrational or that some intervention is preventing the logic of rational leading to good outcomes. In other words, noneconomic factors come into the picture with some force. I also refer to discussions about matters of subsistence—that is, access to economic resources sufficient to survive—and what people will fight for, mainly using the moral economy approach of Scott (1976).

Mainstream DE and markets in agriculture

As we saw in Chapter 10, it can be argued that a key element of DE is the definition of what matters—how the social is brought in. Here we may note how markets and institutions are defined by Ray (1998) as things that matter to economics:

> The goal [of economic analysis] . . . is to look closely at the markets and institutions that form the rural sector and deeply influence the lives of individuals who live in developing countries. In particular, we will study the markets for land, labor, credit, and insurance.
>
> (p. 403)

The thrust of this definition is the idea that what is important to the analysis is the operation of markets. This is worth thinking about, not least in terms of the tensions between WC/PWC and North's NIE, and also the issue of contingency and negotiation of interdisciplinary boundaries to cope with institutions and data creation. As elsewhere, the student should beware. But, as we have learned, Ray is nuanced, and we may read what he says about land reform (pp. 457–461); (we return to this topic later in the chapter).

As we have already seen, conceptually in DE, institutions intrude because of market failure due to such problems as lack of information and limits to what can be contracted (such as an inability to insure against all possible outcomes).[2] If these issues did not exist, then conceptually market exchange and prices would be adequate to secure balances between producers' desires to maximize profits and consumers' desires to maximize their well-being. Yet other common accounts, focusing upon how institutions arise, survive, are reproduced and replaced, place institutions in specific historical, political, cultural, and social contexts. DE tends to avoid this through its use of algebra. Ray notes that imperfection in markets is contagious, because markets are often interrelated. As we shall see, he brings the social in by discussing what happens when perfect competition assumptions are abandoned and, as we have seen, market failure arguments are deployed to show how intervention (perhaps by the state) is justified in terms of its ability to secure better outcomes. This is what Stiglitz is doing in his discussion of market failure (Chapter 9). Ray also remarks tellingly that most students will mainly have studied models of markets with perfect competition and no market failure.

In developing his discussion, Ray makes a strong link between informal institutions and market failure, suggesting that formal institutions correspond to situations where markets work and linking this to perfect competition conditions. This is a similar line of argument to others, such as Bardhan and Agenor and Montiel (Chapter 3): countries are seen as under-developed when the standard modeling framework is viewed as inapplic-able. Is this persuasive? Do you think that information asymmetries, externalities, and so on are more common in *informal* institutions? Do you have any reliable information to base this upon? Fforde (2005) cites evidence from experimental economics that suggests that gender and cultural differences are associated with behavior that is not well-modeled by the standard constrained maximization approach (see Chapter 22).[3]

Consider the examples of market failure given by Ray. He refers to a source of market failure we have already met: information problems, which mean that market price does not provide all relevant information to producers and consumers. For landowners, he links this to the issue of "unobserved actions"—the idea that landowners cannot monitor everything that their tenants or laborers do. In turn, he links this to problems of the enforcement of contracts; for example, because landlords cannot always *observe* tenants or workers, this leads to issues relating to the efficiency of contracts, which are then designed in ways to take account of this. The particular contract design is explained as an attempt to deal with the problem of information: that the landowner cannot know exactly what the tenant does with the land. An economic analysis may be developed that explains why contracts between landowners and their tenants and workers may take particular forms, such as sharecropping in which the landowner is paid, not a monetary rent, but a share of the crop. If the landowner lacks informa-tion about tenants or laborers, the argument goes, and there are costs to enforcing a contract, this analysis offers an explanation of the institutional arrangements (for example, sharecropping) that differ from simple contracts where the landowner receives a monetary amount—a rent payment. This is because the algebra may show that for reasons of lack of information it is more profitable to have such a contract than one that stipulates a rent payment. Institutions for DE are thus deeply associated with deviations from simply buying and selling at a price under conditions that appear to match perfect competition and explained in terms of market failure. Market failure explains the problems in enforcing contracts and so why certain specific arrangements arise instead, such as sharecropping.

We can now step back from this and consider whether all this—what Ray has to tell us about land and the economics of land—satisfies us. Is this a good explanation? Thus we may ask, for instance, whether this is really the most interesting thing about contract enforcement. Who, for example, controls the police? What are we likely to be told about local social attitudes and values—for example, the acceptability of local power relations—that underlie relations that determine access to land? And so on. Here class discussion may be useful, as we are confronting questions that relate to the judgment of an explanation: what makes for a good one?

Another issue Ray (1998) discusses with the market failure conceptualization is that of "unobserved types," which are concerned with lending contracts. This has to do with the costs involved in assessing borrowers and the likelihood of their repaying: what type of borrower is the farmer who is asking for a loan? He knows things that the lender does not know and may have incentives to lie. If the lender is also involved in areas such as fertilizer sales and the buying of agricultural products, it, in turn, probably knows things that the farmer does not. Conceptually, under these conditions, the agreed price of the loan may not reflect enough information: if the farmer cannot convince the lender he will repay, or the lender that it will not gouge the farmer at harvest, a mutually profitable transaction may not occur. Perhaps we observe these issues being overcome through social institutions such as a local church, which reduce the informational problems. Institutions, thus, are explained through ideas of market failure. The problems of asymmetric information are highlighted so as to explain institutions. For example, group lending schemes are thus explained "because the problem is that some borrowers are intrinsically bad risks" (p. 404).

Ray gives more examples of market failure and implicitly suggests that market failure is endemic: "Contracts based on indirect evidence create uncertainty . . . so . . . any lack of insurance constitutes an inefficiency" (p. 405). The inefficiency here is a departure from the situation that would occur if there were markets for everything, so that farmers and landowners could insure fully against all possible risks—the reference point of perfect competition. In some ways Ray seems to chafe at his own exposition. How should we take his remarks about slaves working on plantations, whose lives were good: "[B]ecause people could *own* them they treated them as a capital good and invested in them, particularly in the spheres of nutrition and health" (p. 405). He contrasts them and a "hire and fire" world where employers have little incentive to invest in their workers.

Ray gives more examples of market failure. He is interested in how land as well as credit markets operate in rural areas, for landowners are often involved in the provision of credit, especially in South Asia. Credit rationing may be caused by the lack of equity among borrowers, so that, if they go bust, their creditors bear the whole risk—thus interest rates are kept low to encourage low-risk borrowers. Landowners ration credit to their clients. This violates the standard perfect competition assumption that the supply of loan funds is infinite at the going interest rate. How are credit agreements then to be enforced? If there is no legal recourse, there will be "informal insurance [that rests] on an implicit nexus of social agreement, coupled with the sanction and disciplining of deviators from the agreement" (p. 406). Having prepared the ground, Ray moves on to discuss interactions between factor markets in the rural economy.

Land, labor, capital, and credit

Ray (1998) starts with a model where an unequal asset distribution is assumed (but not explained), such as labor endowments. A market then emerges to permit a mutually beneficial exchange: his basic vision is of capitalist farms hiring labor, each with a similar amount of rented land. He concludes that small family farms are most productive. A landlord maximizes revenues by increasing rents until farmers' profits are equal to each other (nobody earns more profits than anybody else), but Ray argues that the model has to include transactions costs for various reasons: most importantly, because land yields are uncertain, leading to institutions as adjuncts to the simple model of price-based buying and selling. And as landlords and tenants hire labor, they have supervision costs, and again institutions adjust. The perfect competition model is thus unsuitable, and the analysis needs to be adapted. Why do this analytically?

> As soon as we move away from the introductory textbook story of perfect markets, we run into transaction costs in several different markets. Whether a society exhibits a preponderance of land transactions or labor transactions therefore depends on the relative magnitude of these costs.
>
> (p. 411)

Recall that Ray starts with the assumption that there is an unequal distribution of land and labor, and asks how transactions will permit owners to increase their returns and laborers to increase their incomes. He argues that the choice between land and labor as the reallocated factor depends upon transaction costs. What this means is that transactions costs will explain whether we see a large number of small farms or large farms with many laborers. He observes that where land distribution is unequal, management may be concentrated because large landholders can better bear the supervision costs than small landholders. He says that agriculture in many Latin American countries reflects this.

Ray argues that this view of the rural economy is fundamentally correct —markets arise because holdings are unequal—but he accepts that this is simplistic. He considers other inputs—livestock is his first example. He argues that this market is likely to fail, because livestock will likely be overworked and used in time-bound operations (peak demand). Other markets then adjust to this market failure: "[A]nd so it is not surprising to find that the operational distribution of land often follows the operational distribution of bullocks" (p. 413).

His second example is credit. If this market is functioning well, many other inputs can be easily acquired; if not, farmers may have to lease out land and labor. From this discussion he posits a basic rule of analysis—that the more flexible markets adjust to compensate for the less flexible. But it is not exactly clear how we know that one market is more flexible than another or just why we should take the level of flexibility as a given. In part, his discussion suggests that this is a God-given characteristic, but we may also consider that those who are powerful want to make sure the relationships between various markets are in their interests. For example, while it may be hard to change rents, it may also be far easier to change wage rates, such as by influencing the relevant laws. If this were the case, arguably if there is a bad harvest, wage rates will be more flexible than rents, and so workers will be under pressure to bear a greater share of the economic costs. Conversely, if there is a good harvest, the position may be reversed.

It is striking, however, that Ray discusses the interactions between markets *separately* rather than viewing them as being part of a rural economy with important political, social, and cultural characteristics. Note his introductory sentence:

> [A]n economy can react to an unequal distribution of land in a variety of ways. The land market can open up . . . Alternatively, the labor market can become active. . . . We have already discussed how different considerations dictate the relative levels of activity in these two markets.
>
> A proper functioning of the land market is very important for the overall development of the economy.
>
> (p. 415)

Note Ray's rationalization for this:

> [B]ecause if there were heavy inequality people would leave for the cities and this would be politically, environmentally and economically unpalatable.
>
> Input markets exist in order to bring the ratios of various inputs into line for efficient production. Do land markets serve this purpose or are they limited in their operation?
>
> (p. 415)

Here again we see how for DE the criteria by which institutions are to be judged is their static economic efficiency. In his Chapter 12, on the economics of land in developing countries, Ray asks four questions, all concerned with judging the static efficiency of market setups:

1. How does the land rental market deal with inequalities in land ownership?
2. Are land rentals efficient? If not, what alternatives would do better?
3. Is inequality of ownership efficient?
4. If small farms are more efficient, why are they less common than one might expect?

While these arguments appear important, the standard proposed here is static efficiency. The old largely self-serving and ruthlessly pragmatic elite argument against "peasants, the Irish and kaffirs" was that they were *dynamically* inefficient; large capitalist farms would innovate more, improve the land, and so on.[4]

However, consider how Ray exposits his conceptualization. First he considers ownership and tenancy. He has to try to balance a rather general discussion with occasional references to reality. He points to the unequal distribution of land that is often found, which is more unequally distributed (as measured by such indices as the Gini coefficient—see Chapter 16) than income. Further, it tends to be measured as more unequal in many Latin American countries than in many Asian countries; in Africa, ownership is often weakly defined, and land is often held under forms of communal tenure, so that individual claims on plots are often weak. Ray reports that African data is often unreliable and skewed; for example, if legal limits to land concentration are instituted, many recorded as owners lose significant degrees of control and reward. A basic issue is explaining variation in the incidence of two basic forms of tenancy: fixed rent vs. sharecropping.

Ray's argument is that richer tenants prefer fixed-rent contracts "because the landlord is relieved of all risk" (p. 419). His focus here is upon risk as the key factor that drives institutional choice. We can see here the same analytical worries we encountered in the discussion of NIE (Chapter 11), which comes down to the use of the word "choice." How, we may ask, should we conceptualize choice? How does a society choose its institutions? Who exactly has control over land, how did this happen, and what power relationships exist that give some people political and social power, and so relative control over determining which institutions exist?

In this conceptualization, DE has problems maintaining control over disciplinary boundaries. As we have seen in DE, institutions refer to the consequences of market failure—to deviations from perfect competition so there is more to explain than adjustments of what is produced and consumed to maximize profits and consumer well-being. But here, where Ray is trying to discuss the rural economy, treating institutional choice in terms of solutions to market failure raises considerable problems as discussion of institutions almost inevitably seems to bring in historical, social, political, and cultural issues beyond economics. Arguably, under-standing the institutions of the rural economy will include not only choices such as that between fixed rent and sharecropping as economic response to market failure, but will also pose questions about enforcement agencies (are the police and militia neutral?), development resources (who gets the credits?), and local cultural attitudes (local belief, for example, that landlords should and will help in times of trouble).

Market failure as an argument for rural economic institutions

The basic DE analysis of the rural economy in terms of market failure has a long history. Alfred Marshall, the famous nineteenth-century economist,[5] argued that sharecropping generated inefficiency because it gives the tenant—who controls all other inputs—only a fraction of additional output. This for him implies that the tenant will undersupply effort compared with a situation where he pays a fixed rent.

Expressed algebraically, the analysis shows that (because land is a nonproduced input and so costless) economic surplus is maximized if the marginal productivity of labor equals its cost. The tenant has no interest in maximizing this surplus unless he gets paid to do so in some way (i.e. he is paid more than just for his labor). But if he pays a fixed rent, he will be induced to supply labor up to the point at which its marginal product equals its marginal cost. The farmer then gets 100 percent of the marginal return, and the picture is one of static efficiency.

So why could there be, in this conceptualization, sharecropping? Ray's argument now is in terms of risk. Risk-averse behavior implies that as income rises, so the marginal utility of money declines.[6] And farming is a risky business.[7] If a landlord rents to somebody poorer than him, the levels of risk aversion will differ between tenant and landlord. The landlord will be less risk averse than the tenant. For simplicity, Ray assumes that the landlord is risk neutral. He can then compare a fixed-rent contract with one where the landlord chooses a sharecropping arrangement in which his expected return is the same as the fixed-rent contract. This means that the expected return to the landlord is the same under the two different arrangements but for the tenant (assumed to be risk averse), the share-cropping contract is preferred. This is because, compared with the fixed-rent contract, the return to the tenant is *reduced* if the harvest is good but *increased* if the harvest is bad, and the landlord tends to prefer the security of the latter to the possible advantage of the former.

These ideas of risk aversion can be given added power in situations where farm yields are close to subsistence and consumption loans hard to obtain. If there is a bad harvest, to survive, families must confront hard decisions and the need to use resources they do not want to lose (such as the sale of children). This suggests that the downside risk for them to lose 100 kilograms of paddy is far higher than the upside gain of 100 kilograms of paddy. Landlords or richer peasants would value 100 kilograms more or less very differently. We therefore have an explanation for sharecropping. Further, this situation is understood to be one that is suboptimal, with efficiency losses not incurred by fixed-rent contracts. This is a clear argument that is useful to consider as we study DE. We can see what DE does, how it works, and how its metaphysical commitments drive it in a particular direction. The belief in the value of algebra tends to treat historical, social, cultural, and political factors as marginal, and the central thrust in explaining institutions is to relate them to arguments about market failure.

It is now useful to re-examine what Ray (1998) has to say about land ownership. He reported that we find great variations in the equality and inequality of patterns of land ownership in different places. Interestingly, he concludes that one of history's results was enormous inequalities in land holdings. He could have mentioned this earlier in his book in the context of endogenous growth models—that one result of history has been enormous inequalities in formal educational and other standards that are believed to lead to high incomes (Chapter 8)—but he did not. Four questions arise for him.

1. *Is this inequality in land ownership compatible with productive efficiency?* There has been much debate about relationships between farm size and productivity. Ray reminds us of the distinction between technical productivity (total factor productivity) and productivity in the sense of market efficiency. For the latter, resources will need to be allocated into production in ways close to the perfect competition outcome. A priori, it would appear that in terms of pure technology, there should be scale economies or constant returns—that is, smaller farms can never do better than large ones. But use of nonfamily labor creates severe incentive problems, and tenancy also creates incentive problems—in his argument, mainly because of variation in attitudes to risk. The incentive problems here are the familiar DE conceptualization that aspects of the situation prevent maximizing behavior by consumers and producers from leading to optimal outcomes. So there are a range of arguments that the use of family labor has advantages. The evidence suggests that land productivity is highest for family-owned and -run farms, then capitalistic ones, then lastly sharecropping.

2. *If there is an efficiency loss, can rental markets repair this?* Yes, says Ray. Those with larger holdings of land can rent out some or all of it in ways that improve economic efficiency by allowing those with more labor (than landowners) access to land.

3. *If land rental markets are inadequate to restore efficiency, would land sales from rich to poor solve the problem?* All the empirical evidence suggests that land markets fail, Ray says, and land is not sold to the poor by the rich. In part, this is because ownership of land conveys advantages when credit markets are imperfect. For example, land can act as collateral.

4. *If neither land rental markets nor land sales are sufficient to overcome these market failure issues, what is the role of land reform?* Land reform means transferring land when the recipient does not pay full value for it. As Ray argues, this is rare and unlikely to happen, because it "takes tremendous political will" (p. 458). This is a telling phrase as many of the issues flagged already about how societies chose their institutions lie behind it. The historical, cultural, social, and economic factors

associated with any given pattern of land ownership are very often powerful. Land ownership and tenancy relations may be deeply rooted in established and contested ideas of hierarchy and social order. Changing patterns of land holding through programs of land reform engage with these as well as other issues.[8]

One option is to provide tenants with a more secure title (not full ownership) that can still be used as collateral. We can conclude that Ray believes that land tends to be treated inefficiently for reasons that, at the end of the day, are not economic, but that economic arguments offer explanations as to why this may happen and what some of the consequences may be. He does not really seem satisfied with these economic arguments, which explain in terms of market failure.[9]

Before concluding, let me offer three different takes on matters relating to the rural economy.

Some alternative views

The following three readings offer different but interesting views.

Rational choice and revolution

Rutten (2000) studies the ways in which some Filipino farmers shifted their views and abandoned armed struggle "under the impact of counter-insurgency and political liberalization" (p. 241). They were initially willing to engage in armed struggle to secure various goals, including better land access. In some accounts, this is part of the wider historical process of extensive growth in Southeast Asia, an area in modern history abundant in land but with relatively few people (see Chapter 17). As poorer people opened up land and jungles were cleared for agriculture, the land was often taken from them by the more powerful. Rutten thus analyzes the acts of people organizing—or trying to organize—for political power to secure development, a political power that perhaps would be used to secure fair and well-operating markets. This reading may suggest viewing the economy in general and the rural economy in particular as an *effect* of non-economic issues that are political, historical, and cultural.

Do farmers really want "normal markets"? If not, why not?

Kung and Scott both present rationalities that appear on first reading to contradict standard conceptualizations, if not metaphysical commitments. Kung deals with this tension internally, while the "rational peasant" critique of Scott is by Popkin (Popkin 1979).[10]

Does land reallocation have negative long-term effects, as theory suggests that suboptimal land investments are due to the instability of land tenure?

Kung's approach (Kung 2000) points up particular ways in which DE theory operates and that often certain assumptions about behavior are crucial determinants of the direction the analysis takes (refer to the article by Simon discussed in Chapter 11). The issue here is the way in which these assumptions imply that behavior contradictory with that model is inconsistent with rationality, rather than simply inconsistent with those added-on assumptions. What is meant by rational behavior?

Kung asks basic questions about property. Specifically, what is the bundle of property rights associated with the behavior of the people he is studying —in this case, Chinese farmers? He does not look out of his window but collects data on his subjects' subjectivities. He traces their recent history— from Maoist upheaval and nastiness to the household responsibility system.[11] Farmers saw the land taken by large collective farms and then given back to them in various ways and under various forms. He creates data sets for a number of villages, which ask farmers what they think about issues such as landholding; his empirics is thus overtly subjective. He then conceptualizes in terms of process, finding that local implementation of the national system saw villages periodically reallocating land among themselves, behavior opposed by official policy, which envisaged a permanent allocation of land in the form of simple family property.

Kung argues that we can conceptualize family-based land tenure as not the only source of security of land access. He finds "a broader insurance according to an equal entitlement rule," (p. 704) where farmers believe that their village should in some way ensure that all families have some equal rights to land. He also found that 70 percent of reallocations are partial, involving households with changing membership. This meant that, as families gained or lost members through births, deaths, migration and so on, the village gave them more land or took land away. Why is this? He finds that village-wide reallocations are costly in terms of transactions costs and closes in by asking about farmers' perceptions of tenure security. In terms of present security, they value the idea that their plots will not be taken from them before the current leases expire. In terms of future security, they are often keen to keep the plots they have into another lease period.

From this, Kung concludes that farmers treat the reality of partial reallocations as an indicator for the continuing reality of land as a communal resource to which they have reliable access rights in the long term. They believe that loss of land, as family members leave, is offset by the cushion provided for their descendants by the continued existence of the village as a moral community to which their family belongs. Future security is, therefore, positively correlated with the incidence of partial reallocations. The impact of perceptions of collective property rights upon perceptions of security is beneficial to growth. Marginal changes to land allocations are made to cope with changing household dynamics, which works to reduce perceptions of risk and so improve growth. So, contrary to how theory is typically used (with empirical assumptions), he concludes that land reallocation is economically valuable. Farmers are rational to resist the complete allocation of property rights to them envisaged by policy-makers.

The moral economy

The final example of how concepts of land property can be developed comes from a classic text that pushed the idea of a "moral economy" (Scott 1976). This was the idea that farmers near subsistence would act collectively to protect social institutions that could offset risk. If they protect them by violent resistance against perceived threats, this is a theory of peasant rebellion. Scott analyzes the logic of institutions and how they are realized in terms of meaning and values. This refers to the idea that there is a moral aspect to the economy: particular arrangements are viewed as good ones and others as bad. Markets are lacking or incomplete, and this helps to explain farmers' behavior, as we can link, for example, the absence of markets for insurance against harvest failures to the value placed upon social institutions that mobilize communities and provide them with the resources in terms of communal property to deal with natural calamities that face all members. Scott does not bother with this DE argument much, perhaps as it has no easy empirical referent. Subsistence then easily becomes something that is associated with a moral claim: Members of the community have rights to enough food to survive. Forms of exploitation and/or dependent relations that offer security may well be preferred by the population to others and given positive moral value.

In examining farmers' armed risings in colonial Vietnam, Scott argues that people may not be rebelling to secure equality but to secure justice seen as consistent with inequality but providing subsistence—food during hard times. People support local social arrangements that are arguably unfair because they believe these arrangements will ensure their survival if there is a natural disaster. This would be one argument, in other circumstances, for paying rent properly to a local landlord who can be relied upon to provide or secure support in hard times. Of course, much depends upon farmers' own judgments. The moral economy argument thus suggests that farmers may have reason to support economically inefficient forms of social organization (according to DE) because they appear to be in their interest. We saw similar arguments when, for farmers close to starvation, not having a fixed rent to pay made considerable sense. The reader may consult Popkin (1979) to see how Scott's conceptualization was challenged and may then be interested to find and read the wide range of later comments on the debate.

Conclusions

The standard DE explanation of rural economy and the economics of land relies upon market failure and so issues that can be treated within the standard conceptualization. This permits DE to preserve its relative autonomy from other disciplines, but, as we see from Ray's own account, is perhaps perceived by him as inadequate. I tend to agree. DE follows the logic of microeconomics and market failure in treating deviations from optimal situations in terms of market failure—explained with reference to characteristics such as risk aversion that can be treated ahistorically.

Like the juxtaposition of Rigg and Ray in Chapter 12, shifting perspective to study differing rationalities opens the way to economic analysis that can take into account the overriding importance of "the polity," in North's terms. Such analyses are clearly explanatory rather than attempting the apodictic exposition we find in Ray's treatment of market failure, for example, in explaining sharecropping.

Questions for discussion

1. Is Ray's exposition weak in explanatory terms, and if so why?

2. Do you agree with the common view that land access usually provides political and social position and power? And what implication does this have for your views of what DE has to say here?

3. Where can an understanding of DE conceptualizations add to explanations of the politics of rural society and economy?

Notes

1 The reader may have come to see how DE views institutions as *adjuncts* to markets; a perfectly functioning market (perfect competition) in this sense is not an institution. This may be baffling, but recall the arguments in Chapters 9 and 10, especially the discussions of market failure and the importance to NIE of the idea that it is transactions costs that explain institutions. In the simple algebraic model where perfect competition exists, there are, in this way of looking at things, no institutions.

2 If this is slightly baffling, recall that the central point here is the need to articulate a relationship between the algebra of the economic model and some account of reality (see Chapter 9).

3 The literature here is large—for example, Elson (1999).

4 The historical contexts of these arguments are fascinating and important but not something one reads much about in Ray. The central argument for enlightened land ownership that created rental income was that it created sustained improvement in land yields far more than small-scale farmers, dismissed as peasants, uneducated, and ignorant (as in the case of the largely dispossessed Catholic Irish in eighteenth-century Ireland, or Africans in colonies or dependencies—kaffirs, in the old Afrikaaner South African idiom). It takes little thought to realize the considerable social and political force exercised by the powerful in these historical contexts.

5 Marshall pretty much invented the microeconomic analytical framework that analyzed the behavior of firms and consumers in terms of their adjustments of output and purchase levels so as to balance marginal changes in profits and welfare through price signals and so maximize profits and welfare (Chapter 9).

6 As we may learn as children, "a bird in the hand is worth two in the bush."

7 Note that Ray treats risk as exogenous, but we may ask, if this is caused by technology, the weather, or by social arrangements, whose interests are served if the situation stays risky or becomes less risky?

8 Readers may wish to research historical accounts. I recommend at least examination of the compulsory purchase of the land of absentee landlords in Ireland by the British government in the late nineteenth century, as this was part of the background to the early debates among economists on land ownership (Marshall has already been cited), and also the US push for land reform in Japan after World War II, as in other areas including South Vietnam, where this effectively constructed a "middle peasantry" who then, after 1975, confronted Communist attempts to put them into cooperatives (Nguyen Thu Sa 1991).

9 This is suggested by his discussion of two case studies of land reform, which implies that politics is important, probably far more so than economics—and then leaves us somewhat hanging in the air. I do not repeat these here as this is not central to DE.

10 Just what Popkin means by a "rational peasant" has generated a wide literature; it may be thought of as close to the ideas in DE that assert that good explanations of people's actions should be framed in terms of their attempts to maximize their well-being. Many classes on peasants have required students to compare Scott's idea of a 'moral economy' with Popkin's ideas, which are overtly critical of Scott.

11 This was a system used in much of Chinese agriculture as central planning gave way to a market economy; farmers stayed within their collectives but farmed as independent farms, with each household given responsibilities and rights to sell directly on markets.

14 Determinants of economic policy in developing countries
Model and muddle revisited

In this chapter we address some possible answers to the question of what determines economic policy in practice. So far, we have seen how DE tends to preserve its core view of the centrality of economic growth in development by adding on various factors and by treating the ideal of perfect competition as a reference point. This is consistent with its attempt to adopt what it thinks is a natural science methodology, so that, in the view of DE, failure to adopt what is said to be correct policies is best seen as simply a failure to understand the truth of the matter, as DE states it. We saw Ray express dissatisfaction with his own exposition of what DE had to say about the rural economy (Chapter 13). We may put this beside similar problems using the standard DE algebra to analyze rural households noted by Bardhan and Udry (Chapter 9). The Australian experience with the application of such models to farms was also negative, and in some accounts the models were therefore abandoned (McCown and Parton 2006a and 2006b). This raises once again the question of how we understand why certain economic policies prevail and others do not. If we question the idea that an economic policy can be known to be correct, this probably means that we need to look beyond economics to understand what determines policy choice, and this, as we have seen, is not something DE tells us much about.

In this chapter I want to introduce some oxygen to this discussion. DS and common sense suggest many ways of thinking about how policy is determined. DS students will be familiar with basic politics and political economy arguments about interest groups, such as those employed in the formal urban sectors identified in the models of Chapter 12, and the possible roles played by exotic ideas imported into development discourses in developing countries themselves (where we would expect DE to play a major role). I do not intend this to be an exhaustive list. It would be unwise to ignore situations in developing countries where economic policy has been relevant, even by default. But how should its importance be gauged?

Histories refer to efforts to implement ISI, protection, and so on (often by recently independent ex-colonial states); to efforts to disband ISI in favor of WC policies; and in recent years to gathering senses of crisis, reference to failed states, and so on. So far, I have stressed the nature of different positions in DE (the "how"); this is not the same as the question of "why" certain positions prevail. It is easy to conclude that any attempt to understand why a particular economic policy is adopted is not likely to be simple (L&P 2002, at the least). In this chapter I want to introduce some ideas as to *why* this might be the case. The reader may recall Dunn's view (2000) that this is likely to be complicated (Chapter 10). As he put it, referring to the shift from anti-market to pro-market positions in the 1970s and 1980s: "It is extraordinarily difficult to see clearly and steadily quite what is at stake in this drastic shift. . . . Some of the judgments required are essentially causal. . . . [They] are enormously complicated and inherently highly uncertain" (p. 73).

Determinants of economic policy in developing countries

If one takes the view that DE is not best treated in the same way as a predictive natural science, this implies some reflection on possible deter-minants of economic policy, and this, of course, treats DE as part of the game, rather than disinterested observers. But are we likely to get clear answers to questions about why a particular policy is adopted or answers that have persuasive empirics? One useful entry point is the combined effects of belief in certain visions of development, the role of economic growth in development, and the various ways in which DE prescribes the role of the state.

We have encountered the idea that much DE growth theory is usefully seen as reflecting aspects of what DS would call modernization theory: that development is about aligning change *toward* the norms (often but not entirely economic) said to exist in rich countries. Ha-Joon Chang (2003) argues that this ignores evidence that today's rich countries tend to advocate different social and economic change processes and development strategies than those seen in their own countries when they were developing (see Chapter 1).

In thinking about the determinants of economic policy in developing countries in this chapter, I discuss three approaches:

1. *A model of economic policy determination*: Thorstein Veblen and his implications for modern developmentalism (Olson 1998). Here policy is seen as the outcome of social behavior and predatory competition. At this stage of the book, this view may be refreshing.
2. *Models, fads, and economic governance*: implications for economic behavior and economies (L&P 2002 [again]). I focus on a study by William Easterly (Easterly 1999) on the influence of now outdated, so-called gap models of economic growth on the behavior of international lending organizations such as the World Bank. These models, as we shall see,

focus upon the need to manage various gaps, such as a shortfall in domestic savings relative to desired investment in the national economy. Here policy can be seen as an outcome of a combination of past (now discredited) economic theory and institutional interests. Again, at this stage of the book this study brings some fresh air into the room.

3. *Socialization of risk and the heuristic emergence of economic policy belief sets*: focusing upon a study by John Zysman utilized by Wade (Zysman 1983 and Wade 1988). Here policy can be seen as the outcome of learning processes in different institutional contexts with a stress on different patterns of risk bearing and their implications. This more dialectic approach is also refreshing but poses the problem that such learning processes may simply empower students to reach the teacher's correct answer.

Let us start with a look at what a Veblenesque view suggests. One of the original institutionalists, Veblen invented the idea of "conspicuous consumption." An eccentric, he did most of his creative work in the United States in the late nineteenth century, when social differentiation was marked.

Veblen and his implications for modern developmentalism

With Veblen, policy is seen as the outcome of social behavior and competition. What entry points are there to apply such ideas to development? A central issue, which is obvious on reflection, is the importance of *comparability* in development discussions and also the frequent incidence of competition among countries, or, probably more accurately, those who set policy. We see this in the various league tables that rank countries in terms of their success or failure at meeting international targets. These include GDP growth for those economically inclined or the extents to which countries or regions have managed to meet the Millennium Development Goals agreed by members of the United Nations in 2000,[1] or have been successful in attracting FDI, and so forth. Physical manifestations of such competition— modern roads, bridges, cities, export zones, and so on—fit well with ideas about modernization.

Conceptualizing drivers of human behavior along these lines leads to reflection upon the reasons for consumption. Generally, DE assumes that consumption exists to satisfy personal or family wants, just as money is made to finance businesses and taxes collected to finance development. Veblen provides a rather appealing framework for thinking differently.

Veblen himself is writing at a time when "rentier" and land-owning groups were still important in defining lifestyles.[2] "New money" tended to treat them as the objects of "invidious comparison," in Veblen's phrase, as new money sought to emulate these two groups. Thus leisure, a key marker of lifestyle, became a sought-after good, to be consumed either directly or vicariously through family members such as wives (who did not work, dressed well, and were out in society). In this way of thinking, consumption is not entirely instrumental for our own direct needs, but exists in part simply to impress others and to compete. This is because we seek to emulate others and compare ourselves with them. In this comparison we seek to show that we are better off than they are. Veblen thus distinguishes between two sets of drives:

1. Predatory—a desire to be viewed as successful.
2. Purposive—wanting activity to be purposive and instrumental.

These can be contradictory. If consumption is (in part) driven by emulation, it will tend to be visible (conspicuous) and also, because it is predatory and desires to show off "pecuniary prowess" (how rich one is), it will be wasteful, since conspicuous consumption is purposive, as it is thought to imply greater wealth and status. Typically, goods can be used for both ceremonial and instrumental purposes (e.g. cars). Note that over time, as a society becomes on average richer, poorer people have more to spend, and the middle classes can start to buy goods used for ceremonial purposes. Thus status goods become basic needs, and so to maintain their social position and their capacity to act as a reference group, richer people must not only increase their own spending but also develop new goods for their own conspicuous consumption. The situation is dynamic.

This broad stance can be used to think about development, and this is done nicely by Olson (1998). She argues that Veblen's logic still applies contemporarily, but there have been important changes in the reference group for emulation. In his time, this was the wealthy leisure class of the United States and Western Europe in the late nineteenth century. Now, standards are defined (for the moment) by the developed countries for the rest of the world. Global capitalism promotes cross-cultural emulation. Because invidious comparisons are made between people of different cultures, status in the global community is increasingly linked to the ability to successfully emulate the West. This, of course, links, for DS students, neatly to modernization theory, and we can recall Stiglitz's views on what constitutes good political development and his praise for his own society's particular norms (Chapter 9).

Olson (1998) argues that this situation is part of global capitalism, pushed by multinationals and international institutions such as the World Bank. She states that the "balance of world power is held by Western political elites and the corporate interests they represent" (p. 192), and she stresses the ways in which global markets and marketing reinforce pressures for families and individuals in non-Western countries to emulate Western lifestyles; that emulation is most advanced in Asia, based upon a desire for pecuniary prowess. She notes that lifestyle spending is increasingly waste-ful, and we may recall issues such as the extreme size of houses and cars, not to mention food portions, and that, while global tastes are exported, communities often may feel they suffer greatly when incomes are not sufficient to permit emulation.

Coming to the point that interests us here—the determinants of development policy—she argues that by looking at public sector projects (for example, buildings, dams, and military spending), we can see that "there are numerous types of public assets which are symbolic of pecuniary status in the global community" (p. 198)—that is, that they can be understood in terms of the desire to compete with other countries and other elites, through visible and wasteful spending. Of course, not all spending on buildings, dams, and so forth is wasteful. So, by distinguishing between instrumental and ceremonial, she offers a way in which we can analyze such projects and why they exist. She opens the door to the idea that at least some of the perceived value of such projects is in their symbolic value *to those who treat such projects as means for acquiring developmental status*. And she can ask: Who benefits and in what ways?

Posing the question this way allows her to conceptualize the arguments for and against certain development projects. Thus, non-instrumentality is neither a market failure, nor a mistake, nor related to the requirements of capitalist class conflict. Rather, it stems from the desire to compete through emulation, with Western lifestyles and Western development as the goals, since these are the sources of *reference lifestyles*—the standards by which people judge their own social positions.

Olson points to two dangers with this situation:

1. Reductions in conspicuous consumption are difficult, because they imply that the predators—those who use conspicuous consumption as a means to gain advantage—lose.
2. Ecological arguments suggest that current reference lifestyles cannot be adopted too widely. They are too expensive, too damaging to the environment, and in many ways too disruptive of global structures.[3] Perhaps pecuniary values will then become less important, compared with purposive ones.

We may also ponder, early in the twenty-first century, on what may happen if the reference lifestyle itself changes its reference point to something non-Western.

Olson's analysis is a neat one, convincing up to a point. It is worth thinking about how much spending both by individuals and governments —the latter most important to thinking about development policy—is ceremonial and how much instrumental, for the distinction is perhaps not so easy to apply. A central implication of her position is the question of what determines development policy and economic development strategy. To put it more technically, how do we think of policy as *endogenous*? We can note the way in which DE seems to follow global trends that perhaps are related more with the issues and concerns of rich countries, where for DE the relevant intellectual activities are mainly sited.[4] One way to discuss relationships between DE positions and their policy implications is to ask to what extent the stances taken by important organizations such as the World Bank have to do with personality or position: how stable are an organization's preferred policies with respect to shifts in personnel? It is often argued by the recipients of aid, as well as students of it, that the pace of development activities is strikingly linked to patterns of staff rotation and career development. This leads us neatly to Easterly (1999) and the incentives operating on World Bank staff and their origins in DE "1962."

Models, fads, and economic governance: the World Bank and gap models

Easterly (1999) argues that policy is best seen as the outcome of a combination of past economic theory and institutional interests. He discusses so-called gap models and their use to calculate the external finance requirements of developing countries that are clients of international lending agencies such as the World Bank. He discusses problems with these models and their lack of persuasive empirical foundation, and contrasts this with their continued use.

Gap models

Chenery and Strout (1966) developed the Harrod–Domar work to produce the "two-gap" model. This has two key features:

[1] Investment requirements to achieve a given growth rate are proportional to the growth rate by a constant known as the Incremental Capital–Output Ratio (ICOR).
[2] Aid requirements are given by the 'financing gap' between the investment requirements and the financing available from the sum of private [external] financing and domestic saving.

(p. 424)

This is obviously a convenient model if you are in the business of supplying and arranging development loans. Easterly takes a highly rationalist position (he assumes that rational argument matters a lot), reading into this two testable hypotheses:

1. Aid will go into investment one-for-one—that is, there is no **fungibility** (see the list of special terms on p. 323), so that an additional $1 million lent is actually spent on $1 million of investment.
2. There is a fixed linear relationship between growth and investment in the short run—that is, you can assume the ICOR is fixed.

He reports that 90 percent of country desk economists at the World Bank use this model, in which ICOR and prior investment determine GDP, and quotes from many World Bank country reports that use the model to sell the need for external funding. We need to recall that the World Bank, like other international financial agencies, usually has to borrow in order to lend and needs bilateral support for its recurrent funding and for finance of technical assistance and resources to develop lending proposals. We can also note that most international lending institutions do the same, effectively stressing the short-run need for both investment and aid for growth; Easterly quotes the International Monetary Fund (IMF), the European Bank for Reconstruction and Development (EBRD), the Asian Development Bank (ADB), the International Labor Organization (ILO), and also the Swedish International Development Cooperation Agency (Sida). Easterly points out that gap models sit uneasily with WC views that stress efficiency in resource allocation (rapid TFP growth) rather than inputs; all in all, it is easy for Easterly to attack the gap models:

- There is "fungibility." Additional funds lent to the country are not expected to link directly to additional investment spending, as, for example, this may free funds for the government to spend on other purposes.
- The presence of aid frees up local resources that can be used elsewhere (for example, hospitals vs. weapons factories).
- Aid is free, so recipients are encouraged to consume it rather than treat it as capital that should generate a return (for example, higher civil service salaries vs. hospitals).
- If funding comes from a perceived gap, people in the developing country, and/or those keen on lending to them, have an incentive to make sure that a gap is found—for example, no aid equals no hospitals.
- There is no reason to assume that the ICOR is fixed in the short run.

We could also ask what has happened to macrodynamics and changes in the level of capacity utilization (the basis of Keynesianism). And we can also ask whether reforms or other changes may be leading to sharp shifts in the ICOR.[5]

Easterly empirically tests the financing gap model and finds that nobody has ever bothered to do this (because by the time the data existed to do so the models had fallen out of fashion). He also finds little correlation between gross domestic investment as a share of GDP and Official Development Assistance (ODA) as a share of GDP; only 7 percent of his sample of eighty-eight countries showed a positive and significant correlation—two of these were Hong Kong and China, with little ODA. High growth episodes are not well correlated either with prior investment or prior increases in investment (the year before). This relates to arguments that investment is necessary but not sufficient, and Easterly reconstructs what would have happened to Zambian per capita GDP if the ICOR had remained stable: today it would be an industrialized country.

Why does Easterly think the two-gap model is still used? He provides four hypotheses:

1. It is a handy back-of-the-envelope calculation that justifies aid flows as necessary for growth.
2. Everybody does it.
3. There is no profit for an individual who comes up with an alternative.
4. Incentives in the literature do not encourage testing old theories, so up until Easterly nobody bothered.

We may note that he does not offer any empirical evidence for these explanations. He concludes that "Academic researchers should devote more research effort to critiquing models used in practice" (p. 437). Because what he is observing uses vast amounts of money, this short and accessible article tells us something about rational argument in the context of development bank lending.

If Easterly argues that institutional convenience led to a striking stasis in working methods in this case, we turn now to examine ideas about how economic policy may be understood as emerging from and within patterns of learning-by-doing, or *heuristics*.

Socialization of risk and the heuristic emergence of economic policy belief sets

Wade (1988) and Zysman (1983) conceptualized policy as the outcome of learning processes in different institutional contexts with a stress on risk bearing and its implications. The core conceptualization is the effects of different patterns of the "socialization of risk." This underpins ideas about how the economic policy mindset of developmental East Asian EOG emerged and characteristics of it. This has value, in that you can learn much by asking similar questions in other contexts: How do people learn? What are they learning? It also should encourage explanations that make sense to the people who are being explained. Note that Wade is writing rather early (1988), which is consistent with his remark that many believe that inherent market failure is rare and usually caused by government action or inaction (action to restrict market access and inaction in failing to establish a capital market) (p. 129).

These views are clear from the other contributors to the book in which Wade (1988) appeared—*Achieving Industrialization in East Asia* (Cambridge University Press). In this book Wade stands out as unorthodox, for the other contributors assert the value of markets and advise against state intervention. Wade disagrees and presents his arguments in greater detail in

Wade (1990). His text is also part of the contemporary debate about the "East Asian Miracle" (Chapter 18):

> [People argue that t]he superior economic performance of the East Asian capitalist countries has gone with a relatively neutral policy regime: the inferior economic performance elsewhere went with varying degrees of distortion. The causality is from distortions, or lack of them, to results. . . . Whilst [this view] is correct in some respects, it is also, I argue, wrong in others. In particular, Japan, Taiwan and the Republic of Korea have not maintained a close approximation to a neutral policy regime over the post-war period. They have all actively fostered the development of many new industries.
>
> (pp. 129–130)

Central to his argument is the idea that such governments possess a strong capacity for selective intervention. They command a powerful set of policy instruments and enjoy a certain politics that influences how the state is organized and how it is linked to other major economic institutions. In many ways they are successful. Wade asks where this intervention capacity comes from, and his answer balances between a functional conceptual pole and a reference to historical accounts. Although he is a sociologist, he is drawing upon Zysman, who is a political scientist. Wade is concerned about what instruments these governments have and why.

He starts with Zysman's distinction (1983) between capital-market and credit-based financial systems. In the former, firms get external finance mainly from issuing shares, while, in the latter, such funds come from banks. If a group of firms has difficulties and threatens to go bankrupt, this situation has conceptually different implications for the two systems. In the first, so long as the shares are held by a range of agents who can bear the risk, if they lose money that is the end of it. In the latter, when the firms' liabilities take the form of bank loans, there may be wider problems. If the companies cannot repay the banks, and bank depositors start to worry, there may be a run on banks. This amounts to a systemic risk and, with considerable historical experience, one of the learned functions of governments is to require the central bank to advance loans to the banks to tide them over. This is the so-called "lender of last resort" function. The US Federal Reserve was set up, despite political opposition in the United States, after experience with such bank runs and closures during the Great Depression of the 1930s. The basic point made by Zysman and taken up by Wade is that if firms are securing external finance through banks in this way, part of the commercial risk is borne by the state; the socialization of risk in this way pushes officials to learn how to cope and exploit the situation.

Thus in the latter situation, which is not uncommon outside Anglo-Saxon countries, issues about the particular way of sharing risk inherent in such systems provides opportunities for institutional learning (see also Johnson

1982). Zysman's main point is that there is institutional *endogeneity*, referring to the period up until the 1980s. Institutions can develop in two basic ways: banks can become independent of government (for example, Germany) or dependent on government (East Asia). In all cases, governments were wary of the growth of nonbank financial institutions, because this was thought to weaken the dominance of the banks. Taiwan and South Korea used direct control—state ownership of banks—while the Japanese banks relied heavily upon the government for access to credit.

Wade discusses the advantages of such situations. He argues that successful intermediation allows higher investment than just relying upon retained profits, because rapid intersectoral resource mobility, guided by the government (direct credit allocation and reallocation) is then possible. He argues that short-term thinking is avoided because the creditor is locked into the debtor.

More fundamentally, such a political–industrial strategy requires a political base, and so governments use it to build up social coalitions. Again, we can note how odd these ideas may appear to those who believe that markets should on the whole be left alone, with little state intervention. But what is driving this explanatory framework is the idea that government, under these circumstances, has to participate in the socialization of risk. Bank credit entails systemic and other risks (because of high firm leverage or the existence of highly correlated risk—that is, subsectors where firms are vulnerable to trade turndowns). But what happens next? How does government cope with taking on roles in the socialization of risk? It is encouraged to devise interventions that allow it to bail out firms and/or sectors if it chooses to do so, to develop intimacy with company management, to create an ability to discriminate between responsible and irresponsible lending, and so on. All this requires the government to be able to offset the misleading credit price signals that derive from the distortions its own policies have created, by means of knowing which sectors are most profitable. To do this, Wade argues, it has to *learn* how to intervene, and, he concludes, in East Asia, the government was often very successful at doing so.[6]

We may link this idea to how and why certain polities develop and learn (or developed and learned) and others did not in the 1962 world of ISI and protection. In this context perhaps, we could reflect on the idea that Africa and Latin America did not benefit from the Cold War in the same way as the Asian Tigers, since, unlike them, they were not granted access to US domestic markets until far later (Johnson 1998).

Wade completes his analysis by pointing out that companies must be stopped from accessing overseas financial markets that enable them to avoid the various economic and political mechanisms upon which their governments rely:

- Control over the cost of capital.
- Sectoral allocation of credit.

- Effects of large-scale inflows and outflows upon domestic macro-economic stability and thus upon resource allocation and government power.
- Effects of such loss of control upon government's ability to impose politically effective burden-sharing.

In other words, exposure to the global economy weakens the role and meaning of domestic political processes. In this study, written over a decade before the 1997 crisis, we can note Wade's sense of frustration with the arguments and debate over what he calls neoclassical economists (rather like the 1982/WC views). This in part stems from his difficulties in arranging as powerful an argument as the WC position, when what he is really interested in is contingent and messy.

Conclusions

These three readings offer food for thought—for example, regarding the possible presence of inertia and inconsistency in economic thinking when it suits interests such as the lending needs of some international development banks, and the lack of systematic measures to investigate practice (Easterly). The readings encourage looking at practice in order to fit the slogan "Watch what they do not what they say." And it encourages us to look at the question of drivers: just what drives the economics within any particular development policy. Clearly, DE's desire to maintain its relative autonomy from other disciplines poses questions here.

We are encouraged also to think about the importance of learning and cognitive development in the understanding and study of any particular group seeking to attain intentional social change (such as through economic policy and economic development) within a given historical context.

Questions for discussion

1. Can Veblen, as reinterpreted by Olson, be linked to an ascriptive interpretation of cause–effect arguments (see reference to Stoecker in Chapter 5)?

2. Discuss the impact of the World Trade Organization (WTO) upon how officials may learn about the implications of risk socialization and how they can avoid trouble and exploit opportunities.

3. Discuss the incentives issues underlying Easterly's study. For example, what implications could there be for a change in intervention logics of the pace and rhythm of typical career patterns, political cycles, and so on?

Notes

1   See www.un.org/millenniumgoals.
2   The language here is old but the concepts topical. "Rentier" is an old term used to refer to people living off returns from capital investments, such as dividends and bonds. The modern North American equivalent is the "trust fund" and the associated "trust funder." Keynes's remark about the euthanasia of the rentier referred to the collapse of their incomes that would happen if, in a depression, monetary policy pushed interest rates down close to zero. This process increases pressure over time as bonds mature and the reinvestment of the capital at low interest rates cuts yields (old bonds pay more in cash terms as the coupon is fixed). Veblen's remarks about wives have their modern echo in the phrase "trophy wife."
3   It seems to me obvious that the vast processes of urbanization and adoption of Western lifestyles in countries such as China, which started in the 1980s, are, in global terms, quite unsustainable. And much of the global economic turmoil of the first decade of the 2000s was to do with the international macroeconomic imbalances associated with these massive changes in China and other rapidly growing parts of the developing world.
4   DS students are likely aware of the literature on "epistemic communities"— groups sharing common patterns of knowledge production. It does not take long to trace the institutional affiliations of expert contributions to important documents such as the World Bank's annual development reports.
5   This is common in countries undergoing major systemic change, such as that from plan to market. If so, this argues strongly that the ICOR will be changing, perhaps a lot.
6   The classic text on how the Japanese did this is Johnson (1982), in his study of Japan's Ministry of International Trade and Industry (MITI).

15 Policy debacles and their legacies

In this chapter I take the stance of the last chapter and develop it further, using two case studies. Both argue that economic analysis led to various actions, based upon policy advice that was wrong, which failed to have the intended positive results in terms of economic growth and development. This raises the issue of how to cope with such accounts. Ferguson (1997) looks at Lesotho and focuses squarely upon the role of economic analysis in serving the interests of developers/donors. His approach shows how such analyses can misrepresent reality. As the second case study, I take the Philippines (Bello 1982 and 2000; de Dios 2000), because the literature is relatively rich and provides contrasting views of what happened and the role of economic policy.

Examining studies that argue that DE's policy advice resulted in effects not only contrary to what was promised, but arguably bad ones, lends itself to augmentation through student presentations and class discussion. In considering topics for discussion it is important to avoid simply focusing upon arguments that the central issue is mistaken policies, in part because, as we have seen, in predictive terms there is little good reason to trust any policy advice. Also, accounts of policy are situated within extremely complex histories, both of the arguments themselves and of what the arguments are meant to be about, and, as we have seen, much debate attempts to secure support by criticizing "the other position." Such case studies face similar challenges as the DE analyses they are criticizing: problems in prediction and in generating persuasive accounts of what happened and why. What these two case studies offer are clear examples of *unexpected* outcomes. In looking at others, it may also be useful for students to attempt to gauge the *cognitive impact*—that is, the apparent effects of the various histories upon both public and scholarly opinion. One interpretation of the L&P "2002" confusion is precisely that such histories encourage skepticism and reinforce the view that "if you are not confused you are misinformed"—in other words, that apodictic argument and its close relatives are risky.

This chapter is rather short, which could offer the opportunity in class for examination of other relevant case studies. Examples could include failure of other policy sets than those examined here, such as Soviet-style development (Fforde and Paine 1987), ISI, or other similar examples. This is a rather large field. An interesting area to discuss is reform failures that can be explained by "the right reform but in the wrong time or place"; an example is Mexico (Lowe and Kenney 1999).

It is also worth thinking seriously about the likely legacies of these two case studies for human behavior. Such stories are familiar to people in DS and powerfully erode the authority of standard DE prescription. Arguably, these accounts increase perceptions of the risks associated with any given set of policy advice and enhance skepticism about the reliability and respectability of any confident rationality associated with policy advice (recall the quotes from Wolf and Camdessus in Chapter 1).

Lesotho

Ferguson (1997) comes from the post-development tradition in DS and attacks the pretensions to any true rationality of the aid community in Lesotho, a small African nation that suffered considerable external pressure from the end of the eighteenth century. From 1966, the country became an independent kingdom entirely surrounded by the then white-dominated Republic of South Africa.

Ferguson starts from a statement about the aid community's failure to meet stated objectives and develops this by arguing how donor economic analysis of Lesotho was both wrong and served donor interests. Ferguson reports what donors said about Lesotho—that it is a traditional subsistence peasant society—and then uses this to show how the description under-pinned justifications for certain aid activities. We can recall the powerful tendencies within DE to argue that what makes poor countries poor is the absence of the well-functioning markets that DE usually conceptualizes as markers and drivers of development seen as economic growth. Thus, Ferguson views donors as conceiving their mission as one of developing markets where there are none and creating an empirics of a society made up of subsistence farmers to justify this. He then argues that this analysis of the situation in Lesotho is false.

Ferguson's economic analysis of Lesotho paints a different picture: of a country long integrated into regional markets, mainly through the supply of grain and cattle, and more recently through regional labor markets. A decline in agricultural surpluses was, he says, linked to loss of land to Afrikaaners in the mid-1800s, not isolation from the cash economy. More recently, he notes the importance to the economy of labor migration to neigh-bouring South Africa, with families—women, children, and old people—left behind.[1] He argues that the role of cattle in male labor migration processes was important, related to cattle's role as a store of value, as an asset in acquiring and controlling wives, and as a type of consumer good rather than a means of production.[2] When migrant incomes are weak, cattle export sales happen; when wages in South Africa are buoyant, the men buy more cattle and resist attempts to "commercialize" cattle, which would turn them into commodities to be bought and sold for profit, which is what the donors tried to push through.

Ferguson (1997) says donor economic analysis depoliticizes Lesotho, making it into a passive recipient of donor design mediated through a hoped-for neutral local state, which can act simply as a means for implementing the development policies that donors think are correct. On the contrary, in Lesotho, the local state is highly politicized, he argues, and adept at using aid for political ends. He concludes that this sort of situation is quite typical:

> [Lesotho's development outcomes] may be no part of the planners' intentions. It is not necessarily the consequence of any kind of conspiracy to aid capitalist exploitation by incorporating new territories into the world system or working against radical social change, or bribing national elites, or mystifying the real international relationships. The result can be accomplished, as it were, behind the backs of the most sincere participants. It may just happen to be the way things work out. On this view, the planning apparatus is neither mere ornament nor the master key to understanding what happens. Rather than being the blueprint for a machine, it is part of the machine.
>
> (p. 232)

I leave this with some simple questions: How may we cope with Ferguson and similar views? What criteria can be used to assess statements about the nature of particular economies? What drives such practices? What are the possible consequences?

It is perhaps with such analyses as Ferguson's that the risks attached to DE methodologies are most apparent. Without predictive success something is lacking, and into that void may come what (as already quoted) Cohen and Shenton discuss:

> The paradox is that cyclical movement reappeared, whatever the purpose of progressive development, in the intention to develop. It was the intention to development which embraced the internal [the idea] of development, namely the conscious authority of autonomous being to determine and realize its potential.
>
> (Cowen and Shenton 1996: 54, quoted in
> Fforde 2009: 100–101)

By "cyclical movement," they refer to the idea that the movement between various poles—centralization vs. decentralization or much market failure vs. limited market failure—reflects patterns and logics in how development is viewed through trusteeship as correct development. Trusteeship (discussed in Chapter 1) is the belief that the responsibility of the developed is to develop the underdeveloped, who are rightly entrusted with the conditions thought suitable: power, assets, resources, knowledge, and so on. Ferguson's analysis of donor activities in Lesotho suggests that to understand donor views of Lesotho, we need to examine how donor intentions were in the driving seat. To put this another way, it was not what was happening in developing countries that explained changes in development thinking, but what was going on in rich countries, where the intention to develop was, in developmental terms, sited. Thus, one might understand why it is called the *Washington* Consensus.

Development economics and the Philippines

The Philippines is widely seen as a developmental failure, and an examination of its history since World War II may easily confirm this. A range of accounts contrast apparently favorable conditions (examples include a US-inspired political system, high level of education, and geographical positioning in a fast-growing area) with poor outcomes (examples include rather slow GDP growth, poor performance on human development indicators, and political instability).

In terms of thinking about the political economy of aid and development, this case study is useful, because it presents issues such as:

- Why did the Philippines fail? What economic and political factors converged to see such poor developmental results?
- Why should ostensibly democratic institutions such as the World Bank support authoritarian imposition of a certain development model?
- What economic forces resisted imposition of the model?
- What lessons could be drawn from the failure to induce successful EOG under an authoritarian government?

Walden Bello is a left-wing scholar who has produced a range of work. In the study cited here (Bello 1982; see also Bello 2000), he sets up his argument in terms of an attempt by the World Bank and IMF to impose, exploiting President Ferdinand Marcos's martial law, policies in the Philippines similar to the rapidly growing East Asian newly industrializing countries (NICs) (see Chapter 19). This is clearly resonant with arguments that reform-minded economists seek political crises or other opportunities to find ways to push through their policies (Rodrik 1996). This seems quite logical, given the metaphysical commitment of DE positions and an ethics that sees development, believed to benefit the people, centered upon economic growth. What Bello sees is a historical situation where it was hoped that the concentration of power created by martial law offered opportunities to push through correct policies.

What were these policies? According to Bello, a combination of EOG and political authoritarianism sought to create an isolated and insulated technocratic elite that could establish what it saw as good governance in the national interest. It is interesting to note his historical framework. According to Bello, policy debates prior to Marcos had seen the Left and the national bourgeoisie united in supporting protectionism (the "Nationalist Critique"), with weak free-trade forces, as this view was seen as pro-US—the former colonial power still possessing a major military presence in the Subic Bay base. Significantly, in the Philippines, ISI was not seen as "national" because many of the ISI companies were owned by US business interests, which supported the Right. However, the economy was not doing well, and the ISI was partially dismantled in 1962, well before Marcos, but the economic results were poor, an apparent failure of partial liberalization.

Export-oriented policies, according to Bello, came in hard and strong under Marcos's team of technocrats recruited from the United States. Export processing zones (EPZs) were set up, ISI dismantled, and external IMF support provided. But things did not go smoothly. Political struggles meant that ISI was not fully dismantled, and labor unrest ensued as nationalist forces mobilized against US interests. An incentives scheme for exporters, combined with the need to finance infrastructure for the EPZs, was too much for the macroeconomy, leading to balance of payments problems and inflation. By end of the 1970s, export-oriented policies had not generated much exports or employment (failure to attract significant FDI was also a factor). Labor resisted attempts to reduce wages and lay off workers. The macroeconomy was out of balance, and the political and economic situation deteriorated badly.

While we can see factors showing why export growth was limited, at the end of the day it is not exactly clear just why this happened. In economic terms, the response to the changes (the "reforms") did not appear large; growth in GDP per capita did not accelerate and neither did exports. We may note also that the World Bank's policies at the time were, according to Bello, basically political: to defuse social unrest in the context of the Vietnam War and counterinsurgency in both the Philippines and in other developing countries such as Thailand. Recall the story told by Rutten (Chapter 13). Unlike the situation after the fall of the USSR in 1991, such armed resistance in the Philippines and elsewhere could and did secure international material support.

In the urban areas of the Philippines, the World Bank was allegedly seeking to destroy the barriers to the inflow of foreign commodities and forestall the imposition of nationalist controls over investment (Chapter 5). Labor unrest and poor export performance meant that these barriers could not be overcome, and the economy stagnated. In the aftermath, the situation collapsed into the extreme unrest seen later in the Marcos period, with cronyism, martial law, and goon squads.[3] The Marcos regime fell, replaced by that of Cory Aquino and then of Fidel Ramos, a military leader who was crucial to Aquino's position as she came to power.

So what happened after Marcos? Another account shows how politics and economics interact. Emmanuel de Dios, an academic economist, argues that the Marcos period amounted to an attempt to link civil society anew to the executive, and thus central to it was the attack on the old oligarchies (De Dios 2000). Like Bello, though from a different perspective, De Dios's crucial issue is political: obstacles to reform are overcome by the astute use of state power. He argues that changes after the fall of Marcos did not return things to how they were. Traditional patron–client relations had been undermined by new sources of wealth, urbanization and incomplete rural reform, a growing middle class, and mass popular organizations.

More crucially, constitutional change had strengthened the executive while appearing to weaken it. Single-term presidents with six years in office gained in relation to congress members requiring re-election every three years. In looking at obstacles to the use of state power, de Dios analyzes pork-barrel politics, arguing that this had often granted political capacity for the executive to push through reforms. He gives examples of VAT and oil deregulation as two measures pushed through under Ramos by bribing congress members behind closed doors. Compared with the situation analyzed by Bello, the outcome appears more positive, offering scope for step-by-step advance. This process ran into trouble with Ramos's successor, Joseph Estrada, who was unconstitutionally removed from office on the grounds of corruption and abuse of power.

De Dios's view tends to be confirmed by the World Bank 2000, which suggests that the reforms, by now, met little formal political opposition. One reason was that the ideology of EOG and globalization was strong; most importantly, the reforms themselves could be construed as changing the premises for further reform, whether quickly or slowly. Central to the slow pace of change through the first decade of the 2000s, according to the World Bank's report, is the argument that the political economy was such that business remained highly concentrated, leading not only to low levels of competition but great difficulty (given the political power of such groups) in doing anything about it—indicators of this being a range of problems: the weak fiscal position and so poor infrastructure; the poor terms of trade facing farmers; the problems of coping with the liberalized financial system; and the fact that most of the manufactured exports boom was in electronics, as multinational corporations (MNCs) came in.

These two readings, in part supported by Bello from a quite different perspective, argue together that the feasibility of economic reform relies heavily upon the interaction of various factors that influence the polity. This confirms, inter alia, North's view of the primacy of institutions and politics over economics: some of these factors are independent of economic policy at any particular point in time, while some are not. The central issue for reformers, according to these accounts, is to make policy matter rather than to get prices right or to make prices matter; the main question is how to secure change that facilitates further change. And it is likely that conservatives are well aware of this and respond to any such attempts to secure the preconditions for reform by resisting efforts to create any basis for state intervention.

The Philippines is thus a useful case study as it poses many puzzles. For example, the country has long had high levels of education and apparently good institutional development (after the US model) but has been economically unsuccessful in terms of trend GDP growth.

Conclusions

The historical picture is obviously far more detailed and subtle than the readings cited can give justice to. But various messages come through. At root is the tension created by the problems that arise from the central DE position (as laid down in the textbooks cited here) that economic growth is at the centre of development. This leads easily to treatment of political and other matters as simply conditions for the implementation of known correct economic policies. Thus there are extreme difficulties if the logics associated with these other matters are experienced as stronger than economics. In Lesotho and the Philippines, with the apparent output gains to partial reforms leading to negative experiences—unemployment, poor incomes—there was resistance, and the political and social aspects of the situation proved far more important than the hoped-for economic gains. Seeing things in such ways may of course have more general value. But from the perspective of the two case studies, the economic result thus turned out to be simply the effect of these noneconomic factors.

Recall North's remarks that the polity is of overriding importance, but what are the relationships between economic change and politics? It seems obvious that mainstream DE doesn't have much to tell students about these issues. A professionally qualified development economist has no reason to have any specialized understanding of politics, sociology, anthropology, or any of the other areas of knowledge that become important if state power cannot be used to push through reforms (to ignore for the moment the issue of the predictive unreliability of DE).

On the one hand, it seems to me that the great amount of detail and complexity in such case studies, and indeed in general about development experiences, leads to the conclusion that much economic policy advice has to be taken with a large pinch of salt. On the other, this can be taken to imply that DE is simply inadequate, mainly because its approach causes problems when it seeks (or rather, avoids seeking) relationships beyond economics and across disciplinary boundaries.

Further, the effects of such experiences upon economic behavior could be substantial. One can be concerned about the increased perceptions of risk associated with any given set of policy advice and about the possible consequences of any skepticism (such as among voters, investors, and consumers) regarding the rationality and/or the authority associated with any given policy advice.

Questions for discussion

1. Would detailed history, rather than politics, clarify the extent to which the internal of DE explains episodes such as the World Bank's venture in the Philippines?

2. What sort of case studies would be most interesting to further develop the ideas in the two case studies looked at in this chapter?

3. Is it wise to delink economics from other factors? How should this be stopped?

Notes

1 This was the South African Bantustan policy. We can see this in light of the dual economy models discussed in Chapter 12 and making sense in terms of white South African interests.

2 Here we can see interactions between relations of production and relations of reproduction, as discussed in Robertson (1991). Bardhan and Udry, from Ferguson's point of view, are quite right to stress how family practices make the standard models inapplicable (Chapter 9).

3 There appear to be important differences between the situation at the start of Marcos's period as president of the Philippines (1965) and what happened later. Martial law was declared in 1972 and he eventually left office in 1986.

Part II

Topics and issues

As mentioned in the Preface, this text has a classic pattern that moves from introducing arguments and concepts to discussing ways of dealing with them in practice. The Preface broached key issues, above all, different ways of treating subjectivity. Chapters 1 through 3 then discussed general issues arising in development and how problems emerge with traditional or mainstream treatments of knowledge. Chapter 4 introduced some internal discussions of the importance of DE within economics, flagging the issue of whether or not standard models should be applied to developing economies and relating this to the extent of market failure, which, in turn, opened the door to discussions of how economists view economic relations. This was discussed in detail in Chapter 9, but before that we went through two detours. The first, in Chapters 5 and 6, offered a quick introduction to approaches to the study of knowledges, such as DE, followed in Chapters 7 and 8 by accounts of what economists actually do.

By this stage, readers should be familiar with the overall approach of the book and the basic issues involved in understanding DE. In turn, this should suggest the value of the main theme of this book, which is that, while DE should not be taken at face value, the failure of its overall approach to generate robust predictive knowledge is extremely suggestive for wider problems in DS. The exemplar of such problems is belief in the known value of participation (the technique that involves aid project stakeholders in areas such as project design, monitoring, and evaluation) and its ability to ensure better development outcomes (Mosse 2005). DE failure to generate predictive knowledge suggests, in turn, that DE is best appreciated as explanatory, and an indicator of good explanations is their willingness to appreciate others' contributions—that is, to happily negotiate across disciplinary boundaries. The second detour, Chapters 7 and 8, therefore exposited the core elements of economic growth theory and followed Ray (1998) rather closely. This showed how DE seeks to define development as platformed upon—in other words, conceptually less robust than—economic growth. The study of development thus is said to require, above all, the study of economics, because economic logics are assumed to prevail. This leads to various conceptual tangles but shows how DE shrinks from open engagement with other aspects of development.

Chapter 9 examined microeconomics, explaining the central role played by DE conceptualizations of markets that do not fail and revealing the lack of empirical argument to point students toward fair judgment of the extent to which markets succeed. This empirical problem of market failure, it was argued, exists *despite* economists' arguments about the valid role of non-market institutions, above all, the state, in development.

Chapters 10 through 15 then drew upon these foundations to discuss how DE coped with various issues.

Chapter 10 discussed internal debates about the extent of market failure and the tensions created by different views of this, expressed in the Washington Consensus and the post-Washington Consensus. These positions are often strongly criticized from outside DE by mainstream DS. Chapter 11 provided perspectives on these debates, offering a heterodox economic explanation for why there should be ignorance and arguing that critiques often present recoding and reconstruction as decoding and deconstruction —that is, they argue that while their antagonists—those they argue against, such as DE—are inconsistent, a true position can be arrived at through analysis of that inconsistency. From the perspectives of this book, such views take the familiar risk, which is that faced in general by approaches assuming that debate may progress through apodictic argument: the demonstration of the validity of a position through logical argument. Clearly, this starts to develop the possibility that it may be wiser, so long as stable predictive knowledge is unavailable, to treat knowledges as better accompanied by dialectic argument, in the sense of being consciously process-oriented, with acceptability criteria understood as contextual.

Chapters 12 through 15 then explored a variety of issues, contrasting and exploring differences between DE and alternative accounts of how these issues should be understood. Common themes were: the value of exploring the particular assumptions contained in DE models used to generate ideas about development, for these assumptions often appear as parameters in the models and are crucial to their solutions; the value of considering wider sets of ideas to explain beliefs, such as the drivers of economic planning (Veblen); the possibility of learning by doing (Zysman and Wade); and particular beliefs in the local characteristics of markets and likely output responses (Lesotho and the Philippines). Such discussions enrich debate about development experiences by making it easier to understand explanations offered by DE and where they are coming from. My assumption is that ideas are not best seen as either wrong or right (and, if so, reflecting some stable reality) but as part of accounts and histories.

In the coming chapters I will platform upon the ideas and discussion in these chapters to explore various topics and issues, including reference to DE as exposited by Ray. Often the discussion will be more open to student participation and presentations.

Part II thus starts with Chapter 16 and a discussion of poverty, inequality and the impacts of globalization. This includes explanation of technical issues arising in different ways of measuring inequality, both within DE and between DE and DS. Chapter 17 offers students a pathway to thinking about markets for 'factors of production' – land, labor and capital – and how DE (as presented by Ray) copes with markets for credit, with a look at informal markets.

Chapter 18 then presents a discussion of development dogmas and their histories. There is much of interest to be learnt from an examination of treatments of the Western European "economic miracle" of the decades immediately after World War II, and this is then followed by a discussion of the World Bank's 1993 account of the Asian "economic miracles." I look at this in context, though this is a subject that has generated a very large literature, and examine some critiques of it. Chapter 19 follows with a re-examination of the development policy set typically taught nowadays in the mainstream as "wrong." Again, we can examine dogmatic differences. Chapters 20 and 21 permit students to look at two topics that have also generated strong beliefs and debates—globalization, and explanations for East Asian economic success.

The penultimate chapter reviews experimental economics and the problem of empirics, and moves to the end of the book by focusing upon arguments for and against belief, as a basis for action, in empirical research that suggests the existence of reliably known cause–effect relationships. There is much of interest here, including the question of whether some experimental work may in effect abandon the instrumental rationality hypothesis. Chapter 23 concludes. Its first section confronts the issue of "spin" as part of DE arguments, looking at particular published pieces of work. The chapter then suggests ways of thinking of economic matters in terms of broad explanatory concepts, and enjoys exploring various ideas, such as the notion that the economy may be viewed as an "effect" of other more fundamental factors.

The list of special terms can be found after the final chapter.

16 Poverty, inequality, and accounts of the impacts of globalization

In this chapter we focus upon issues relating to poverty. We quickly cover materials dealing with measurement (Ray 1998, Chapter 6), inequality and growth (Ray 1998, Chapter 7); also work by Ravallion, a leading mainstream development economist with a wide range of publications and reports. We also refer to concepts of exclusion (Rigg 1997; see also Chapters 12 and 17).

For students who wish to explore further, two particularly interesting lines of attack are:

- Delving deeper into the empirics behind global statements. Ravallion (2004) points the way, and it is a useful exercise to disaggregate cited facts. This encourages caution about the use of such terms as *global poverty*.
- Examining different accounts of poverty and seeing how they contradict each other because their authors tend to view causation and evaluate situations differently.

Economic inequality: measurement

According to Ray, the shift in focus here, as we saw in the discussion of structural issues in Chapter 12, is from an aggregate to a disaggregate view: from countries in their entirety to the distribution of income, or wealth, among different groups in society. He also argues that there are *functional* reasons for being interested in matters of inequality. Even if we are not concerned about inequality per se, it may have some relationship to growth, as we have already seen in a number of places. Thus in Chapter 7 we saw him argue that investable savings derive from decisions to defer consumption, which conceptually shifts the focus of our interest from how corporations or business people may accrue investable resources. And in Chapter 13 we saw Ray lacking enthusiasm for strictly economic explanations of landholding patterns, whether through landlords or in political opposition to land reform. Thus we can appreciate the canonical DE definition of economic inequality as differences in measured (dollars) wealth or income. This contrasts with what Rigg said about social position:

that differences in wealth or income should be conceptualized as the *effects* of such forces.

Ray makes various analytical points that explain how such variables are linked to formal algebra. He stresses the importance of distinguishing between current expenditure or income flows; the distribution of wealth or asset stocks; and the distribution of lifetime income. This is related to whether we are talking about long-term or short-term considerations. Such distinctions also permit consistency in linking variables to optimization models and clarity of thinking within that conceptualization.

Ray also links these ideas to "real" economic issues, arguing that differences in incomes in the short run matter differently if the society is mobile. Just how income is earned may also be important. This functional distribution of income relates, of course, to how factors are owned. A household can receive income from different factors of production—rent, profits, or labor returns, which can influence esteem through social positioning. But these different income sources are also linked to how economic growth takes place, and this is related to functional income: the increased returns to factors of production accompanying economic growth. We can see how Ray puts all incomes into a black box and then takes them all out again (in the next chapter), so here we discuss measuring inequality with a summary statistic. This is not as simple as it sounds, and understanding this facilitates seeing how DE works with such empirics.

A single summary statistic to measure inequality, Ray argues, needs to follow four principles:

1. *Anonymity*: The particular entity (household, person, etc.) to which income is attached should not influence the value of measure calculated. This means that we can arrange the entities by income or whatever the metric is. In common language—"my income is as good as yours"—the significance of an Aboriginal earning $35,000 is the same as that of a Lebanese. This flies in the face of the idea that we are all different and the value of incomes varies and is not objectively comparable.
2. The *population principle*: The size of the population should not matter, so that doubling the population does not change the value of the measure. This means that inequality in small groups is assumed to be the same as in large groups.

These two principles allow us to draw a histogram of population arranged in groups by income range. A third principle gets us to another histogram: the percentage of total income by quintiles.

3. The *relative income principle*: Absolute incomes do not matter, only relative incomes, and it assumes that proportionate shifts do not matter.[1] DE students with knowledge of consumer theory will know that this,

of course, assumes something about the shapes of utility curves as well as how interpersonal comparisons of welfare are managed.

4. The so-called *Dalton principle*: If two income distributions are compared, and one can be obtained from the other by a series of income redistributions, from richer to poorer individuals, then the former is more unequal.

What can be seen here is how the effort to produce a single summary statistic requires, if these principles are to be followed, making assumptions about the world and how it is to be understood. There are no logical reasons to *necessarily* make these assumptions.

Economic inequality: the Lorenz curve

The Lorenz curve is a standard method for discussing inequality based upon these four principles and is constructed by ranking the percentage share of total income received by each equal-sized population group. For example, the lowest 25 percent of the population receive 10 percent of national income; the next 25 percent get 15 percent; the next 25 percent get 20 percent; and the highest 25 percent get 55 percent. You then add to get the total income—the sum of earnings—received by the *cumulative* percentage of groups: the lowest 25 percent get 10 percent (of total income); the lowest 50 percent, 25 percent; the lowest 75 percent, 45 percent; and the total (100 percent), of course, get 100 percent. The graph you plot is the Lorenz curve.

The Lorenz criterion is that if the curves of two distributions do not cross, one distribution is unambiguously less equal than the other, which means it satisfies all of the four conditions. If they cross, one cannot move to the other by a series of income transfers in the same direction, so there is no unambiguous change in inequality. This gives DE a nice single number, a summary statistic that can be quoted, cited, taught, examined, and compared with others. But, in constructing it, various choices have been made as the assumptions are selected. Central to these assumptions is the basic idea that a dollar is the same whoever earns it; this is, of course, contradicted by a wide range of social practices, such as the variation of income tax with income levels and social policies and practices that support groups seen as worthy.

A crude but useful alternative is the range: calculating the value of the maximum income less the minimum (in the income survey that is being used) as a ratio to the mean. Another method that is also crude but useful is the Kuznets ratio: the ratio of the total incomes of the richest x percent to the poorest y percent. Ray reports another statistic: the mean absolute deviation (MAD) from the mean calculated as a share of the mean. But this does not satisfy the Dalton principle, because if a transfer is made between two people above the mean, the MAD will not change, so he advises against using it.

The coefficient of variation (CoV)—the standard deviation divided by the mean—gives more weight to incomes further from the mean. This satisfies the Dalton principle, because if a regressive transfer is made, the CoV always changes.

Then there is the Gini coefficient, which is the ratio of two areas. This is best understood by looking at a graph, but it equals the ratio between the area between the actual Lorenz curve and the Lorenz curve that would obtain if all incomes were equal, and the total area is under the latter. Thus if all incomes are actually equal, the Gini coefficient equals 0, and if completely unequal (one individual has all available income), it equals 1.

The Gini coefficient and the CoV will both show shifts in the same direction so long as the Lorenz curves do not cross; if they do, they can give different answers. Ray argues this is because our intuitive sense of inequality is essentially incomplete, so we must look at the curves. Lorenz curves typically cross when the Kuznets ratio is doing funny things—for example, when the poorest x percent and richest y percent both lose shares of total income.

Ray points out that sometimes there is no unambiguous measure of changes in inequality, so one can try to find a better measure or accept that relative inequality may simply not be measurable. This implies that use of a single summary statistic should not be accepted uncritically, suggesting caution, and one should avoid and be suspicious of categorical thinking that links aggregate concepts to single statistics such as the Gini coefficient. After all, Stats 101 will tell us that if this conceptualization is used to generate a model and this model is false, the results of statistical inference will be spurious.

Measuring inequality: DE and DS

Discussions of inequality are one of the areas where the tensions between DE and DS are often great. As we saw from the discussion in Chapter 12, DE's objective measurements are DS's attempts to valorize social patterns that may be argued to *cause* inequality. Although Ray has little to say about how choices should be made between different measures, he discusses how participants in debates about the effects of globalization stress different measures: variation between people or between countries. He also mentions ways in which different people focus upon vertical vs. horizontal inequality and relative inequality vs. absolute inequality. This is further discussed by Ravallion (2004).

Ravallion argues that antagonists often have different values; economics has not become divorced from ethics. What is more important: economic differences between countries (said to be rising) or within countries (said to be falling)? How can a discussion value the effects of reform? Should one look at differences in impacts as income varies or differences in impact at given income levels? Answering these questions will tend to involve

choosing between a metric that stresses aggregate gains and one that empha-
sizes negative effects on the poor. Critics of globalization usually focus
upon absolute inequality—the income gap—while economists tend to focus
on the relative income distribution. Much research suggests that growth is
often distribution-neutral at the country level, and the Kuznets hypothesis
is not confirmed.

Research on global inequality has mixed results, and discussion rapidly
shows the problems of aggregation. The world poverty rate, as recorded,
has been falling. Based on the $1 a day poverty standard that is widely used,
and measured between 1981 and 2001, the number of poor fell from 40
percent to 21 percent of the world's population. But does this mean that the
global problem of poverty has been easing? Here there is debate. Yes, some
poor countries are being left behind, so that absolute differences are rising
as the rich get richer; statistics on relative poverty obviously gives worse
results than the percentages, which are *absolute* data. Furthermore, the
decreases in poverty have mainly taken place in China and mainly in the
early 1980s, when around 200 million Chinese saw their incomes go over
$1 day in 1981–1984. This change is arguably linked to the decollectivization
of agriculture at the time (Ravallion 2004: 8).[2] He argues that while growth
seems clearly good for reducing absolute poverty, there is also evidence that
trade openness tends to increase inequality and that such processes are
perhaps stronger in poor countries and occur with other processes that *lower*
inequality in high-income countries.

We can see clearly here how empirics are embedded in normal human
subjectivities. We may ask: Why focus upon the average impact of reforms
in a country rather than upon variations between rich and poor population
groups? This is common among pro-globalizers, as focusing on a country
permits them to use an empirics that is favorable to their position. Those
opposed to globalism, though, look at the losers, using empirics that argue
that the poor lose out.

Thus arguments about globalization's reported positive effects on
inequality rely upon a focus upon relative inequality. Looked at in terms of
absolute inequality, clearly there is an issue:

> [T]here is little obvious reason for assuming that it is the relative inequal-
> ities in incomes (rather than absolute inequalities) that matter instru-
> mentally to valued social outcomes. Arguable inequalities in power
> relate more to absolute inequality of income than relative inequality.
>
> (Ravallion 2004: 24)

If we assume that a dollar is a dollar and if growth is distribution neutral,
then the rich obviously do much better than the poor: a 10 percent gain in
a large income is more than a 10 percent gain in a small income, *if measured
in dollar terms*. Ravallion thus concludes that it is vital to look at what
underpins the statistics used to refer to poverty.

Causality in economic inequality

Some concept of inequality is fundamental to any thinking about development—not just what it is but why it is and what it does. The DE analysis is therefore important. A central issue, in a nutshell, is whether it can be argued that we *need* the rich. Ray grapples with this, arguing that "With low incomes distributed unequally, the consequences for poverty, under-nutrition, and sheer waste of human life are simply unthinkable" (Ray 1998: 197). But it is not clear whether this implies for Ray that in poor countries incomes should be redistributed rather equally. Are rich people, whose high incomes perhaps offer potential for high savings, necessary for growth?

Ray concludes that causality runs in both directions: inequality causes and is caused by other aspects of development. He starts with the question: Why is the distribution of endowments as it is? As we have seen a number of times, powerful forces in mainstream DE step around this question, treating endowments as exogenous to the modeling process. This creates tensions: "At another level, though, the question of what determines endowments is useless" (p. 198). The tensions arise because an apparently central element of the DE growth story, the supply of savings, risks becoming something that cannot be explained by economics. Rather, the conceptualization starts to link it to the distribution of endowments, including assets such as land (see Chapter 13).

Ray's analysis initially starts by taking a particular endowment distribution as given, and then seeing what might happen to it over time. Central to this is the so-called inverted-U hypothesis, usually identified with Kuznets. Ray measured the ratio of the total incomes of the top 20 percent to the bottom 60 percent and found it was more extreme—that is, higher—in developing countries than in rich countries. This implied that economic development was a *sequential and uneven* process: distribution worsened and then improved. This, of course, creates a story about what happens over time from an observation about what is happening at a point in time.

This is a neat example of how powerful ideas can be constructed. The conceptualization here may suggest that poor people will tolerate worsening inequality if they believe it will lead to increased incomes/development that will eventually benefit all. In caricature, it offers a reason why we may welcome an unequal distribution of incomes now because it creates savings that lead to growth and so high incomes for all later. This trickle-down argument, to be plausible, requires some belief that this is what people *actually* feel and that they can do something to change the pattern of income distribution if they wish.

The hypothesis can be grappled with, if not neatly tested. Time series analysis is difficult, mainly because of data limitations (not much data exists on incomes distribution). Alternatively, one can use cross-section analysis, which relies upon the idea that there is a development process, so that it makes sense to compare countries in this way. Broadly speaking, this data shows that inequality rises and falls against current per capita GDP. This seems to work also with Gini coefficients and cross-country regressions that regress on a quadratic of per cap GDP.

Ray notes that variations in income inequality between countries does not explain even half of the observed inequality in average incomes across countries (but it could be masked by government policy). The data is also confusing, because, if people shift between low- and high-income sectors, Lorenz curves may be crossing as this happens, so what does a changing Gini coefficient mean?

More fundamentally, "The implicit assumption is made that all countries have the same inequality-income relationship" (p. 206)—that is, that the relationship between income inequality and average incomes is the same in all countries. Ray argues that this is not reasonable, and the data shows some interesting issues—for example, the Latin effect. Most of the higher-inequality, middle-income countries are Latin American, and they sit in the middle of the U-graphing inequality against per capita GDP. Their inequality may be explained through other structural reasons, but their presence in the data gives a Kuznets inverted-U. Although it is risky to cope with this by using a dummy variable,[3] if you do, the Kuznets curve vanishes: "This suggests that structural differences across countries or regions may create the illusion of an inverted-U, when indeed there is no such relationship in reality" (p. 208).

Ray then offers a textured discussion of income and inequality. His standard growth story argues that with everyday change people accumulate wealth, acquire skills, increase work productivity, and so on. This may be more uneven—for example, a sector may take off, leading to a big increase in the demand for resources that it can use, which drives up incomes and prices. This then leads to compensatory—second-round—effects through incomes, prices, and so forth. Ray uses the concept of the multiplier (see "Externalities, technical progress and growth" on pp. 116–117) to argue that this may drive prices for the inputs to the point sector back down again. At any point in time, all three processes are likely to be at work. He asks why these might lead to more inequality at lower income levels. Much development shifts poor people from low-income agriculture to high-income progressive sectors, at which point the process may stop.

Readers may have heard of the "middle-income trap," or the lost decades discussed by Easterly (2001) (Chapter 8). The former is the idea that per capita GDP levels of around $1,000–12,000, which are said to mark middle-income levels for countries, are a level of development that is challenging (Gill and Kharas 2007).[4] Many countries reach those levels but few continue to grow economically. Some reach those levels and then fall back again. This fate was suffered by a number of countries that adopted WC policies in the 1980s, some of which had been reported as success stories before then, and their growth problems are part of the reason for the lost decades reported by Easterly, as per capita GDP growth slumped in many countries from the early 1980s.

Ray argues that technical progress may initially benefit the modern sectors, because using modern techniques in backward agriculture is hard. Although technical progress may be biased against unskilled labor, eventually shortages and education erode skill differences. Industrialization often initially brings vast profits to a minority, which do not trickle down until labor surpluses in agriculture have been used up (recall the dual economy models of Chapter 12).

Ray offers a useful exposition of how DE shifts from theory to explanation. As a more dialectical approach (rather than apodictic) appears to invite discussion, we can note conceptually that these dichotomous categories—skilled/unskilled, agriculture/industry—will likely be influenced differently by change, so that aggregation is a problem. In some ways the theory is too simple, in that historical accounts of particular regions or examples may not find it easy to use these categories.

DE returns to its basic positions. As Ray argues, the central *analytical* puzzle here is the relationship between inequality and the savings rate. This points back to apodictic argument and tends to assume that growth is accumulation and we are in the conceptual world of economic growth modeling (Chapters 7 and 8). Politically, the argument that high savings are needed to finance development, so you need rich people, is appealing to some, but others argue that redistribution can push up savings. Ray's argument involves a thought experiment: if you replace a worker on $5,000 and an executive on $55,000 with two professors on $30,000, what happens? If we look at marginal savings rates, the argument is that if rich people have a higher marginal savings rate, obviously shifts in income to them raise savings. A range of issues can be brought in. Thinking about subsistence needs suggests that pushing down the incomes of the very poor is risky.[5] As we saw in Chapter 12 in the discussion of moral economy issues and in Chapter 13 when discussing share-cropping, if incomes are close to subsistence— starvation—levels, the poor may respond violently. This can be risky for rich and poor alike.

We may think also about conspicuous consumption: the very rich may spend a lot, so encouraging them to save and invest may not work. Arguments against, for example, the absentee Protestant landlords of eighteenth-century Ireland often asserted that they spent their rents, not on improving the yields of their estates, but upon conspicuous consumption in England. Ray prefers to focus on the nonpoor who are not yet well off— that is, the emerging middle class that may save a lot as a result of their move up, especially intergenerationally. For him, this suggests an S-shaped curve: initially, improvements in incomes are largely consumed, then savings rocket as people see possibilities for advance, and later level off.

All this means that the conceptualization of the effects of changes in inequality is likely to become difficult and tense if it starts to engage with accounts from particular regions or social groups. Complex and non-economic factors will tend to force themselves into the discussion; as Ray wrote earlier, "the question of what determines endowments is useless" (p. 198).Yet Ray tries for a "stylized story" that seeks to offer a general explanation for a complex set of phenomena. If many people are very poor, redistribution from the rich may reduce savings and so growth; if the country is middle-income, redistribution from the rich to the middle may sharply increase savings because the middle classes will save more, as they do not have the wasteful consumption patterns of the rich. He ends up with a comfortable commitment to the existence of two long-term patterns: (1) starting with low inequality and, as growth kicks in, high savings and distribution rise together; (2) starting with high inequality, in cross-section, as income falls, savings drop sharply; the people low on the incomes distribution are so poor that they save very little. In modeling terms, savings are influenced by the existing level of inequality; so the starting point has a big influence.

If we turn to evidence, it is striking that, in standard empirical terms, this is not clear. Some cross-country regressions show strong negative correlations between indicators of inequality and subsequent growth (especially land ownership). To a certain extent, as we have seen, this is partly Latin America vs. East Asia, because countries in East Asia have some of the highest savings rates in the world and Latin American countries are lower. Ray notes that the result—the negative correlation between inequality and later growth—remains even when a dummy for democracy is introduced.

Inequality can also be linked to the composition of demand. Causation arguably may run both ways since the derived demands for certain types of spending vary. This means that the demands for goods created by high incomes and low incomes are different; one of the few stable statistical relations in economics is that the share of spending on food tends to rise with income for very poor people. A society with a mass of very poor farmers and a few very rich landlords will have a different pattern of demand than the same society after a radical revolution that pushes through land reform and introduces mass education. This can be studied by looking at the commodity bundles of different income groups and then at the implications for equality of each group. This data allows for a modeling of the changes in demand for each type of commodity as incomes are redistributed. Shifting land from absentee landlords to local capitalist farmers, for example, would arguably increase demand for modern agricultural inputs as the new owners sought to maximize profits. Again, the results suggest the importance of path-dependency, for apparently similar societies may evolve differently, given different starting points.[6]

Before concluding, Ray looks at the issues of inequality relating capital markets to development. Central to his argument is the issue of *collateral*. Social measures that ensure payment for goods and services are easier to arrange than for loan repayments. It is easier to ensure that buyers pay for their purchases than it is to make them pay their debts. This, he argues, can influence occupational choice as some opportunities cannot be realized by people who have the talents but not the collateralizable assets, which leads to less entrepreneurship.

Ray concludes that inequality tends to be inefficient as limits to access to credit keep people from creating employment. The poor tend to have less access to credit than the rich. At rather low levels, inequality reduces the supply of creativity and entrepreneurship. "Inequality has a built-in tendency to beget inefficiency, because it does not permit people at the lower end of the wealth or income scale to fully exploit their capabilities" (p. 237).

Conclusions

The aggregate global data is heavily influenced by regional differences, often called structural: historical and societal differences between China, Latin America, East Asia, and other developing countries can explain as well as any of the general economic theories. While at an aggregate global level the numbers of people who earn less than $1 a day has fallen sharply, this statistic is heavily influenced by China and India. As growth continues in many countries, and many people remain poor farmers, absolute inequality is increasing. At the same time, middle-income countries such as Latin America and the nonoil exporting (or problematic) countries of the Middle East face major issues as their populations confront the task of moving beyond middle-income status.

The tendency to argue in aggregate terms, and the pitfalls in doing so, is particularly marked in the case of inequality and growth. The Kuznets curve issue remains deeply important, because it goes to the root of the tension between the creative and the destructive forces unleashed by markets.

Questions for discussion

1. What conclusions might be drawn from a situation where authority exerts pressure for agreement on how to define and measure poverty?

2. Imagine a situation where a researcher has assessed welfare levels in a poor village at two points in time and concluded that welfare has fallen, yet the villagers disagree. Why might this be?

3. Find two case studies—one that plausibly show how inequality was good for development and another that shows it was bad.

Notes

1   Absolute incomes are measured in dollars or some other currency; relative incomes are measured in terms relative to some yardstick, such as "an income equal to 35 percent of average income."

2   There are other arguments; one that a crucial element of the real income gains of Chinese farmers at the time was not mainly a shift toward what mainstream DE would say gives static economic efficiency (decollectivization) but rather the effects of substantial improvements of farmers' terms of trade as the state pushed up the prices of payments for their outputs. (See Wong 1992 and Bramall 1993 and 1995.)

3   See "proxy" in the list of special terms, on p. 327.

4   "At a turning point that differs across countries, but that occurs *systematically* at middle-income levels, countries begin to specialize in production and employment once more. Scale economies in production appear to win out. This suggests that new strategies that favor specialization must be adopted at some point by middle-income countries if they are to become rich" (Gill and Kharas 2007: 5). For definitions of middle-income status, see the websites of any of the large international development organizations (for example, http://data.world bank.org/about/country-classifications).

5   Standard Stalinist industrialization policy sought ferocious reductions in farmers' incomes.

6   A good and accessible study, comparing Nordic success with troubles in South America, is Blomstrom and Meller (1991). In particular, Danish rural institutions developed greatly during a period of near-complete absence of state policy toward them in the late nineteenth century. There are many ways to skin a cat.

17 The economics of factor markets in economic development

Viewed from a distance, perhaps coming from other disciplinary backgrounds or DS, many of the points made by DE disconnect from arguably important economic and noneconomic issues. How this is done should by now be increasingly clear. In part, DE fails to obtain predictive power suited to its formal method, which, in turn, is associated with problems in negotiating disciplinary boundaries. In consequence, developmental accounts of the economic aspects of change are usually inward looking and weakly linked to other explanations. Economic matters thus often start to appear as little more than the *effect* of other logics. This is not helped, as we have seen many times, by DE empirics.

Let us return to the simple periodization of Lindauer and Pritchett, who end their discussion in "2002." Given readers' own particular values and metaphysical commitments, imagine what a good economic history of the two decades after 2002, written around one generation later, say in 2022, should include. Probably one should expect explanations that refer to institutions such as businesses, labor regimes, farmers, government, and political parties (recalling North's views of the importance of the polity—see Chapter 11). Also included would be the underlying behavior—the nature of markets and other vital parts of the economy— but how much reference should be made to the unobservable conditions of perfect competition that DE formal modeling uses as an integral part of its methods? Does this reference suggest that, at the end of the day, "markets work" and market failure is relatively unimportant?

Surely, a plausible history would include discussion of the relative importance of policy compared with other causes of change, stressing comparisons of "model with muddle." In addition, we would learn also what poverty meant for power relations, recalling Ravallion's remarks (Chapter 16) about the problems caused by a focus on relative poverty. The history would also probably include reference to the AFC of the late 1990s and link this to the GFC of the late "noughties"; these two events would likely dominate popular memories of the two decades from 2002 to 2022. If we follow the same line of argument as Lindauer and Pritchett, these events would be expected to negatively influence beliefs in the reliability of free markets, as did the Great Depression of the 1930s (see Chapter 2). In turn, we would expect that economists' views would have to change again, and this would be reflected in changed techniques and approaches.

After the discussion in Chapter 6 of what economists actually do, we may expect that the writing of such a history would require major changes in how economists decide what to model, and we could link these changes to how economists' changing beliefs link to policy, and how certain policy options may be shut out by the approaches taken by DE at any point in time. What the study of DE's history shows is how this dialectic between changing beliefs and DE's basic approach—at root, reliance upon algebra— works itself out.

In this chapter we will discuss elements of the economic history of South-east Asia (SEA) in recent years and link this to various positions, including Ray's (1998) on rural credit. This throws light upon how various ideas from DE can be considered within economic history. The focus here is upon how we treat markets within an economic history.

Students may wish to explore the debate about interlocking markets in rural areas and their effects on the poor, and seek case studies that discuss this issue. They are not hard to find.[1] The point here is, in part, that if markets such as land and labor or capital and commodities (such as for inputs such as fertilizer) are not assumed to be independent from each other, then, as we have seen, the standard DE analytical framework runs into trouble.

It is worth recalling the idea of class: societies that base much of their transactions upon markets may be divided according to the means of production—between those who own land and capital and those who sell their labor. Even though this concept is largely absent from mainstream DE, in some ways it is fundamental to a wide range of analytical frameworks, including the system of NIA, which, as we have seen, is a way of measuring factor incomes—the returns to land, labor, and capital.

Now largely forgotten classical economists such as David Ricardo, later joined by Piero Sraffa and Michal Kalecki, stressed the importance of viewing economics in such terms, and, in the case of Sraffa and Ricardo, based their theory of prices upon the effects of the distribution of incomes between wages and profits. Such views are now widely disparaged, and the micro-foundations of DE are largely a theory of how technology and preferences combine with optimization behavior to determine prices and resource allocation. In this chapter, let us explore different approaches to interactions between land, labor, and capital in recent SEA history. Largely, these are stories of development, and we can use them to see how DE relates to other perspectives, including that of DS.

SEA and the big numbers[2]

In contemporary SEA, long-settled areas of "population saturation" are relatively rare: the Red River Delta, parts of Java, and upper Burma come to mind. In these parts of SEA, over the centuries before recent urbanization and shifts from agriculture, high population densities created pressure to migrate and find new land. Historically, in most of SEA, land was relatively abundant and migration thus a viable option. Prior to World War II, a significant part of the Western colonial impact was a rapid expansion of cultivated area to provide large export surpluses, partly of rice to the coastal cities of China and partly of such commodity crops as rubber, coffee, timber, and tea. In this expansion, colonial histories emphasize how land access was influenced by colonial interests, with a strong tendency to ensure that those interests gained control through various devices (such as a racist legislature that kept the local population out of the market) intended to create scope for plantations or some other form of agriculture that benefited select groups to exploit these new market opportunities. These groups were usually selected to support the interests of colonial powers, and so were either foreigners or those chosen for their alliance with colonial interests. Profits from exports of agricultural products were thus channeled toward colonial interests, possibly in trade companies as well as in agriculture directly. It is rare to find situations where local indigenous[3] populations gained colonial support for expanding such exports. One consequence of this was a general pressure against smallholder involvement in export agriculture.

The argument can be made that SEA, like Eastern Europe, is in recent history best seen as an area of relatively abundant land and relatively scarce people. Historians used the comparison between Eastern Europe's apparent land abundance and Western Europe's large population to explain such puzzles as the far later end to serfdom (bondage to the land) in Eastern Europe, the powerful effects (in the West) of the Black Death's reduction of labor supply upon social relations as labor's bargaining position improved, and so on.[4]

Such economic histories encourage reflection on the importance of how land is opened up, who gets it, and how; we have already touched on this through the work of Rutten (Chapter 13). Moreover, it is easy to link such accounts to the focus of DE growth theory on inputs. In SEA, there are frequent reports of the politically powerful strategizing how to get politically weak people to work land rather than control it, which is consistent with a situation of relative land abundance compared to labor. An obvious example is the use of Chinese and Indian immigration to supply labor for plantations, such as in Malaya and lower Burma. In Vietnam, where poor people easily could be found and so the powerful did not need to import workers, equivalent stories can be found related to the Central Highlands. In Vietnam, regional distinctions were important, so internal migration helped boost the profits of colonial plantations in the newly opened up areas.

When land stops being abundant, then conceptually societies and their institutions and their cultures should be expected to face new challenges.

We found this echoed in the Lewis model (Chapter 12), but now it is land that is scarce, not labor. The Harris and Todaro model looked at urban–rural migration patterns, and the underlying assumption was that the rural economy was one of poor access to land (see Chapter 12).

From a DS perspective, a frequent issue that can be found in many writings, such as international nongovernmental organizations (INGOs), are the tensions created by a developmentalism that supports agribusiness, often manifested in conflicts between smallholders and large-scale producers. Ray's cautious discussion of land access and land reform and its limits partly reflects this. It is possible to see export-oriented growth and exports of labor-intensive manufactures as a political response to global geopolitics and the political conflicts of the Cold War.[5] Certainly, some accounts stress the importance of the Cold War in allowing certain countries and regions of Asia to gain access to US and other developed country markets (Johnson 1998): the US gave privileged access to its markets to countries thought strategically important to the global struggle against Communism (see Chapter 21).

Finally, at the level of food, culture, demography, and the good life, it is useful to bear in mind the effects of transition from land abundance to land shortage. The Mekong Delta and its emerging contemporary problems are but one possible example, as a region whose population had long experienced an easy life based upon abundant land and opportunities but find after two decades of rapid market-based growth since the end of central-planning in 1989–1991 that life has changed: that increasing numbers of people lack land, are pushed into wage labor, and see their incomes squeezed (World Vision and Adam Fforde & Associates, p/1 2004).

Markets as institutions

Treating markets as institutions throws up useful questions and insights— for example: In what contexts are markets located? What agencies define, enforce, and change the rules? And, how do economic logics work themselves out, if at all?

We have already seen how the standard DE microeconomic framework has difficulties when consumption and production occur within the same unit (Chapter 9). Added to this are issues of gender and interactions between relations of production and relations of reproduction (Robertson 1991), because the shifting of tasks (such as caring for the young or old) and intergenerational resource transfers beyond the family (such as by hiring care workers or putting old people into retirement homes) implies institutional variation and redefinition of core social identities and roles: what it means to be a child, a son, a mother, and so forth. Whether these are seen as fundamental or not depends upon values and emotions: whether there is some sense of obligation to care for such family members, how this is experienced, and whether that obligation may be met by shifting from direct caring to one mediated by the hiring of services, such as care workers, a retirement home, and so on. These are open questions to which there are different answers, but the extent of debate and emotional engagement suggests that for many they are very important. This suggests that discussions of labor may well encounter the impossibility of removing nonmarket relations from calculations of what is done and why. Even if a hired child caretaker or retirement facility is seen as acceptable, the criteria imposed to judge acceptability surely reflect emotional issues of mutual and direct responsibility: the comparison is with a nonmarket solution, where the care is provided by family members. Usually, such calculations are not easy, which is surely the point.

Labor

Discussions of decisions about choices between market and nonmarket solutions quickly shift attention beyond the company or business to include trade unions, conglomeration effects, migration (permanent and temporary), and other institutions of great importance to workers' calculations. It is possible to conceptualize far more broadly than the simple supply-and-demand framework would suggest and to adopt a "labor regime" with narrow or broad definitions depending upon the scope of the analysis. By labor regime, I mean, to put it simply, the wide range of factors that are included in a broad history of labor—for example, political and cultural factors. This leads to reflection upon trade unions and their varying position within labor regimes in Asia, and the frequent existence of radical labor action, with strikes, a radical labor leadership, and frequent strong state opposition. This has generated a literature that is contentious and should be examined critically.

For SEA generally, Deyo (1997) asks:

> Why are East and Southeast Asian patterns of flexible production predominantly static in nature and, where dynamic, more autocratic than their counterparts in industrially more advanced countries? To adequately address this question, it is necessary to understand patterns of economic governance across the region.
>
> (p. 108)

Deyo's *economic governance* refers to a wide range of factors that would be included in a broad history of labor, especially those that create order in relations between labor and employers as part of the labor regime. In the case of Thailand, Ji Ungpakorn (1995) poses the question of whether nationalism or class offers the better basis for radical political organization. Though writing over a decade ago, his points are provocative, given the increasing radical unrest through the first decade of the 2000s:

The Marxist definition of class is based, not on life style or income, but on the relationship with the means of production. Anyone who has little or no control over their work process and has nothing except their manual or mental labor to sell, is defined as working class. In this way, in modern capitalist Thailand, teachers, low-ranking civil servants, white collar office workers and university Chapters are working class, along with train drivers, lorry drivers, laborers and factory workers . . .

The Marxist definition of middle class in modern society covers those people who are neither capitalists nor workers.

(p. 376)

Like DE, such views have powerful metaphysical commitments. At root, this is the belief that the core issue in understanding historical change is the relationship between those who control economic assets—"the means of production"—and labor.

Land

Turning now to land, we find in SEA many accounts of land markets that have often or usually coexisted with preexisting institutions, such as land access based upon community land rights and so, for a given family, resulted from its membership in a particular community. In Vietnam these are well documented, in part because of the desire of analysts to understand the origins of revolt, especially against the French colonial regime during the 1930s, and in part because sympathizers to the Hanoi regime and its own writers sought to explain rural collectivization under Communist rule. Since the opening of the country in the early 1990s, other studies have added to this picture, often arguing that the spread of market-based ways of accessing land involved the weakening or destruction of older institutions, such as the common land system in parts of Vietnam, which broke down as the colonial presence pushed into villages and saw such lands often taken over by individuals (Scott 1976).

We find in these accounts reference to communal traditions among farmers in the long-settled areas, with rather large areas referred to as communal land, along with practices of sharecropping on newly cultivated land in the recently opened-up Mekong Delta. In the hill areas where wet rice was grown, populations were relatively settled, while in the mountains it was common to find swidden cultivation, where populations tended to be relatively mobile, often moving to new areas as land yields fell. Such patterns appear common in SEA. Again, studies often argue that while these systems tended to be relatively sustainable, changes in the modern period have often been damaging both to the environment and the older institutional set-ups, and linked to the spread of market relations.

Consider Cleary and Eaton (1996):

> The real tragedy of the commons is the process whereby indigenous property-rights have been undermined and de-legitimised. This destruction of local-level authority systems will be seen as the principle cause of natural resource degradation.
>
>   Frequently, traditional local communal powers were assumed by the state which then allocated rights of exploitation to alien commercial interests. This is often exemplified by the fate of forests in the region.
>
> (p. 5)

Cleary and Eaton thus offer an account of changing institutions within which histories of markets may be situated, and in which economics appears as the *effect* of other logics (such as the developmental ideas of local states).

Capital

A central question that arises when reading such accounts is how realistic it is to treat capital as just another commodity or factor of production. Heuristic accounts report a parallel evolution of capital intermediation and state policy, as in Wade (1990) and Zysman (1983) (Chapter 14), and in some ways these echo rather old arguments from Polanyi (1976; see also North 1995a) that capital is better seen as a fictitious commodity, but what does this mean?

Polanyi presents an analysis in which the state is important in creating national markets and coping with the consequences. It also poses interesting questions about the conditions required for internationalization of markets, the differences between goods and factor markets, and the importance of political and social problems in pushing for state reactions. According to Polanyi, the growth of national markets and the exercise of state power were historically inseparable, and the former was not the natural outcome of market development but the result of the exercise of state power. He argues that the chaos caused by the three "fictitious commodities" (land, labor, and capital) led to state intervention.[6] Clearly, NIA conventions argue that these three fictitious commodities differ essentially from others. GDP sums the returns to land, labor, and capital.

Discussing the pre-industrial revolution in Europe, Polanyi argues that production for national markets was significantly different from long-term international trade.[7] Production for markets had to arise in towns while obtaining food and other inputs from a hinterland. Towns tended to oppose the establishment of national markets, because local markets were controllable and offset the uncontrollability of profitable long-distance international trade that was not subject to any single political power but often of great importance to urban merchants. State intervention and sovereignty had therefore to be used to break down these local trade barriers.

This is a neat contention, often cited in the argument that markets are located in institutional contexts (recall North and compare with the DE microeconomics in Chapter 9). The conceptualization can be used to generate implications for the present process of globalization—for example, in the particular roles of the IMF and World Bank and the need for a world order that treats local states as sovereign agents within a rule-governed system. This brings us back to DE as part of how economics, and so policy and intentionality in social change, is construed. We have already found that DE, with its problems in negotiating disciplinary boundaries and avoidance of overtly explanatory methods, itself tells us rather little about policy and politics, for a start. Let us return now to see what Ray (1998) has to say about DE and credit markets (Chapter 14).

DE and its treatment of credit

Ray places the analytical framework, as usual, in the context of market failure stemming from the absence of markets. Recall Stiglitz's argument that the absence of market failure "explained why markets result in Pareto efficient outcomes" (Chapter 9). This involved an interpretation of the algebra that meant, among other things, that anything and everything was available through markets, at prices that would not alter as more or less was bought by an individual consumer (perfect competition); in other words, there were no "missing markets." The conceptual point of reference is thus theoretical. Ray takes it as empirically given that credit markets are not likely to operate smoothly and stresses the importance of this to his analysis of rural economies.

The platform is the problem of information, so he argues that the problems are insuperable in monitoring what is done with a loan, facilitating debtor voluntary or strategic default, stemming from issues with enforcement. Here we see DE starting with a statement about "model" and using this to establish the important characteristics of the "muddle." Ray illustrates this muddle with examples from international debt and from poor countries, where, he says, justice is neither cheap nor reliable, and so it is expensive to transact; resources have to be used to check up on clients, to reduce risks, and so on. Credit should not therefore be seen as something as easy and reliable to buy as, say, a cup of coffee. He moves quickly to the conceptual conclusion that credit arrangements are likely to have a large institutional-informal—that is, nonmarket—component. Here, then, we have a strong statement about the importance of the noneconomic.

Ray argues that it is important to distinguish between working capital, consumption credits, and fixed capital. Involuntary default and strategic default are both seen as outcomes of informational imperfections, and both lead to suboptimal lending. This means it is important to distinguish between formal and informal lenders. Because the formal lenders lack information about borrowers, they cannot easily accept nonmonetized collateral. The analysis then turns to look at informal markets.

Informal markets and their treatment by mainstream DE

Informal markets are characterized by:

- Informational constraints (higher risk of nonrepayment, resulting in higher risk and costs of transacting).
- Segmentation (lenders only deal with some but not all borrowers).
- Interlinkage (transactions occur in other markets simultaneously, spreading the costs of risk-bearing).
- Interest-rate variation (rule of one price does not hold or have to hold).
- Credit-rationing (interest rates are below equilibrium and so supplier choice of client prevails).
- Exclusivity (borrower is locked into one lender at a time).

All this adds up to a powerful social position for the asset-rich side of the transaction. This could be the lender but also the borrower if, for example, the lender is a relatively unimportant member of a politically weak ethnic/ religious minority.

The policy implications of these analyses can be important. They include the warning that state credits to traders and landlords may not be passed on to borrowers, and, by contrast, the value of institutions such as micro-finance that capture the informational and positional capital of lenders. We may note in passing that such policy concerns naturally focus attention upon the political power of those who control these institutions, likely, in part, to be INGOs or donors. In some countries, this is far-reaching, such as accounts of INGOs having major influence upon local politics in aid-dependent countries such as Bangladesh. What is going on here is that DE offers an explanation—the absence of markets—for the existence of situations where the powerful capture economic benefits. Interestingly, this explanation appears to rely upon the idea that what is crucial is the non-existence of the conditions of perfect competition. Perhaps, as reflection on Stiglitz suggests, these conditions are mainly presented within DE to permit it to be argued, with Stiglitz, that "markets result in Pareto efficient outcomes," so Ray here is offering a warning.

Conclusions[8]

In the analysis of factor markets, it is striking that DE and DS seem to have a relatively easy relationship in their different approaches to capital markets. To put it in a "realist" manner, when analysis is "up close"—situated in a particular historical context—things are complex and interesting, because markets seem obviously to fail and so nonmarket issues appear important.

This comes up in any consideration of what is cause and what is effect, and it is not hard to argue that in many areas the economy is both cause and effect.

Some issues where economics seems both the subject and object of effect include:

- *The importance of the agency of property-rights enforcement.* The particular ways in which property rights are enforced may be seen as both affected by economic issues and a cause of them.
- *Why factors of production are not like other commodities.* Economic arguments help explain why land, labor, and capital are different from other things that are bought and sold, in that they are not produced in the same way, while how land, labor, and capital appear economically is illuminated by noneconomic issues, such as how labor copes with care for the old and the young, and whether this relies upon market or nonmarket arrangements.
- *The inevitability of resource allocation decisions beyond the market.* Reflection on why Polanyi insists that markets for land, labor, and capital are markets for fictitious commodities makes the point that, as they are not produced in the same way as ordinary goods and services, their availability depends on factors that include nonmarket forces (such as the willingness or reluctance of old people to go into retirement homes).

Questions for discussion

1. How might one criticize historical explanations posed in terms of "land abundance" vs. "people abundance"?

2. Reflect on other areas where, conceptually, a dominant impression is that what is being discussed may usefully be seen as the *effect* of factors external to it.

3. Is it possible to discuss possible "de-development" in North America in terms of the loss of a growth pattern that exploited an open frontier?

Notes

1 Much of this debate was accelerated by Newberry (1975), who downplayed the issue. It is a revealing debate.

2 Like the idea of the "fundamentals" (see Chapter 5, note 2), the notion of the "big numbers" reflects the belief that certain basic numerical characteristics of a large group of people are meaningful. This may appear trite, but deserves reflection. It is, once again, an attempt to conceptualize a host of local contingent events as in some way sharing common elements; the tension under the surface here is

that of the apodictic illusion—the idea that simply because one can refer to the average level of measured GDP per capita for a large group of people that this is a good way of thinking.

3   The linguistic issue here is caused by the presence within SEA of substantial migrations, so that English has problems finding a suitable term for the subject populations. "Indigenous" may refer to those present *before* late "natives" arrived—or not. This is striking given that the region now called England contained a large Celtic population before the arrival of Anglo-Saxon and then Norse migrants in the first millennium, but has retained no easy linguistic solution to the problem of what to call the natives. "Welsh" etymologically means "foreign," but that does not help much either.

4   These issues have been deeply discussed in the academic literature.

5   This may also be thought of as part of a strategy to relocate population from the countryside into the cities. Maoist insurgency thinking argued strongly that it was the peasantry not the urban proletariat that would provide the basis for armed struggle against the forces of imperialism.

6   Polanyi uses the term "fictitious commodities" because he argues that, unlike normal goods and services, land, labor, and capital are not produced for profit; thus, for him they are not commodities. Land, labor, and capital are all paid for, but these payments are not then used—unlike, say, payments for purchase of a car—to buy inputs and to pay factors of production.

7   The phrase "industrial revolution" usually refers to complicated historical factors that saw, initially in the UK, the rise of economies that were no longer dominated by agriculture, tended to grow and change fast, were highly urbanized, and widely dependent upon machines of various kinds. Historical accounts usually focus upon the eighteenth and nineteenth centuries. From the second half of the twentieth century the richest of these economies started to deindustrialize and shift toward services.

8   The perceptive reader may well notice that in parts of this chapter my own "metaphysical commitments" are active – I am stating what I believe likely to be the case "out there". Students may wish to re-read the section "A note on language" in the Preface and think about how, seeking here to persuade the reader about what "really is", I reduce the use of caveats and become more assertive in my language, rhetorically referencing the idea that there is a knowable reality (and I know it).

18 Development dogmas and their histories

In the next chapter I will examine aspects of the shift from import substituting industrialization (ISI) to export-oriented growth (EOG) that is arguably part of the drastic shift that Dunn (2000) referred to "as the massive impetus towards economic liberalisation of the last two decades of the twentieth century" (p. 184) (Chapter 10).[1] In this chapter, I want to prepare the ground for Chapter 19. Since this shift is so important, it risks attacking "straw men," and indeed it is valid to suggest that the reader be particularly careful in forming a judgment as to what actually happened. DS students will be well aware of the powerful attacks made upon the Washington Consensus as the cause of considerable problems in many poor countries, as well as the idea of the "lost decades" (Easterly 2001 and Chapter 8). Others will be aware of the powerful arguments that economic growth relies upon allowing the market to work and so deregulating and liberalizing. I will suggest ways of dealing with this dilemma, which mainly demands a clear understanding of how positions in the debate are formed. Recall the discussion in Chapter 16 of the frequently confused nature of different ways of gauging poverty. In my opinion, it is clearly, as Dunn states, "extraordinarily difficult to see clearly and steadily quite what is at stake in this drastic shift" (p. 184).[2] In part, this is because apodictic arguments invite conceptualization at rather high levels of abstraction—one reason why straw men are so useful, for they support attempts to make the conclusions of an argument appear necessary—that is, that x = yz.

Many convincing contemporary accounts suggest caution in reaching conclusions about how ideas changed and why too quickly and too generally.[3] For example, for a discussion of the 1950s and statist development in Western Europe, the background to the 1970s and the 1980s shift in economic perspectives, see Shonfield (1976). In Shonfield's account, for example, it would be quite wrong to attribute to "Keynesianism" the post-World War II economic success in continental Europe.

The shift from ISI to EOG is fundamental to understanding many current positions in DE. Shonfield provides the background to this shift and offers remarks on the post-World War II economic development "miracle" in Western Europe. Before then it is useful to see by contrast how the East Asian "miracle" is construed. This can be assessed by examining the 1993 "Miracle Study" of East Asian success (World Bank 1993) and two of its critics. It is also useful to discuss what can be learned about ISI from more historical accounts. In the next chapter I will discuss accounts of the history of the shift in DE and its practice from ISI to EOG—from 1962 to 1982, in L&P's (2002) terms.

The immediate origins to the 1993 World Bank study were official Japanese responses to Bank criticisms of its targeted lending programs.[4] The Japanese government therefore decided to pay for a Bank study to investigate successful growth in Asia. Concluding that Japanese-supported targeted lending programs had little positive effect, the study can also be viewed as a marker of interventionist policies—the shift from 1962 to 1982 beliefs. It is important to discuss other accounts of what underpinned the first miracle (*Wirtschaftwunder*) in Western Europe after World War II. Broadly speaking, we find arguments that this economic growth had relied on protection (with growing free trade in the Common Market) with, in some countries, indicative planning,[5] controls on capital movements, frequent use of price controls, and state involvement in the allocation of credit and foreign exchange in various ways, with extensive use of SOEs (nationalized industries). It was thus very 1962, and extremely successful in terms of economic growth, social stability, and the preservation of peace in a region stricken by two awful wars in two generations. This latter factor need not be forgotten, given the experience of East and Southeast Asia.

As time passes, the possible range of case studies that examine development doctrines naturally has expanded. Students may wish to explore those off the radar screen of current DE (and DS), since heterodox experiences can be interesting and revealing. For me, candidates include the various colonial experiences discussed in Cowen and Shenton (1996) (although they are hard to read), experiences in Eastern Europe between World War I and II, failures of partial reform (for example, the Philippines), and heterodox transitions to fast economic growth.

The European economic miracle

Shonfield (1976) offers what is now a heterodox account of the post-war European economic miracle. His main explanations for the unprecedented economic success of the 1950s and 1960s were:

- Stable employment without major fluctuations in output levels.
- Rapid growth of production across and shared by a large number of countries (the only previous example was the United States prior to World War I), with falling share of business investment in GDP.
- Wide diffusion of the benefits of economic advance, supported in Western Europe by welfare services and pension schemes.
- Rising savings as a share of private incomes.

To this list Shonfield added some particular historical factors:

- The sustained expansion of international trade after World War II.
- The 1950s building boom.
- Major structural changes as labor moved from agriculture to industry and services (largely finished by the 1960s).

It is worth recalling that, from a DS perspective, countries such as France and Sweden were still strikingly rural at the end of World War II. The UK and the Netherlands were two exceptions in the degree of urbanization and industrialization they enjoyed. He adds to this two other factors: policy, meaning the conscious pursuit of full employment (which stimulates international trade), and rapid technological change.

But, most significantly for the ISI vs. EOG debate as expressed through DE, Shonfield discounts the influence of Keynes. He argues that Keynes's focus was upon short-term dynamics, not growth, and other ideas than his drove and defined state interventions. He discusses in some detail the patterns of state intervention in developed countries after World War II and argues that those countries that most heavily adopted Keynesianism (UK and US) "were least successful in managing their economies after WWII" (p. 65).

The patterns of state intervention seen in Continental Europe were for a short time imitated by the UK and the US—the Kennedy Democrats in the early 1960s and the Labor government that came to power in the UK during the mid-1960s. Although patterns varied among countries, he points to a range of activities that could be termed state intervention.

The degree and extent of public authorities' influence over the economy had vastly increased, operating through different mechanisms—here the banks, there SOEs—but in almost all countries large volumes of state spending came to be considered normal. Large amounts of social welfare spending become pervasive in Western Europe, especially education and pensions. This was combined with a radical shift in attitudes towards social relations, such as the power of employers and owners, compared with the pre-war period: "In the private sector the violence of the market has been tamed" (Shonfield 1976: 66).

With competition regulated and controlled,[6] this encouraged long-term collaboration between firms, supported by agreed government policies. To a large extent part of this shift was driven by improvements in technology. In most countries, we find institutions arranging for R&D, training and use of scarce manpower, and so on.

Finally, Shonfield refers to the conceptual underpinnings of these profound social changes as "the pursuit of intellectual coherence. Its most obvious manifestation is long-range national planning" (p. 67). This is a telling statement and is suggestive of the tensions created for DE when confronted with alternatives that imply state intervention; here it is important conceptually to match the intentionality of long-range national plans with assertions of the rationality of markets left to their own devices.

It is thus in the area of indicative planning that Shonfield's remarks are most interesting. He notes the French experience, where the state sought to accelerate growth by guiding investment so as to increase returns (to reduce the ICOR), but made this subordinate to social goals: what to produce, where, and so on. This produced a detailed and textured conceptualization of the change process and contrasts with the British focus upon aggregates.[7] We have seen this willingness to think in terms of big numbers in the economic growth theory of Harrod and Domar (Chapter 7).

The East Asian economic miracle

The World Bank's 1993 study offers a clear canonical statement, laying down what the Bank had concluded were the causes of the success of the high-performing Asian economies (HPAEs—Hong Kong, Singapore, Japan, Taiwan, Republic of Korea, Malaysia, Indonesia, and Thailand). This was expressed in the form of eight lessons, mainly related to economic policy, thus doing far more than simply presenting an economic analysis. These are squarely within the WC or 1982 (L&P) perspective.

The Bank's account of East Asian developmental success

The study stressed fast GDP growth, with improving income distribution (as measured by Gini coefficients). Development is thus understood as a combination of economic growth as the central point, with social advance largely measured by poverty reduction (see Chapter 16). "The HPAEs are the only economies that have high growth and declining inequality" (World Bank 1993: 3–4). This combination produced dramatic gains in human welfare: life expectancy, reduced numbers of people in absolute poverty, access to clean water, and so forth all improved. This was caused by getting the basics right:

- Rapid gains in private investment and human capital as the principal engines of growth, sustained by high levels of domestic savings.
- Rapid growth in agriculture.
- Rapid decreases in population growth.

In this sense there is nothing miraculous about the East Asian growth, and the study attributes the economic success as largely due to superior accumulation of physical and human capital. This is then quite clearly understandable in terms of the basic elements of DE. The driver is economic growth, which is understood in terms of the ability to generate and utilize increased resources, understood as capital in both physical and human terms.

Intentionality enters the account in ways that are now familiar to us, with development conceptualized as an intentional but known process. Therefore, the World Bank study argues that getting the basics right was accompanied by fundamentally sound development policy, which allowed the apodictic logics of DE appropriate rein:

• Good macroeconomic management.
• Policies to increase the integrity of the financial system.
• Education policies focused on primary and secondary levels.
• Agricultural policies that stressed productivity and did not tax agriculture unduly.
• Price distortions kept within reasonable bounds.

Markets were, thus, allowed to work properly, and institutions were market friendly.

The study manages the question of interventions by accepting that these often violated the dictum of a neutral incentives regime. In a few countries, these were successful, but "the prerequisites for success were so rigorous that policy-makers seeking to follow similar paths in other developing countries have often met with failure" (p. 6). There were, it was argued, two prerequisites: institutional mechanisms to establish clear performance criteria and situations where the costs of intervention did not become large. The World Bank study contrasts East Asia and SEA, saying that the latter saw far less intervention and may be more relevant to other countries.

The World Bank's eight lessons

The study focused upon subject areas where the analysis could argue that markets were allowed to work. Clearly, there is an underlying belief that market failure was limited in scope, and where it did occur was viewed in typically mainstream ways that made it relatively easy to handle analytically (for example, the classic public goods such as education). This we can see from the detail:

1. *Macroeconomic stability*: Inflation was kept low, and the exchange rate kept competitive in East Asia. The success was both in terms of long-term growth trends and in the management of macroeconomic balance over the short term in the face of shocks such as the oil price rise. Success resulted from correct policies that relied upon a technocratic elite in government that was insulated from political pressures, either via laws or convention.
2. *Building human capital*: Public and private resources were put into high levels of education. Tertiary education tended to be vocational, and female participation high.

3. *The creation of effective and secure financial systems*: Popular financial savings were mobilized (mediated) in rather high volumes via a shift toward positive real interest rates (later in the process) and the creation of secure and stable banking systems through protection and regulation (although this reduced the level of competition). Also, state development banks were often used along with commercial banks.

4. *Limited macro price distortions*: Wages were kept near what the World Bank considered to be correct levels through flexible labor markets, and interest rates were kept positive in real terms (after an initial period). This meant that resources flowed toward sectors that reflected comparative advantage (enhancing the efficiency of growth), meaning labor-intensive and resource sectors early on and more capital-intensive areas later.

5. *Openness to foreign technology*: When countries started rapid growth, it was possible to obtain technology through licensing, importation of machinery, and reverse engineering. This is now harder but the Southeast Asian HPAEs can still do so.

6. *Little if any bias against agriculture*: Unlike some other countries, agriculture was not seen as a source of capital for industrialization. Rural incomes benefited from state spending on rural infrastructure, from the green revolution, and from low direct and indirect taxation.

7. *Secure environment for private investment*: A core of technocratic managers (relatively insulated from commerce, less so in Thailand and Indonesia) created a secure environment through a combination of good pay, rule-governed methods of organization, and granting high status to public employment. Also, institutions were set up that linked bureaucracy to the public sector.

8. *Sometimes positive effects of market intervention*: These tended to be carried out within limits. There were three types:

    1. *Promotion of specific industries*: This was ineffective; instead, the economic structure that emerged resulted from market forces and relative factor prices/comparative advantage.
    2. *Directed credit*: This was effective but brought high risks.
    3. *Export promotion*: This was effective.

Above all, the Bank supported exports and the use of export performance as a way to manage relations with businesses in the context of controls on interest rates to create rents that could accrue to businesses rather than banks or depositors.

Contextualization

Let me attempt to put these conclusions into contexts. Above all, it is useful to appreciate that most countries went through an ISI stage after

World War II when this was established development doctrine. World Bank reports at the time show this clearly, and it is illuminating to read these from the 1950s. The experiences of the Philippines (Chapter 15) are but one example of a shift in mainstream prescriptions, in which one "one size fits all" solution is replaced by another. Ultimately, this may be traced to the belief in apodictic argument that seeks to demonstrate the validity of abstract propositions. This is why it is important to fully appreciate the significance of the view, shown in L&P (2002), that around a decade after the publication of this World Bank report in 1993, there was no longer any clear certainty— no "big idea." As we have seen, however, this does not fit well with DE core elements. The World Bank's support for export credit subsidies stands out as a deviation from the overall direction of the Bank's argument, which sought to limit state intervention to situations where there is said to be market failure. This is the core platform upon which the intellectual coherence of the Bank's position rests.

A key issue is the insulation of domestic capital markets from external forces. It is common to argue that this is now no longer possible, but the argument is belied by the experiences of countries such as Malaysia after the AFC. If it were argued, in the aftermath of the GFC, that financial markets are saturated with market failure, due to problems of moral hazard,[8] information asymmetries, and poor attention to public assets such as the environment (with large external costs imposed on others by polluters), it is clearly conceptually possible to support, within DE, policies that insulated domestic capital markets and that saw states intervene in them. But, to be managed within DE, this would involve arguments about market failure.

A further historical discussion involves the origins of the SEA export push that is placed by the Bank so centrally in its analysis. Accounts explain this in terms of the effects of the removal of import protection, as ISI was abandoned to suit new external doctrines, which led to Bank support for the supply of duty-free import of inputs to exporters so as to push the new model (EOG).

This leads to a more profound discussion about the nature of the policy advice here. Just where does the intention to develop come from? Why do all this? Based upon what values? Why assume that technocrats, even when insulated, believe in the World Bank thinking? One is reminded of the point made by Lewis Carroll, author of *Alice in Wonderland*, that, if one disagreed with a logical inference, logic would "take you by the throat and force you to agree."[9]

A heterodox view would hypothesize that these arguments support a generalized syndrome of extensive state subsidy to exports, as well as private sector and non-state social spending to support EOG. One can ask what the implications are for competition between exporters, if costs are influenced by these subsidies, accumulated capital investments, and other input costs. There is some evidence from Vietnam in the 1990s that these subsidies led to what DE would presumably call a vast market distortion.[10] This is because, while capital moved freely throughout Vietnam in the 1990s, little went into those areas that the EOG conceptualization predicted: light manufactures and other labor-intensive sectors. Instead, by the end of the decade, employment creation in foreign-invested firms (which the theory would have expected to be focused on light manufactures but often were not) was only some 300,000 in a country with a total population near 80 million. Investment instead tended to go into real estate and minerals extraction. The argument is that, because the vast subsidies (infrastructure especially) designed to support EOG, which were enjoyed by Vietnam's regional competitors, were absent in Vietnam, capital therefore went elsewhere after Vietnam returned to world markets in 1990–1991 after it abandoned central planning. It was only in the first decade of the new millennium that the Vietnamese economy started to look like other countries of SEA, and employment growth in foreign-invested firms accelerated. But, without a powerful commitment to EOG, many observers saw even this growth in foreign investment as rather low.

I turn now to examine two critics of the Bank study from the mainstream. I start with Rodrik, rightly famous as a liberal economist and previously cited (Chapters 5 and 15). Wade (discussed in Chapter 14) made his name with a famous book that argued, against the Bank, that Taiwan and South Korea had successfully intervened in markets (Wade 1990). There is a large literature on the developmental state concept.

Critics of the study: Rodrik

Upfront, Rodrik (1994) stresses that the World Bank study puts the positive value of intervention back on the map, which, he says, is a major change in Bank thinking. In terms of an analytical critique, he argues that much can be explained by the starting point, if the analysis is done with statistics, and he points to the flat resource allocation—especially land—caused by the relative absence of landlords and high education levels.[11] For him, statistics also suggest that high levels of investment and rising labor force participation are the main correlates with high growth, and that the HPAEs have not actually shown high rates of labor productivity growth—that is, these are cases of *perspiration* not *inspiration* (Krugman 1994). This poses questions about the economic efficiency of their institutions and, in terms of economic history, the question is how to explain high investment. Is it the cause or the result of rapid growth?

Rodrik also argues that it is not clear what is meant by either economic openness (economies that trade a high proportion of their output) or creating an environment that encourages private investment and competition. Nor is it clear to what extent export orientation actually encourages growth. More fundamentally, he questions whether we actually know what government was really doing in the HPAEs. This echoes the view of Shore and

Wright that policy tends to become conceptually more fragmented the closer one gets to it (Shore and Wright 1997: 5 and Chapter 3).

Critics of the study: Haggard

Haggard (1994) argues in a similar way to Rodrik, asserting that existing income and asset distributions reflect the starting point more than the pattern of development. Unlike Rodrik, he tends to accept arguments that exports enhance growth. But he is more concerned with the question of just why these policies were adopted. Reform in the HPAEs tended to be preceded by a concentration of authority in the executive, followed by at least some of that authority being delegated to technocrats. But what happened to wider support for reforms thereafter? In part, he argues, the World Bank is asserting that the regimes gained legitimacy through shared growth, but his counterargument is that sharing was caused as much by the starting point. More tellingly, these countries tended not to be democratic, so the fairness or unfairness of how the benefits of growth were distributed did not matter at that time. And he notes that Bank praise for flexible labor markets referred to prohibitions upon free trade unions and the use of violence.

Conclusions

The World Bank stresses that interventions make sense only when markets fail, yet the lack of any clear empirical foundation for arguments about the extent of market failure in a particular context and the lack of a clear concept in DE of dynamic efficiency suggest that this is an empty criterion. Nothing here explains *where* policy is to come from but instead the prescriptions are linked to universals: squarely, the assertion that markets rarely tend not to fail, so at the level of the national economy and in most general terms success was because the market was allowed to work. This is straightforward 1982 L&P thinking and can be understood in those terms.

We can contrast this with Shonfield, who stresses the historical process and the variation between SEA countries' experiences and practices, finding variation within commonalities. This expands our understanding of what was meant by 1962 L&P thinking and can be understood in those terms.

If we contrast these two belief sets ("1962" in L&P terms and Shonfield), we may learn something: perhaps most simply expressed in the idea that there are many ways to skin a cat. Also, if we consider economy as an effect, it is not wise to view any success after the shift from ISI as isolated from the social and institutional changes that preceded it. Shonfield's view that capitalism had been tamed is for me telling, as it points to profound shifts in the position of society and ordinary people vis-à-vis powerful people and governments. Developed market economies in, say, 1962, were countries whose populations' views of social order and the role of government were arguably very different from the conflict-ridden interwar years. As Dunn reminds us, such historical changes are very hard to be sure about, and therefore one should not trust accounts that seek to explain these changes, as perhaps the contrasting views we have discussed in this chapter confirms. This suggests that any simple story about what caused what should be viewed either skeptically or as but one account among many. From that perspective, it is instructive how DE seems to support strongly any view, such as that of WC, that is *premised* on the idea that policy is vital and that change should contain intentionality.

Questions for discussion

1. What is the point of comparing the Western European and East Asian economic miracles?

2. Discuss the extent to which the presence of straw men in argument accompanies apodictic argument.

3. Discuss justifications for the export credit subsidies advocated by the World Bank in its miracle study, given mainstream DE approaches.

Notes

1 See Box 2.1 on p. 20 for a short explanation of these two phrases. See also the sections "Development economists' unstable views" on pp. 21–23 and "International trade"on pp. 56–57.

2 Thus, while it would seem obvious that the shifts in thinking about development at these times were consistent with the shifts from ISI to EOG, I agree with Dunn that one should be skeptical of accounts that suggest that these changes are easily and accurately explained.

3 While Dunn, in the quote above, refers to the last two decades of the twentieth century, even dating these discussions and debates is contentious. The reader may recall my quote from Gillespie in Chapter 5 (p. 71), who refers to theological debates centuries ago.

4 Robert Wade, personal communication.

5 The phrase "indicative planning" refers to French practices that saw government indicate to key businesses what economic direction was sought, and so supported these goals through allocation of credits, infrastructure, and so on. The sense is that the plan was not legally binding.

6 It does not take much reading in the histories of European countries and the US between the wars to find evidence of levels of social unrest far higher and more violent than what was to become normal after 1945. A good source on labor unrest in the US is *Strike!*, by Jeremy Brecher (1972).

7 If the reader has access to a good library, it is interesting to compare national statistical yearbooks for the two countries at this time. The British variant attempts intellectual coherence through a stress on NIA, while the French contains a range of surveys and other exercises apparently designed to meet particular problems. This might be taken to suggest something about the relationship between data

and metaphysical commitment—whether reality is really messy or really muddled.

8 "Moral hazard" is a peculiar term, I believe derived from the insurance business, that points out that once one is insured against a risk, one may well be inclined to take greater risks, thus increasing insurers' liabilities. For example, if investors think they will be bailed out, they will take higher risks. Arguably, for insurers if this happens a lot they will reduce the amount of insurance they offer, so there is market failure.

9 The phrase comes from an article by Carroll in the journal *Mind* (see Winch (1958)). See also www.mathacademy.com/pr/prime/articles/carroll/index.asp.

10 I thank Warwick McKibben for pointing this out to me in private.

11 The relative absence of landlords is in part a reflection of US policy just after World War II. Because accounts of the Japanese militarism often stressed the problems facing rural areas, the occupying regimes in other countries often pushed through land reform. With Vietnam, as immediate post-war Democrats close to the New Deal were replaced by others, South Vietnamese conservatives were able to delay land reform until rather late, though the middle peasantry that confronted Communist collectivization after 1975 was mainly a US creation (Nguyen Thu Sa 1991). With a different political history, the US colonial power in the Philippines did not push through land reform.

19 Import substituting industrialization revisited

In this chapter we revisit ISI and in so doing examine DE arguments against it, using Ray (1998), Chapter 17.2, "Trade Policy: Import Substitution." We also see what he says about the move away from import substitution (his Chapter 17, Section 4). In the next chapter we will explore in greater detail how DE approaches globalization and economic development.

A useful study of ISI with regard to relationships between economics, political economy, and institutional stability is Waterbury (1999). It is important to appreciate how ISI is often used as a straw man. For mainstream DE, working within what it considers a natural science methodology, the shift from ISI to EOG is often presented as a Kuhnian paradigm shift, with a new theory dealing with anomalies that earlier theory could not explain. This way of explaining the shift is in some ways misleading, not least because of the importance of the extent of market failure to the internal of DE and the lack of empirics to underpin such views.

For students looking for topics for presentations and class discussion, what may be most interesting is not further general debate as to the nature of ISI, but investigation of two issues, through case studies:

1. Details of different histories of change processes in countries said to have implemented ISI (Brazil is a good example); some of these are accounts of what was in the past referred to as success. These same periods were then analyzed by other accounts as failures, as the policies adopted were later considered to be wrong. Students may then track how changing beliefs interpret and reinterpret history. Knowledge of these different historical accounts is often both off the radar screen and revealing when, as is sometimes the case nowadays, such countries again receive favorable publicity as their development performance improves. The meaning of this performance may be read into contemporary debates in different ways. These case studies have the added advantage of offering an opportunity to read texts that support development doctrines that are now anathema to particular belief sets as beliefs change (WC and PWC are good straw men here).
2. Details of how particular sets of development policies were abandoned and/or introduced.

A central issue that Ray has to deal with is to explain and justify abandonment of ISI policies and their replacement by market-friendly EOG strategies.

Trade policy: import substitution

Ray starts by considering why trade policy might exist, and he answers with a common position, which is that it benefits certain groups. Conceptually, this way of entering the argument is striking, as it sets up the discussion in terms of a focus upon factors that interfere with the operation of markets, which suggests that market left alone will, on the whole, lead to good outcomes—that is, that market failure is not generally extensive. In Lindauer and Pritchett's terms, this presents a 1982 position. But we will see that Ray himself appears to disagree with this.

Import tariffs and/or direct controls on foreign trade are supported by those who benefit from them directly, such as firms protected from foreign competition or those allocated rights to import certain goods. These groups then act politically to create lobbies that ensure that these policies stay in place, so that markets cannot work freely, which is clearly consistent with the underlying idea that markets rarely fail. This can be compared with ISI views, where such lobbies are legitimized by the view that they protect domestic interests and permit them to contribute to national economic growth. Ray introduces this pro-ISI viewpoint by referring to the possible desire of a country to break free from the stranglehold of primary production. Conceptually, this opens the door to thinking that an existing pattern of trade, with markets operating freely, may be bad for development. So what we have here, in terms of Ray's argument, are two quite different political stories: the anti-ISI one that is optimistic about free markets and sees export policy as creating interests that lobby to preserve obstacles to deregulation, and the pro-ISI one that is presented as a poor country keen to industrialize and move away from dependency upon primary (likely agricultural) exports.

By bringing in the political, Ray highlights a conceptual tension between the short-term or static framework we saw in Chapter 9—the micro-foundations of DE—and growth economics. This tension comes down to the possibility of long-term gains from trade policies. In terms of the interests of DS, Ray suggests that the introduction of intentionality pushes for an analysis that justifies intervention, for the lobbies he mentions are unconcerned with development as they focus upon their own short-term interests.

From this, for Ray, comes the basic policy issue, which is how to create an artificial competitiveness for domestic producers. Exploitation of local markets arguably can be done through import substitution, in two steps: (1) the creation of barriers to imports, and (2) substituting for these goods by producing them domestically. These have different implications. Barriers to imports alone may be effectively invisible to domestic producers, while policies to support producers that can take over their markets are likely to be more visible and so different politically.[1]

Ray discusses various options. Treatment of different types of imports may be unequal, which poses the question of which are preferred, and to what degree, and the perceived consequences of different patterns of support. Ray argues that there is a strong likelihood of discrimination between imports of inputs to production and consumer goods imports, because the protection of the former directly affects producers' costs, while the latter appears as changes to prices of consumer goods. Again, here, we see Ray pointing to the politics of the situation.

There is also a choice between tariffs and quotas. Ray constructs a model that shows how to gauge the different effects. A tariff or a quota arguably increases the domestic price of an import and so (hopefully) domestic profitability and so output. Both are expected to shift the exchange rate, making the domestic currency usually more valuable. This then gives a basis for a comparative static analysis, which initially suggests that tariffs and quotas have the same effect but differ in which entity receives the benefits of the policy. Domestic producers gain more in the case of quotas (unless they are auctioned), and the government gains more in the case of tariffs.

The political analysis Ray generates proceeds in terms of who or what benefits and discusses the associated interests linked to the trade policy: for example, TV manufacturers will lobby for a quota, hoping that by reducing imports this will improve their profitability by cutting competition. He also points out that governments may be ignorant of economic conditions. For example, because they may not know the precise level of imports that correspond to a given tariff level and thus the corresponding level of domestic production, they may impose a quota that is not effective in its outcome. Ray's analysis divides welfare effects into the static and dynamic.[2] We know that DE can explain for static effects but will struggle with dynamics, affecting the discussion by essentially giving greater weight to the apparent clarity of the static arguments over the apparent lack of clarity of the dynamic arguments.

The basic conclusion of Ray's analysis is that the static arguments show that domestic buyers lose. He uses the common "consumer surplus" methodology, without dealing with the problem that the marginal utility of income may not be fixed.[3] Based on the assumption that the utility of income is fixed, producers and the government gain, while consumers lose.

Further, a dollar is a dollar, and its value is assumed the same for everybody no matter their income levels. Based on this assumption, there is a net loss (if the changes for producers, consumers and government are summed). But he points out that if the consumers are rich, the government revenue is spent on the poor, and producers' gains are valued highly, there will be a net gain in the static analysis. If consumers are very rich, the very poor benefit, and producers' gains are valued very highly, then the net gain will be even larger. Ray notes also that the import "world" price may not stay the same (if the country is not a price taker), and this could also lead to a net static welfare gain. The mechanism here is the sort of thing that noneconomists may not notice and stems from the fall in demand for that good from that country.

Turning to dynamic effects, Ray points to three possibilities:

1. Learning by doing: reductions in costs over time result from the increased level of domestic economic activity caused by the protection.
2. Spillovers: learning by doing in sectors other than that protected through derived demand. The protected sector expands, which affects its suppliers.
3. Increasing returns: the increased scale of production itself reduces unit costs.

Rather than develop these arguments, Ray points to the central issue for him: whether the protection can be removed once a certain level of development has been reached. This focuses the argument on whether the government is relatively autonomous from interest groups that benefit from the protection. This argument relies upon a narrow definition of interests. If resources are mobile, it would be possible to convince people that, even if they have to change sectors, they will have a better life in an economy growing faster than one growing slowly. Once convinced of the "creative forces of destruction" (Schumpeter 1975 [1942]), Ray's argument, the standard DE one, assumes that these people—those who move from one sector to another—focus upon how they benefit from the status quo in certain limited ways and so are unable to think about the effects of future growth. If we recall the basic way of thinking of the world in microeconomics (Chapter 9), the focus is upon their own consumption today and not upon the outlook for their community or their children. But whether this is the case or not is a matter of empirics.[4] Arguably, whether and how change may actually occur is a matter for them and their political and community leaders. We can thus see that the standard discussion of the costs and benefits of ISI appears clear on the static disadvantages (though these depend on valuations of the welfare effects upon different groups) and unclear on the dynamic position.

The move from import substitution

Ray (1998) reports that many ISI countries faced economic difficulties in the 1970s, often associated with balance of payments problems. Because of this, many moved away from ISI, often pushed by the IMF and World Bank. The main problem with ISI, he says, was the creation of vested domestic interests

> that use protection as a monopolistic (or oligopolistic) right, rather than a temporary measure to increase competitiveness. Thus, exports are

stifled by the overvaluation of the exchange rates, but imports are never adequately replaced by domestic substitutes. Instead, protection acts as a wall for continued inefficiencies.

(p. 685)

Is this plausible? What political and political–economic arguments underpin this? As mentioned, this theory contains important assumptions about the nature of interests.

Ray then develops a standard account of ISI, arguing that ISI can only continue while the external environment remains favorable, as was the case for Latin America in the 1970s. Thus he explains the shift from ISI in terms of the 1980s crisis, which grew out of the OPEC oil shocks of 1973–1974 and bank lending to developing countries of the recycled "petro dollars." The situation depended upon banks' perceptions of the risks attached to their loans. Initially, countries like Brazil used these loans to finance further ISI, as did Turkey (using them for public investment projects). Ray argues that, by the end of the 1970s, the trends in debt-export ratios were actually not that bad, but, by 1982, lending had stopped, causing a debt crisis. ISI was abandoned as the debts were renegotiated, with the IMF pushing for policy changes conditional on its participation, and we enter the world of *structural adjustment*. Before examining this, it is worth making two key points.

First, this period deserves further detailed study, for, as we know from the AFC and the GFC, financial markets remain subject to powerful subjective forces. It is possible to argue that, with the gathering shift in global thinking away from ISI and toward support for market forces, whatever the truth, financial judgments would write down the value of loans to countries implementing ISI policies, resulting in increased risk of default and increased likelihood of balance of payments crises. These issues were also bound up with domestic politics in the United States and the UK, containing Wall Street and London as dominant financial centres.

Second, as governments in the United States and the UK came to be strong advocates (under Ronald Reagan from 1982 and Margaret Thatcher from 1979) of free market policies, international banks—whatever their own analyses—may have felt that support from these governments in their negotiations with borrowers required adherence to the new thinking. And, of course, the United States and the UK between them had strong influence on the World Bank and the IMF, in part through their governance structures but also through the beliefs of their staff.[5]

From the early 1980s, WC ideas were expressed in the so-called structural adjustment loans (SAPs). The main elements of a SAP were pretty much those required to shift the development policy from ISI to EOG, and included import and export liberalization (or keeping the exchange rate competitive) and fiscal and monetary discipline (with privatization). There is a vast literature discussing the social costs of such policies, which the reader may consult. We have seen already the problems facing Easterly (1999) in analysing why these policies seemed to have such poor results (Chapter 10).

One of the more interesting conclusions drawn from experiences with SAPs is that it is difficult to ensure that these policies are actually implemented. The Philippines case study (Chapter 15) would suggest that a central element is the local experience: whether economic activity, leading to job creation, is believed to cause increases in real incomes, and other pointers to popular agreement that the economy is doing well. It is not too farfetched to suggest that the relative clarity of the static arguments and the relative opacity of the dynamic ones mean that the former are more convincing but the latter more important. This is what can be expected from approaches that highly value apodictic thinking. In normal English, it looks good on paper, but the proof of the pudding is in the eating.

Let us now examine an accessible account of ISI from a historical perspective (Waterbury 1999).

ISI: economics, political economy, and institutional stability

In understanding DE, one of the most useful aspects of ISI is to appreciate its role as a straw man. Many countries either have protected or often attempt to protect domestic markets for domestic producers, which can be foreign or domestically owned. Many of these countries are now rich. Protection of the markets against imports pushes up domestic prices, increasing producers' profits. In order to encourage investment and business activity, it is useful for those who oppose protection to set up a straw man that can be used to show that this policy option should not be followed.

Because ISI is a part of most courses on development, DE, and development policy, it is worth asking the essentialist and realist question: What was it? Waterbury (1999) argues that ISI is not a pure type[6] and often set the conditions for successful export promotion. He points to commonalities among countries with ISI strategies:

- Industrialization was usually (but not always) conceived of as heavy industrialization and often aimed at autarky—economic self-sufficiency.
- Tariffs, quotas, and quantitative trade restrictions were used everywhere.
- ISI was often driven by military/strategic aims.
- The agricultural sector was seen as the major source of surplus for industrial investment.
- It was believed that markets could be tamed by the use of plans and policy interventions.

Waterbury argues also that there was no commonality regarding the following:

- the role of FDI;
- the role of the private sector;
- the extent and presence in different sectors of SOEs;
- macroeconomic policies—exchange rate, fiscal, and monetary;
- policies toward agriculture;
- redistributive policies.

This suggests, therefore, that a modern ISI, if positive in attitude toward light industry, agriculture, and markets, could/would return to old arguments in favor of infant industries—the idea that start-up industrial development firms would simply be too weak and immature to cope with open competition. To avoid criticism, a modern ISI would be presented as quite different from classic ISI. Such a contemporary neo-ISI would have to be WTO-proof and would therefore involve methods of non-tariff protection that did not require high import tariffs, though many developing countries have negotiated significant "tariff bounds" as part of WTO membership. Arguably, these policies would include goals of political stability and would seek rapid employment creation, thus encouraging FDI for light manufactures, as well as steady growth in rural incomes, thus encouraging high levels of state spending in rural places on areas such as infrastructure, social spending, and credits to local business. Further, to manage all this, whoever is in the driving seat would seek a capable state to do this, able to cope with hard-line EOG and neoliberal foreign policy advice. I would argue that this style is becoming visible in some parts of the world.

Conclusions

It is important to distinguish the theoretical arguments from the history of the shift from ISI and the context of the debt crisis. It is also important to consider the historical failure of periods in which ISI strategies were adopted to result in sustainable growth in many countries and its continuation in some developmental successes, such as China, India, and Vietnam. In many ways the particular developmental histories of these countries challenge the standard prescriptions of mainstream DE and this suggests that the contingency and uncertainty identified in L&P and linked to 2002 may be persuasive.

Questions for discussion

1. Discuss the extent to which the accounts of Shonfield and Waterbury contrast with standard accounts of the weaknesses of policies that do not stress the value of export-orientation.

2. Discuss whether the absence of clear dynamic efficiency arguments within DE leads to arguments to focus on static efficiency issues, which can be argued more clearly.

3. Consult the WTO website and discuss options for policies that protect domestic firms and are acceptable in WTO terms (in other words, policies that would be hard for competitors to deal with through WTO mechanisms). Comment on likely domestic political implication.

Notes

1   See Ha-Joon Chang (2003) for a comparison of US protection in the nineteenth century, which involved little more than tariffs, and that of others, which made the state far more directly involved in the economy. These contrasting learning experiences are illuminated by the work of Zysman (1983) and Wade (1988 and 1990).

2   The difference between static and dynamic analysis in DE has been discussed in Chapter 9. Discussing microeconomics, the former is the idea of changes in how the economy allocates resources to competing ends, but with important variables, such as the capital stock and the supply of labor, assumed not to change. When the analytical focus is on growth—as we saw in Chapters 7 and 8—these variables are now said to change.

3   The issue here, which is somewhat technical, is that this technique relies upon the idea that the value of a dollar is the same as income changes. This allows, if extended empirically, reference to be made to the so-called Marshallian observable (fixed-income or uncompensated) rather than the Hicksian unobservable (fixed utility or compensated) demand curve. There is little reason to suppose that the value of a dollar does not vary with income, either for the same individual or between individuals. The reader may consult Stiglitz (2000: 109–111) to see how he gets around this ("since the compensated and uncompensated demand curves are almost the same, typically"). He gives no empirical justification for his view that the value of income does not vary significantly as income rises and falls. The reader may wish to refer to the discussion of risk-averse behavior in Chapter 13.

4   The reader may wish to review the discussion of work by Kung (2000) in Chapter 13 that showed Chinese farmers able to think in terms of ensuring land access to their descendants through their villages.

5   See Rodgers and Cooley (1999), already cited, for histories of what happened in the early 1980s to the careers of World Bank staff who did not rapidly shift their belief sets to the new 1982 (L&P) pattern.

6   To quote: "ISI, both conceptually and in practice, is a very big tent. The variety of experiences that can fit within it is so great that generalizations either wash

out important variations and the reasons for them, or lose all analytic sharpness. Moreover, most countries pursued a mix of inward-oriented and export-oriented policies, sometimes simultaneously, sometimes in sequence. In a number of countries ISI set the conditions for successful export promotion. Thus, neither ISI nor export-led growth are pure types, and the balance between them tended to shift over time" (p. 323).

20 Globalization and economic development

Some issues

In this chapter we examine what Ray (1998) has to tell us about international trade and contrast this with some empirics. A useful study (Zebregs 1998) tells us whether flows of capital between developed and developing countries follow patterns predicted by mainstream DE. Two other studies (Prasad et al. 2003 and Wood 1997) tell us something about the empirics of discussions about who gains from globalization. The chapter includes an examination of the changing doctrinal position of the IMF. Students should find it extremely easy to select topics for presentation and discussion, since globalization is a hot topic.[1]

The wider context to the economics of globalization

If the core issue is how to understand the pattern of international economic relations, then the patterns of trade and of capital flows are arguably simply the *effects* of powerful forces. This relates to the question of who benefits from international economic relations and globalization, and why. It is worth recalling that until World War II the dominant relation between poor and rich countries was one based upon force; most poor countries were subject to foreign rule or close to it. This included Japan's empire—parts of southern China and Manchuria, Taiwan, and Korea—and countries such as the UK, France, and the Netherlands, which worked through familiar systems of colonial rule. Considered in this context are the European and US empires/spheres of influence. For example, the United States had the Monroe Doctrine and its various influences over Latin America, with only the Philippines as a significant former colony. World War I saw the removal from the field of international relations, and so from the colonial game, of the Ottoman and Austro-Hungarian empires, while Germany lost her colonies. But on the eve of World War II most of what are now developing countries in Africa, the Middle East, East, and Southeast and South Asia were colonies. The main exception was Latin America, which had largely thrown off Spanish and Portuguese rule in the nineteenth century. The British Empire had seen various colonies gain substantial degrees of independence (usually those with white populations) and had lost Ireland in the face of armed resistance.

The post-World War II international order saw this international system, with its empires and colonies, replaced by a system of formally sovereign nation-states expressed by the UN system, and through the next decade and a half most of the old imperial structures were disbanded. This immediately posed the problem of how relations between weak and powerful nations would be managed. This issue was aggravated by the Cold War until the rapprochement between the United States and China in the early 1970s and then the fall of the USSR in 1990–1991. By the time of writing, the changing pattern of relations between rich and poor countries and the current situation of greatly reduced respect for poor country sovereignty[2] have combined with major shifts in relative geopolitical power (the rise of China and India, the decline of the United States, and the slow pace of change in the European Union). There remains a rule-governed but anarchic order —in the sense that there is no global sovereign—with a range of international organizations associated with the UN system, such as the General Agreement on Tariffs and Trade (GATT), United Nations Conference on Trade and Development , WTO, and the IMF/World Bank.

Mainstream DE and the economics of trade

Since World War II, international trade has grown fast (Ray 1998, Chapter 16). This was true in the first twenty-five years after 1945, despite the predominance of ISI as the main development paradigm. For poor countries, performance has been mixed. One can argue that there are three broad groups of countries with somewhat similar conditions:

1. Successful EOG: East Asia and some of SEA.
2. Some export success but without a sustained breakthrough: parts of Latin America.
3. Failure, with the focus on many African countries.

Until around 2000 the terms of trade tended to move against primary producers. Since then, as countries like Australia have learned to their advantage, the trend has reversed. The composition of exports from poor countries as a whole has generally shifted toward manufactures (although this hides the great variation among them). Ray argues that this largely reflected deliberate government policy in East Asia, with other countries trying to imitate East Asian success. Standard DE theory would suggest that developing countries export primary products and import manufactures, but while globally there is an apparent trend of manufactures as a share of exports rising with GDP, there is no apparent trend of primary imports rising as a share of imports with GDP.

Economic theory contributes the concept of *comparative advantage* to discussions of foreign trade. If you assume that only one input is needed to produce two different goods, with fixed but different input/output ratios, then trade should involve specialization in the goods that a country is relatively efficient in producing. One way of thinking about this is that each country uses the relative abundance in another country of the input it lacks—through trade. The *absolute* cost of production does not matter, and all benefit.

Comparative advantage comes from various factors, including technology, so that transformation ratios (inputs into outputs) differ between places, and factor endowments—even if technologies are the same, a model can show that mutually beneficial trade can occur. The analysis looks at the production possibility frontiers for each country. These are the different ways in which fixed available resources can be combined to produce different quantities of given sets of outputs and will differ according to the different factor endowments. When there is trade, the relative prices of goods and services will change in each country, cheapening goods and services that use more relatively scarce inputs (now accessed through trade). This is the so-called Heckscher–Ohlin theory of trade. It is not entirely consistent with observations (Ray 1998: 636).

Preferences may also affect trade, because if personal preferences vary to *support* differences in factor availability (for example, poor people eat more food), this will reduce trade. If preferences vary to *offset* differences in factor availability (for example, rich people prefer labor-intensive tradable services such as tourism), this will encourage trade.

Specialization poses additional problems for theory, because the presence of economies of scale makes most models unstable. Specialization can also be seen as a form of concentration, so that we find regions highly focused on particular products, such as airplanes or electronic chips.

Issues of globalization

Looking at the global picture, the pattern seems to be one of limited success, in that some but not all poor countries benefit strongly from globalization. In other words, some fail while some succeed. In most global aggregates, the overall picture is heavily influenced by the different trends in East Asia (as we have already seen from the discussions of poverty in Chapter 16). We will address the question—Why East Asia?—in the next chapter. We saw both critics of the World Bank miracle study argue that these differences between the countries they studied and other developing countries tend to reflect the importance of circumstance (for example, starting point) rather than reliance upon free markets.

For many economists who work on developing countries, clearly an important aspect of current globalization processes is that they be seen as leading to convergence—that is, that income and welfare differences between rich and poor countries tend to decrease rather than increase. Again, this is related to export orientation and the openness of the economy (the extent to which it trades and sees capital flow across its borders). A range of ideas can be found that take this direction, including the view (for example, Yamazawa 1992) that the pattern of development globally is essentially progressive, in that latecomers to globalization would see incomes and welfare rise, and, as this happened, old sectors (typically labor intensive) would become uncompetitive, while new sectors using higher technological levels and more capital would become more competitive.

In some textbooks, this derives from theories attributable to Heckscher–Ohlin and at root to predictions of factor price equalization (Krugman and Obstfeld 2000: 77–79). The Heckscher–Ohlin theory reportedly states that "the model doesn't give us an accurate prediction [and] in the real world factor prices are *not* equalized" (p. 78). This has important implications for the political economy of export-oriented growth. It is certainly appealing, not least on intellectual grounds, to accept arguments that growth patterns that involve openness will lead to a rapid growth in employment if that growth is in labor-intensive sectors (such as light manufactures). It is far less appealing to consider alternatives, which is that population growth and relative intersectoral growth rates, combined with the nature of wage determination, could lead to negligible shifts in relative rewards to factors of production, so that wages stagnate.

Empirics relating to international economic interactions

At this point it is useful to examine a study of the empirics of international capital flows. We recall from Chapter 18 how DE orthodoxy of "1982" argued strongly that free movements of capital would be rational, flowing from where it is most abundant to where other factors are most abundant. We saw also in Chapters 7 and 8 that this issue was treated as fundamental in discussing reasons for nonconvergence in the context of economic growth theory, arguing that high levels of human capital and R&D were probably offsetting declining returns to capital.

What has been happening? Zebregs (1998) reported an inability to find any clear relationship between what the neoclassical model most often used by DE predicted and the resulting flows of FDI. According to him, most FDI is going to a small number of middle-income countries rather than to the poorest (where wages are lowest). The paper argues that the basic empirics of FDI are that it flows to a small number of relatively high per capita GDP developing countries and is highly concentrated within developing countries arranged by levels of GDP. It does not follow simple neoclassical theory, which would expect FDI to flow to countries with low relative labor costs, nor does it follow patterns that would be expected with models that account for variation in technology by country. Zebregs (1998) concludes: "The marginal product of capital, as defined by the standard neoclassical model, cannot explain the observed distribution of FDI flows to developing countries" (p. 23).

This poses a second question. If not price, what other factors influence perceived interests, and are these influenced by changing DE views on the correct way to do development—ISI, EOG, and so forth? What influences investor and policymaker expectations? In looking for doctrinal positions, we can examine what the IMF has said.

It would make sense to take the IMF's views as a good proxy for important global opinion, and we can recall the history of the transition from ISI and the early 1980s debt renegotiations (Chapter 19). Until the early 1970s, the IMF supported the existing regime of fixed exchange rates and restrictions on capital flows but moved to support liberalization of the capital account of the balance of payments in keeping with new thinking in favor of market liberalization (the shift from 1962 to 1982, in L&P terms).

We have seen the somewhat apocalyptic opinions of Michel Camdessus, IMF head during the AFC. Certainly, the crisis suggested that premature liberalization of capital flows was risky, exposing the IMF to moral hazard problems in its role as international lender of last resort. A few years later, L&P (2002) suggests that the mainstream consensus position was a mixed view, and we can find evidence that IMF doctrine has indeed shifted. This shift, clearly related to that discussed by Dunn (2000; see quote in Chapter 10), is striking. In terms of empirics, clearly the past has not changed, but the interpretation of it has. We may note that the shift in doctrine took two rather different lines.

First, an empirical study (Prasad et al. 2003) argued that the key issue was the inability to identify clear causality: while countries with a high degree of financial integration had indeed grown faster than those without (a simple correlation), a detailed examination of the data could not identify a robust causal relationship between the degree of financial integration and growth performance, nor was there evidence for financial integration reducing fluctuations in consumption. This was despite the fact that "In theory, there are many channels by which financial openness could enhance growth" (Prasad et al. 2003: 6 and 26). Correlation, of course, is not causality.

Second, if this was what research argued, a public statement by senior IMF officials (in the *Financial Times*) argued in clear L&P (2002) terms that countries

> do enjoy the benefits of financial integration, in terms of both higher growth and lower instability, once they have crossed a certain threshold in terms of the soundness of their domestic monetary and fiscal policies and the quality of the social and economic institutions.
>
> (Prasad and Rogoff 2003)

Yet, they argued that:

> Economic theory leaves a number of complex and crucial questions unanswered. For instance, in order to control the risks associated with

opening up to capital inflows, it seems necessary for countries to have strong institutions. On the other hand, inflows of capital, especially foreign direct investment, may bring technological know-how and knowledge of best practices in other countries that can improve domestic institutions. So should a country postpone opening its capital markets until it has good institutions? Or should it use financial integration as a tool to improve its institutions? Unfortunately, there are *no definitive answers to these issues, which are best approached by each country depending upon its circumstances.*

(*Idem*, emphasis added)

This appears to be a call both for central banking practice to be improved and for an integration of economics with other logics/approaches. It is an encouragement for economists to actively negotiate across disciplinary boundaries, and it is far less certain about what should be done than would earlier have been the case.[3] Comparison can be made with the position taken in the 1993 World Bank study, which, similar to the 1982 views we saw in L&P, was very certain about what should be done and why.

In early 2003, George W. Bush came to power in the United States, and neoliberal foreign policy advocates gained considerable influence, running into the sands of Iraq and Afghanistan, and acting as a backdrop to the GFC (the reader may wish to recall Martin Wolf's apocalyptic statements in Chapter 1: "we are seeing at least the beginning of the end not just of an illusory 'unipolar moment' for the US, but of western supremacy, in general, and of Anglo-American power, in particular" (Wolf 2009).

The apodictic reasoning of microeconomic theory and economic growth theory (Chapters 7, 8, and 9) lacks traction. The rather simple stories of neoclassical economics argued that free markets tend to shift resources to areas where they can be used most efficiently, to areas where capital is scarce and labor relatively cheap. Yet Zebregs presents empirics that this is not the case. IMF doctrine from the early noughties argues that economic theory tells us little about the value, a priori, of capital account liberalization, thus rejecting (though perhaps this would be denied) apodictic reasoning.

Globalization and labor

We can go further and ask what economists were saying about the effects of globalization on returns to labor. Here we examine the work of Adrian Wood (1997), one-time chief economist of the UK Department for International Development. He argues that the conventional wisdom, as of the mid 1990s, was that

Greater openness to trade has been accompanied by rising rather than falling wage inequality. In contrast, the debate over trade and inequality in developed countries is now over the magnitude of the effects, with their direction – adverse to unskilled workers – being largely agreed.

(p. 33)

This is because naive neoclassical theory expected that trade openness would boost the relative demand for unskilled labor (the factor in relatively abundant supply in poor countries). But Latin American experience since the mid-1980s—that is, the abandonment of ISI—has been to the contrary, with widening differentials between skilled and unskilled workers. This tends to contradict what is thought to have happened in East Asia in the 1960s and 1970s: a massive incorporation into the workforce of low-skilled workers. Wood looks at two classes of explanations.

The first treats differences between East Asia and Latin America as central. This, he argues, is not easy to cope with empirically. The second explanation looks at differences between the two periods of the global economy before and after the massive growth of Chinese exports in the 1980s. First, the entry of China and other large low-income Asian countries meant that unskilled workers in Latin American middle-income countries faced far greater global competition. Second, technical progress shifted in ways that were biased against unskilled workers, since technology required greater skills. Wood concludes that the data does not permit strong conclusions to be drawn. In any case, where does this leave the simple arguments about the value of free markets in the absence of market failure?

Conclusions

Quite apart from L&Z (1993), there is strong evidence that simple DE expectations do not fit well with the evidence provided by scholars such as Zebregs and Wood. This may be taken to suggest that market failure is widespread, and so context and institutions are extremely important to plausible explanations, not to mention hopes of predictive success. This argument fits with the positions taken by economists, such as Agenor and Montiel (1999) and Bardhan (1993), that conditions in developing countries do not suit standard economic theory. This was confirmed by our examination of Bardhan and Udry (1999) (in Chapter 9). This argument is quite independent of the discussion of the more general point as to how often, in general, markets fail.

Again, this evidence implies that the 1982 project, and the associated high stress upon the relative power of economic logics (as then construed), had weak intellectual foundations. We can see this in how arguments about the efficiency of markets usually refer to statics, and so offer access to the statements we found in Chapter 9, echoed by Stiglitz, about how markets work. These are apodictic, founded upon the attributes of models, and, as we found in Chapter 6 and in this chapter, links between these models and reality are vague rather than predictive, as their form hopefully suggests. Further, these arguments are, in their form, universalist, leading to belief that what works there works here, but with empirical difficulties.

Questions for discussion

1. Discuss, starting with Rodrik (1998), confusions in the empirics of globalization comparable to what Ravallion had to say about poverty in Chapter 16.

2. Since the late 1990s, Australia, a country that largely exports primary commodities, has seen its terms of trade improve and improve faster during periods of slower global growth. Discuss in the context of standard arguments about the value of export-oriented growth.

3. Discuss tensions in arguments about free trade, which stem from the end of the Cold War, and the geopolitical need to bind poor countries, especially China, into global economic relations.

Notes

1   Rodrik (1998) is an accessible introduction.
2   DS students are hopefully aware of arguments behind this: fears of failed states, mistrust of Third World elites, and rising problems of corruption. I cannot develop these ideas here and leave it to students and class discussion to examine the question of how the status of DE may fit into such debates.
3   This lack of certainty fits well with how L&P characterize economists' beliefs in "2002" (see Chapter 2).

21 Why East Asia?

In this chapter we look at discussions that aim to answer the question: Why has East Asia apparently seen such economic success? We have seen often how the empirics of global economic development are crucially influenced by East Asia and, in recent years, also by India. With the GFC, attention also started to focus upon the so-called BRIC countries: Brazil, Russia, India, and China.[1]

We will examine Johnson (1998), who argues strongly for the importance of the context. We will also look at an important add-on to mainstream DE—the concept of commodity chains (Gereffi 1999)—and at a useful discussion from outside DE that compares SEA with Northeast Asia (NEA) (Macintyre 1994). A central issue here, which talks to the relationship between DE and DS, is the importance of economic policy and whether it has become more or less important for a country to have the capacity to devise and implement good policy.

The question of geographical context is arguably interesting in thinking about how history could have been very different and trying to compare what happened in East Asia with somewhere else. If India, for example, after World War II, had shown the same rapid changes as East Asia, what would have happened to regions comparable to SEA? If SEA was drawn into dynamic change processes by its proximity to NEA, which regions could have been similarly influenced had India grown rapidly in the years just after the war? Thus consider the differences between SEA, which contains the immigrant group, the Tamils, and East Africa, which is home to another common immigrant group from India, the Gujeratis. The fates of these two Indian migrant groups turned out to be very different as SEA benefited from Japanese economic power, while in East Africa there was no equivalent to Japan. Could these situations have been different?

After World War II, India was a democracy, militarily linked to the USSR, hostile to China (border wars), and with not much local industrial development. Indian post-war growth was autarchic, with policy driven by high levels of government control and regulation. Until the 1990s, its growth was slow and had little effect upon its neighbors. For East Africa, there is no equivalent to Japan as a powerful driver of regional economic development dating back to before World War I. Iran, for example, never had equivalent mass in modern times. SEA economic history is deeply bound up with Japan's post-World War II export drive. The comparison with East Africa is stark. With a different history, one can imagine Indian global firms starting to push overseas, as local costs rose (which, of course, is not such a persuasive comparison because Indian labor reserves are far larger than Japan's, given the limits to Japan's global reach).

But even since the 1980s, as India has been growing about as fast as China (a little slower, but still very fast), the East African story is still quite different from SEA: the forces pushing for global integration differ in these two regions. In other words, context and history can be argued to be very important. Obviously, just how important, and in what ways, is a matter for comparative explanations, and it is likely that these will include a wide range of factors, such as culture, nineteenth- and early twentieth-century histories, and local elite and popular attitudes. While these cannot be discussed here, as our focus is upon understanding DE, these considerations should point students to a range of topics for presentations and discussion.

An issue here is the combination of the obvious importance of geopolitical issues with problems in addressing them (this is not a book on international relations). Topics worth considering include the ways in which privileged market access granted to particular countries and not others sometimes appears to lack positive developmental impact (Mexico's economic relations with the United States in the 1960s are a useful example), examples of how market access was negotiated (Vietnam was granted early access to EU markets despite US counterpressure), and the overall effects of the low contemporary tariff levels (Hill 2000). If possible, students may also search out equivalent analyses to those of Johnson and Gereffi, which also offer alternative explanations of aspects of globalization.

The Cold War

Why East Asia? Chalmers Johnson (Johnson 1998) argues that the AFC raised important long-term issues. He focuses his argument on the question of whether East Asia was miracle or design. This implies focusing upon the role of policy, the causes of change, and implications for the present. He argues that the ultimate reasons for the AFC remain unclear, but arguments so far have tended to support the revisionists rather than the Anglo–American economic orthodoxy—that markets on the whole should be left unregulated. His position is that the entire Asian development picture cannot be understood outside of the global and cultural context. He asserts that the focused and effective drive to export and grow, as shown by Japan and South Korea, relied upon various factors, including access to the US market. This was predicated upon subordination to US geopolitical interests, with major political consequences in terms of countries' abilities to depart from US interests. He argues that SEA countries responded rather passively to some of the consequences of this situation, compared with the ways in which Japan, South Korea, and Taiwan in different ways actively exploited access to US domestic markets. In the run-up to the AFC, Japanese and Korean companies responded to cost pressures, including the refusal of the US government to confront structural barriers to market access in Japan, leading to the forced revaluation of the yen. At the same time, partial deregulation of Japanese financial markets had led to excessive monetary expansion and a "bubble" economy, with grossly inflated real- estate values and excess lending.

The increase in the value of the yen led to an export of the Japanese bubble economy to SEA, and, he argues, without use of state power to control the consequences, eventually the markets turned against the bubble. The details of this history are not important to us here. What is important are the issues he is raising: on the one hand, his view that SEA growth is mainly to be explained by context, not by policy; and on the other, the idea that this also helps to explain the problems of the AFC—the lack of appropriate policy. Thus the question of the presence and impact of policy becomes central, and explaining the AFC becomes a way of testing for the presence of policy and state power. Johnson examines three alternative approaches that he says have been advanced for explaining the crisis:

1. *Liquidity crunch*: Was the crisis essentially financial? He points to the emergence of China as a global competitor and its rising exports prior to the crisis, helped by the devaluation of 1994. He cites political dealings between Japan and the United States designed to secure President Bill Clinton's re-election in 1996, the yen devaluation, and the adverse effects upon SEA exporters. Also, Japanese proposals to support crisis-hit countries were rejected by the United States in favor of the IMF, which imposed (initially) deflation and high interest rates, worsening the crisis.[2] He seems to conclude that the crisis was not essentially financial.
2. *Overcapacity*: This is similar to the liquidity-crunch argument but more depressing. Johnson argues that SEA economics do not rest on good fundamentals. There is chronic oversupply in core sectors of East Asia, resulting from overinvestment, and demand for these goods is increasingly weak and oversaturated. This suggests that EOG policies, with the associated heavy investments in support of them, may be running out of steam globally, and that maintaining competitive edge may be the new dominant issue for lower-income countries. He seems to conclude that EOG policies need to be seen as problematic, mainly in their destabilizing effects on the global economy. This is an interesting pointer to the nature of the GFC a decade later and the increasing problems with the Chinese export surplus.
3. *The end of the Cold War*: Johnson appears to like this approach the best. He argues that the basic question is the fundamental origins of the East

Asian model, with its major impact upon SEA economic development. If the answer is the Cold War and the desire to bind Asia economically to US influence, trading market access, and EOG driven by powerful state measures, then the end of the Cold War must logically have major consequences. The underlying question here is whether economic success in East Asia, unlike during the Cold War, is now seen by the US as tending to weaken rather than increase US political influence.

I ask the reader to compare such considerations with the standard approach of DE as exposited in Ray (1998) or T&S (2006).

East Asia and commodity chains

If we look for explanations of how East Asia operates economically as a region, we can find one in what Gereffi (1999) has to say about commodity chains, where the focus is upon the dynamics of position. Analytically, the question is how to define position and this is done through the concept of the commodity chain, which is the "whole range of activities involved in the design, production and marketing of a product" (p. 38).

This is a view from business studies but is arguably about economics. The starting point is fundamentally that of asymmetry in markets, resource costs, control and technology, and how this evolves. He argues that people learn from this process by being part of it. It is highly competitive and the outcome of context: the evolution of economic relationships, which includes established high-cost economies that export globally and manage their production processes across international borders.

Gereffi makes a distinction between chains for "buyer-driven" (in which the central organizer is a retailer, branded manufacturer, or branded marketer selling, for example, garments, footwear, and toys) and "producer-driven" (the central organizer is a large company or producer selling, for example, cars and airplanes). He believes that Asian success has involved mastering the dynamics (that is, how to change over time) of shifting from low local value-added work involving the assembly of imported inputs to original equipment manufacturing and finally to production of its own brand goods. But the question is what controls these chains—which country and which agency. Profitability tends to be highest where entry barriers are highest; this is the same for both buyer-driven and producer-driven changes, as the point of the barriers to entry is to reserve high-value positions in the chains for certain groups. This is because, in buyer-driven chains, high entry barriers are not related to control over technology and backward and forward linkages but to advantages, based upon research and marketing, in shaping mass consumption via strong brand names and using global sourcing to meet this demand.[3] Thus, as a firm within the chain seeks to get closer in position to brand names, which use highly sophisticated marketing techniques (with proprietary information sources) and similar central sources of profit, it gets more difficult: entry barriers increase. It is the position within the chain that is crucial to understand what a particular agent does, and moves up the chain seeks to secure high profits and are therefore resisted by incumbents, such as putting up entry barriers (setting the standards for style is a good example).

This came about because of the importance of establishing close linkages with lead firms in buyer-driven chains, so that a network of business relations results. The lead firms are primary material sources, which grant technology for transfer and knowledge, and sell to retailers and marketers. The next step is "industrial upgrading"—that is, moving within these networks to points where profits are higher. This may or not involve actually physically moving the site of activity. This upgrading is not simply caused by changes in prices (that is, rising wages) but is linked with organizational capacity and within this to learning processes. Firms do not move outside the chain, but alter their position within it. In the garments industry, for example, the crucial step is to go beyond assembly to original equipment manufacturing and to a situation where the local firm is also actively involved in upstream and downstream linkages, in order to buy in inputs (which means ensuring quality) and extend its supply reach toward the retailer. Therefore, the big issue is related to the positions occupied within the network, or the commodity chain.

Although both sorts of chains have been involved in the internationalization of SEA, the capacity to move to more profitable niches in buyer-driven chains derives from business strategies within the chain that are different from those in a producer-driven chain. High profits in producer-driven chains come from technology and organization, while in buyer-driven chains they come from relational aspects (your position in the chain), trade policy (quotas), and brand names.

In terms of DE and its position within DS, it seems clear that the commodity chain approach is far easier to access from a DS perspective, because the approach denies the all-determining importance of price in economic behavior taught in DE mainstream microeconomics (Chapter 9). Historically grounded, the approach denies the instrumental rationality hypothesis by taking learning processes seriously and treating them as open—that is, part of the evolutionary process.

Before concluding this chapter, and moving toward the end of the book by examining spin in DE, it is useful to see how political scientists have treated issues arising from the role of policy in economic growth in SEA and NEA.[4]

Politics and political economy

Macintyre (1994) offers a clear overview of the pre-crisis (1997) literature on SEA and NEA and how to explain and analyze rapid economic growth when the role of government and the state is seen as crucial. He divides the literature by its focus upon two related issues: (1) the nature of the involvement of government in markets, and (2) the effects of business upon political life.

It is evident that the NEA/SEA comparison reveals much about the literature. A key question is the extent to which SEA states are developmental—whether they offer coherent narratives of how, guided by policy, their governments did development. This question is given added meaning by accounts of NEA that stress the importance of developmental states, with the nature of the relationship between state and business as a central variable underpinning spectacular economic performance (Johnson 1982 on Japan). MacIntyre sees two broad clusters of ideas used to analyze and compare development in NEA and SEA:

1. *State strength*: A slippery concept about the extent to which officials and politicians are isolated from political pressures and coherent in their policy formulation.
2. *Strategic intervention in markets*: How the officials and politicians developed their countries.

He notes that in neither cluster is business seen as important in determining state action. The situation with SEA, on the other hand, is different. As defined in the literature he surveys, state strength is far less than in NEA, while SEA states are far closer to business and far less coherent in formulating development policies and intervening in markets. The shift toward EOG in SEA is said to have made this difference more striking. There is evidence from both Thailand and Vietnam that shifts in policy often follow shifts in economic direction. However, SEA economies have tended also to show spectacular growth.

MacIntyre points to two important possible conclusions from this:

1. SEA poses a challenge to orthodox views of the key to successful development—that is, the need for active measures to secure development, for developmentalism. Is a strong state needed?
2. SEA political and economic development is unsustainable, for political reasons, because no strong state exists. When major restructuring is politically resisted by important interest groups, the state is not strong enough to overcome resistance from the interest groups and so does not occur.

Like Gereffi, such accounts are informative about economic issues, are a long way from standard DE as we find it exposited by the canonical textbooks (Ray and TS), and are accessible.

Conclusions

To conclude, we may note the fundamental tensions created by the idea that East Asia's success was not intentional. If it was not intentional, then logically it was accidental, and that means that policy—and so policy advisers—was not necessary. The classic view of policy that underpins DE encourages viewing success as a combination of good policy (either imported or locally derived, or a combination), and effective government (to implement good policy). Remove intentionality and it makes things seem far less stable, especially if the context seems to have fundamentally changed. Since the Cold War has ended, we see the emergence of large rapidly growing economies—China and India—rather than the trickle down model of East Asian derived growth. Perhaps Martin Wolf is right to be so concerned that we are seeing the "beginning of the end . . . of western supremacy" (Wolf 2009). And perhaps that pushes DE to be more accessible to DS.

Questions for discussion

1. Discuss the implications for DE of MacIntyre's view that economic development in SEA happened rather than being caused by policy and politics.

2. Compare the concept of a commodity chain with the mainstream DE microeconomic conceptualization of how consumers and firms are interrelated.

3. Would you expect that the local change rationalities of Asian interventionists would make sense to those trained in standard DE conceptualizations of how economies work? And vice versa?

Notes

1 When I first studied development economics, in the mid-1970s, Brazil was an emerging economic giant, with a military government driving sophisticated ISI.
2 Johnson could have added other comments here, not least that it is not exactly clear how the political dealings between Japan and the US affected the issue.
3 This recalls the discussion of Veblen's ideas of conspicuous consumption in Chapter 14.
4 While here NEA now includes China, Taiwan, South Korea, and Japan, at the time Macintyre was writing China was not so clearly part of successful NEA. The other country within China's historical cultural sphere is, of course, Vietnam, but it is conventionally seen as part of SEA and again, at the time Macintyre was writing, was not obviously a success story.

22 Experimental economics, the problem of empirics, and the challenge to development studies

Introduction

This chapter starts with a discussion of why experimental economics is valuable and stresses the nature and thrust of its empirical focus. Next, an overview is followed by a summary of how the standard positions within DE appear in light of the results of experimental economics: first, we learn about the extent of market failure, and, second, the assumption of instrumental rationality. A short section points out that much positive comes from experimental economists' work, followed by a discussion of how these results challenge DS and standard intervention models in development work that assume knowable cause–effect relations—predictive knowledge.

A discussion of experimental economics gives us a good opportunity to review some important issues raised in this book and to explore just how development economics challenges development studies and aid workers.[1] A core element of this challenge is the debate about whether international development aid fosters attention upon issues of mainstream practice that is based upon the belief that interventions can and should organize around knowledge of cause–effect relations, which is predictive and so known beforehand. This raises the question as to whether such relationships are indeed knowable in a predictive sense.

DE presents, as we have seen many times, as possessing such knowledge, but, as we have seen, there are many good reasons to question this. In turn, this alerts us to the wider issue of whether it is wise to organize development interventions around the assumption that we can predict what will happen. I have argued, stressing in particular the Levine and Zervos study, that DE, if it wishes to, has good grounds for skepticism. Experimental economics adds further empirical support for skepticism about mainstream beliefs. Such issues should resonate, for international workers and development studies scholars, with concerns about power asymmetries and their mediation through experts positioning themselves on a base of "knowledge."[2] The literature is full of worries about such tangles; historically, creators of techniques of rapid rural appraisal (RRA) and participatory rural appraisal (PRA) aimed squarely at a generation of knowledges that would avoid perceived adverse consequences of power asymmetries (Chambers 1983). The discussion of development debacles in Chapter 15 explored links between adverse developmental impacts and development doctrines. The discussion of participatory methods in the context of Mosse (2005, Chapter 9; Fforde 2010) suggests that misplaced predictive confidence is not at all the unique property of development economists—Mosse is an anthropologist.[3]

The argument runs both ways. In social terms, while a given academic community of development economists will usually, as economists generally, contain a rather high proportion of theoreticians building models (Chapter 6; Yonay and Breslau 2006), a similar community of development studies academics will have a rather high proportion of people involved in practice, often through international development consultancies. Few aid workers "do theory," building formal models, although they are often far better informed about comparative theories of change than academics credit them (Fechter and Hindman 2011). The knowledge assumptions that underpin aid projects and programs within international development easily confront aid workers with tangled puzzles. They confront the core question of whether an aid project as usually organized actually does what it should do: do the available resources reliably lead to its desired results? If there are difficulties, is this because of ignorance or because of diversity? Is it that we do not know what works, or that what works "there" is not working "here"? Or would it be better to intervene in ways that side-step predictive assumptions and abandon them entirely?

If an intervention such as an aid project or government policy should, for example, reduce infant mortality in its target groups through improved education for fathers, then practitioners face the question of whether infant mortality actually fell, whether male education really improved, and whether this actually resulted in the reduced child deaths. Such questions are bound up with questions of empirics (did mortality fall, did male education improve?) and causality (why did this happen?). Further, in contested situations, these questions are all debatable: precisely *which* measures of mortality and male education were used, and is there agreement about whether they were suitable and accurate? Who, actually, gets to say what caused what and who decides on the adoption of—or belief in—one causative explanation rather than another? DS students are well aware of how addressing such issues will readily involve them in discussions of power relations, of how discourses operate to define and exclude content, and so on (Chapter 5). The tone of such concerns will note very readily any suggestion that purportedly predictive explanations have only "vague" relations to reality, to recall what we found in the discussions of Chapter 6. Further, as McCloskey (1985) pointed out, a decision that a parameter in a statistically estimated model is not significantly different from zero will, in some areas of aid practice, clearly depend on the stakes. No decent person would abandon trials of an intervention if, say, half the children in a district were dying before they were one year old simply because the variation in the sample available was far too small to place the estimated parameter far enough away from zero.[4] Therefore, good reasons exist for thinking that, in the absence of reliable predictive knowledge, practitioners should be careful to avoid reckless commitment to unreliable beliefs.

There are tensions in the experimental economics literature between two positions. On the one hand, some argue that recent changes in development economics have seen a considerable expansion of empirical work, often through experiments, leading to better policies or at least the chance of having them.[5] On the other, some argue, somewhat to the contrary, that policy work in the main still relies upon ideas, supported by theory rather than evidence, that relies on the assumption that market failure is not extensive and the key to development is to address market failure.

Experimental economics involves the use of various techniques to generate data under conditions influenced by the experimenters—"the experiment" or (when used more directly to explore policy interventions) the "trial."[6] The degree to which these conditions are determined by the experimenters has caused interesting discussions, not least as this relates to the question of the extent, or manner, in which experimental results are those sought by experimenters; thus, in order to understand the results, we need to know what experimenters themselves want. Some observers of these activities argue that results most certainly need interpretation in terms of the inclinations and prior beliefs of experimenters.

A large part of the literature is indeed concerned with arguments as to whether or not economic behavior in reality does conform to the assumptions found in microeconomic textbooks. This in itself is striking, as, were economics empirically founded, the question would be highly irregular. One very common question that experimenters address is thus whether there is market failure. An important example is whether externalities exist in consumption, where people appear empirically not to seek to maximize their immediate personal gains and act (as the experimental economics literature usually puts it) *altruistically* or (as one might ponder) in ways that support strategies that assume common interests, perhaps unknown, so that sharing makes fundamental sense. We therefore find many experiments that examine results from situations where people confront the "Prisoner's Dilemma" or play what is called the "Ultimatum Game." The point here, sociologically, is that it is natural for the outsider to think that the interest in market failure arises from the belief that markets in reality usually do *not* fail (in this very particular sense—Chapter 9) and that "basically" markets work.

A reading of many of the results of experimental economics suggests, to put it simply, two conclusions. First is that market failure, because of externalities, is the norm rather than the exception. To indulge in some ad hoc reasoning: humans, as any parent of a feisty two-year-old with a four-year-old sibling will tell you, are taught to share willy-nilly. It is dangerous, in the kindergarten, to refuse to learn to share. Second, mainstream economics, for reasons we do not understand very well, faces enormous problems in accepting this. How credible is the following critique?

> {A} major problem is not so much to do with development economics theory as with development economics policy analysis. No matter how sophisticated our theory and empirics become, it seems that in the debates on great policy issues of the day – on exchange rates, trade policy, labor market policy, deregulation etc – simple "ECON 101" economics is very important. For many if not most policy analysts, the basic competitive model . . . is the workhorse tool – it is the framework that slips most easily into mind when thinking about economic policy. . . . At the very least one can say that this position needs to be tested in theory and in empirics.
>
> (Kanbur 2005: 43–44)

If Kanbur is to be trusted, then what we should observe in the impact of experimental economics upon mainstream empirical beliefs is that even when these beliefs are tested empirically and found lacking, they will tend to remain intact (see also Fforde 2005 and Chapter 2). This is worth knowing or at least suspecting.

An overview of experimental economics

Cardenas and Carpenter (2008) give us a good overview of experimental economics from the perspective of lessons learned "from the field labs in the developing world" (p. 311). Before examining what they say, consider Banerjee and Duflo (2011), a popular and influential book, for this shows how the stance of experimental economics offers a platform for a confident knowledge of how to "do development."

Banerjee and Duflo do not appear greatly concerned with the politics of knowledge production, nor do they mention PRA or RRA. In epistemological terms, their stance fits with positions taken by Kuhn and Popper (see Chapter 5) rather than those of more contemporary scholars such as Said, Escobar, and Foucault, who are concerned about *whose* knowledge we are discussing while showing relative lack of interest in ideas that knowledge "progresses." Banerjee and Duflo present a commitment to the idea that knowledge progresses and that their knowledge is better. Banerjee and Duflo's work, though, is (perhaps implicitly) highly political, arguing for their gaining resources and power so that their doctrines, which entail extensive use of experimental techniques, may better establish causes and their effects—what will lead to what, so development can, in this sense be "done," with correct research as they define it. The politics of knowledge production here is to replace one set of allegedly false ideas with another, allegedly true in a predictive sense. Banerjee and Duflo are judiciously skeptical about what is reliably known but confident that, with proper research, the behavior of the poor can be correctly modeled so as to secure predictive power.[7]

Cardenas and Carpenter (2008) is a very good survey of experimental economics. They share the focus of DE upon explaining underdevelopment *within* economics (see Chapter 4). This is clear when they state that "explanations of poverty, growth and development depend on the assumptions made about individual preferences and the willingness to engage in strategic " (p. 311). There is nothing here about power relations or relevant histories that could explain factor endowments such as land (recall the tangles facing DE in explaining land-ownership patterns discussed in Chapter 13). The explanations offered by experimental economics, they argue, assume that "behavioral hypotheses {are} at the core of why, after decades of attempts to induce development . . . a few countries have escaped poverty while others remain severely poor" (p. 311). It is correct for them, thus, and consistent with the epistemological stance they take (see Chapter 5) to focus upon "a topic that has always been at the heart of development economics – individual preferences . . . [and look for] insights in four categories of experiments: the propensity to cooperate in social dilemmas; trust and reciprocity; norms of fairness and altruism; and, risk and time preferences" (p. 311). We can see that, for students from a DS background, the focal issues are very particular, if not provincial, and this situation derives from the disciplinary assumption that *economic* arguments explain development or the lack of it (see Chapter 3).

Any propensity to cooperate in situations of social dilemmas poses problems for mainstream DE when, as is the case, basic microeconomic models suggest that the rational thing for individuals to do is *not* to co-operate. We saw in Chapter 9 how the basic model of microeconomic behavior was that people acted to maximize their own welfare, given prices and incomes. Their own welfare was determined by what they themselves consumed: they gained no pleasure from others' joys. If this particular rationality is assumed to determine behavior, certain things will happen. For example, people will "free ride" by enjoying what taxes fund—such as investment in clean public water supplies—but avoid payment of taxes. The decision whether to pay taxes or not, when the tax bill comes, is obviously easier to model and rationalize than decide whether in principle taxes are worth paying, for if nobody did, there would be no tax revenues with which to pay the bondholders.

Experiments can show whether people do behave like this. Thus, Cardenas and Carpenter (2008) report that economic experiments show the existence of, and measurable variation, in social tendencies to cooperate. They also report that these indicators are correlated with GDP, the fraction of the population in poverty, and other broad gauges of development (p. 312). They find similar patterns in the results of experiments that measure other aspects of behavior, which reveal departures from standard models, and again find that these patterns vary and appear correlated with levels of development. However, they report that indicators of propensities to cooperate tend to *fall* with indicators of the level of development (though they take the US as the epitome of "developed" status). They note that "cooperation increases when social sanctions are allowed" in experiments (p. 317). They generalize that in experiments to gauge cooperation, trust, and reciprocity, "average play is nowhere near the prediction based on egoistic preferences" (p. 320).

In detail, they report results of various types of games, including something called the Dictator Game, where the first participant offers a transfer from a pot to the second person—that is all. This is different from the Ultimatum Game, where, if the offer is accepted, the share-out follows what was offered, but if it is not accepted, both get nothing. The Ultimatum Game is thus rather simple.

To return to my ad hoc sociology, for a two-year-old, "A," with a pile of sweets in front of her, the nasty adult says "share with little 'B' or you get nothing because I am far bigger than you and will take all the sweets away," and so "B" in turn (these children are, of course, compliers, in the end, as socio-pathology is very limited) learns (to produce a happy adult) that if he declines "A"'s offer to share, "A" will lose her sweets, and unless "A" is really angry, cross and wants to kick the table over, she in her turn will learn fast to offer at least something. "A" learns to offer to share with "B," and "B" learns to accept. This is the "horrors of sharing." The grown-up word for it is *socialization*, but adults tend to cloak their dictatorial exercises of power in long words.

In terms of the language of Cardenas and Carpenter, adults teach the horrible two-year-olds that egoistic behavior has severe costs attached to it. So, to be reasonably satisfied by life, with a reasonable amount of sweets, don't be caught being egoistic and, perhaps, don't actually be. Now, Cardenas and Carpenter also report the results of the so-called Trust Game, where the first participant sends as much of his money to the other player as he wants; this amount is then tripled by the experimenter so the second player actually gets three times what the first sent her, and the second player can then send back as much as she wants. Again, mainstream economic rationality predicts a rational outcome where the second player will send back nothing, and so the first should in turn rationally send nothing—and thus no game. But experiments show that people do play, and the percentages sent and returned can be measured. Again, these show variations from place to place, and on this basis experimental economists can link such indicators to levels of development. They report that correlations here are significant. Less poverty is correlated with more trust (p. 322).

Cardenas and Carpenter discuss variations between geographic places in the results of the Ultimatum Game and again find that "most behavior deviates from the subgame perfect equilibrium (of very small offers) in systematic ways" (p. 323). Again, they find that experimental measures of trust correlate with development indicators. Here their argument refers to research done by economic anthropologists (Henrich et al. 2006; see also Henrich et al. 2001) who report that "community level differences explain far more of the variation in play than individual differences" (p. 324). These arguments consistently point to variations in behavior as ways of explaining (through correlation evidence) variations in levels of development, whether of countries or communities.

The last of Cardenas and Carpenter's four issues is related to the idea that varying attitudes to time and risk lead to different patterns of behavior. One belief they quote is that poor people are poor because they have high discount rates (they place very low values on things in the future compared to things here and now) and are risk-averse. They look at experimental evidence and conclude that "there does not appear to be much support for the idea that poor people in developing countries are more risk-averse than richer people in developed countries" (p. 326). They make similar conclusions about time preferences (p. 328).

Their survey thus offers *two* key findings: first, that experiments show that behavior is not crudely egoistical, contrary to what the standard models assume; and, second, that variation in behavior between places is correlated with levels of development. These results are primarily and above all *empiric*, though, as we shall shortly see, understanding their empirics requires an understanding of their theory and practice. As Cardenas and Carpenter conclude, these correlations have then to be explained. Naturally, as economists they seek to offer economic explanations, but we are dealing with issues that likely refuse to stay within economic boxes, such as culture, politics, national social norms, and so forth, and it seems likely that the usual tensions and troubled explorations of interdisciplinary boundaries will arise. They state:

> As the reader can see, there is already a substantial body of experimental work on preferences in developing countries. While some questions have been answered, the main contribution of the current literature is the establishment of a field methodology [that is, for carrying out experiments (AJF)]. We also think that these methods will now set the stage for new, more policy-oriented research. If policies are aimed at inducing changes in to improve outcomes, experiments can provide detailed behavioral data about the effects of certain incentives, institutions or information on a specific context or group. In the future, these data may also make it feasible to calibrate and tailor policies at the local level.
>
> (p. 333)

This conclusion appears at first sight as sound common sense. But we need to appreciate the deeper question behind it—the need to argue that mainstream assumptions about behavior are awry. Why does this point need to be made at all? The answer has something to do, most likely, with the way in which economics, and so DE, offers predictive knowledge but, as it is not set up to select models based upon their predictive power, does not deliver predictive power (Chapter 6).

If we look at the history of experimental economics we find that evidence of departure from the basic beliefs about behavior embodied in the assumptions of mainstream economics is by now very old. Cardenas and Carpenter produce new research, but evidence against the mainstream has been there for a long time. Surveys such as Guala (2008) show early evidence of experimental economics contradicting mainstream beliefs. Similarly, lack of robust relationships between policy and outcomes reported by L&Z was likely obvious to statisticians rather soon after the datasets became available and as published individual studies contradicted one another (Chapter 2), yet most citations of L&Z failed to engage with this central message (Fforde 2005). Again, we are back in the familiar puzzle caused by the generally "vague" relationships between mainstream DE models and empirics despite the evidently predictive nature of the models, with their variables for "t"—time. Yet, as also should be clearer by now, DE, through various mechanisms, is relatively clear, if it cares to be, about what it does and does not know, empirically speaking. This is its challenge to development studies.

A summary of standard positions within DE, in light of experimental economics

The extent of market failure

A central issue within DE is the extent in reality of market failure. We discussed the meaning of this term in Chapter 9, linking it to the view that in its absence markets would work well, delivering good outcomes. Conversely, in its presence intervention was justified. Thus, poor outcomes and ways to deal with them appeared to involve finding ways of reducing the extent of market failure. The argument in Lindauer and Pritchett (see Chapter 1) was that between the early 1960s and the early "noughties" mainstream economists' view shifted from the belief that market failure was widespread through the belief that it was not to a somewhat confused position. Further, these shifts were not driven by changing interactions between models and data as the world changed but by broad experiences and disenchantment with old ideas. As Dunn put it (see Chapter 10), the clear result was the *negative* result—that existing beliefs were thought false. As we have seen, experimental economics has long provided evidence that market failure is widespread, though this has not greatly influenced mainstream economic beliefs.[8]

The meaning of the instrumental rationality hypothesis and justifications for the use of formal algebraic models

I have argued that a basic justification for the use of algebra to model human behavior, with its implicit suggestion of predictability, is the *instrumental rationality hypothesis*: "the assumption is required to support a way of understanding decisions and behavior that uses a formal algebraic model and treats the human as no different from a non-sentient machine" (Box 1.4, p. 14; see also Chapter 11).[9] Various issues arise here.

First, there is the question of the response of those studied to their being studied. As we shall see, based in part upon experimental economics, we find development interventions drawing upon *randomized field trials* to generate interventions (Levitt and List 2009). For comparison, new assessment methods would use a sample of students to seek to predict outcomes. As students are not machines, any canny teacher will expect them to "game" the trial. Even if not told that it is a trial, shrewd ones will easily guess, adjusting their answers to suit their interests, perhaps as individuals, perhaps as a group (perhaps if the new methods are designed to "reduce gender bias," known to students to be a hot topic). Similarly, informed local NGOs working in a population, or the people themselves, can seek to "game" such trials. In almost all surveys of income and expenditure, the lowest income groups usually have incomes from all sources (as reported) that are *lower* than expenditure: no wise person automatically tells an outsider the truth about such things. It would seem to be in the nature of such things that, information being what it is, any particular instrumental rationality the modeler assumes to be operating will easily become the object of such "gaming." The modeler can never fully know what exactly is going on (for that is the point of the gaming) and so stands a strong chance of being unable to predict outcomes (unless those modeled decide to go along with the "man in the white coat" for their own reasons, which does not change much).

Second, there is the response of experimenters to their interactions between their models and their data, and vice versa. This is very interesting, for it is possible to argue that some patterns of interaction change model choice, "endogenizing" it so that, in effect, the instrumental rationality hypothesis does not hold.

Examination of the large experimental economics literature and especially discussions of methodology show a wide range of opinion. Much methodological discussion involves attempts to attack ways in which experimental economics appears to confound standard assumptions.

Examination of this literature adds to the evidence that questions the commitment of much economics to predictive empirical validation. Rabin (1998) argues that:

> Economics has conventionally assumed that each individual has stable and coherent preference, and that she rationally maximises these preferences. Given a set of options and probabilistic beliefs, a person is assumed to maximise the expected value of a utility function $U(x)$.
>
> (p. 11)

After an extensive review, Rabin reports what he sees as the common response of economists to evidence that suggests rejection of this canonical assumption:

> Over the years, economists have proffered many reasons for down-playing the relevance of behavioral research challenging [these] assumptions. . . . It is common when presenting psychological findings to discuss broad methodological objections and attempt to rebut them.
>
> (p. 41)

Rabin, writing in the mid-1990s, says that he hopes for empirical valida-tion of theory (the article was published in 1998 in the *Journal of Economic Literature*). Yet on my reading, the theory he seems to have in mind is based upon, like that of the conventional approaches he refers to, a wide range of assumptions, not the least of which is that theory does *not* need to be empirically validated in a predictive sense, which is what experimental methods come up hard against. In this sense one can suspect that method-ological discussions are simply a smoke-screen, as the customary "vague" relation between model-choice and reality (Chapter 6) has to confront other competing criteria and results that confound standard beliefs by negating them.

However, recent research suggests that there may be more to it than this —at root concerned with the negotiation that takes place between experi-menter and his/her experiment (which, obviously, has people in it). This takes our discussion away from the question of the validity of mainstream beliefs and into new areas. In a more DS language, does experimental economics offer an opportunity to develop a "post-positivist" production of knowledges that go beyond the instrumental rationality hypothesis? At the core of this are the linked questions of process (the evolution of knowledge over time) and the relationship between scholar and subject.

Santos (2009) argues:

> Experimenting in the social sciences is informed by the trade-off between the exercise of control over the actions of the experimental

participants and the potential to provide understanding about human behavior. Control is a requirement of the experimental method to produce pertinent and intelligible results for scientific inquiry. But the more control is exercised the more the experimental results are the outcome of economists' actions. Economic experiments must therefore achieve a difficult balance. They must elicit intelligible behavior while ensuring that the actions of those taking part in the experiment are not determined by the design set-up and the rules of the experiment.

(p. 71)

If human subjects are treated as non-sentient machines, then this suggests that one can have as much control over them as over a machine—usually a lot more than one usually has over a human, whether two or twenty years old. Santos's insight is that the *lack* of control generates valuable results: the experimental trade-off is between control and human agency. One might add to illuminate her point that humans, if asked to behave "like machines," may well ask "how?" and the experimenter will then simply watch a dance of their own creation, learning nothing new.

In viewing comments from psychologists comparing their own experimental methods with those of economists, Santos interprets the latter as:

deemed 'regulatory' which contrasted with those of psychology which were deemed comparatively 'laissez-faire' . . . the mandatory practices in economics are highly controversial in psychology . . . perceived by the psychologist critic as illegitimate procedures that extricate rational behavior by "beating subjects over the head" through constant repetition, feedback, complete and detailed information, and anonymity

(p. 72)

And so experiments were allegedly set up to paint a picture of subjects acting in accordance with standard economic rationality. Santos adds criticisms of experiments by economists where:

The most common charge is that the experimental economist dismissed some crucial variable . . . (t)his is particularly evident when economists fail to elicit rational behavior or to confirm the predictions of economic theory that presuppose rationality. The experimental setup is then accountable for not having provided subjects the opportunity to behave rationally. Underlying these criticisms is then a demand for new controlled experiments.

(p. 73)

Then:

It comes out very straightforwardly that the 'regulatory' procedures of experimental economics attempt to induce self-interest by rendering as a salient course of action the pursuit of monetary gains that are contingent on individual performance, and by omitting the impact of individual actions on others.

(p. 73)

She provides support for this view, with evidence for setting up an experiment to generate selfish rational behavior. As we have seen, of course, there is abundant evidence from experiments assembled in other ways that reveals very different behavior that is *not* in accordance with standard rationality assumptions. As she puts it, though, all this requires *effort* on the part of the experimenter, who, willy-nilly, has to engage with his or her experimental subjects: "The fact that economists are equally able to generate behavior that conforms to and conflicts with the model of rational economic men does not undermine the experimental exercise" (p. 75).

Why not? Her answer is that "the experimental set-up must allow room for the participants' agency" (p. 75), and this can only be assessed by looking at their scope for *autonomous action*. Machines do not usually engage with humans by using autonomous action; if they do, humans worry about this, and a range of films and writings explore the consequences.

Others have also observed similar tensions. Hertwig and Ortmann (2001) are struck by ways in which some experimental economists repeat experiments with the same subjects, allowing both sides to learn. They also stress their concern that methodological issues are given insufficient attention, calling for "more research on the consequences of methodological preferences" (p. 383). The central interest here is the mutual interactions between experiments and their subjects, on the one hand, and among experimenters as a social group on the other.

This perspective perhaps turns the standard "positivist" assessment of experimental economics on its head.[10] Thus scholars such as Santos appear to believe that it is very possible to negotiate with experimental subjects over issues such as just what game will be played, what behavioral models will be used (with them perhaps constructed ad hoc for a particular situation), what interpretations placed on the behavioral models used, and so on. Something similar could be done with field trials. In such practices the goal of the exercise is understood, it would appear, as being to cooperate in an evolving knowledge production process that reflects subjects' views of the real world where experimenters do *not* assume that "it is unnecessary to distinguish between the real world and decision makers' perceptions of it" (see Box 1.4, p. 14). In this sentence the "real world" is what experimenters think it is, and negotiation accepts and manages differences between what experimenters think and what subjects think. But will this actually happen? Maybe yes and maybe no seems to be the answer. The crucial point is that it can. My own discussions with some experimental economists suggest very much that it can happen; typically, such practitioners *consciously* learn from their trials and experiments. In a DS language they adopt a "self-reflective practice," treating their subjects in ways that are quite different from how they would research non-sentient machines.

These problems are well illuminated by Bardsley (2005) who discusses problems confronting economic experiments that arise from the specifically human nature of what they study. He makes the simple point that what is being studied, the "social psychological phenomena" to which the experiment refers ("in the real world"), are *relational*. This means that they depend jointly on certain relationships between people *and on people's perceptions that these same relational criteria are satisfied*" (Bardsley 2005: 241, stress added). This makes the point that humans are well aware of the difference between actually being a consumer, or a manager, and simply pretending to be one, so that "experimenters ought to pay attention to subjects' interpretations *of the experiment* in order to interpret their results" (idem; stress added). The issue, then, put simply, is that there is no ontological stability: somebody who is participating in an experiment is different from when they are not (Chapter 3). This is crucial. To return to the analogy I made in Chapter 2 (Box 2.3, p. 29) about how humans react to their situations: assuming that a rock there and a rock here are the same thing is one thing, but assuming that Mary there and Mary in the lab are the same thing is quite different. Bardsley (2005) cites evidence for this so-called "Hawthorne Effect" (Adair 1984); as he puts it:

> The strict identity of laboratory and target variables, from which natural scientific experiments derive their demonstrative force, does not hold [in economic experiments]. There are two aspects of laboratory experiments which allegedly undermine this identity. Both arise from the experimenter-subject relationship (t)hat gives rise both to the non-identity of certain laboratory relationships and institutions with the real counterparts . . . and the peculiar theory-ladenness of experimental stimuli . . .
>
> (p. 245)

To repeat, because social phenomena are relational—concerned with relations between humans—if you change the relationship, the object you are studying changes; an experiment changes the relationship. Precisely because of this, experimental economics is pushed into practices that abandon the instrumental rationality hypothesis, effectively endogenizing the process of model-selection and knowledge production that comes with the interaction between the humans involved—the experimenters and their subjects. However, to be pushed is one thing, and to actually move is another.

On the issue of the response of experimenters, again we find useful arguments. Many of these arise from interactions between economics and psychology and are concerned with *behavioral economics*, and that is complicated. Part of the complication arises from two things. First are the ways in which mainstream economics came to prefer particular models of human behavior *by abandoning psychological arguments in favor of a notion of rational choice* and the arguments about human nature that underpinned this (Bruni and Sugden 2007). Second is the question of whether "better" models that use different algebraic formulations—the techniques used by behavioral economists—do any better. I argue that the central issue, for practitioners who use intervention logics that entail cause-and-effect relationships, is reliable predictability. Bruni and Sugden argue that for much of the twentieth century "mainstream economics represented itself as a separate science without bothering too much about these problems," including not worrying much about the lack of successful prediction (p. 171).

The impossibility of DE standard modeling under plausibly common conditions in poor countries

We saw in Chapter 9 that where "household economics" exist, people are clearly making simultaneous decisions about production and consumption, usually in families. One can think of family farms and family businesses. As developing countries have urbanized, work is rarely just wage labor; rather, in what is often called the "informal" sector, families (or groups operating similarly) take both production and consumption decisions. As already quoted, the textbook we referred to (Bardhan and Udry 1999) concludes:

> The available empirical evidence casts serious doubt on the validity of the unitary model. While the available work is mostly supportive of the more general model of efficient households, there is some evidence, particularly in Africa, that calls even this weaker model into question. More research is required before the general validity of the efficient household model can be accepted. If the efficient household model cannot adequately account for the intra-household allocation of resources, it appears that it will be necessary to move towards more detailed, culturally and institutionally informed noncooperative models of the interaction between household members.
>
> (p. 18, emphasis added)

What experimental economics offers, in combination with the engagement through behavioral economics of adaptive modeling processes, are ways of generating applied research that is culturally and institutionally informed. Clearly, we can see efforts to do so within the experimental economics. However, a sociologist, anthropologist, or historian reading texts such as Cardenas and Carpenter (2008) is likely to come away with concerns that concepts of culture and institutions are still weakly developed, not least by the pressure to generalize—for example, concern about the idea that countries such as Kenya have sufficiently homogenous populations that it makes sense to talk of "Kenyan" cultural tendencies to cooperate, etc.

It seems far easier to generate the negative result than a positive one with predictive power, far easier to show that mainstream beliefs are false than to generate robust comparable new ones, and hard to abandon the instrumental rationality hypothesis.

Experimental economics: empirical implications

One is confronted with the bald statement from Henrich et al. (2001) that "the canonical model is not supported in any society studied" (p. 73). Further,

> the canonical model of the self-interested material payoff-maximising actor is systematically violated [11] . . . [and] preferences over economic choices are not exogenous as the canonical model would have it, but rather are shaped by the economic and social interactions of everyday life. This result implies that judgements in welfare economics [12] that assume exogenous preferences are questionable, as are predictions of the effects of changing economic policies and institutions that fail to take account of behavioral change.
>
> (p. 77)

At a rather common-sense level, the simplest point to make about experimental economics is that there *are* useful empirical implications beyond the somewhat negative one that mainstream DE has severe empirical weaknesses. Experimental economics reconstructs as it deconstructs: it does not reject modeling but advises changes to it, showing its retention of behavioral assumptions.

Cameron et al. (2013) is a good example.[13] The research team investigated the effects of China's one-child policy; as is well known from the school playground, children without siblings are often different (perhaps as the "horrors of sharing" that confront two-year-olds and others occurs outside the immediate family). They report that this policy has "produced significantly less trusting, less trustworthy, more risk-averse, less competitive, more pessimistic, and less conscientious individuals" (p. 1). Those familiar with team sports might at once conclude (without any scientific basis) that such children would be easier to beat, as their teamwork would be poor.

It is useful to see how Cameron et al. came to these conclusions and what they did with them. They argue in blanket terms (compare Bardsley) that "Behaviour in economic games has been widely shown to be correlated with actions outside the experimental setting" (p. 1)—their citations here show that this view is empirically based, without direct testing of the context they research, so it may or not be true for their setting. They deploy a range of games and use these to compare results for people born in Beijing just before and after the policy came in—1979. These results lead them to the conclusions already stated. They cite other research (on a different topic) that they say concludes that "differences between only children and others in Beijing is similar to that in other urban areas" (p. 3) and state that "our results are generalizable to other urban areas of China where the [policy] was strictly implemented" (p. 3). We see a familiar desire to generalize results: the researchers say that conclusions from a piece of research in the capital city are generally valid for two alleged reasons. First, generally experimental results apply outside the experimental setting, and, second, their particular results apply to the general situation because another different piece of research supports this. We therefore see, as often occurs, that tight argument within the particular piece of research then gives way to relying upon somewhat risky bases in order to generalize. The rhetorical thrust is to produce generalizations rather than reliably predictive statements. This suggests that the aim is *not* so much at the development of interventions that require predictive power but rather at influencing ideas and beliefs.

Development studies challenged: prerequisites to challenges to belief systems—DE and DS as contrasting examples

Do people want to know?

It has been wisely said that some questions are valuable, not in their answers, but in the posing of them. An introduction to this, of great historical power, is a remark by a German woman, Traudl Junge, who had been one of Adolf Hitler's last secretaries, when she was in her very early twenties. She wrote her memoirs (Junge 2004), which reported, amid much fascinating historical detail, that she spent much of her life after the war trying to deal with how she had come to do what she had done—to work, in some sense willingly, for Hitler. These memoirs came to be the basis for a film, called in English *Downfall*, at the end of which she appears in an interview. Asked about the Holocaust camps, Junge first replied that they (one supposes, Germans of that time and place) did not know, but then continued: "we could have known if we had wanted to." For our purposes here, this question's power is exacting and penetrating: for a belief to be challenged, those who hold it must in some way accept that challenge, for if they do not, it seems that we humans have a vast capacity to protect our beliefs.

As we have seen, to understand DE it seems vital to understand the nature and quality of beliefs within it; in particular, the ways in which models and theories relate to reality. I have argued that the particular approach of DE permits a far finer understanding of how this happens and a far better basis for judging the reliability of predictions than DS often appreciates. Consider microfinance as an example. Like other common aspects of development interventions, such as participation, for example, any student of DS researching microfinance will easily find a wide range of confident statements that "it works" and that resources spent on microfinance will have positive developmental outcomes. Consider now, however, the arguments deployed in Banerjee et al. (2009). At the same time consider whether these same arguments "could have been known if we had wanted to" far earlier.

Microfinance as a telling example: is it "known to work"?

Consider the research reported by Banerjee et al. (2009). Superficially, this appears straightforward. They assert that *no* randomized trials of the impact of introducing microcredit exist prior to the one they carried out and report on (p. 2). They find very little evidence for impact of microfinance upon monthly spending per capita. Although expenditure on durable goods did increase, this was mainly households with existing businesses, whose profits rose. What happened was that the roll-out of microfinance in Hyderabad was randomized, so that in 2005, 52 out of 104 neighborhoods were randomly selected for opening of a branch of a fast-growing micro-finance institution, and the rest were not (p. 2). They cite, pejoratively, a wide range of opinions that would expect poverty alleviation to follow from the introduction of microfinance.

> In 1999, Jonathan Morduch wrote that "the 'win-win' rhetoric promising poverty alleviation with profits has moved far ahead of the evidence, and even the most fundamental claims remain unsubstantiated." In 2005, Beatriz Armendáriz de Aghion and Morduch reiterated the same uncertainty, noting that the relatively few carefully conducted longi-tudinal or cross-sectional impact studies yielded conclusions much more measured than . . . anecdotes would suggest.
>
> (p. 2)

Their conclusions are nuanced, stating, in addition to the basic results already mentioned, that it is hard to assess the long-run impact of the program (p. 21).

We conclude that, epistemologically, we have a familiar pattern. New research engages with a situation of strongly held but allegedly unfounded beliefs. Its research method generates results said to be valuable and which suggest that earlier unfounded beliefs were recklessly held, in that they are not supported by the new knowledge created. A somewhat novel element is the researchers' conclusion that the effects of the intervention are hetero-geneous, in ways uncovered by their data. This contributes to one general effect of experimental economics, which is to juxtapose the tendency to universalistic assumptions in the mainstream with evidence that the world is diverse and far from homogeneous. Assertions of diversity and complexity drawing on experiments can push against assertions of similarity and simplicity that too easily preserve asymmetric power relations.

A cautionary discussion of the value of randomized controlled experi-ments can be found in Shaffer (2011). He links these trials squarely to the

relationships we find in mainstream development projects and other interventions that rely upon cause–effect notions: *inputs* lead to *activities* that
lead to *outputs* that lead to *outcomes* that lead to *impacts* (p. 1621).[14] With
great clarity Shaffer goes through various problems with thinking causally
in these terms, related to the extent to which such ideas are capable of
empirical foundation. Central to this is the problem that a trial by definition
excludes the control area, and argument about whether they—the trial and
the control—are ontologically different or not has no natural "God-given"
end point. What happens in the control group and what happens in the
trial have to be analyzed, and the managers of the trial cannot be absolutely
sure about what is going on. An example he gives is a trial where subjects
excluded from the trial responded by looking elsewhere for alternatives, a
fact unknown to the experimenters, who therefore concluded that the program was highly ineffective. Shaffer's response to this is to seek methodological openness, so that research methods may serve the questions at hand
rather than the researchers and those seeking to use their results to justify
intervention activity.

The challenge to development studies

The challenge to development studies is then clear: the ways that beliefs
are constructed mean that, despite pretensions to predictive power, they
offer little reliable ability to plan for the future and allocate resources to
attain certain goals. Experimental economics shows how such beliefs can
be challenged, in what is once again a largely negative result. The positive
result, since robust prediction appears a chimera, is that research processes
that treat their subjects as autonomous sentient humans tend to emerge from
these tangles. The research processes have to fight off enemies who attack
them, usually on methodological grounds (obviously, as they lack empirical
power). They tend to redefine research in ways that see knowledges as
outcomes of processes where power relations are better managed. This seems
to involve far greater awareness of diversity and complexity, and moves
away from beliefs in simplicity and similarity.

Conclusions

Much of the discussion can be perceived from the point of view of reckless
behavior. In some jurisdictions, violation of another is judged to happen if
there is a clear violation of will, or if the violator does not properly check
that he or she is not violating the other person's will. This means making
sure that the other person, reasonably freely, has voice and the opportunity
to use it.

It is only the existence of power asymmetries that allows much of what
we discussed in this chapter to happen, but these are influenced by
particular habits of thought and incentive structures that accompany them.

As we will see in the discussion of "spin" in the next chapter, consumers of research wisely need much information about where the research is coming from and how it is produced before buying in to any proposals for action.

Questions for discussion

1. Discuss how, as students or poor farmers, you would "game" a randomized trial carried out in your class or village.

2. Discuss how you would investigate whether or not an experimental economist was or was not holding to the instrumental rationality hypothesis.

3. Does experimental economics suggest that ignorance or diversity is the main obstacle to good international development work?

Notes

1 I thank colleagues in Melbourne interested in experimental economics for taking time to discuss with me—Ian MacDonald, Lata Gangadharan, Nisvan Erkal, and Guy Mayraz. For surveys of experimental and behavioral economics, see McDonald (2008); Chakravarty et al. (2011); Guala (2008); Roth (1995).

2 Thus I found the opinion, in the group mentioned in note 1, that "because it is costly to run trials successful academics like Banerjee and Duflo are at an advantage," so that knowledge production reflects this power asymmetry. The sense was that this did not happen because Banerjee and Duflo were "better scholars," but because they had more power (reflected in better access to resources that enabled them, rather than others, to decide what knowledge would be created).

3 Olken (2007) reports his field experiment research findings as arguing that "The evidence on grassroots participation showed that increasing grassroots participation in monitoring *reduced missing expenditures only under a limited set of circumstances . . . "* —hardly an enthusiastic endorsement (p. 243, stress added).

4 For those who do not understand the statistics here: the ability to gauge whether an estimated value—here of child mortality—depends on the extent to which it is likely to be far from the real value, and this depends on the extent to which the child mortality varies between children, which will be harder to gauge right if the sample is small. The bigger the sample, the easier to gauge whether your estimated values are close to the real value; the more money you spend, the bigger the sample and the more reliable your estimate.

5 Banerjee and Duflo (2011), said to be the "bible" of this trend, is a good example.

6 See the discussion of "randomized field trials" below.

7 I admit that my respect for this book is considerable, in that it presents a mass of empirical evidence. It reminds me of studies I used to read in the 1970s written by development scholars who had comparably wide experience and questioning minds, but different theoretical perspectives. Banerjee and Duflo are familiar with what they study, but this does mean that they have reliable predictive

capacity. A passing remark of theirs about Vietnam, a country about which I have expertise, is to my mind clearly off the mark. In a discussion of introduction of democracy at local level, they refer to Vietnamese "local elections" being introduced in 1998 (p. 243). Formally, this was not the case at all as the Communist Party sought to retain control, through its Leninist structures, and this would be found if one looked at the formal documentation (Fforde 2011b).

8   Interviews with the group mentioned in note 1 suggested that this remained the case and that take-up of these ideas in development practice in Australia was particularly slow. This reflected the particular nature of dominant belief sets among development economists and, in Australia, those who hired them. Compare Riedl (2009) and Banerjee and Duflo (2011).

9   By contrast, Gramajo (2008) treats rationality as a social construct, identifying two different rationalities associated with different social groups in the community he studied.

10 By contrast, Green and Tusicisny (2012) treat much of what I discuss here as sources of bias. For them, relaxation of the instrumental rationality hypothesis is a mistake.

11 This is an Ultimatum Game result, and interestingly "rejections of positive offers in some societies occur at a considerable rate" (p. 77), they do *not*, in my naive interpretation, share.

12 See Box 1.2 on p. 9. For a quick discussion of the possible influence of such research on public spending, see Ng (2005).

13 See also Olken (2007), Cameron et al. (2009) and Dasgupta et al. (2012). Also Fletschner et al. (2010).

14 DS students will be familiar with this framework from such project management tools as the "logframe."

23 Conclusions

In concluding, I will look first at what I call *spin* in economics and then at two useful metaphors—aggregation economies and economies of scope—to show how DE may deliberately produce explanations, usually to support a particular set of beliefs. I will finish with some thoughts on how DE's position within DS may evolve.

An issue that has lurked behind the development of this book is the relationship between apodictic argument and the basic DE conceptualization of markets and market failure that relies heavily upon an "ideal" (perfect competition) rather than upon robust relationships between model and empirics. Perfect competition is conceptualized as an ideal to which competition will push as long as it is allowed to. If this process does not happen, market failures and excessive regulation are the candidates for blame.[1] In this sense, discussion of a DE model relies for its persuasive power on its logic: *if* the algebra is accepted as meaningful, then it follows that, as Stiglitz put it, we have a reason "why markets result in Pareto efficient outcomes" (Stiglitz 2000: 77). But this is a big if. Is the model real?

Even if it is real, there still arises the realization problem: the conceptual link between the model and reality in terms of how we might actually attain the conditions it describes—an issue we have touched on many times. I mentioned the argument about the "second best"—even if some target may be maximally attractive, it may be better to settle for a second best alternative because of the costs of getting to the top (Chapters 9 and 13). A wide range of ideas and sayings warrant caution in such cases, which come down to how, if at all, one may transit across the gap between here and there, between reality and model.

Further, the particular algebra formulas used to model the conditions under which the solutions to the equations can be said to represent efficient outcomes may confuse these issues, perhaps by adopting particular functional forms that, of themselves, suggest that the transit is easy. I conclude that apodictic argument encourages risks in that it tends to set up belief in the value of certain situations rather than others and, because of weaknesses in just how such arguments are related to realities, to underplay the possibility of problems that may arise if attempts are made to attain those situations. In this sense, policy debacles (such as with Lesotho and the Philippines discussed in Chapter 15, not to mention the "lost decades" of economic growth in the 1980s and 1990s discussed in Chapter 10) have profound implications and can be seen as partly the consequences of the mainstream interpretation of the problem of development, which seeks to define correct development through reference to authority. What confuses the situation are the issues of power and politics that accompany such processes, which tend to subject students and others to a series of arguments about development and its nature. As an example of such arguments, I turn now to a quick discussion of spin in DE.

Spin as part of DE arguments

It should be relatively obvious to the reader, not least from the L&Z (1993) saga, that published articles in the DE field may not be empirically sound. I have argued (Chapter 2) that this is partly the result of the universalism encouraged by both our language and DE's particular conceptualizations, which leads to a tendency to assume that sampling is from a single population, when it may well not be. L&Z are engaging with econometric research that seeks to explain variations in economic growth across countries by seeking statistical relationship between growth and variations in certain policy settings. This assumes various things, not least that "policy" refers to the same thing in different contexts, as do the various economic variables: sampling is from a single population.[2] Basic statistical theory argues that this helps explain a situation where a plethora of published results contradict each other but, given the basic assumptions, are each meeting reviewers' beliefs about the requirements of statistical method—that is, if reviewers share the same belief in universalism of the authors of a particular paper, they will accept the assumptions that support the results of each piece of research, so recommend that the paper be published.

If we step back, we can think of this in terms of epistemological analysis. Each paper is a research project that stands on its own terms. The question is how to judge the overall research program, as we may call the body of research made up of the research projects. It is evident that while there is disagreement at the level of the research program, each research project, as published, assumes there should be a certain agreement. We may thus learn from the differences between the results of the research program (disagreement) and the particular results of each research project (asserted new knowledge).

We have also learned that many of the standard facts of global change, such as poverty reduction, rely upon aggregation that, when reversed, suggests that regional or other differences make all the difference. Thus, most recent economic growth in developing countries has taken place in a few countries; because two of them—China and India—are very large, this influences the data. As we shall see, one revealing element of spin in DE published results is the tendency to exploit this characteristic of the data by actively constructing indicators that are proposed as proxies in ways that support the position of the protagonist.³ Digging into this requires more than appreciating problems caused by ontological universalism, and, at a minimum, shows how the internal policing of publications in DE is not something to take for granted.

The significance of spin therefore is that it is not simply a mistake but rather a desire to push the argument in certain directions. As such, the mistake says something about the problems that the protagonist—usually the author of a paper or book—is facing in advancing his or her interests or metaphysical commitments. It is not, though, so easy to explain such mistakes (indeed it may be better not simply to label them as mistakes) and is facile to simply assert when we find such things that they are part of the system, a reflection of asymmetric power relations or some global conspiracy. It may be, but that needs research.

Let us recall some of the arguments already cited. The rereading of Converse by Friedman (Chapter 5) suggested that we are dealing with belief systems that are (to recall Yonay) only vaguely, if at all, related to empirics. This is not to say that they are isolated from reality but to ask just what that relationship is. The reading of Colander et al. (2004) (Chapter 6) suggested that what was likely to be of primary importance to the authority of a particular position in economics generally, as well as in DE, was what the community— economists themselves—valued most highly. The response to L&Z, tracked through citations (Fforde 2005), suggests that this practice is not quite the same as that of engineers but rather a reflection of metaphysical commitments. To quote:

> This historical inquiry concludes that more realistic elements (such as general utility compared with additive utility) are introduced into consumption theory only if they do not weaken the systematic order of the conceptual representation of the phenomenon (consumption) already achieved. If the inclusion of elements that correspond better to common-sense evidence, empirical data or experimental verifications jeopardizes the determinateness and the systematic unity of the theory, they are simply put aside. This does not mean that the search for realism is irrelevant in neoclassical theorizing about consumption, but just that the pursuit of conceptual integrity is stronger than that of realism. *One can say that neoclassical economics tries to maximize the realism of the theory under the constraint of preserving its systematic view.*
>
> . . . such a hierarchy between systematic character and realism is not an idiosyncrasy of neoclassical consumer theory or of neoclassical economics in general, but is rooted in a broader character of scientific understanding.
>
> (Moscati 2003; emphasis added)

If we examine how spin was used, we can learn something about how DE "tries to maximize the realism of the theory under the constraint or preserving its systematic view"—that is, how it copes with its facts.

Examples of spin

Rodriguez and Rodrik (1999) examine work by Dollar, and Sachs and Warner, who all argue that there is a reliable relationship between indicators of trade policy and growth. Rodriguez and Rodrik, however, conclude with somewhat similar results to L&Z—that is, when the econometric research is looked at in detail, it is far less compelling than it would appear at first sight. This compares methodologically with robustness testing:

> Do countries with lower barriers to international trade experience faster economic progress? . . . The prevailing view in policy circles in North America and Europe is that recent economic history provides a conclusive answer in the affirmative. Multilateral institutions such as the World Bank, IMF and the OECD regularly promulgate advice predicated on the belief that openness generates predictable and positive consequences for growth.
>
> (p. 1)

> . . . we are sceptical that there is a strong negative relationship in the data between trade barriers and economic growth, at least for levels of trade restrictions observed in practice. We view the search for such a relationship as futile.
>
> (pp. 38–39)

It is worth reflecting on the tensions between these two paragraphs. On the one hand, the authors observe that policy circles believe that evidence strongly supports their belief that lower barriers to trade (EOG policies) are associated with faster growth. On the other hand, they not only state that there is no such relationship, so that higher trade barriers are not known to reduce growth (the negative relationship), but that such a relationship cannot be found—for some reason, this is not knowable.

Standard teaching in statistical method often instructs the researcher to examine data in as raw a state as possible, before adjusting it to suit estimation and analysis. This requires that researchers be capable of tolerating confusion while they become better informed (see note 1 in Chapter 11). In DE empirical work, we often find studies that use proxies and dummy variables. Because these have to be chosen or constructed, there is obvious scope for spin. This can be found discussed in Rodriguez and Rodrik (1999).

In the proxies for openness devised by Dollar (1992) and Sachs and Warner (1995), they make various remarks that are consistent with the previous quotation, which is insightful in terms of the history of knowledge production and I think rather convincing. They argue that the particular choices of proxies made by these researchers ensure that their results support their beliefs and so advance their interests—a good example of spin. The reader may consult these for themselves. Additionally, however, we need to ask whether Rodriguez and Rodrik are willing to consider not only that established and firmly held beliefs may be wrong, but that what those beliefs are about may, actually, be unknowable. Their analysis of Sachs and Warner engages with the question of how an argument is developed that supports established and firmly held beliefs that are arguably ill-founded. For example, they point out that the Sachs and Warner index of openness[4] is based upon a dummy variable, which can take the value of zero or unity depending upon a yes or no answer to a range of questions. Rodriguez and Rodrik comment as follows:

> The Sachs–Warner dummy's strength derives mainly from the combination of the black market premium (BMP) and the state monopoly of exports (MON) variables. Very little of the dummy's statistical power would be lost if it were constructed using only these two indicators. In particular, there is little action in the two variables that are the most direct measures of trade policy: tariff and non-tariff barriers (TAR and NTB).
>
>   . . .
>
> The extent to which [BMP and MON have] . . . significance in explaining growth can be traced to their correlation with other determinants of growth: macroeconomic problems in the case of the black-market premium, and location in Sub-Saharan Africa in the case of the state monopoly variable . . . [the dummy variable] serves as a proxy for a wide range of policy and institutional differences, and *yields an upwardly-biased estimate of the effects of trade restrictions proper.*
>
> (p. 15 et seq.; emphasis added)

What is happening here is a deconstruction of the constructed variable (the dummy) used to show empirically that open economies grow faster.[5] What Rodriguez and Rodrik suggest is that economists have considerable choice in how they construct these variables. This is in part because of the "vague" relationships between theory and data previously identified (to repeat Yonay's use of the word *vague* from Chapter 6). Again, this is partly because theories say little about functional form (see the list of special terms on p. 323). Finally, though, it is because DE practice, lacking as it does robust predictive power, has nowhere else to go other than to offer such choices to its practitioners. And there seems nothing robust in the empirical practice, in terms of what can be said to work statistically, to prevent publication of such a paper.

Mistakes and rhetoric

We need to return to McCloskey's (1985) point about the difference between economists and their data:

> The numbers are necessary material. *But they are not sufficient to bring the matter to a scientific conclusion.* Only the scientists can do that, because "conclusion" is a human idea, not Nature's. It is a property of human minds, not of the statistics.
>
> (p. 112)

In other words, if you want to prove the point, construct a suitable index. But, as is true for all performance, while the scientist may conclude one thing, whether the rhetoric actually works is up to the audience. It is therefore consistent with what McCloskey is saying, but yet, in part, internally consistent, for Rodriguez and Rodrik to argue that their antagonists' results are an "upwardly-biased estimate." To start with, if the economic relationship is, as they suggest, unknowable, then it is not plausible to refer to bias. The particular choice of proxy both produces a publishable result and generates results that are consistent with the aims of the authors—to show that EOG works. This by now should be familiar to readers. Buying into the beliefs, the reader has to be willing to assume that the theory is true in order to interpret the estimates as anything other than spurious—in other words, to treat the research project as meaningful (see the list of special terms on p. 323 and Box 2.2 on p. 21). And it is also partly because, and this is consistent with DE method, the main goal is to add parameters to belief. The problem, of course, is that precisely because theory lacks the wherewithal to generate functional form, the natural tendency is to try to show that effects are more rather than less powerful and so to select data (proxies and dummy variables) that may be interpreted as showing that relationships are strong. For a certain amount of policy XX, you get lots of YY. This is not a wise basis for actually doing anything.

Kenny and Williams (2001) point out that:

> Overall, attempts to divine the cause or causes of long-term economic growth, testing a wide range of possible determinants using statistical techniques, have produced results . . . that are frequently contradictory to results reported elsewhere. That is, empirical evidence is hardly unanimous in support of a particular view of the growth process.
>
> (p. 1)

What does this suggest about what was done by Sachs and Warner and by Dollar? Why were their papers published?

Gundlach (1999) provides an interesting insight about human capital. We can ask, as we have done before, whether human capital is better conceptualized as an input, so that more of it adds to output, or, following Veblen and others, as a positional good, generating access to rents or other ways of dividing up the rewards of economic advance. Gundlach argues that economic theory is well ahead of measurement in assessing the role of human capital in development (Gundlach 1999). By this he means that one can find relatively confident statements in the literature, usually treating human capital as an input (recall the discussion of endogenous growth models in Chapter 8 that did so), that for him lack empirical foundation. Again, we see a tendency in DE to trust to apodictic reasoning, in other words to believe in the algebra—to believe in DE theory. This, like so many other examples of the internal empirics of DE, suggests that it is the internal sociology of the DE community and its method, with its preference for apodicity and avoidance of dialectic and discussion, that protects its core beliefs—its metaphysical commitments. And, clearly, so long as development is organized on the basis of knowable cause–effect relations, this will place DE in an uneasy position with DS. In this sense, DE and DS both deal with the problem of development, conceptualized as the attempt to cope with the simultaneous beliefs that development is both done and something that happens—both *product* and *process*.

There is nothing strange about theory driving statements ahead of data, and this is what Isaac Newton and Gottfried Leibniz tended to do (Kline 1980). These men, founders of much modern mathematics and physics, often skipped over important steps in their theoretical development, returning to them later once they had their final results, sure in their own minds that they were right. However, their empirics were experienced as internally predictive. Clearly, though, there are persuasive arguments, if we review the previous discussion that reviewers who share the basic beliefs of the authors whose work they review cannot be trusted to reveal methods that are fragile to the sort of deconstruction mounted by Rodriguez and Rodrik; at the end, it is the issue of universalism that is intriguing.

Economics and metaphor

In expositing the basics of DE I have stressed that one valuable aspect of DE is that it shows, clearly and with much data, that robust predictive knowledge is absent. It is unwise to do development based upon the idea that we know cause–effect relationships well enough to organize around them. This suggests that we remain largely within the confines of the problem of development as conceived by Cowen and Shenton (Chapter 1, et al.). Thus we tend to organize around unstable beliefs that we know what causes what and, at the end of the day, we rely upon authority to tell us what those beliefs are. This can and does lead to spectacular problems as we experience unforeseen consequences, and it also means that we end up protected from those consequences. [6] The discussion of spin shows that DE practice has great freedom in its use of empirics, while the discussion of method shows that DE practice faces great constraints in the ways it can negotiate interdisciplinary boundaries and approach core discussions, such as the correct role of policy. These latter constraints can be eased by use of revised modeling techniques to extend the field to market failure, but the sensation of *float*—theory and concepts that are meant to rather clearly relate to reality but do not—continues. For students of DE and DS, this is at root because of the contrasts between the apparent predictive form of DE algebra and the pressures upon DS to take account of diversity, variation, and multiple beliefs that sit badly with the assumptions associated in DE with its algebra.

The tensions created for DS by the problem of development, as construed, are not minor. In some ways, DE is at an advantage to DS precisely because of DE's commitment to quantitative data and formulation, in the sense that it robustly knows (if it wishes) the experience of predictive failure. Although DS suffers similar difficulties, in many ways it is far less aware of them. In this sense the dual questions are: how does DE develop explanatory knowledge that is accessible to others with different beliefs (such as, I would argue, important elements within DS), and how does, in effect, a rejection of apodictic judgments in favor of process-oriented discussion platform on the failure of prediction? An idea I offer is to consider the economy, not as an autonomous field subject to logics so powerful that development in general is an expression of economic growth, but as an *effect* of other logics or disciplines. Adding to this is the idea that, in becoming such an effect, economics has coped by generating various explanatory concepts that help to link together a range of knowledge and practices. After all, in this sense, the economy is a field where a range of disciplines interact and engage, but it is also a field where ignorance is well known.

The state as effect

A useful and telling point of comparison between DE and DS is the concept of the state. While it is possible to argue that the term has such a wide field of reference as to suggest avoiding it, people still use it. To quote Dunn (2000):

> Each of these two conceptions (the state as sociological fact and the state as normative political proposal) must relate in some way to most of the entities which we now call states, but neither makes quite clear how to apply it in practice.
>
> (p. 69)

By comparison, when is the economy seen as sociological fact, and when is it seen as a political proposal? Surely the discussion of spin shows that DE attempts a similar dance. In this sense, we can start to ask whether the dance is satisfying and acceptable (to whom?).

In a critical essay, an eminence grise of US political science, Gabriel Almond, clinically dissects the current in political science that sought to bring the state back in to discussions and in so doing create a platform for a wide range of studies that presented analyses in terms of state–society relations. As I have argued, these analyses fit well with the classic approach to intentionality that so suits DE, where development is done and intentionality is sited upon a state that, guided by advice as to what good policy is, acts as the main agency of development. Almond argues that this conceptualization requires treatment of the state in ways that are problematic and led earlier to abandonment of the term in his part of the academic world—US political science. In part, he argues, this was because it was extremely hard to develop a satisfactory empirics—crucially, to develop definitions that made it easier rather than harder to establish where the state or indeed a particular state started and stopped. What were its boundaries?

This issue was taken up by another political scientist, Timothy Mitchell, in a famous article that argued that the state was, in effect, epiphenomenal—a reflection of other things—and in itself no more than that (Mitchell 1991). As Mitchell put it, the state is an effect of certain techniques of rule. Many thinkers had put great efforts into:

> The statist approach [that] always begins from the assumption that the state is a distinct entity, opposed to and set apart from a larger entity called society. Arguments are confined to assessing how much independence one object enjoys from the other.
>
> (p. 89)

In concluding, Mitchell argues for five propositions:

1. The state should not be taken as a free-standing entity.
2. The "distinction between state and society should nevertheless be taken seriously, as the defining characteristic of the modern political order" (p. 95).
3. The state should not be seen as a "phenomenon of decision-making," because such views are "inadequate."
4. The state should be seen as an "effect of detailed processes of spatial organization, temporal arrangement, functional specification, and supervision and surveillance, which create the appearance of a world fundamentally divided into state and society."
5. These "processes create the effect of a state" (p. 95).

This way of looking at things is useful when we turn to re-examine the problems facing DE. These problems come down to the attempt to adopt certain analytical categories and methodologies, which assume that what they are applied to is suited to the assumption of instrumental rationality and that homogeneity "out there" is sufficient to generate explanations accompanied by robust empirics. If we turn this on its head and start conceptualizing the economy as an effect, many of these tensions relax. This is because, as we have seen, concepts associated with economic analysis provide powerful explanatory metaphors that offer potential for coping with economic issues. Treating these as metaphors makes it far easier to exploit their power, while treating them as characteristics of algebraic models driven in the mainstream DE style tends to neuter them.

If we re-examine in this light what Mitchell has to say about the state as an effect, much of what this book has been about becomes easier to grasp. DE imagines, quite in conformity with our contexts, the economy as something upon which state policy operates and which is the focus of consumer desires, businesses' searches for profits, and other conventionally accepted views of the economy. In this way (and obviously there may be others) various processes create the effect of an economy that can be simultaneously treated as both sociological fact and the object of normative propositions. By this is meant that statements about the economy, like statements about the state, imply both that they exist, as facts, and that they should have certain characteristics, rather than others, inviting the listener or reader to take sides.

What our examination of DE centrally suggests is not so much that its portrayals of sociological facts are awry, for that is obvious, but that its ability to contribute to discussions of normative propositions lags well behind other disciplines, which have abandoned the limitations of naive scientific method, in part because of the poor returns to investments in trying to secure predictive power as a basis for policy science (Fforde 2010). It seems likely that this will reverse for DE, as it did for others, through the use of explanatory metaphors that draw on existing ideas, and somersault over the problems caused by the algebraic method. Such a method would sharply reduce the value of technical skills and raise the value of those who can, just like state–society theorists in political science, treat the central concept of their rhetoric—the economy—as an effect; in other words, as a way to bounce their ideas and influence into those academic areas that appear to be the sources of that effect or theory, and thus to construct arguments about developing economies that enable others to make better sense of their necks of the wood: sociology, gender, anthropology, history, political science, and so on. And we know from McCloskey that rhetoric will play a central part.

Consider two metaphors: agglomeration economies and economies of scope. These pose major technical problems for algebra but offer potentially powerful explanations of social change and its possibilities that reach beyond economics. Discussion of these metaphors helps show how the quite understandable assumptions of DE—crucially and centrally, the value of apodicity, that is, of a method that searches for predictability—generate the thickets and tangles that we have moved through. The discussion suggests that these assumptions need to be relaxed so as to support the persuasive arguments that make sense to the rest of DS and that these beliefs in algebra need to be abandoned. If it seems obvious to many outside DE that these beliefs are unwise, it is probably also obvious to many within it. But, as for any discipline, what worries members in the privacy of their own thoughts is one thing, and what can and should profitably be said in seminars is quite another. This book is not a sociological analysis of DE, but it is plausible that the benefits of not changing remain large, even if it is not exactly clear what they are. Why do taxpayers continue to finance quantitative economic research projects? Why do students continue to study economics? The reader may recall the contrast (in Chapter 6) between the excited reporting of the "cutting edge" of economics by Colander and the more sober arguments of McCloskey and Yonay. Colander took it for granted that economics was an important and vital discipline. McCloskey and Yonay suggest that its wider influence faces considerable threats, not least to its authority. Readers may feel that this book shows that if DE is exposed to criticism from outside and so likely to be questioned, mainstream DE is increasingly vulnerable.[7] Yet economics contains many powerful and useful explanatory concepts.

Agglomeration economies

The concept of agglomeration economies is deployed with great success in studies like Ball and Sunderland (2001). This book provides an explanation of the economic history of London (1800–1914) that treats, like Zysman (1983), ideas as part of history and uses a range of concepts, such as that of agglomeration economics, to develop its analysis. One can read about how problems in a large industrial and services conurbation were identified, and problematical and various solutions were discussed and trialed by its population and leaders. Against this, such matters as the London economy within the national (and international) contexts are discussed with reference to how various factors interact.

Thus Ball and Sunderland, after pointing out that London was the first city with a system of suburbs, linked to the center by public transport systems, say that economic theory is useful because it enables deductions to be made about real world processes (it acts like a normal natural science model). Although this use of theory also gives life to the available information, they also use it to explain the interconnectedness of urban life—how it hangs together. And their use of theory helps explain how an urban economy is related to the wider context.

Ball and Sunderland argue that agglomeration economies are caused by the crowding together of economic activities, and they reduce and offset various costs that increase with city size. For workers, such economies are useful and exist because of the range of opportunities available; if one sector is in a cyclical downturn, work can be found elsewhere, thus reducing the amount of savings needed for a rainy day. The London economy therefore was more efficient than it would have been had agglomeration economies not been present. These economies are offset by competition for the available resources in a city—land, labor, and other inputs—and this can push up costs. This tension provides a simple model that explains the reason for a city's size.

Their argument is more detailed than this would suggest. They refer to economics of scale that are *internal*—felt directly by the producer or consumer. Thus a greater scale of production, for example, would allow the costs of a large indivisible investment by a producer, such as a dock, to be spread over a higher volume of output, reducing unit costs. But other economies are *external*—experienced indirectly and so do not influence the scale of production[8] or consumption by the owner of the asset and are called agglomeration economies, of which there are two types: those that influence the productive potential of a particular industry—*localization economies*, and those that influence a variety of urban activities—*urbanization economies*. These are rich concepts and the effects of the two phenomena can be broad and wide-ranging. A localization economy is associated with the various ways in which industries gain from clustering together and point to ways in which "[c]lustering enables specialised out-sourcing and leads to a greater amount and variety of available shared inputs" (p. 20). On the other hand, the concept of urbanization economies are benefits "that are not specific to a particular industrial sector [and] come in a variety of guises: innovation, scope and insurance effects are three of the most important" (p. 21). In general, these economies are hard to measure, Ball and Sunderland argue, but surely exist because firms and consumers are willing to pay far more to be in cities and so enjoy these lower costs. This would seem to be an argument that provides an aggregating and abstracting argument that can make sense to a wide range of readers. But it does not use algebra.

Ball and Sunderland argue that while the upper classes and professionals seemed to benefit from city life more than the poor, the latter, in London, tended to live better than elsewhere. Wage rates were often higher in real terms, and family income strategies could be more easily diversified, so the poor were less likely to be heavily unemployed. Spatial differentiation in part reflected land values, so that in nineteenth-century London, the poor lived far more centrally because they could not afford public transport, but the better-off managed to avoid them, in part through suburbanization and in part through the "vestry" structure of poor rate support.[9]

Economies of scope

The concept of economies of scope is similar to that of agglomeration economies and is also a powerful method for linking together ideas from other disciplines. It also provides intriguing evidence for the internal of mainstream economies, more precisely the use of optimization and associated specific techniques for its algebraic formulation. As we shall see, the concept of economies of scope, despite its apparent power, saw limited application and thus perhaps epitomizes the destructive effects of the drive for rigor offered by mathematicization. The technical issue, as economists probably know, is that with joint production no cost curve can be constructed without assumptions that, in effect, deny joint production. The analytical edifice used in microeconomics (Chapter 9) relies upon the construction of a function that shows how the cost of the given good varies with the level of output.

Alfred Chandler was a highly influential economist and business historian at Harvard University. His influential and seminal work (Chandler 1977 and 1990) uses the notion to develop a series of detailed histories of his topic (joint production in large firms) and is mainly explanatory rather than algebraic in its form of argument. But William Baumol and others[10] found ways of managing the notion *within* the orbit of their particular mathematics, opening the door to the treatment of contestable markets as a real phenomenon. Contestable markets is the idea that, for markets to operate efficiently, firms need to behave *as if* there were high levels of competition, which can (conceptually) happen if they think that high levels of profits (because, for example, of their use of market power) will attract new competitors, and so they restrain their behavior. Thus, what is theoretically important shifts from the idea that markets are competitive to the idea that they are contestable.

A definitive (in disciplinary terms) treatment of economies of scope may be found in Bailey and Friedlaender (1982). Their focus is upon the theoretical value of such economies where production is treated as the activities of a single firm. While the superficial form of theory appears applicable to joint production under any circumstances, we have already seen how this may lead to problems if there is simultaneously consumption and production within the same unit (Chapter 6). They report:

> There are said to be positive economies of scope when a single firm can produce a given level of output of each product line more cheaply than a combination of separate firms, each producing a single product at the given output level. As a general matter, the authors state that economies of scope arise from the sharing or joint utilization of inputs.
>
> (p. 1026)

They also confirm the algebraic problems I mentioned earlier (the difficulties in constructing a cost curve):

> In essence, the new literature argues that . . . conventional measures of average cost are not well defined for a multiproduct firm. There is no single economically meaningful way to aggregate output.
>
> (pp. 1025–1026)

My argument is that a broader conceptualization of what is meant by inputs leads to more useful arguments. This conceptualization includes interactions, usually highly gendered, between activities directly aimed at sale for the market as well as activities directly aimed at caring for the household (such as child care). Consider the treatment of the farming family from Bardhan and Udry in Chapter 9 that stressed ways in which family decisions covered interactions between consumption and production. When examined through the lens of economies of scope, voluntary participation simultaneously in consumption and production, with the associated need for resource valuations and transfers in various forms, arguably becomes an area of high potential for rapid development.

Let us reflect on recent Vietnamese experiences from such a perspective. By the late 1980s, prior to the loss of Soviet bloc economic assistance and the unexpected economic break-out to rapid growth of the early 1990s, it is possible to point to many areas where the *rationality of informal* makes change understandable (de Vylder and Fforde 1996).[11] In many cases, informal patterns of behavior appear to have formed a basis for the generation and exploitation of considerable economies of scope in the next two decades. Let us consider a range of noneconomic fields and see their economic effects. While these areas are highly gendered, it is the complementarities involving aspects of gender, rather than essential difference, that are interesting.

Long-established cultural practices usually grant women (especially when married and with children) a range of valid commercial opportunities, and such stereotypical female roles as participants in highly gendered local street or village markets, as controllers of family cash resources, and especially in cash-based networking in informal capital markets. We may note that transfers of real property are typically expressed and recorded as transfers between families, not individuals, with the head of family signing as such. Thus, in this Vietnamese account, records of transfers of large assets should (for them to be treated as low risk) be signed by relevant adults (male and female). Discussions of such gender issues in the context of economies of scope are usefully informed by work stressing the tendency for relations of production to be subordinated in many ways to relations of reproduction (see Robertson 1991 in Chapter 17). Observations by sociologists that gender relations may be viewed as complementary are also instructive (Ireson 1992).[12] The sense, so far as I can see, is that a useful way in which gender can be conceptualized is not so much that men and women work in complementary ways, though this is what it often comes down to, but that it is all about interaction between things that are inseparable. This seems to me evidently to lead us to focus upon ways in which, at the level of the family, decision-making will seek to adapt to new opportunities by rearranging existing exploitation of complementarities, providing a platform for exploiting economies of scope.

If the family thus offers entry points for discussion of economic change, other areas may also be mentioned. It has often been strongly argued that Vietnamese rural communities' traditional society, especially in the north and center, possessed strongly communal aspects. Counter-arguments question images of a traditional rural life (Kleinen 1999). Nevertheless, in areas such as the treatment of land and an apparent manipulation of formal structures (such as Communist Party-sponsored cooperatives), in order to turn them into interfaces between local interests and external powers, it is relatively easy to point to issues that affect group interests. Scott's work on the moral economy of the peasantry arguably points in similar directions (Scott 1976, Chapter 15).

With regard to land, while it is well known that perhaps 25 percent of rural land in Vietnam was in some sense communal in the nineteenth century (again, in the north and center), it is perhaps less well known that treatment of the so-called 5 percent land (the Vietnamese Communist equivalent of Stalin's private plots, which was not farmed collectively but left to individual families to work, with rights to sell the produce from it on local markets while produce on the cooperative's land had usually to go to the state) often involved local collusion against external pressures. Therefore, field research in the 1990s, when much of the cooperative structures were no longer doctrinally supported, could find both farmers and cadres gleefully report that in their cooperative/commune the 5 percent land was far more than 5 percent of the agricultural land area (Fforde 1989). In other words, cadres and farmers colluded to reduce the land worked by the cooperative whose output had to be delivered to the state and to increase the land worked by families whose output could be sold on local markets. Further, reports of the evolution of land regimes after 1988, when "Decree 10" marked a major shift in doctrine as the Communist Party moved policy from support to cooperatives, show variations that appear to reflect local concerns for balances between equity and efficiency, with, at times, land being leased out by the village or commune and not allocated to families on a long-term basis, and so available as a buffer against future contingencies. Naturally, such areas were often used to benefit the locally powerful.[13]

By contrast, emergence of standard organizational responses to market failure after 1989–1991 appears to have been slow. It was only around the end of the decade that a rich map of informal farmers' groups started to emerge, as farmers organized non-market economic relations to exploit opportunities in ways better than markets. Further research is needed, but these groups often seemed to operate in areas of market failure (see Chapter 9). By the middle of the first decade of the 2000s it could be reported that:

> Our fieldwork suggests that one should expect, in areas such as those surveyed, the majority of families to belong to at least one Informal Farmers' Group (IFG). In a village of around 100 families, one could expect easily to find 6 or 8 credit IFGs with 10 members each, perhaps as much as dozen labor IFGs of various types, 2 or 3 artisanal IFGs and, depending on the situation, 'quasi-public asset' IFGs. This suggests that there are at least a dozen people acting as IFG leaders, soundly

entrenched in these local informal organizations, negotiating, convincing, winning and losing arguments. This is rather a lot of activity in a situation where, a generation ago (before Decree 10), there would perhaps have been simply a cooperative brigade, operating mechanically and inefficiently. The impact of IFG activity upon the wider community should not, therefore, be underestimated. The quality of IFG leadership was usually impressive.

(Fforde 2008: 29–30)

If the family and the rural community suggest considerable facility for exploiting opportunities to organize, then what may be said about state-owned enterprises (SEOs)? Fforde (2007) paints a picture of rapid transformations as, having learned to do one thing, companies then changed to doing another. This study argues that the real motor of the Vietnamese transition from plan to market was the commercialization of SOEs (Fforde 2007). By the end of the 1980s, at times supported by policy and at times opposed by it, SOEs had become highly market-oriented. Informal capital markets had evolved so that, by the end of the 1990s, many SOEs were usefully seen as virtual share companies: While not legally structured as share companies, it was possible to identify virtual shares of various types, with different rights (over issues such as large investments). The ability and facility with such ways of doing business allowed SOEs to exploit commercial opportunities (some corrupt) and to operate in relatively business-like ways; surpluses tended to be treated as capital that should generate a return rather than as objects of conspicuous consumption. Like families and villagers, state capital had learned how to use methods that work in one place to make money in another. Scope had been created to better exploit economic opportunities.

If this rapid dance through some particular economic history is suggestive, it argues that the concept of economies of scope requires treatment of the economy as partly the effect of noneconomic factors. This sits rather uncomfortably with the way in which DE platforms on the idea that economic growth is central to development (Chapter 3). To return to Bailey and Friedlaender (1982), as already stated, they report the inability of their formal modeling methods to deal with the internal problem of the construction of a cost function. And then the argument lurches to the seductive idea of contestable markets, with what are by now widely accepted negative consequences.

It is in the generation of a historical account, however, that the notion of economies of scope is productive.[14] It is not hard to argue persuasively that a population such as the Vietnamese, possessing the social capitals alluded to in the previous section, would find it, under suitable contexts, easy to shift abilities and organizational resources from one activity to another as economic growth changes the pattern of incentives and makes some sectors less profitable as others become more profitable. Of itself, this is an argument that can explain economic dynamism and adaptability. And such a population, well equipped to exploit opportunities, would surely enjoy considerable natural protection from competitors. This then starts to offer a persuasive account of Vietnam's success since the final emergence of a market economy in 1989–1991.

Confusion and its power

Many of these discussions, as I have already mentioned, can become somewhat precious. It is easy to demonstrate the power of elements outside the DE rules of the game:

> The Devil (expecting an agreed sexual favor): *But you promised!*
>
> Frenchwoman: Yes, but I lied.
> > (*Les Visiteurs du Soir*, Dir. Marcel Carné, France, 1942)

The quotation shows a familiar opacity, powerful in that it may generate closure as well as continued engagement with noncompliance; a rabbit hole in that, perhaps precisely in the nature of its power, it defies authoritative response. This is not a matter of pretence, though; rather, it points to the idea that ignorance is inescapable—is she still lying? And, it is well known that the latent pre-Ockham realism in our languages suggests often that we confront, not ignorance, but bias, dissimulation, and other identifiable attempts to pretend that things are different from how they really, truly are (Gillespie 2008). In analytical terms, ontological issues are inadequately developed: the meanings of words may be insufficiently stable for reliable and repeated use. As the Devil appears to have found out, she did not mean what he thought she said. And nobody has to believe in either mainstream DE or what I have to say about it.

In a recent study, Butler has argued that this opacity is not only an inescapable part of human interactions but fundamental to a "giving of accounts"—the justifications of actions and intentions that, so the young are often taught, must accompany ethical behaving (Butler 2005). Thus, discussions may refer to the philosophy of action, which include the notion that arguments about cause and effect are mainly concerned with ascription—of responsibility, of bad behavior—a view that is intriguing (Stoecker 2007). Such attribution of cause and effect as an integral part of behavior is thus distinguished from arguments about cause and effect in themselves—that is, analysis may be simply a blame game and uninterested in accessing robust underlying causes. Such judgments often attribute intentionality and agency—or deny them. At the end of the day, there is a chasm between an argument and what it means to a particular person at a particular place and time (Winch 1958). What can we then learn about the position of DE in DS from our examination of DE? Three points stand out.

First, DE has consistently attempted to act as though development was a knowable process. This situates it within views that expect DE to confront evident predictive failure by recourse to authority in order to defend its positions. DE defends itself by a combination of tactics that are revealing. First, it returns to apodictic arguments that come down to algebra; and, second, it restricts the domain of relevant knowability to economics, manifest in the idea that economic growth is the center of development. Both tactics tend to make DE unfriendly, and so its position within DS is a prickly and defensive one. DE finds it hard to negotiate disciplinary boundaries, despite its possession of a range of powerful explanatory metaphors and command of a territory—the economy—that remains accepted as important.

Second, this situation, viewed from a distance, suggests that the economy, or economic matters, contain little that offers, under current conditions, powerful explanations. Rather, as what often appear as an *effect*, economic matters are most persuasive when integrated with explanations that draw upon other fields. Thus, situated within DS, economics is most powerful when it works cooperatively; put in other terms, economists within DS are most persuasive when they know about other disciplines and how to negotiate with them. This view turns on its head the standard DE problem of isolation and presents this as an opportunity to exploit these possible links. Clearly, though, given the nature of the situation, in working cooperatively, much of the existing core of DE is useless, primarily in that it starts from the wrong premises in DS terms. In some ways it is astonishing how fragile so many of the hard-taught positions of DE are. This teaches the lesson that it is the failure of DE to generate knowledge, similar to the natural sciences (essentially predictive capacity), that is most important. From this, DS learns that dialectical, not apodictic, argument is respectable.

Finally, such an opening up of DE within DS exerts considerable pressure upon DS itself. As I have pointed out, often using the example of participatory methods, large parts of DS, for all the overt genuflection to multiple truths, are more than happy to accept the classic policy logics epitomized by the conceptualization behind practices such as the logical framework approach: that developmental acts, such as aid interventions, should be organized on the basis of known cause–effect relationships. The experience of DE shows that these are a chimera. It follows that serious treatment of the lessons of DE within DS will require abandonment of such tendencies within DS. This is far harder than it may appear.[15] To put it another way, if they are honest, development economists know far more reliably than the core disciplines within DS that, in predictive terms and using the standard terms, they do not know. Yet a plethora of studies from within DS are used as the basis for aid interventions, which assert that they know the effects of certain actions.

In my experience, it is development practitioners who find this message least threatening. Therefore, acceptance of DE within DS is most likely to be successful when it is bound up tightly with practice. A suitable metaphor is the role of the midwife as a professional standing ready to help a pregnant woman who may or may not need assistance from other professions, such as doctors. That is the role of the practitioner. And practitioners, at least in my opinion the good ones, live well with ignorance.

Question for discussion

1. Read Godley (2005) as an introduction to the concept of flows of funds accounting. Understand that this concept, like NIA and Harrod–Domar growth modeling, is about identities. Read the parts of the IMF *World Economic Outlook* (2007), which discuss global macroeconomic imbalances (Chapter 2, up to about p. 66). Think about what this means for possible and actual relationships between Chinese household savings, the Chinese balance of payments surplus, and the US fiscal deficit and household savings. Read Bernanke (2005) (before the GFC) and note how he seems to believe that, with readjustment of exchange rates, China's balance of payments surplus will reduce fast. Read Bloom and Williamson (1998) and Higgins and Williamson (1997) — focus upon the conclusions and skip the econometrics if you want — and consider whether the effects of demographic factors upon Chinese savings, of which the global macroeconomic imbalances are in part, thus, an *effect*, appear more or less robust than other factors, such as the effects of exchange rate changes. Think again about Bernanke's views. Reflect on how cultural, social, and political issues have their economic effects.

Notes

1 Thus a definition of an economic rent is a "gain or advantage that cannot be competed away" (Milgrom and Roberts 1992: 420).
2 To use an everyday analogy, think of a research program whose projects assume that variation in academic performance is caused by race or sexual orientation, and where the research projects give a series of empirical results that contradict each other. Each project has to assume that the codings for race or sexual orientation refer to the same things in different contexts. One possible conclusion is that they do not: two people who both reply "yes" to "Caucasian, heterosexual" may be very different in terms of factors that influence academic performance, and do not amount to a single population.
3 "Spin" is a term familiar to most of us; here I simply use it to create discussion around the idea that what is said or put into a research project is there to support some ulterior motive; it is not what it seems, and caution is advisable.
4 This is a proxy variable, also called a dummy (see the list of special terms, p. 323). Clearly, the discussion here shows the rather wide freedom that may be enjoyed by those seeking to construct such variables.

5 In passing I would remark that such a deconstruction is, in practice, far easier to carry out than it may appear. One should be wary of proxies (see the list of special terms, p. 323).

6 Although this book is not a sociological study of DE, comparable to Yonay (1998), it is to me striking that, so far at least, the costs of the predictive failure of DE do not appear to be borne either by its advocates or those living in rich countries. Just how and why remains, I think, unclear.

7 One consequence of the trends in modern tertiary education is, as discussed in the Preface, a tendency for economics to be sited in faculties with commerce and business. While large student numbers can thus be secured for the standard core subjects such as microeconomics and macroeconomics, the "tail" of specialized subjects, such as DE, risks coming on to the radar of cost-cutting exercises. As a large document prepared for Australian high school students keen to select suitable tertiary courses put it, "Economics, being about things like consumers, business, labour and so on, should be really interesting, but as a topic for most people it is deadly boring."

8 For example, the presence of the dock may have external benefits, encouraging, say, transport companies to increase their scale of activities because their clients are in one place, by the dock.

9 Public support for the poor was organized through the local parishes of the city, whose committees were named vestries, after the room in the parish churches where the vestments, vessels, and parish records were kept, and where the committee would meet. After the middle of the nineteenth century, reforms to local administration saw these committees developed into non-ecclesiastical bodies. A result of this system of local government was that, as poor relief was paid for from local property taxes, this "involved a substantial redistribution from the better-off. The latter tried to avoid this through sustaining a localised 'vestry' structure of poor rate support, so that the vestries in which the better-off lived [in the nineteenth century] . . . paid a far lower poor rate. The other option was to leave the city centre and move to suburbs beyond the remit of the tax net, which the middle classes did in droves as soon as transport systems made it feasible" (p. 24). American readers will be well aware of similar processes in their own cities ("white flight") after World War II, many decades later.

10 Baumol et al. (1988); also Lloyd (1983); Baumol's earliest article on this is Baumol (1977). See Bailey and Friedlaender (1982) for a decent review.

11 Fforde (2007) offers a historical analysis of the commercialization of Vietnam's state enterprises, which treats the informal activities of these businesses as they became involved with markets from the late 1970s as far more important than formal legality or policy.

12 Ireson is discussing Laos, but the idea that elements of a duality (here, male–female) are usefully seen as largely inseparable complements are common culturally in many parts of the world.

13 Kung (2000) (already cited) describes similar local facility with land access organization at local levels.

14 For textured studies, see, for example, Weaver and Deolalikar (2004) and Mekhora and Fleming (2004).

15 See the rapid discussion of Mosse (2005) in Chapter 9 above and in Fforde (2010). Mosse, an anthropologist, was convinced that participatory methods would work, and his book shows him coping with the consequences of their failure.

Special terms

apodictic: propositions that can be *demonstrated* to be true, *given their premises* (for example, $1 + 1 = 2$).[1] Much argument tries to do this, in effect assuming that by doing so the argument will capture in some way the truth of what it is said to be about. This assumes also that if the proposition is apodictic, it will be based upon good argument. And this is a tricky position. To some people, often those familiar with formal argument and mathematics, these ways of developing an argument are familiar. The key issue is that because apodictic propositions can be demonstrated to be true, they are bound to rules of what can be said, definitions of terms, and so on. Since they are formal, such propositions also tend to be open to a range of possible interpretations in their relation to reality. They contrast with other propositions whose acceptance does not rely upon some demonstration of their truth, such as "If you like that coat I will give it to you," or "If you invest in Africa you will tend to lose money."

ascriptivism: the idea that discussions about cause and effect are usefully seen as part of human processes of negotiation, manipulation, mutual enjoyment, and so on.

canonical: the texts of a discipline or approach, such as DE, that are accepted (such as by professional bodies) as what should be taught and so what is accepted as true (for then students can be examined on their knowledge of it without dispute between examiners).

contingent: the meaning of a topic that is not fixed but depends upon something. Thus, the meaning of GDP depends upon the context; just because there are two numbers, each called GDP, does not mean anything if the meaning of GDP is contingent.

correlate: the statistical result that variable "x" varies in such a way that its changes are related to the changes in variable "y." Grass grows faster or slower, and when you water it, up to a point, it grows faster. The correlate of watering is the rate at which grass grows. It is just a matter of the numbers and not causation. You could as well say that the correlate of grass growing faster is more watering. Ideas of causation depend largely upon how any regularity in the data is explained; for example, one could explain pressures from house owners to increase the supply of water from the mains supply to their gardens in a suburb where changes in grass varieties have occurred by arguing that it is because the grass is growing faster that more water is supplied. DE is full of attempts to support arguments about cause—that is, underlying relationships—with reference to correlation. The two are quite different (see the discussion of McCloskey in Chapter 6).

data: this isn't as simple as it looks. A stream of numbers is meaningless without some idea of what they mean; giving them meaning is what DE does, and whether you accept that meaning or not is contingent—for example, on whether you think that meaning is realistic or the politics associated with it are acceptable to you—and so to a certain extent you choose to accept it or not. To be part of DE is to accept certain meanings and to reject others.

econometrics: a body of economists' practices that involves an algebraic model derived from economic conceptualization, which argue that the model is true and that observed data deviates from it because of errors (perhaps in measurement), assume something about these errors, and then do a statistical exercise to estimate the parameters of the model.

empirics: the combination of facts and arguments that give the facts meaning for a given approach—that is, the combination of facts with ideas that define the facts in a practice or set of arguments. Here I am following Imre Lakatos (Chapter 5) in thinking in terms of the importance, for a set of facts, of the observation theory of a practice that gives them their specific meanings. Thus the use of GDP within growth theory in DE uses facts—the measures of GDP available to it—and deals with its empirics by giving particular meanings to this GDP data.

endogenous: in an argument or a model, the variables whose values are conceptually determined within the model. Contrast this with *exogenous:* a variable whose values are set outside the model. The choice is made by the designer of the model.

epistemological: how things are understood. The term allows us to step back and think about different approaches to knowledge. Thus, a view that quite different models should be used when circumstances differ may be said to argue that one should not assume *epistemological universalism*—that the same knowledge should work everywhere (see also Chapter 5).

exogenous: in an argument or a model, those variables whose values are conceptually determined outside the model. Contrast this with *endogenous:* a variable whose values are set inside the model. The choice is made by the designer of the model.

export-oriented growth (EOG): the idea that economic development would happen if policy encouraged exports.

external: the ideas and concepts outside a science or field of knowledge, such as DE, and not part of it. For DE, this would include the acceptance of multiple truths now so common in modern social sciences.

externalities: costs and benefits external to the calculations of a particular consumer or producer but caused by their behavior.

facts: alleged reality specific to a particular set of practices or methodology, thus related to what could be called ways of observing or what have been called "observation theories."

factor incomes: incomes paid to factors of production—labor, capital, and land.

factors of production: labor, capital, and land.

functional form: particular forms taken by natural science equations. For example, Newton's law of gravity is that the force varies with the inverse square of the distance between the centers of gravity of the two bodies, and you can write this down in algebra. It does *not* say that the force gets less as they get farther apart, which you can only write down in general form; the functional form is not given by the theory. Newton's law has a functional form. Generally, economic theories lack precise functional form in algebraic terms (though the allowable range of functional forms may be limited), which means that when they are used empirically the researcher has considerable freedom.

fundamentals: a common term adopted by economists, which tends to mean, in combination, elements of the context of the economy that support good growth, on the one hand, and parameters of the economy that do the same, on the other.

fungibility: anything that can equally well be used in different ways or situations. The issue comes up in discussions of economic assistance. Because aid is fungible, if a donor pays for a hospital the government has money to spend on, say, political repression instead. This means that paying for hospitals is not as ethically simple as it may at first appear.

gross domestic product (GDP): factor incomes generated within the territory controlled by the nation.

gross national product (GNP): factor incomes generated by entities that belong to the nation.

import substitution industrialization (ISI): the idea that economic development would occur if local producers were able to take back domestic markets from foreign imports, which implies that policies are necessary to protect and support them, such as through import taxes (tariffs) and targeted support.

internal: the ideas and concepts that are of or part of a science or field of knowledge, such as DE. For DE, this means that arguments should be expressed in formal logical terms, meaning algebra.

metaphysical commitments: the untestable assumptions of an approach, such as the idea that competition tends to push markets toward the characteristics described by models of perfect competition (see Chapter 9), except under particular and knowable conditions. I take this phrase from Gillespie (2008) (see Chapter 5). It is not so much that these views are not based in reality but that the particular approach does not usually test or query them.

model: a conceptual device used to manage argument and discussion. It may be expressed in algebraic terms but this is often unwieldy. A model may be systematic without using algebra. Humans (some of them) are extremely good at managing particular problems in systematic ways that do not lend themselves to algebra—for example, when relationships that appear clear and fixed in language are better seen as contingent or variable. A good example is the work done by switchboard operators in hospitals when they manage emergency calls. If they are good at their job, they will balance such factors as the changing traffic conditions facing ambulance drivers of different levels of fatigue and aptitude, and the variable relations between different prickly but talented medical specialists (again adjusting for fatigue, mood, and varying presence of colleagues). They may talk, for example, in terms of the number of nurses on call, but the particular realities of each nurse is what they think about. This example does not lend itself well to algebra.

moral hazard: once one is insured against a risk (say of crashing one's car) there are different incentives to avoiding that risk, which may mean that one takes greater risks (say of a road accident), increasing insurers' liabilities. For investors, this means that if they think they will be bailed out, they will take higher risks. Arguably, for insurers if this happens a lot they will reduce the amount of insurance they offer, and so there is market failure.

National Income Accounting (NIA): fundamental to the particular empirics of both macroeconomics and growth economics. It measures the incomes accruing to factors of production in a given time period and provides measures of the level of real economic activity when the effects of price changes are removed.

neoclassical: the dominant school within modern mainstream economic thinking. The term is called "neo" to differentiate it from earlier groups, called "classical." Much of the detail of DE exposited in this book is based upon neoclassical economics, of which it is part.

observation theory: the idea that data of itself is meaningless unless it is explained and given meaning by some theory or explanation.

ontological: concerned with what things are said to be. Another way of looking at this is that it is concerned with the nature of things, especially whether these things are stable, and, if not, how they change. It is therefore closely related, in the use of algebra, to what the algebraic terms refer to.

perfect competition: a technical term in economics referring to particular conditions in certain algebraic models, specifically that consumers and producers take prices as given—that is, they do not experience changes in prices as the amounts produced or consumed change. This has important conceptual effects because such conditions imply that markets will lead to good things: levels of production and consumption that allow firms to maximize profits and consumers to maximize welfare.

priors: the prior assumptions and beliefs that people bring to their study of something. These are related to their metaphysical commitments but are often far simpler. For example, people may believe that knowable laws determine how humans behave and specifically economic laws that tell us how the economy works. If so, it is not likely that they will find it easy to experience reality in ways that deny this, as their empirics will tend to reinforce these beliefs.

proxy: a variable that can be used in place of another one, where the second is usually unobservable. The extent to which the proxy moves in close parallel to that which it proxies is often insufficiently discussed, and the exercise is often somewhat ad hoc. Sometimes a dummy variable is constructed to proxy for something, such as "economic openness" (see Chapter 23).

rent: a return to ownership that cannot be competed away, either because of some inherent issue (such as the productivity of land or increasing returns that create higher profits for producers) or because of some institutional problem such as government intervention—for example, rationing that creates shortage, so that those with coupons can sell them, if they wish.

rent-seeking: behavior that seeks to gain access to rents when rents are created by some institutional set-up, such as chatting up the supplier of ration books to get additional coupons. Clearly, it is also interesting to think about the factors that create such rents.

statistical inference: the practice that concludes, from an examination of data in the model, what can be said about the parameters of that model and with what reliability.

straw man: in argument, the familiar tactic of setting up a characterization of what you want to attack and then attacking it, rather than directly confronting your antagonist.

Note

1   If the "1" refers to each of a pair of rabbits, then logically 1 + 1 = "many," not 2, under reasonable assumptions.

References

Adair, G. (1984) The Hawthorne effect: a reconsideration of the methodological artefact, *Journal of Applied Psychology*, 69: 334–345.

Agenor, Pierre-Richard and Montiel, Peter J. (1999) *Development Macroeconomics* (2nd edn), Princeton, NJ: Princeton University Press.

Almond, Gabriel A. (1988) The return to the state, *American Political Science Review*, 82(3) (September): 853–874.

Armendáriz de Aghion, B. and Morduch, J. (2005) *The Economics of Microfinance*, Cambridge, MA: MIT Press.

Arndt, H.W. (1981) Economic development: a semantic history, *Economic Development and Cultural Change*, 29(3).

Arndt, Heinz (1987) *Economic Development: The History of an Idea*, Chicago: University of Chicago Press.

Bailey, E.E. and Friedlaender, F. (1982) Market structure and multiproduct industries, *Journal of Economic Literature*, 20 (September): 1024–1048.

Ball, Michael and Sunderland, David (2001) *Economic History of London, 1800–1914*, New York: Routledge.

Banerjee, A.B., Duflo, E., Glennerster, R., and Kinnan, C. (2009) The Miracle of Micro-Finance? Evidence from a Randomized Evaluation, Cambridge, MA: MIT Press (mimeo).

Banerjee, A.B. and Duflo, E. (2011) *Poor Economics: A Radical Rethinking of the Way to Fight Global Poverty*, New York: Public Affairs.

Bardhan, Pranab and Udry, Christopher (1999) *Development Microeconomics*, Oxford: Oxford University Press.

Bardhan, Pranab (1993) Economics of development and the development of economics, *The Journal of Economic perspectives*, 7(2) (Spring): 129–142.

Bardsley, N. (2005) Experimental economics and the artificiality of alteration, *Journal of Economic Methodology*, 12(2) (June): 239–251.

Barro, R. (1991) Economic growth in a cross-section of countries, *Quarterly Journal of Economics*, 106: 407–444.

Barro, R. (1996) Democracy and growth, *Journal of Economic Growth*, 1: 1–27.

Baumol, W.J., Panzar, J. and Willig, R. (1988) *Contestable Markets and the Theory of Industry Structure*, San Diego, CA: Harcourt Brace Jovanovich.

Baumol, William J. (1977) On the proper cost tests for natural monopoly in a multiproduct industry, *American Economic Review*, 67(5) (December): 809–822.

Bello, Walden (1982) Export-oriented industrialization: the short-lived illusion (Chapter 5), in Bello, W. et al. (Eds.) *Development Debacle: The World Bank in the Philippines*, San Francisco, CA: Institute of Food and Development Policy.

Bello, Walden (2000) The Philippines: the making of a neo-classical tragedy, in Robison, Richard, Beeson, Mark, Jayasuriya, Kanishka, and Kim, Hyuk-Rae (Eds.), *Politics and Markets in the Wake of the Asian Crisis*, London: Routledge.

Bernanke, Ben S. (2005) The global saving glut and the US current account deficit, US Federal Reserve (speech). Available at www.bis.org/review/r050318d.pdf (accessed August 2010).

Blomstrom, Magnus and Meller, P. (Eds.) (1991) *Divergent Paths: Comparing a Century of Scandinavian and Latin American Economic Development*, Baltimore, MD: Johns Hopkins Press.

Bloom, David E. and Williamson, Jeffrey G. (1998) Demographic transitions and economic miracles in emerging Asia, *World Bank Economic Review*, 12(3).

Bramall, Chris (1993) The role of decollectivisation in China's agricultural miracle, 1978–90, *Journal of Peasant Studies*, 20(2) (January): 271–295.

Bramall, Chris (1995) Origins of the agricultural 'miracle': some evidence from Sichuan, *China Quarterly*, 143 (September).

Brecher, Jeremy (1972) *Strike!*, San Francisco, CA: Straight Arrow Books.

Bruni, L. and Sugden, R. (2007) The road not taken: how psychology was removed from economics, and how it might be brought back, *The Economic Journal*, 117 (January): 146–173.

Butler, Judith (2005) *Giving an Account of Oneself*, New York: Fordham University Press.

Camdessus, Michel (1999) From the Crises of the 1990s to the New Millennium. Remarks by Michel Camdessus, Managing Director of the International Monetary Fund, to the International Graduate School of Management (IESE) Palacio de Congresos, Madrid, Spain, November 27.

Cameron, L., Chaudhuri, A., Erkal, N., and Gangadharan, L. (2009) Propensities to engage in and punish corrupt behavior? Experimental evidence from Australia, India, Indonesia and Singapore, *Journal of Public Economics*, 93(7–8): 843–851.

Cameron, L., Erkal, N., Gangadharan, L., and Meng, X. (2013) The little emperors: behavioral impacts of China's one-child policy, *Science*, 339(6122): 953–957.

Cardenas, Juan Camilo and Carpenter, Jeffrey (2008) Behavioural development economics: lessons from field labs in the developing world, *The Journal of Development Studies*, 44(3): 311–338.

Cassen, Robert (Ed.) (1985) *Soviet Interests in the Third World*, London: Sage.

Chakravarty, S., Friedman, D., Gupta, G., Hatekar, N., Mitra, S., and Sunda, S. (2011) Experimental economics: a survey, *Economic and Political Weekly*, 46(35) August 27: 39–78.

Chambers, Robert (1983) *Rural Development: Putting The Last First*. Essex, UK: Longmans Scientific and Technical Publishers; New York: John Wiley.

Chambers, Robert (1995) Poverty and livelihoods: whose reality counts?, *Environment and Urbanization* 7(1): 173–204.

Chandler, Alfred D. (1977) *The Visible Hand: The Managerial Revolution in American Business*, Cambridge, MA: Belknap Press.

Chandler, Alfred D. (1990) *Scale and Scope: The Dynamics of Industrial Capitalism*, Cambridge, MA: Belknap Press.

Chang, Ha-Joon (2003) *Kicking Away the Ladder: Development Strategy in Historical Perspective*, London: Anthem Press.

Chenery, H.B. and Strout, A.M. (1966) Foreign assistance and economic development, *The American Economic Review*, 56(4), Part I (September): 679–733.

Chenery, H. and Srinivasan, T.N. (Eds.) (1995) *Handbook of Development Economics*, New York: North-Holland.

Chenery, Hollis (1974) *Redistribution with Growth: Policies to Improve Income Distribution in Developing Countries in the Context of Economic Growth: A Joint Study* [commissioned] by the World Bank's Development Research Center and the Institute of Development Studies, University of Sussex, London; published for the World Bank and the Institute of Development Studies, University of Sussex [by] Oxford University Press.

Clark, J.C.D. (2000) *English Society 1660–1832: Religion, Ideology and Politics During the Ancien Regime* (2nd edn), Cambridge: Cambridge University Press.

Cleary, Mark and Eaton, Peter (1996) *Tradition and Reform: Land Tenure and Rural Development in South-East Asia*, New York: Oxford University Press.

Cohen, J. (1994) The earth is round (p<0.5), *American Psychologist*, 49(12): 997–1003.

Colander, David, Holt, Richard P.F., and Barkley Rosser Jr, J. (Eds.) (2004) *The Changing Face of Economics: Conversations with Cutting Edge Economists*, Ann Arbor, MI: University of Michigan Press.

Converse, P.E. (1964) The nature of belief systems in mass publics, in Apter, David E. (Ed.) *Ideology and its Discontents*, New York: The Free Press of Glencoe, reprinted in *Critical Review* 18(1–3) (2006): 1–74.

Cowen, Michael and Shenton, Robert (1996) *Doctrines of Development*, London: Routledge.

Dasgupta, U., Gangadharan, L., Maitra, P., Mani, S., and Subramanian, S. (2012) Choosing to be trained: evidence using observational and experimental Data, working paper.

Descartes, René (1985) *The Philosophical Writings of Descartes*, trans. Cottingham, Stoothoff, and Murdoch (3 vols.) Cambridge: Cambridge University Press.

Deyo, Frederic C. (1997) Labor and post-Fordist industrial restructuring in East and Southeast Asia, *Work and Occupations*, 24(1), February.

Diamond, Jared M. (2005) *Guns, Germs, and Steel: The Fates of Human Societies*, New York: Norton.

de Dios, Emmanuel S. (2000) Executive-legislative relations in the Philippines: continuity and change, in Barlow, Colin (Ed.), *Institutions and Economic Change in Southeast Asia: The Context of Development from the 1960s to the 1990s*, Cheltenham, UK: Edward Elgar.

Dollar, David (1992) Outward-oriented developing countries really do grow more rapidly: evidence from 95 LDCs, *Economic Development and Cultural Change*, 523–544.

Dunn, John (2000) *The Cunning of Unreason: Making Sense of Politics*, New York: Basic Books.

Easterly, W. (2001) The lost decade: developing countries' stagnation in spite of policy reforms 1980–1998, *Journal of Economic Growth*, 6: 135–157.

Easterly, William (1999) The ghost of financing gap: testing the growth model used in the international financial institutions, *World Development*, 60: 423–438.

Elson, Diane (1999) Labor markets as gendered institutions: equality, efficiency and empowerment issues, *World Development*, 27(4): 611–627.

Escobar, Arturo (1995) *Encountering Development: The Making and Unmaking of the Third World*, Princeton, NJ: Princeton University Press, Princeton Studies in Culture/Power/History.

Eurostat-OECD (2012) Eurostat-OECD, Methodological Manual on Purchasing Power Parities, European Commission. Downloaded from www.oecd.org/document/3/0,3746,en_2825_495691_37961859_1_1_1_1,00.html (accessed May 11, 2011).

Fairclough, Norman (1992) *Discourse and Social Change*, Cambridge: Polity Press.

Fechter, Anne-Meike and Hindman, Heather (Eds.) (2011) *Inside the Everyday Lives of Development Workers: The Challenges and Futures of Aidland*, Sterling,VA: Kumarian Press.

Ferguson, James (1997) Development and bureaucratic power in Lesotho, in Rahnema, Majid and Bawtree, Victoria (Eds.), *The Post-Development Reader*, London: Zed Books.

Fernandez, C., Ley, Eduardo, and Steel, Mark F.J. (2001) Model uncertainty in cross-country growth regressions, *Journal of Applied Econometrics*, 16: 563–576.

Fforde, Adam and Paine, Suzanne H. (1987) *The Limits of National Liberation: Problems of Economic Management in the Democratic Republic of Vietnam, with a Statistical Appendix*), London: Croom-Helm.

Fforde, Adam (1989) *The Agrarian Question in North Vietnam 1974–79: A Study of Cooperator Resistance to State Policy*, New York: M.E. Sharpe.

Fforde, Adam (2005) Persuasion: reflections on economics, data and the 'homogeneity assumption', *Journal of Economic Methodology*, 12(1) (March): 63–91.

Fforde, Adam (2007) *Vietnamese State Industry and the Political Economy of Commercial Renaissance: Dragon's Tooth or Curate's Egg?* Oxford: Chandos.

Fforde, Adam (2008) Vietnam's informal farmers' groups: narratives and policy implications, *Suedostasien aktuell – Journal of Current Southeast Asian Affairs*, 1.

Fforde, Adam (2009) *Coping with Facts: A Sceptic's Guide to the Problem of Development*, Bloomfield, CT: Kumarian Press.

Fforde, Adam (2010) Responses to the policy science problem: reflections on the politics of development, *Development in Practice*, April 20.

Fforde, Adam (2011a) Policy recommendations as spurious predictions: toward a theory of economists' ignorance, *Critical Review*, 23(1–2): 105–115.

Fforde, Adam (2011b) Contemporary Vietnam: political opportunities, conservative formal politics and patterns of radical change, *Asian Politics and Policy*, 3(2), 165–184.

Fine, Ben (1999) The development state is dead: long live social capital, *Development and Change*, 30 (January): 1.

Fletschner, Diana, Leigh Anderson, C., and Cullen, Alison (2010) Are women as likely to take risks and compete? Behavioural findings from Central Vietnam, *Journal of Development Studies*, 46(8): 1459–1479.

Friedman, Jeffrey (2006) Public competence in normative and positive theory: neglected implications of "The nature of belief systems in mass publics," *Critical Review*, 18(1–3): i–xliii.

Friedman, Milton (1966 [1953]) *The Methodology of Positive Economics*, in *Essays in Positive Economics*, Chicago: University of Chicago Press.

Galbraith, John Kenneth (1998 [1958]) *The Affluent Society*, 40th Anniversary Edition, New York: Houghton Mifflin Company.

Gereffi, Gary (1999) International trade and industrial upgrading in the apparel commodity chains, *Journal of International Economics*, 48: 37–70.

Gill, Indermit S. and Kharas, Homi (2007) *An East Asian Renaissance: Ideas for Economic Growth*, Washington, DC: World Bank.

Gillespie, M.A. (1999) The theological origins of modernity, *Critical Review*, 13(1–2), Winter: 1–30.

Gillespie, M.A. (2008) *The Theological Origins of Modernity*, Chicago: University of Chicago Press.

Gillis, Malcolm (1987) *Economics of Development*, New York: Norton.

Godley, Wynn (2005) Some unpleasant American arithmetic, The Levy Economics Institute of Bard College, Policy Note 5.

Gramajo, A.M. (2008) Rationality as a social construction: what does individual have to say about development in an Amazon community? *Journal of Economic Issues*, 42(1), March: 115–132.

Granger, C.W.J. (1990) Spurious regression, in Eatwell, John, Milgate, Murray and Newman, Peter (Eds.), *Econometrics*, London: W.W. Norton & Company, pp. 246–248.

Granger, C.W.J. and Newbold, P. (1974) Spurious regressions in econometrics, *Journal of Econometrics*, 2(2), July: 111–120.

Green, D.P. and Tusicisny, Andrej (2012) Statistical analysis of results from laboratory studies in experimental economics: a critique of current practice, paper presented at the 2012 North American Economic Science Association (ESA) Conference, Tucson, AZ, November 16–17.

Guala, F. (2008) Experimental economics, History of, in Durlauf, Steven and Bloom, Lawrence (Eds.), *The New Palgrave Dictionary of Economics* (2nd ed.), Palgrave-Macmillan.

Gundlach, Erich (1999) The impact of human capital on economic development: problems and perspectives in Tan, Joseph L.H. (Ed.), *Human Capital Formation as an Engine of Growth: The East Asian Experience*, Singapore: ISEAS.

Haggard, Stephan (1994) Politics and institutions in the World Bank's East Asia in Fishlow, Albert, Gwin, Catherine, Haggard, Stephan, Rodrik, Dani, and Wade, Robert (Eds.), *Miracle or Design? Lessons from the East Asian Experience*, Washington, DC: Overseas Development Council.

Henrich, J., Boyd, R., Bowles, S., Camerer, C., Fehr, E., Gintis, H., and McElreath, R. (2001) In search of homo economicus: behavioral experiments in 15 small-scale societies, *American Economic Review*, 91(2): 73–78.

Henrich, J., McElreath, R., Barr, A., Ensminger, J., Barrett, C., Bolyanatz, A. et al. (2006) Costly punishment across human societies, *Science*, 312 (June 23): 1767–1770.

Hertwig, R. and Ortmann, Andreas (2001) Experimental practices in economics: a methodological challenge for psychologists?, *Behavioral and brain sciences*, 24: 383–451.

Higgins, Matthew and Williamson, Jeffrey G. (1997) Age structure dynamics in Asia and dependence on foreign capital, *Population and Development Review*, 23(2) (June).

Hill, Hal (2000) Export success against the odds: a Vietnamese case study, *World Development*, 28(2).

Hindess, Barry (1996) *Discourses of Power: From Hobbes to Foucault*, Oxford: Blackwell.

Hoover, Kevin and Perez, Stephen (2005) Truth and robustness in cross-country growth regressions, *Oxford Bulletin of Economics and Statistics*, 66: 765–798.

IMF (2007) World Economic Outlook April 2007. Available at www.imf.org/Pubs/FT/weo/2007/01/index.htm (accessed August 2010).

Ireson, Carol (1992) Changes in field, forest, and family: rural women's work and status in post-revolutionary Laos, *Bulletin of Concerned Asian Scholars*, 24(4) (October–December).

Jameson, K.P. and Wilbur, C.K. (Eds.) (1979) *Directions in Economic Development*, Notre Dame, IN: University of Notre Dame Press.

Jehle, G.A. and Reny, P.J. (1998) *Advanced Microeconomic Theory*, New York: Addison-Wesley.

Johnson, Chalmers (1982) *MITI and the Japanese Miracle: The Growth of Industrial Policy, 1925–1975*, Stanford, CA: Stanford University Press.

Johnson, Chalmers (1998) Economic crisis in East Asia: the clash of capitalisms, *Cambridge Journal of Economics*, 22: 653–661.

Junge, Traudll and Müller, Melissa (Eds.) (2004) *Until the Final Hour: Hitler's Last Secretary*, Arcade Publishing.

Kanbur, Ravi (Ed.) (2005) New directions in development economics: theory or empirics? A symposium in economic and political weekly with contributions from Abhijit Banerjee, Pranab Bardhan, Kaushik Basu, Ravi Kanbur (editor) and Dilip Mookherjee, August, Working Paper 2005–24, Department of Applied Economics and Management, Cornell University, Ithaca, New York, 14853–7801.

Kenny, Charles and Williams, David (2001) What do we know about economic growth? Or, why don't we know very much?, *World Development*, 29(1).

Kleinen, John (1999) *Facing the Future, Reviving the Past: A Study of Social Change in a Northern Vietnamese Village*, Singapore: Institute of Southeast Asian Studies.

Kline, Morris (1980) *Mathematics: The Loss of Certainty*, Oxford: Oxford University Press.

Krugman, Paul (1994) The myth of Asia's miracle, *Foreign Affairs*, 73(6) (November–December): 62–78.

Krugman, Paul R. and Obstfeld, M. (2000) *International Economics: Theory and Policy*, Reading, MA; Harlow: Addison-Wesley.

Kuhn, Thomas, 1962, *The Structure of Scientific Revolutions*, Chicago: Chicago University Press.

Kung, James Kai-Sing (2000) Common property rights and land reallocation in rural China: evidence from a village survey, *World Development*, 28(4): 701–719.

Lakatos, Imre (1970) Falsification and the methodology of scientific research programmes, in Lakatos, Imre and Musgrave, Alan (Eds.), *Criticism and the Growth of Knowledge*, Cambridge: Cambridge University Press.

Lal, Deepak (Ed.) (1992) *Development Economics*, Aldershot, UK: Edward Elgar.

Ledgerwood, J.L. (1995) Khmer kinship: the matriline/matriarchy myth, *Journal of Anthropological Research*, 51(3) (Autumn): 247–261.

Levine, Ross and Zervos, Sara J. (1993) What have we learnt about policy and growth from cross-country regressions?, *The American Economic Review*, 82(2), papers and proceedings (May): 426–430.

Levitt, S.D. and List, J.A. (2009) Field experiments in economics: the past, the present, and the future, *European Economic Review*, 53: 1–18.

Lindauer, David L. and Pritchett, Lant (2002) What's the big idea? The third generation of policies for economic growth, *Economia*, 3(1) (Fall): 1–39.

Lindauer, J. (Ed.) (1968) *Macroeconomic Readings*, New York: Free Press.

Lloyd, Peter (1983) Why do firms produce multiple outputs? *Journal of Economic Behavior and Organization*, 4: 41–451.

Lowe, Nichola and Kenney, Martin (1999) Foreign investment and the global geography of production: why the Mexican consumer electronics industry failed, *World Development*, 27(8): 1427–1443.

Lucas, Robert (1976) Econometric policy evaluation: a critique, Carnegie-Rochester Conference Series on Public Policy, 1: 19–46.

Lumer, Christopher and Nannini, Sandro (2007) *Intentionality, Deliberation and Autonomy*, Aldershot, UK: Ashgate.

McCloskey, Deirdre M. (1985) *The Rhetoric of Economics*, Madison, WI: University of Wisconsin Press.

McCloskey D. and Ziliak S.T. (1996). The standard error of regressions, *Journal of Economic Literature*, 34: 97–114.

McCone, R.L. and Parton, K.A. (2006a) Learning from the historical failure of farm management models to aid management practice, Part 1: The rise and demise of theoretical models of farm economics, *Australian Journal of Agricultural Research*, 57: 143–156.

McCown, R.L. and Parton, K.A. (2006b) Learning from the historical failure of farm management models to aid management practice, Part 2: Three systems approaches, *Australian Journal of Agricultural Research*, 57: 157–172.

McDonald, Ian (2008) Behavioural economics, *The Australian Economic Review*, 41(2): 222–228.

MacIntyre, A. (1994) Business, government and development: northeast and southeast Asian comparisons, in MacIntyre, Andrew, *Business and Government in Industrialising Asia*, Sydney: Allen & Unwin.

Mekhora, Tham and Fleming, Euan (2004) An analysis of scope economies and specialization efficiencies among Thai shrimp and rice smallholders, 2004–10, Working Paper Series in Agricultural and Resource Economics.

Milgrom, Paul and Roberts, John (1992) *Economics, Organization and Management*, Englewood Cliffs, NJ: Prentice Hall.

Mitchell, Timothy (1991) The limits of the state: beyond statist approaches and their critics, *The American Political Science Review*, 85(1): 77–96.

Moscati, Ivan (2003) History of neoclassical consumer theory: a neo-Kantian epistemological perspective, *La matematica nella storia dell.economia*, Primo workshop, Torino, October 16–17.

Mosse, David (2005) *Cultivating Development: An Ethnography of Aid Policy and Practice*, London: Ann Arbor, MI: Pluto Press.

Newberry, D.M.G. (1975) Tenurial obstacles to innovation, *Journal of Development Studies*, 11: 263–277.

Ng, Y-K. (2005) Policy implications of behavioral economics: with special reference to the optimal level of public spending, *The Australian Economic Review*, 38(3): 298–306.

Nguyen, Thu Sa (1991) *Ve nhan vat trung tam o nong thon Nam bo: Nguoi Trung nong* (On the central personality of the rural South: the middle peasant), *Tap chi KHXH* So 9, 3.

North, Douglass (1995a) Markets and other allocation systems in history: the challenge of Karl Polanyi in Richard Swedberg (Ed.), *Economic Sociology*, Cheltenham, UK: Edward Elgar.

North, Douglass (1995b) The new institutional economics and third world development, in Harriss, J., Hunter, J., and Lewis, C.M. (Eds.) *The New Institutional Economics and Third World Development*, London: Routledge.

Olken, B. (2007) Monitoring corruption: evidence from a field experiment in Indonesia, *Journal of Political Economy*, 115: 200–249.

Olson, Paulette (1998) My dam is bigger than yours: emulation in global capitalism, in Brown, Doug (Ed.) *Thorstein Veblen in the twenty-first century: A commemoration of The Theory of the Leisure Class (1899–1999)*, Cheltenham, UK: Edward Elgar.

Polanyi, Karl (1976) *The Great Transformation*, New York: Octagon Books.

Popkin, Samuel (1979) *The Rational Peasant: The Political Economy of Rural Society in Vietnam*, Berkeley, CA: University of California Press.

Popper, Karl (1959) *The Logic of Scientific Discovery*, London: Hutchinson.

Porter, Doug, Allen, Bryant, and Thompson, Gaye (1991) *Development in Practice: Paved with Good Intentions*, London: Routledge.

Prasad, Eswar and Rogoff, Kenneth (2003) The emerging truth of going global, London: *Financial Times*, September 1.

Prasad, Eswar, Rogoff, Kenneth, Wei, Shang-Jin, and Kose, M. Ayhan (2003) *Effects of Financial Market Liberalisation on Developing Countries: Some Empirical Evidence*, Washington, DC: IMF.

Rabin, M. (1998) Psychology and economics, *Journal of Economic Literature*, 36(1) (March): 11–46.

Ravallion, Martin (2004) Competing concepts of inequality in the globalization debate, World Bank Research Working Paper 3243, Washington, DC: World Bank.

Ray, Debraj (1998) *Development Economics*, Princeton, NJ: Princeton University Press.

Riedl, A. (2009) Behavioral and experimental economics can inform public policy: some thoughts, RM/10/002, Maastricht University.

Rigg, Jonathan (1997) *Southeast Asia: The Human Landscape of Modernization and Development*, London: Routledge.

Robertson, A.F. (1991) *Beyond the Family: The Social Organization of Human Reproduction*, Cambridge: Polity Press.

Rodgers, Yana van der Meulen and Cooley, Jane C. (1999) Outstanding female economists in the analysis and practice of development economics, *World Development*, 27(4): 1397–1444.

Rodriguez, Francisco and Rodrik, Dani (1999) Trade policy and economic growth: a skeptic's guide to the cross-national evidence, NBER Working Paper 7081, April.

Rodrik, Dani (1994) King Kong meets Godzilla, in Fishlow, Albert, Gwin, Catherine, Haggard, Stephan, Rodrik, Dani, and Wade, Robert (Eds.), *Miracle or Design? Lessons from the East Asian Experience*, Washington, DC: Overseas Development Council.

Rodrik, Dani (1996) Understanding economic policy reform, *Journal of Economic Literature*, 34 (March): 9–41.

Rodrik, Dani (1998) Symposium on globalization in perspective: an introduction, *Journal of Economic Perspectives*, 12(4) (Fall).

Rodrik, Dani (2003) Chapter 1, Introduction: What do we learn from country narratives, in Rodrik, Dani (Ed.) *In Search of Prosperity: Analytic Narratives on Economic Growth*, Princeton, NJ: Princeton University Press.

Rose, Jonathan (2003) *The Intellectual Life of the British Working Classes*, New Haven, CT: Yale University Press.

Roth, A. (1995) Introduction to experimental economics, in Kagel, J.H. and Roth, A.E., *The Handbook of Experimental Economics*, Princeton, NJ: Princeton University Press, 3–109.

Rothschild, M. and Stiglitz, J. (1976) Equilibrium in competitive insurance markets: an essay on the economics of imperfect information, *The Quarterly Journal of Economics*, 90(4) (November): 629–649.

Rutten, Rosanne (2000) High-cost activism and the worker household: interests, commitments and the costs of revolutionary activism in a Philippine plantation region, *Theory and Society*, 29: 215–252.

Sachs, Jeffrey and Warner, Andrew (1995) Economic reform and the process of global integration, *Brookings Papers on Economic Activity*, 1: 1–118.

Said, Edward W. (1978) *Orientalism*, New York: Pantheon Books.

Samuelson, Paul A. (1947) *Foundations of Economic Analysis*, Cambridge, MA: Harvard University Press.

Santos, A.C. (2009) Behavioral experiments: how and what can we learn about human, *Journal of Economic Methodology*, 16(1) (March): 71–88.

Schumpeter, Joseph A. (1975 [1942]) *Capitalism, Socialism and Democracy*, New York: Harper.

Scott, J.C.R. (1976) *The Moral Economy of the Peasant: Rebellion and Subsistence in Southeast Asia*, New Haven, CT: Yale University Press.

Scott, James (1998) *Seeing Like a State: How Certain Schemes to Improve the Human Condition Have Failed*, New Haven, CT: Yale University Press.

Shaffer, Paul (2011) Against excessive rhetoric in impact assessment: overstating the case for randomised controlled experiments, *The Journal of Development Studies*, 47(11): 1619–1635.

Shonfield, Andrew (1976) *Modern Capitalism*, New York: Oxford University Press.

Shore, C. and Wright, Susan (1997) Policy: a new field of anthropology, in Shore, Chris and Wright, Susan (Ed.), *Anthropology of Policy: Critical Perspectives on Governance and Power*, London: Routledge.

Simon, Herbert A. (1986) Rationality in psychology and economics, *Journal of Business*, 59(4), Part 2 (October): S209–S224.

Springer, Kimberly (2002) Third Wave black feminism?, *Signs*, 27(1), (Summer): 1059–1082.

Stigler, George J. (1947) *The Theory of Price*, New York: Macmillan.

Stiglitz, Joseph E. (1998) More instruments and broader goals: moving towards the post-Washington consensus, WIDER, Helsinki.

Stiglitz, Joseph E. (2000) *Economics of the Public Sector* (3rd edn), New York: W.W. Norton & Company.

Stoecker, Ralf (2007) Action and responsibility – a second look at ascriptivism, in Lumer, Christoph and Nannini, Sandro (Eds.), *Intentionality, Deliberation and Autonomy*, Aldershot, UK: Ashgate.

Sylvester, Christine (1999) Development studies and postcolonial studies: disparate tales of the Third World, *Third World Quarterly*, 20(4): 703–721.

Thirlwall, A.P. (2003) *Growth and Development with Special Reference to Developing Countries* (7th ed.), London: Palgrave Macmillan.

Todaro, Michael P. and Smith, Stephen C. (2006) *Economic Development* (9th edn), Boston, MA: Pearson Addison Wesley.

Ungpakorn, J. (1995) The tradition of urban working-class struggle in Thailand, *Journal of Contemporary Asia*, 25(3): 366–379.

Vietnam Poverty Update Report (2006) Poverty and poverty reduction in Vietnam 1993–2004, Nguyen Thang (Ed.), Vietnamese Academy of Social Sciences, Hanoi, December.

de Vylder, Stefan and Fforde, Adam (1988) *Vietnam – An Economy in Transition*, Stockholm: SIDA.

de Vylder, Stefan and Fforde, Adam (1996) *From Plan to Market: The Economic Transition in Vietnam*, Boulder, CO: Westview.

Wade, Robert (1988) The role of government in overcoming market failure: Taiwan, Republic of Korea and Taiwan, in Hughes, Helen (Ed.), *Achieving Industrialization in East Asia*, Cambridge: Cambridge University Press.

Wade, Robert (1990) *Governing the Market: Economic Theory and the Role of Government in East Asian Industrialization*, Princeton, NJ: Princeton University Press.

Wallis, W. and Roberts, H. (1956) *Statistics: A New Approach*, Glencoe, IL: Free Press.

Warren, Bill (1971) The internationalization of capital and the nation state: a comment, *New Left Review* I/68 (July–August).

Waterbury, John (1999) The long gestation and brief triumph of import-substituting industrialization, *World Development*, 27(2): 323–341.

Weaver, Marcia and Deolalikar, Anil (2004) Economics of scale and scope in Vietnamese hospitals, *Social Science and Medicine*, 59: 199–208.

Williams, Alan (1996) Interpersonal comparisons of welfare, Discussion Paper 151, University of York, Centre for Health Economics.

Williamson, John (1990) *Latin American Adjustment*, Washington, DC: Institute of International Economics.

Williamson, John (2000) What should the World Bank think about the Washington Consensus? *The World Bank Research Observer*, 15(2) (August): 251–264.

Winch, Peter (1958) *The Idea of a Social Science and its Relation to Philosophy*, London: Routledge.

Wolf, Martin (2009) How the noughties were a hinge of history, London: *Financial Times*, December 23.

Wong, Christine (1992) Fiscal reform and local industrialization: the problematic sequencing of reform in post-Mao China, *Modern China*, 18(2) (April).

Wood, Adrian (1997) Openness and wage inequality in developing countries: the Latin American challenge to East Asian conventional wisdom, *The World Bank Economic Review*, 11(1): 33–57.

Woodside, A.B. (2006) *Lost Modernities: China, Vietnam, Korea, and the Hazards of World History*, Cambridge, MA: Harvard University Press.

World Bank (1993) *The East Asian Miracle: Economic Growth and Public Policy*, Washington, DC: World Bank.

World Bank (1994) *Lao People's Democratic Republic – Country Economic Memorandum*, Washington, DC.

World Bank (2000) *Philippines: Growth with Equity – The remaining agenda – A World Bank Social and Structural Review*, Washington, DC: World Bank.

World Vision and Adam Fforde & Associates p/l (2004) *Mekong Delta Poverty Analysis*, Canberra: AusAID, downloadable at www.ausaid.gov.au/publications/pdf/mekong_poverty_report_04.pdf.

Yamazawa, Ippei (1992) On Pacific economic integration, *Economic Journal*, 102(415): 1519–1529.

Yonay, Y.P. (1994) When black boxes clash: competing ideas of what science is in economics, 1924–39, *Social Studies of Science*, 24: 39–80.

Yonay, Yuval P. (1998) *The Struggle Over the Soul of Economics*, Princeton, NJ: Princeton University Press.

Yonay, Y.P. (2000) Explaining scientific practices versus explaining the history: answers to my critics, in *Research in the History of Economic Thought and Methodology: A Research Annual.* Bingley [u.a.] Emerald, ISSN 0743-4154, ZDB-ID 868255, 18: 169–178.

Yonay, Yuval P. and Breslau, Daniel (2006) Marketing models: the culture of mathematical economics, *Sociological Forum*.

Young, Alwyn (1995) The Tyranny of Numbers: Confronting The Statistical Realities of The East Asian Growth Experience, *Quarterly Journal of Economics*, 110(3): 641–680.

Zebregs, Harm (1998) Can the neo-classical model explain the distribution of foreign direct investment across developing countries? Washington, DC: IMF Working Paper 139.

Zysman, John (1983) *Governments, Markets and Growth: Financial Systems and the Politics of Industrial Change*, Ithaca, NY: Cornell University Press.

Index

Note: Page references to Notes are followed by the letter 'n'.